D0984673

World Holiday, Festival, and Calendar Books

World Holiday, Festival, and Calendar Books

An Annotated Bibliography of More Than 1,000 Books on Contemporary and Historic Religious, Folk, Ethnic, and National Holidays, Festivals, Celebrations, Holy Days, Commemorations, Seasonal Celebrations, and Calendar Systems from around the World. Arranged by Topic, Supplemented by Descriptive Lists of Periodicals, Associations, and Web Sites, and Indexed by Author, Title, and Subject

Edited by
Tanya Gulevich

Omnigraphics, Inc.

Penobscot Building • Detroit, MI 48226

Tanya Gulevich, *Editor*

Omnigraphics, Inc.

Matthew Barbour, *Manager, Production and Fulfillment*
Laurie Lanzen Harris, *Vice President, Editorial Director*
Peter E. Ruffner, *Vice President, Administration*
James A. Sellgren, *Vice President, Operations and Finance*
Jane Steele, *Marketing Consultant*

***

Frederick G. Ruffner, Jr., *Publisher*

ISBN 0-7808-0073-7

Library of Congress Cataloging-in-Publication Data

World holiday, festival, and calendar books / edited by Tanya Gulevich.
p. cm.
Subtitle: An annotated bibliography of more than 1,000 books on contemporary and historic religious, folk, ethnic and national holidays, festivals, celebrations, holy days, commamorations, seasonal celebrations, and calendar systems from around the world. Arranged by topic, supplemented by descriptive lists of periodicals, association, and web sites, and indexed by author, title, and subject
Includes index.
ISBN 0-7808-0073-7 (1 lb. bdg. ; acid-free paper)
1. Holidays-Bibliography. 2. Festivals--Bibliography.
3. Calendar--Bibliography I. Gulevich, Tanya
Z5710.W67 1997
[GT3930]
016.394.26--DC21 97-37784
CIP

∞

This book is printed on acid-free paper meeting the ANSI Z39.48 Standard. The infinity symbol that appears above indicates that the paper in this book meets that standard.

Contents

Appendix

Indexes

Introduction

The world's holidays and festivals present remarkable occasions to increase our understanding of the cultural, religious, and historical traditions of our nation and our world. In addition to illuminating the world's diversity, holidays and festivals also provide the opportunity to deepen our appreciation of cultural similarities. Some festivals have been celebrated since ancient times, reflecting enduring human fascination with and reverence for certain ideas and events. Seasonal holidays, new years' festivals, and celebrations of thanksgiving represent these kinds of perennial human festivities. Other festivals have contemporary origins. Many of these honor ideals, events, or institutions that have become important today. The African-American holiday of Kwanzaa, Earth Day, and the commemoration of such recent historical events as the founding of the United Nations are twentieth-century examples of this kind of holiday. Contemporary social concerns may also reshape older traditions of observance. For example, feminist influence on Jewish traditions has sparked renewed interest in Rosh Hodesh. Reviewing the heritage of past celebrations can even lead to the revival of ancient traditions, such as the Olympic Games and solstice ceremonies. Alongside these revivals stand many holidays with continuous histories of celebration, for example, such ethnic and religious observances as the Japanese Shichi-go-san (Seven Five Three) Festival and the Muslim observance of Ramadan. These kinds of celebrations embody the values of various ethnic groups, nations, and religious traditions. The customs associated with them reveal distinctive cultural styles of joyous celebration or solemn observance. Given this diversity of subject, style, and content, the study of holidays has much to offer the general reader, student, and researcher.

Purpose

World Holiday, Festival, and Calendar Books (*WHFCB*) provides organized access to English-language literature on the world's holidays, festivals, and calendars. The structure, scope, and content of *WHFCB* enables the reader to identify interesting and appropriate materials on holidays for many audiences.

Scope

The books listed in *WHFCB* treat holidays, festivals, and calendar systems from all parts of the globe and from many historical periods. Most of the books cover holidays and events that are currently celebrated, though they often trace their histories back to previous eras. A small but significant number deal with festivals of ancient peoples, such as the ancient Greeks, Aztecs, and Celts, that have continuing relevance in the modern era. Some address the festivities of more recent historical eras, such as colonial America or medieval Europe.

WHFCB covers seven world regions: Africa, Asia, Europe, Latin America, the Middle East and North Africa, North America, and the Pacific. Some books address the festivals of an entire region, such as *Fiesta Time in Latin America* and *I Am Not Myself: The Art of African Masquerade,* but most limit themselves to the holidays of a single ethnic or national group. Examples of these kinds of titles include *Annual Customs of Korea* and *Welsh Folk Customs.* Some specialize even further, focusing on a single festival of a specific ethnic group or geographic region, such as *The Iroquois Midwinter Ceremonial* and *Christmas in Spain.*

WHFCB also directs the reader to information on the celebration of religious holidays. Individual volumes cover the beliefs and observances of Bahá'í, Buddhism, Christianity, Hinduism, Islam, Judaism, Neopaganism, Shinto, Sikhism, and Zoroastrianism, among others. Additional information on the holidays of these and other religious traditions may be found in many of the reference works listed in *WHFCB,* such as *Holidays, Festivals, and Celebrations of the World Dictionary, 2nd Edition,* and *The Encyclopedia of Religion.*

COVERAGE

Although *WHFCB* lists a wide variety of books, it focuses on titles written for the general reader. *WHFCB* includes about 175 children's books as well as many more volumes directed towards young readers. Some of these volumes may also be of interest to older readers due to the information offered or the level of presentation. *WHFCB* also covers about 100 scholarly books from the fields of anthropology, ethnic studies, history, folklore, philosophy, and theology. This number does not include books written by scholars for a general audience. Some special interest volumes also appear, including several directed specifically towards teachers or festival planners. *WHFCB* lists about 50 general reference works on holidays and festivals and about 40 religious reference works.

Holidays, festivals, and calendar systems form the main subject of most of the books listed in *WHFCB*, but for some ethnic and religious groups about which less information is available in English, works were included in which holidays, festivals, and calendars constitute only a minor subject. The unevenness of coverage among the various ethnic, national, and religious traditions reflects the availability of accessible English-language books on the subject. Thus the reader will find that *WHFCB* lists more titles addressing various aspects of Christian observances than Hindu observances, more books on United States holidays than on Russian holidays. Given the scope of the literature, *WHFCB* makes no claims to offer a complete listing of books on holidays, festivals, and calendar systems, but rather represents a very large sample of the most accessible works in terms of approach, content, level of difficulty, and availability. For our purposes, books with current publication dates and those which could be found in well-stocked public libraries were judged more widely available than older works and titles which were more likely to be held only by specialty libraries. Older volumes were included, however, if they are considered classic works on the subject of holidays, such as Chambers's *Book of Days*, first published in the 1860s and reprinted in 1990. *WHFCB* lists about 30 such works. The vast majority of titles covered are much more recent, however, with more than 55 percent published in or after 1980.

Organization

The more than 1,000 bibliographic annotations contained in WHFCB are divided into four chapters. These chapters contain books that share either a similar subject matter or approach. The books in Chapter One treat world holidays; Chapter Two consists of books focusing on religious holidays; Chapter Three lists works concentrating on the holidays of ethnic and national groups; and Chapter Four contains books on calendar and time-reckoning systems.

CONTENTS OF CHAPTERS

The first chapter of *WHFCB*, entitled "World Holidays," consists of nearly 150 books which take an international, comparative, or theoretical approach to holidays. These works are subdivided by topic and approach and are listed under five separate headings. The books listed under the first heading, "General Works," survey the many holidays observed around the globe. This group includes such reference works as *Anniversaries and Holidays*, as well as more descriptive volumes, such as *The Book of Fairs*. Books listed under the second heading, "Seasonal Holidays and International Events," focus on a single event or on a specific type of festival that is celebrated in many countries. This heading includes titles such as *The Olympics: A History of the Games* and *Harvest Festivals Around the World*. Books that appear under the third heading, "Historic Events Commemorated Around the World," examine the history and observance of such internationally recognized days as Columbus Day, Hiroshima Day, and Holocaust Remembrance Day. If a book treats the holiday or international event from the perspective of a single nation, however, such as *America at D- Day: A Book of Remembrance*, it appears in Chapter Three under the heading for that nation. The fourth heading in Chapter One is entitled "Holiday Preparations, Activities, and Advice." It groups together such titles as *Folk Festivals: A Handbook for Organization and Management*, *Fireworks! Pyrotechnics on Display*, and *The Alternate Celebrations Catalogue*. The last heading of Chapter One, "Anthropological, Historical, Philosophical, and Theological Approaches," contains works on the nature of festivity from the disciplines of anthropology, sociology, history, philosophy, and theology. Here the reader will find such volumes as *Models and Mirrors: Towards an Anthropology of Public Events* and *The Feast of Fools: A Theological Essay on Festivity and Fantasy*.

Chapter Two of *WHFCB* lists about 300 books that provide information on religious holidays. The first heading in Chapter Two, "General Works," offers reference titles on world religions, comparative studies of religion, and other useful background readings on aspects of religious celebration and observance. Examples of these titles include *The World's Religions*, *The Dictionary of Non-Christian Religions*, and *Sacred Dance: Encounter with the Gods*. Works which focus on the festivals of a single religious tradition are listed under separate headings for that religion. Bahá'í, Buddhism, Christianity, Hinduism, Islam, Judaism, Neopaganism, Shinto, Sikhism, and Zoroastrianism each have their own headings. The books under each of these headings may be further subdivided into general works which cover many different holidays or provide background information, as well as works which treat individual holidays, such as Passover or Easter. Thus, under the main heading "Christianity" and the subheading "General Works," the reader will find such titles as *Christian Symbols and How to Use Them* and *The Christian Year: Its Purpose and History*. The religions of many native and ancient peoples are specific to their ethnic group. Since readers are more likely to identify these peoples as ethnic rather than religious groups, books about their holidays and festivals have been placed in Chapter Three, which treats the celebrations of ethnic groups and nations. There the reader will find texts about such indigenous celebrations as the Hopi Snake Dance, as well as investigations of such ancient holidays as the Eleusinian Mystery Cult Festival of ancient Greece. Much information about the holidays of religious traditions which are not represented by individual volumes on the subject may still be gleaned from many of the general works on religious holidays, as well as from the reference works listed in Chapter One.

Chapter Three, "Holidays of Ethnic Groups and Nations," concentrates on cultural traditions of celebration. Within this chapter, nearly 550 books appear under eight major headings representing seven world regions—Africa, Asia, Europe, Latin America, the Middle East and North Africa, North America, and the Pacific—and one historical period, Ancient. Titles listed under these headings may be further subdivided into general works and works that treat specific countries or ethnic groups within those countries. The major heading "North America," for example, contains four subheadings: General Works, Canada, Native North America, and the United States. Books about United States holidays are further divided into general works, such as *All About American Holidays*, and volumes that treat specific holidays or ethnic traditions of celebration, such as *Thanksgiving: An American Holiday, An American History* and *Fiesta U.S.A.*

Readers interested in the holidays of Africa should note that books on the subject may appear under two major headings, "Africa" and "Middle East and North Africa." As in the Middle East, many of the holidays celebrated in North Africa are Muslim. The heading "Middle East and North Africa" reflects this element of cultural continuity between the two regions.

The fourth and final chapter of *WHFCB* contains citations on nearly 50 books about calendar and time-measuring systems. These books appear under five different subheadings that cover general works on calendar systems, books addressing units of time, such as days, weeks, and months, and volumes concentrating on the calendar systems of specific ethnic or religious traditions.

FORMAT OF ENTRIES

Within each heading and subheading, books are listed in alphabetical order by title. Each entry provides the reader with a full bibliographic citation that also notes the book's special features, such as illustrations, indexes, bibliographies, and appendices, and lists the total number of pages. Annotations summarize content, organization, and approach, and identify any specialized target audience. Children's books are marked with a for easy identification. Call numbers and ISBN numbers are given for each title, as available, and appear just below the annotation. Finally, each entry is numbered. These numbers are used to identify books in the indexes.

Due to the limitations of local library holdings, a very small number of books whose annotations appear in *WHFCB* were not reviewed by the editor. Their annotations were taken from *Holidays and Festivals Index*, edited by Helene Henderson and Barry Puckett (Detroit, MI: Omnigraphics, Inc., 1995). The annotations that were not reviewed by the editor are marked (NR).

SPELLINGS AND FORMS USED

Translations and transliterations of many foreign words relating to holidays can be found throughout *WHFCB*. Every attempt has been made to standardize the spellings of these words as they appear in the annotations. *The Encyclopedia of Religion* (1987), edited by Mircea Eliade, was used as a guide for the spelling of many foreign words related to religious holidays. Michael Strassfeld's *The Jewish Holidays* (1985) provided an additional source for spellings related to Jewish holidays. For Asian and African holidays, no single standard was used. The spelling that appears in the annotations is the one most often found in the sources consulted.

Special Features

INDEXES

While the books contained in *WHFCB* are organized topically, three separate indexes also provide access to specific information. Author and title indexes allow the reader to locate individual works quickly and easily. The subject index covers holidays, countries, ethnic groups, activities, people, objects, and events. This enables the user to identify, for example, all the books listed in *WHFCB* which treat Chinese New Year or the people of Ethiopia, or to investigate a variety of holidays that honor the solstices, include the element of fasting, or are celebrated with masks. All index references are to **entry numbers**, not page numbers.

APPENDICES

Readers interested in further sources of information may consult the appendix, which contains a list of journals that publish articles on holidays, festivals, and calendar systems; associations that promote celebrations or offer resources on holidays and festivals; and an annotated list of web sites that address these topics.

Audience

WHFCB is intended for middle school, high school, college, and public libraries, as well as churches, synagogues, mosques, community organizations, and any other institutions or individuals interested in researching holidays, festivals, and calendar systems.

Acknowledgments

Several people and institutions contributed to the compilation of this book. First and foremost I would like to thank Omnigraphics editor Helene Henderson for her unstinting availability and sound advice. I am also grateful for the help of Jenifer Swanson, who researched and wrote annotations for the web sites listed in the appendix. In addition I thank Barry Puckett for tracking down a number of books which eluded me in local library systems. Finally, I would also like to acknowledge the wonderfully efficient Santa Clara County Library system, through whose facilities most of the research for this book was done. The Palo Alto City Library as well as Stanford University Libraries were also helpful sources of books.

CHAPTER ONE

World Holidays

General Works

♦ 1 ♦

The Almanac of Anniversaries. **Kim Long. Santa Barbara, CA: ABC-Clio, Inc., 1992. 270 pp. Bibliography. Index.**

Covers United States history, births and deaths of noted individuals, founding dates of public institutions and businesses, literary and musical debuts, inventions, and unusual events. Gives chapter for each year between 1993 and 2001. Notes 25-year, 50-year, 75-year, 100-year, 150-year, 200-year, 150-year, 300-year, 350-year, 400-year, 450-year, and 500-year anniversaries which occur in that calendar year. Emphasis on observances in the U.S.

DEWEY: 394.2 LC: D11.5 L64 ISBN 0-87436-6753

♦ 2 ♦

Anniversaries and Holidays. **Ruth W. Gregory. Fourth Edition. Chicago: American Library Association, 1983. 262 pp. Bibliography. Index.**

Identifies 2,637 anniversaries and holidays from 183 nations, with special emphasis on observances in the U.S. Covers holy days, feast days, holidays, civic days, anniversaries and special events. Part one provides a calendar of fixed days, part two several calendars of movable days, and part three an annotated bibliography of books concerning anniversaries, holidays, and special events.

DEWEY: 394.26 LC: GT 3930. G74 ISBN 0-8389-0389-4

♦ 3 ♦

The Book of Days: A Miscellany of Popular Antiquities in Connection with the Calendar, Including Anecdote, Biography, and History, Curiosities from Literature, and Oddities of Human Life and Character. **Robert Chambers. New introduction by Tristram Potter Coffin. Two volumes. 1862-1864.**

Reprint. Detroit, MI: Omnigraphics, Inc., 1990. Volume I, 832 pp. Volume II, 840 pp. Illustrated. Index in Volume II.

An assortment of materials related to the Christian church calendar, seasonal changes and the folklore of Great Britain. Includes events, biographies, anecdotes connected with the days of the year, and other commentaries. Detailed entries.

DEWEY: 394 C445 LC: DA 110.C52 ISBN 1-55888-849-9

♦ 4 ♦

The Book of Fairs. **Helen Augur. Introduction by Hendrik Willem Van Loon. Illustrated by James MacDonald. 1939. Reprint. Detroit, MI: Omnigraphics, Inc., 1992. 308 pp. Index.**

Traces the development of trade, customs, and social life in connection with fairs in history up to the 1939 World's Fair. Includes discussion of fairs and festivals in ancient Tyre, Athens, and Rome, the Kinsai Fairs in thirteenth-century Cathay, and assorted fairs in thirteenth-century France, fifteenth-century Belgium and Germany, medieval England, Ireland, and Scotland, and nineteenth-century Russia. Also covers the modern expositions.

DEWEY: 381.18 LC: HF5471.A8 ISBN 1-55888-892-6

♦ 5 ♦

The Book of Festivals. **Dorothy Gladys Spicer. 1937. Reprint. Detroit, MI: Omnigraphics, Inc., 1990. 429 pp. Appendix. Bibliography. Glossary.**

Describes the celebration of the most important festivals of 35 different ethnic and religious groups, chosen from among those most represented in the U.S. population. Arranged alphabetically by ethnicity and religion. Briefly explains the Armenian, Chinese, Gregorian, Hindu, Jewish, Julian, and Muslim calendars.

DEWEY: 394 S LC: GT3930.S58 ISBN 1-55888-841-1

♦ 6 ♦

The Book of Holidays and Festivals. **Marguerite Ickis. New York: Dodd, Mead and Company, 1970. 164 pp. Illustrated. Index.**

Describes festivities and holiday celebrations around the world. Written for older children.

DEWEY: 394.2 ISBN 0-396-06250-4

♦ 7 ♦

The Book of Holidays Around the World. **Alice Van Straalen. New York: E. P. Dutton, 1986. 192 pp. Appendices. Glossary. Illustrated. Indexes.**

Presents one holiday for every day of the year from countries around the world. Beautifully illustrated, with over 80 photographs, drawings and other works of art. Explains movable holidays associated with Buddhist, Chinese, Christian, Hindu, Islamic, and Jewish calendars.

DEWEY: 394.26 LC: GT 3933.V36 ISBN 0-525-44270-7

♦ 8 ♦

A Calendar of Festivals: Traditional Celebrations, Songs, Seasonal Recipes, and Things to Make. **Marian Green. Shaftesbury, Dorset, England: Element Books, 1991. 160 pp. Bibliography. Illustrated. Index.**

Offers a collection of holidays, saints' days, customs, lore, recipes, crafts, songs, and symbols for each month of the year. Covers ancient, Christian, Jewish, and folk holidays from Britain and the United States. Emphasis on British customs and lore. Lists zodiac symbols and characteristics of people born under each sign.

DEWEY: 394.26 ISBN 1-85230-204-6

♦ 9 ♦

Celebrate the Sun. **Betty Nickerson. Philadelphia, PA: J. B. Lippincott Company, 1969. 128 pp. Bibliography. Illustrated. Index.**

Conveys the meaning and spirit of 50 seasonal festivals and other celebrations from around the world. Text describes celebrations, customs, and atmosphere. Illustrations consist of 51 color drawings made by children of many nations. Covers Mardi Gras, the Durbar (Ghana), Muharram (Islam), May Day, Hanukkah, Gion (Japan), Perahera (Sri Lanka), La Cueca Chilena (Chile), and more. For children.

DEWEY: 394.2

♦ 10 ♦

Celebrate the World: Twenty Tellable Folktales for Multicultural Festivals. **Margaret Read MacDonald. Illustrations by Roxane Murphy Smith. New York: H. W. Wilson Company, 1994. 225 pp. Appendix. Bibliography. Illustrated. Index.**

Offers 20 simple folktales from around the world with tips on how to tell the tale to children, notes on sources, and suggestions for further reading. Also introduces a festival for each folktale, and offers suggestions on how to organize your own celebration of the festival. Appendix lists audience participation tales, stories which incorporate improvisation, and appropriate age-grade for each tale. Illustrated with black-and-white drawings.

DEWEY: 398 M135

♦ 11 ♦

Celestially Auspicious Occasions: Seasons, Cycles, and Celebrations. **Donna Henes. Illustrations by Joonhee Lee. New York: Perigee Books, 1996. 236 pp. Bibliography.**

A collection of lore, legend, customs, and celebrations of calendrical and seasonal cycles from cultures past and present. Covers solstices, equinoxes, quarter days, seasons, days, weeks, and months, and unusual celestial occurrences, such as blue moons and eclipses. Also treats New Year celebrations and birthdays. Contrasts lineal and cyclical conceptions of time.

DEWEY: 299.93 LC: BP 605. N48 H45 ISBN 0-399-52210-7

♦ 12 ♦

Chase's Calendar of Events: The Day-by-Day Directory to Special Days, Weeks and Months. **Chicago: Contemporary Books, Inc. Annual. Approximately 600 pp. Index. Tables.**

More than 10,000 brief entries listing religious and other holidays, ethnic and international observances, sponsored events, presidential proclamations, sporting events, awards, historic anniversaries, birthdays, weather, calendrical, and astronomical phenomena. United States emphasis. Contact information given for many events.

DEWEY: 394.26 LC: D11.5 C48 ISBN 0-8092-2361

♦ 13 ♦

Concise Dictionary of Holidays. **Raymond Jahn. New York: Philosophical Library, 1958. 102 pp. Illustrated.**

Provides brief explanations of holidays and days of commemoration or observance from around the world. Emphasizes those observances which Americans are most likely to see or experience.

DEWEY: 394.26 J25 LC: GT 3930 J2

♦ 14 ♦

Curiosities of Popular Customs and of Rites, Ceremonies, Observances, and Miscellaneous Antiquities. **William S. Walsh. 1898. Reprint. Detroit, MI: Omnigraphics, Inc., 1966. 1018 pp. Illustrated.**

A dictionary-style compendium of commentary on, and explanation of, customary practices, rituals, ceremonies, legends, and observances. Covers saint's days, festivals from around the world and throughout history, feasts, fasts, and days of observance or commemoration. Also treats a variety of customs, such as blood covenants and the churching of women, as well as things and places associated with popular customs, ceremonies, beliefs, or legends.

LC: GT 31 W2

♦ 15 ♦

Customs and Holidays of the World. **Lavinia Dobler. Illustrated by Josephine Little. New York: Fleet Publishing, 1962. 186 pp. Index.**

Features more than 70 festivals from Europe, Asia, the Middle East, the Americas, and Africa. Entries explain festival's significance and how it is celebrated. For widely celebrated holidays, notes festivities and customs of many lands. Organized by season. Includes further reading list and guide to pronunciation.

DEWEY: 394 D633c

♦ 16 ♦

The Customs of Mankind. **Lillian Eichler. Garden City, NY: Garden City Publishing, Inc., 1937. 753 pp. Bibliography. Illustrated. Index.**

Presents the customs of many lands and times concerning etiquette, speech, introductions, courtship, marriage, gifts, correspondence, hospitality, table manners, holidays, dance, dress, funerals, children, superstitions, and games. Holidays covered include New Year, Lincoln's Birthday, Valentine's Day, Washington's Birthday, St. Patrick's Day, April Fool's Day, Easter, May Day, Mother's Day, Arbor Day, Flag Day, Independence Day, Labor Day, Columbus Day, Halloween, Armistice Day, Thanksgiving, and Christmas.

DEWEY: 390 LC: GT75. W35

♦ 17 ♦

Days and Customs of All Faiths. **Howard V. Harper. 1957. Reprint. Detroit, MI: Omnigraphics, Inc., 1990. 399 pp. Index.**

Describes the origins and history of religious celebrations, customs, and lore associated with specific calendar dates and times of the year. Focuses on Christian traditions, with some coverage of Judaism as well.

DEWEY: 291.3 6 LC: GR 930 H3 ISBN 1-55888-850-0

♦ 18 ♦

A Dictionary of Days: The Curious Stories Behind More Than 850 Named Days Celebrated in Literature and Real Life. **Leslie Dunkling. New York: Facts on File Publications, 1988. 156 pp.**

Covers North American and British named days of all kinds. Includes nationally and locally celebrated days, currently and formerly celebrated days, as well as fictional day celebrations from literature. Also documents common expressions, scientific terms, and cultural events invoking the concept of "day." Much cross-referencing.

DEWEY: 394.2603 ISBN 0-8160-1416-9

♦ 19 ♦

Dictionary of Festivals. **J. C. Cooper. 1990. Reprint. London: Thorsons, 1995. 231 pp. Bibliography.**

Covers festivals of the world, both ancient and contemporary, including their gods, symbols, rituals, and customs; also provides summary articles on festival types, ethnic and religious traditions of celebration. Entry length ranges from about a paragraph to two pages. Treats ancient Greek, Roman, Babylonian, Egyptian, Celtic, and Mayan festivals, as well as Chinese, Japanese, European, Native American, Christian, Muslim, Hindu, Sikh, Jewish, Buddhist, Zoroastrian, Jain festivals, and more. Cross-referenced.

ISBN 0-7225-3193-1

♦ 20 ♦

Dictionary of Mythology, Folklore and Symbols. **Gertrude Jobes. Three volumes. New York: Scarecrow, 1962. 1759 pp., plus 482 pp. index (volume three). Bibliography.**

Exhaustive listing of symbols and their meanings. Covers world mythology and folklore, as well as letters of various alphabets, names, plants, animals, minerals, characters from fiction, activities, attributes, and everyday objects. Index made up of two parts containing a total of approximately 22,000 listings. Part one devoted to deities and mythological characters, part two devoted to mythological affinities, attributes and things.

DEWEY: 398.03

♦ 21 ♦

Do You Know What Day Tomorrow Is? A Teacher's Almanac. **Lee Bennett Hopkins and Misha Arenstein. New York: Citation Press, 1975. 223 pp. Appendices.**

An almanac for elementary school teachers. Lists holidays, birthdays of noted individuals, historic events, inventions, discoveries, and firsts. Provides brief biography for individuals, background information and explanation of events and celebrations; many entries give further reading suggestions for students. Arranged by month and date. Appendices list reference materials and cited works.

DEWEY: 909 LC: D11.5.H65 ISBN 0-590-07444-X

♦ 22 ♦

The Every-Day Book; or, Everlasting Calendar of Popular Amusements, Sports, Pastimes, Ceremonies, Manners, Customs, and Events, Incident to Each of the Three Hundred and Sixty-Five Days, in Past and Present Times; Forming a Complete History of the Year, Months, and Seasons, and a Perpetual Key to the Almanack ; Including Accounts of the Weather, Rules for Health and Conduct, Remarkable and Important Anecdotes, Facts, and Notices, in Chronology, Antiquities, Topography, Biography, Natural History, Art, Science, and General Literature; Derived from the Most Authentic Sources, and Valuable Original Communications, with Poetical Elucidations, for Daily Use and Diversion. **William Hone. Introduction by Leslie Shepard. Two volumes. 1827. Reprint. Detroit, MI: Omnigraphics, Inc., 1967. Volume one, 1720 pp. Volume two, 1711 pp. Illustrated. Indexes.**

Each volume presents a wealth of information and anecdote about the events, customs, objects, and celebrations associated with the days of the year. Organized in chronological order. Illustrated with black-and-white engravings. Indexes of general subjects, Catholic saints, poetry, and flowers found in both volumes.

LC: RO32.02 ISBN 1-55888-905-1

♦ 23 ♦

Every Day's a Holiday. **Ruth Hutchinson and Ruth Adams. New York: Harper, 1951. 304 pp. Bibliography. Index.**

Discusses one festival for every day of the year. Includes folk holidays, religious holidays, saint's days, and fairs from around the world. Explains the reason for the celebration and describes festivities and customs.

DEWEY: 394.26 H97 ISBN 1-55888-172-7

♦ 24 ♦

Festivals. **Ruth Manning-Saunders, ed. Illustrated by Raymond Briggs. New York: E. P. Dutton and Co., Inc., 1973. 188 pp.**

An anthology of stories and poems about festivals and holidays from around the world. Each celebration introduced by a brief summary of its history and customs. European and United States emphasis. Illustrated with color and black-and-white drawings. For children.

DEWEY: 394.2 ISBN 0-525-29675-1

♦ 25 ♦

Festivals and Saints Days: A Calendar of Festivals for School and Home. **Victor J. Green. Poole, Dorset, England: Blandford Press Ltd., 1978. 161 pp. Index.**

Beginning with New Year's Day and following the calendar, the book covers over 30 secular, Christian, Jewish, Hindu and Muslim holidays observed in Britain. Also includes Independence Day and Thanksgiving in the United States. Further reading list. (NR)

DEWEY: 394.2 LC: GT3932.G73 ISBN 0-71370889-1

♦ 26 ♦

Festivals for You to Celebrate. **Susan Purdy. Philadelphia, PA: J. B. Lippincott and Company, 1969. 192 pp. Bibliography. Illustrated. Indexes.**

Suggests craft projects for 29 holidays from around the world. Entries relate significance of holiday, describe holiday customs, and give illustrated instructions for craft projects suitable for ages eight and above. Covers the Green Squash Festival (Mexico), Noruz (Iran), and selected European, American, Asian, Christian, and Jewish holidays. Furnishes activities index, which ranks activities according to difficulty, and a general index.

DEWEY: 745.5

♦ 27 ♦

The Folklore of World Holidays. **Margaret Read MacDonald. Detroit, MI: Gale Research, Inc., 1992. 739 pp. Index.**

Documents folklore and folk practices surrounding 340 holidays and festivals from more than 150 countries. Presented by calendar date. Referenced excerpts from other works provide material for entries. Covers non-Western nations. Does not include most political holidays, local holidays, or holidays of tribal groups.

DEWEY: 394.26 LC: GT 3930. F65 ISBN 0-8103-7577

♦ 28 ♦

Foreign Festival Customs. **Revised edition. Marian Schibsy and Hanny Cohrsen. New York: American Council for Nationalities Service, 1974. 74 pp.**

Christmas, New Year, and Easter customs, traditions, and recipes from more than thirty immigrant groups to the United States. Discusses Thanksgiving and harvest traditions from Europe. (NR)

DEWEY: 394.2 LC: GT3932. S34

♦ 29 ♦

Funk and Wagnalls Standard Dictionary of Folklore, Mythology and Legend. **Maria Leach, ed. New York: Funk and Wagnalls, 1972. Revised in 1984. 1236 pp. Index.**

Comprehensive treatment of the world's folklore. More than 8,000 entries, including 55 survey articles characterizing various folklore genres and the folk traditions of many ethnic groups. Compiled by prominent folklorists, anthropologists, linguists, musicologists, and other scholars. First one-volume printing of this work.

DEWEY: 398.042 LC: GR 35. F82 ISBN 0-06-250511-4

♦ 30 ♦

A Guide to World Fairs and Festivals. **Frances Shemanski. Westport, CT: Greenwood Press, 1985. 309 pp. Appendix. Index.**

Covers 75 countries (with the United States covered in a separate volume; see entry ♦ 790 ♦). Celebrations around cultural programs, sports, religion, humor, agriculture, flowers, holidays, folklore, history, patriotism, and community included. Entries explain the origins, history, purpose, events, and activities of each festival. Festival listings are organized by country. Appendix lists festivals by type.

DEWEY: 394.2 69 LC: GT 3930. S43 ISBN 0-313-20786-0

♦ 31 ♦

Holiday Folklore, Phobias and Fun: Mythical Origins, Scientific Treatments and Superstitious "Cures." **Donald E. Dossey. Los Angeles, CA: Outcomes Unlimited Press, Inc., 1992. 231 pp. Appendices. Bibliography. Index.**

Covers New Year, St. Valentine's Day, St. Patrick's Day, Friday the 13th, Easter, April Fool's Day, Halloween, Thanksgiving, and Christmas. Explains holiday's origin, relates holiday folklore, including customs, symbols, sayings, and superstitions, and tells how to enjoy the holiday and/or overcome holiday-related fears or depression. Chapter on miscellaneous superstitions, spells, omens, rites, and predictions. Appendix I gives recipes; II, the author's suggestions on improving attitudes and redirecting emotions; and III, a list of fears and phobias.

DEWEY: 398.33 LC: GR 930.D67 ISBN 0-925640-06-9

♦ 32 ♦

Holidays. **Lloyd Champlin Eddy. Boston, MA: The Christopher Publishing House, 1928. 304 pp. Index.**

Day-by-day listing of holidays and birthdays worldwide, followed by chapters on various religious and secular events observed in many lands. Discusses New Year's Days, Arbor Days, Memorial Days, Flag Days, Independence Days, Thanksgiving Days, Carnival, Armistice and Peace Days, and more.

DEWEY: 394.26

♦ 33 ♦

Holidays: A Reference First Book. **Revised edition. Bernice Burnett. New York: Franklin Watts, 1983. 87 pp. Illustrated.**

An abbreviated holidays encyclopedia for children. Covers holidays observed in the U.S., holidays of many American ethnic groups, and major holidays of many foreign countries. Also lists national holidays around the world. Arranged in alphabetical order by holiday, country, or ethnic group. Illustrated with black-and-white photos.

DEWEY: 394.2 6 LC: GT 3933.B87 ISBN 0-531-04646-X

♦ 34 ♦

Holidays and Anniversaries of the World: A Comprehensive Catalogue Containing Detailed Information on Every Month and Day of the Year, with Coverage of 23,000 Holidays, Anniversaries, Fasts and Feasts, Holy Days, Days of Saints, the Blesseds, and Other Days of Heortological Significance, Birthdays of the Famous, Important Dates in History, and Special Events and Their Sponsors. **Jennifer Mossman, ed. Second edition. Detroit, MI: Gale Research, 1990. 1080 pp. Index.**

Offers a day-by-day listing of 23,000 secular, religious, and historic holidays, birthdays of notable individuals, special observances, and historic events. Covers state, national, and international holidays. Introduction gives a brief history of the calendar, glossary of English words, abbreviations, and Latin words referring to time. Perpetual calendar covers the years 1753-2100.

DEWEY: 394.2 H717 ISBN 0-8103-4870-5

♦ 35 ♦

Holidays and Festivals Index: A Descriptive Guide to Information on More Than 3,000 Holidays, Festivals, Fairs, Rituals, Celebrations, Commemorations, Holy Days and Saints' Days, Feasts and Fasts, and Other Observances, Including Ethnic, Seasonal, Art, Music, Dance, Theater, Folk, Historic, National, and Ancient Events from All Parts of the World, as Found in Standard Reference Works. Includes Location, Date, Alternative Names, Cross References, and Indexes by Ethnic Group and Geographical Location, Personal Name, Religion, and Calendar. **Helene Henderson and Barry Puckett, eds. Detroit, MI: Omnigraphics, Inc., 1995. 782 pp. Bibliography. Indexes.**

Directs the reader to information about more than 3,000 holidays, festivals, celebrations, commemorative days, feasts and fasts from all over the world as cited in 26 of the most widely known and held reference works on holidays and observances. Covers religious and secular events from more than 150 countries. Entries list holidays and events in alphabetical order by name, and note place celebrated, date observed, ethnic or religious group, title and page number of reference book providing more information, and, where applicable, date established and person or event for which observance is named. Includes lists of legal holidays by American state and foreign country, glossary of words relating to time reckoning, brief explanation of the Julian, Gregorian, Jewish, Islamic, Hindu, Buddhist and Chinese calendars, and a comparative table of calendar systems. Provides annotated bibliography of sources indexed, as well as an annotated bibliography of more than 200 other source works on holidays, festivals, and special events. Multiple indexes allow reader to search for holidays and events by ethnicity and geographic location, event name, religion, and calendar system.

DEWEY: 394.2 69 LC: GT 3925. H65 ISBN 0-7808-0012-5

♦ 36 ♦

Holidays Around the World. **Joseph Gaer. Illustrated by Anne Marie Jauss. Boston, MA: Little, Brown and Company, 1953. 212 pp. Index.**

Introduces the reader to holidays from around the world. Gives chapters on Chinese holidays, Hindu holidays, Jewish holidays, Christian holidays, Muslim holidays, holidays of the Jains and Parsis, and one international holiday—United Nations Day. Entries explain significance of the holiday, describe activities of celebration or observance, relate customs, and retell legends and stories. Provides list of major holidays celebrated in the United States.

DEWEY: 394

♦ 37 ♦

Holidays, Festivals, and Celebrations of the World Dictionary: Detailing More Than 2,000 Observances from All 50 States and More Than 100 Nations. A Compendious Reference Guide to Popular, Ethnic, Religious, National, and Ancient Holidays, Festivals, Celebrations, Commemorations, Holy Days, Feasts, and Fasts, Supplemented by Special Sections on Calendar Systems, the Millennium, Admission Days and Facts about the States and Territories, Presidents of the United States, Tourism Information Sources, and Web Sites on Holidays; Special Indexes of Chronological, Ethnic and Geographic, Historical, Religious, Ancient, Folkloric, Calendar, Promotional and Sports Holidays, State and National Legal Holidays, General, and Subject Indexes. **Second edition. Helene Henderson and Sue Ellen Thompson, eds. Detroit, MI: Omnigraphics, Inc., 1997. 822 pp. Bibliography. Indexes.**

Describes 2,000 religious and secular holidays, festivals, commemorations, and observances from 100 countries and all 50 states, including independence, republic, and liberation days. Entries contain source and contact information. Emphasis on currently celebrated events. Arranged alphabetically by key-word in holiday name. Amply cross-referenced. Special section on the upcoming millennium and expanded coverage of calendar systems. Six appendices provide information on U.S. states and territories, U.S. presidents, domestic and international tourism information sources, an annotated bibliography, and an annotated listing of holiday-related web sites on the Internet. Multiple indexes including ethnic and geographic, religious, chronological, ancient, calendar, folkloric, historical, promotional, sporting, legal holidays by state, legal holidays by country, general, alphabetical by name and by key-word, and subject.

DEWEY: 394.26 LC: GT3925.T46 ISBN 0-7808-0074-5

♦ 38 ♦

Holiday Symbols: A Guide to the Legend and Lore Behind the People, Places, Food, Animals, and Other Symbols Associated with Holidays and Holy Days, Feasts and Fasts, and Other Celebrations, Covering Popular, Ethnic, Religious, National, and Ancient Events, as Observed in the United States and Around the World. **Sue Ellen Thompson. Detroit, MI: Omnigraphics, Inc., 1998. 558 pp. Index.**

Explains lore, history, and customs associated with more than 750 holiday symbols. Covers symbols of 174 religious, national, folk, and ethnic holidays from around the world. Includes some ancient holidays. Entries, in alphabetical order by holiday name, list type of holiday, date of observation, where celebrated, symbols, colors, and related holidays. Brief essay on holiday origins begins each entry, discussion of holiday symbols follows. Offers further reading for each holiday. Cross-referenced. General index and symbols index.

DEWEY: 394.26 01 48 LC: GT3930.T48 ISBN 0-7808-0072-9

♦ 39 ♦

The Illuminated Book of Days. **Kay Lee and Marshall Lee, eds. Illustrations by Kate Greenaway and Eugène Grasset. New York: G. P. Putnam's Sons, 1979. 213 pp.**

Offers an entertaining collection of facts, anecdotes, folklore, anniversaries, holidays, saints' days, rhymes, household hints, birthdays, recipes, and farming lore associated with specific days, months, or seasons. Amply illustrated with color and black-and-white drawings.

DEWEY: 394 I29 LC: AY 71 1979 051 ISBN 0-399-12406-3

♦ 40 ♦

International Directory of Theatre, Dance, and Folklore Festivals. **Jennifer Merin with Elizabeth B. Burdick. Westport, CT: Greenwood Press, 1979. 480 pp. Appendix. Bibliography.**

Lists 850 festivals in 56 different countries. Entries give name of festival, contact address and telephone, approximate dates, and a brief description. Listings organized by country, indexed by festival name.

DEWEY: 790.2 025 LC: PN 1590 F47 M47 ISBN 0-313-2099306

♦ 41 ♦

International Holidays: 204 Countries from 1994-2015. **Robert S. Weaver. Jefferson, NC: McFarland and Company, Inc., 1995. 361 pp. Appendices. Index.**

Lists the observed holidays, religious and secular, for 204 countries from 1994 to 2015. Listing is arranged by month and year, beginning with January 1994 and ending with December 2015. Entries give date, country, and holiday name. Appendices list fixed holidays (including bank holidays) and movable holidays, provide tables for determining the Gregorian calendar date of selected movable holidays from the major religious and ethnic groups for the years 1900-2100, and furnish a table of holidays honored by each country. Appendices cross-referenced. Index of countries and holiday names.

DEWEY: 394.2 6 LC: GT 3930. W38 ISBN 0-89950-953-3

♦ 42 ♦

Manners and Customs of Mankind: An Entirely New Pictorial Work of Great Educational Value Describing the Most Fascinating Side of Human Life. **J. A. Hammerton. Four volumes. London: The Amalgamated Press, Ltd.; New York: Wm.. H. Wise & Co., 193?. 1356 pp. Illustrated. Indexes.**

Essays cover such topics as Animal Dances of the East, Midsummer Beliefs and Practices, and Food Taboos and Their Meaning. Subject headings under which essays are grouped are: Agricultural Customs; Children and the Young; Costume, Special Customs; The Dance; Death and the Disposal of the Dead; Education, Customs in; Etiquette and Conventions; The Family; Fetish and Fetish Worship; Folk Lore; Food and Food Gathering; Games and Amusement; Habitations; Law and Justice; Local Customs; Magic, Primitive; Marriage; Medicine and Treatment of the Sick; Miscellaneous; Music; Nature Lore and Superstitions; Naval and Sea Customs; Personal Adornment; Racial Manners; Religion and Religious Customs; Seasonal Customs; Sex Customs; Sport; Springtide; Summer; Taboo; War and Military Customs; and Witch Doctors and Witchcraft. Classified index to chapter titles. General index (including illustrations). (NR)

♦ 43 ♦

Manners, Customs, and Observances: Their Origin and Signification. **Leopold Wagner. 1894. Reprint. Detroit, MI: Omnigraphics, Inc., 1968. 318 pp. Index.**

Gives the origins and explains the meaning of a wealth of popular practices, symbols, and days of observance. Materials organized by topic. Covers royalty, the Church, the armed services, government, the law, community, society, courtship, marriage, death, burial, popular amusements, saints, Church festivals, Jewish festivals, and secular holidays or commemorations. British emphasis.

DEWEY: 390 LC: GT 75 W3 ISBN 1-55888-186-7

♦ 44 ♦

Mort's Guide to Festivals Feasts Fairs and Fiestas: International Edition. **Mort Barish and Michaela M. Mole. Princeton, NJ: C.M.G. Publishing Company, Inc., 1974. 191 pp. Index.**

Provides a calendar listing of thousands of festivals, fairs, and holiday celebrations in 115 countries of Asia, Africa, the Caribbean, Europe, North and South America, the Middle East, and the Pacific. Covers folk, religious, food, cultural, sports, national, patriotic, and other festivals. Gives date and location, and most listings include major attractions. Also gives address of national tourism office for each country.

DEWEY: 394 ISBN 0-9600718-5-7

♦ 45 ♦

Multicultural Holidays. **Julia Jasmine. Illustrated by Sue Fullman and Theresa M. Wright. Huntington Beach, CA: Teacher Created Materials, Inc., 1994. 304 pp. Index.**

An aid to elementary school teachers in presenting ethnic diversity. Gives a brief explanation of over 75 holidays from around the world, including American ethnic holidays. Organized by season. Suggests classroom exercises, activities, and crafts, introduces foreign words and foods, gives teaching tips.

DEWEY: 394.26 ISBN 1-55734-615-1

♦ 46 ♦

Music Festivals of the World: A Guide to Leading Festivals of Music, Opera, and Ballet. **Dennis Gray Stoll. Oxford, England: Pergamon Press Ltd., 1963. 310 pp. Illustrated. Index.**

Divided into 21 chapters, each featuring the important festivals of a country or region of the world. Heavy coverage of western and central Europe. Detailed information given for 70 festivals, including an account of the festival's origin, history, location, composers, and featured music. Contact information given for many festivals.

DEWEY: 780.9 LC: ML 35 S 875

♦ 47 ♦

The Mystical Year. **Editors of Time Life Books. Alexandria, VA: Time Life Books, 1992. 144 pp. Bibliography. Illustrated. Index.**

Presents a holiday, festival, or paranormal occurrence for each day of the year, selecting those which celebrate mystical traditions or mysterious forces. Includes ancient and contemporary celebrations and events from around the world. Each of the four seasons introduced with a brief essay. Richly illustrated with color photographs and drawings of sites, artifacts, and celebrations.

DEWEY: 291.3 6 LC: BL 590.M97 ISBN 0-8094-6537-X

♦ 48 ♦

1996 World Holiday and Time Guide. **Annual. New York: J. P. Morgan and Co., Inc., 1996. 155 pp.**

Offers a country by country listing of holiday dates, time zones, bank hours, and business hour overlaps (for countries with more than one time zone). Gives holiday dates and time zones for all U.S. states. Lists holidays of the world and U.S. state holidays by date. Provides time difference tables. Reviews the services and philosophy of J.P. Morgan and lists its office locations. Interactive version of this booklet is available through the J. P. Morgan website at http://www.jpmorgan.com.

LC: GT 3930 W6

♦ 49 ♦

Observations on the Popular Antiquities of Great Britain: Chiefly Illustrating the Origin of Our Vulgar and Provincial Customs, Ceremonies, and Superstitions. **John Brand. Arranged, revised, and greatly enlarged by Sir Henry Ellis. Three volumes. Volume one (1895), 539 pp.; volume two (1900), 522 pp.; volume three (1901), 499 pp. Reprint. New introduction by Leslie Shepard. Detroit, MI: Omnigraphics, Inc., 1969. Index.**

Describes, provides commentary on, and gives history of British holidays, customs, and folk beliefs. Lengthy entries refer to popular beliefs and customs of the day, as well as references made in historic documents and literary texts. Covers folk and religious holidays, calendar customs, amusements, superstitions, games, ceremonies, beliefs, practices relating to the supernatural, and more. Volume one treats holidays and calendar customs. Volume two treats customs and ceremonies not associated with the calendar, and volume three addresses popular beliefs and practices relating to divination and the supernatural. Original edition published in the eighteenth century. Index to all volumes in volume three.

DEWEY: 390.00942 LC: DA 110 B83 ISBN 1-55888-915-9

♦ 50 ♦

Round the Year with the World's Religions. **Royston Pike. 1950. Reprint. Detroit, MI: Omnigraphics, Inc., 1993. 208 pp. Illustrated. Index.**

Chronologically arranged chapters covering customs, legends, and stories behind religious observances in ancient Rome and Greece, Europe, India, Tibet, China, Japan, and Ceylon, and among ancient Romans, Greeks and Egyptians, Jews, Christians, Hindus, Jains, Muslims, Buddhists, Incans, and Aztecs.

DEWEY: 394.2 P 635r ISBN 1-55888-996-5

♦ 51 ♦

Seasons of the Sun: Celebrations from the World's Spiritual Traditions. **Patricia Telesco. York Beach, MN: Samuel Weiser, Inc., 1996. 307 pp. Bibliography. Illustrated. Indexes.**

A book of days directed towards those interested in home celebration of diverse holidays. Introduces 129 holidays and festivals from more than 40 cultural traditions, ancient and contemporary. Entries summarize the magical themes, history, and lore of each holiday and suggest decorating ideas, garments, ritual food and drink, incense, activities, and invocations, incantations, spells, and blessings. Also covers life-cycle event celebrations. Holiday, recipe, and general index. Black-and-white drawings illustrate.

DEWEY: 291.36 LC: BF 1623.R6T45 ISBN 0-87728-872-0

♦ 52 ♦

Small World Celebrations. **Jean Warren and Elizabeth McKinnon. Illustrated by Marion Hopping Ekberg. Everett, WA: Warren Publishing House, Inc., 1988. 160 pp.**

Introduces 16 festivals and celebrations from around the world and tells how to organize a celebration of each event for children. Covers the Winter Festival (Russia), Chinese New Year, Doll's Day and Boy's Day (Japan), Saint Patrick's Day (Ireland), May Day (England), Lei Day (Hawaii), Bastille Day (France), Inter-tribal Indian Ceremonial (Native America), Diwali (India), Hanukkah (Jewish), Christmas (Mexico and Germany), Kwanzaa (African American), and the World Eskimo Indian Olympics (Alaska). Furnishes brief explanation of the event and its celebration, presents craft activities, songs, and foods, and furnishes a folk tale from the culture.

DEWEY: 745.5941 ISBN 0-911019-19-7

♦ 53 ♦

Stories of the World's Holidays. **Grace Humphrey. 1924. Reprint. Detroit, MI: Omnigraphics, Inc., 1990. 335 pp. Index.**

A collection of stories about the people, events, and ideas celebrated in holidays from around the world. Includes stories about Robert E. Lee, the Chinese Feast of Lanterns, Abraham Lincoln, St.Valentine, George Washington, Japanese festivals, St. Patrick, Lexington Day, Poland's Constitution, Memorial Day, the Declaration of Independence, Jan Hus, Bastille Day, Simon Bolívar, the Star-Spangled Banner, the unification of Italy, Christopher Columbus, the Gunpowder Plot (England), Thanksgiving, and Christmas. Offers suggestions for further reading.

DEWEY: 394.2 6 LC: GT 3933 H86 ISBN 1-55888-882-9

♦ 54 ♦

UNICEF'S Festival Book. **Judith Spiegelman. Illustrations by Audrey Preissler. New York: United States Committee for UNICEF, 1966. 25 pp.**

Tells how 12 festivals from around the world are celebrated. Treats Ethiopian New Year, Divali (India), No-Ruz (Iran), Hanukkah (Israel), the Doll Festival (Japan), Posadas (Mexico), St. Nicholas's Day (the Netherlands), Id-al-Fitr (Pakistan), Easter (Poland), St. Lucia Day (Sweden), Songkran (Thailand), and Halloween (the United States and Canada). Illustrated with color drawings. For children.

DEWEY: 394 S755

♦ 55 ♦

Wild Planet! 1,001 Extraordinary Events for the Inspired Traveler. **Tom Clynes. Detroit, MI: Visible Ink Press, 1995. 669 pp. Illustrated. Indexes.**

Describes the celebration of 1,001 festivals, holidays, and special events from around the world. Treats events in 17 West European countries, nine East European countries, five Middle Eastern countries, nine African countries, seven South and Central Asian countries, six East Asian countries, eight Southeast Asian countries, five Pacific countries, eight South American countries, two Central American countries, 11 Caribbean Islands, Canada and the United States. Entries give date, location, transportation tips, accommodations, and organizations to contact for more information. Provides a list of tourist information organizations for each country. Illustrated with black-and-white photos. Indexed by festival activity, by month, and by country and event name.

DEWEY: 910.2 C649w ISBN 0-7876-0203-5

♦ 56 ♦

The World of Festivals. **Philip Steele. Rand McNally and Company, 1996. 46 pp. Illustrated. Glossary. Index.**

Introduces children to many different types of festivals and celebrations, and identifies examples of these festival types from around the world. Festivals are grouped together by the following themes: family festivals, life-cycle celebrations, celebrations of the past, special days, change and renewal, seasonal festivals, world gatherings, arts festivals, and unusual festivals. Also groups together Jewish, Christian, Islamic, Hindu, Sikh, Buddhist, and other spiritual festivals. Gives festival calendar. Color photos and drawings illustrate.

DEWEY: 394.2 LC: GT 3933.S73 ISBN 0-528-83758-3

♦ 57 ♦

A World of Holidays. **Louisa Campbell. Illustrated by Michael Bryant. New York: Silver Moon Press, 1993. 61 pp. Glossary.**

Offers short stories for children which depict the customs and festivities of five international holidays. Covers New Year in Japan, Ramadan and Eid-ul-Fitr in Pakistan, Independence Day in Namibia, Thanksgiving among the Canadian Iroquois, and Christmas in Mexico. Also discusses the variety of customs found in new year festivals around the world. Illustrated with black-and-white drawings and photographs.

DEWEY: 394.2 6 LC: GT 3933. C36 ISBN 1-881889-08-4

♦ 58 ♦

The Year's Festivals. **Helen Philbrook Patten. Boston, MA: Dana Estes and Company, 1903. 270 pp. Illustrated.**

Describes the customs and celebrations of nine holidays: New Year's Day, Twelfth Night, St. Valentine's Day, All Fools' Day, Easter, May Day, Halloween, Thanksgiving, and Christmas. Includes material from many historical periods and different countries. European emphasis.

Seasonal Holidays and International Events

♦ 59 ♦

All Saints All Souls and Halloween. **Catherine Chambers. Austin, TX: Raintree Steck-Vaughn Publishers, 1997. 31 pp. Illustrated. Glossary. Index.**

Gives history, customs, and symbols of three autumn holidays honoring souls, spirits and the dead: All Saints Day, All Souls Day, and Halloween. Provides two craft projects, a scary story, and further reading list. Color photos of celebrations in Europe, Latin America, Africa, the United States and Mexico illustrate. Further reading list. For children. One book in a series entitled *A World of Holidays.*

DEWEY: 394.2 646 LC: GT4965.C47 ISBN 0-8172-4606-1

♦ 60 ♦

Autumn Festivals. **Mike Rosen. New York: The Bookwright Press, 1990. 32 pp. Glossary. Illustrated. Index.**

Introduces children to autumn festivals from around the world. Illustrated with color photos. Explains food and harvest festivals. Treats various Thanksgiving and tropical harvest festivals, Hanukkah, Bonfire Night (Britain), Diwali (India), the Moon Festival (China), Dussehra and Durga Puja (India), various festivals of remembrance, the Festival of Kali (Bengal), and Rosh Hashanah. Gives festival significance and highlights. Illustrated with color photos. Further reading list. One book in a series on seasonal festivals.

DEWEY: 394.2 683 LC: GT 4380.R67 ISBN 0-531-18352-1

♦ 61 ♦

Calendar Moon. **Natalia Belting. Illustrated by Bernarda Bryson. New York: Holt, Rinehart and Winston, 1964. 58 pp.**

Furnishes verses celebrating the lunar months. Based on the natural events, legends, and the often-poetic names that peoples from around the world have associated with lunar months. Two-tone drawings illustrate. For young readers.

DEWEY: 398

♦ 62 ♦

Celebrate the Solstice: Honoring the Earth's Seasonal Rhythms Through Festival and Ceremony. **Richard Heinberg. Foreword by Dolores La Chapelle. Wheaton, IL: Quest Books, The Theosophical Publishing House, 1993. 199 pp. Illustrated. Bibliography. Index.**

Discusses the celebration of winter and summer solstices and world renewal rites and myths throughout history and around the world. Suggests activities for contemporary observance. Notes. (NR)

DEWEY: 394.2 LC: GT4995.W55 H45 ISBN 0-8356-0693-7

♦ 63 ♦

Celebrating Nature: Rites and Ceremonies Around the World. **Elizabeth S. Helfman. Illustrated by Carolyn Cather. New York: Seabury Press, 1969. 165 pp. Index.**

Describes ancient and contemporary celebrations of nature from around the world. Links a number of more contemporary European and American holidays to ancient rites celebrating nature. Covers the ancient Egyptians, Greeks, Hebrews, Romans, and European peoples, contemporary Japan and China, and ethnic groups from sub-Saharan Africa, South and South East Asia, North and South America. Written for older children. Further reading list.

DEWEY: J 394.2 LC: GR 930. H44

♦ 64 ♦

The Complete Book of the Olympics. **David Wallechinsky. New York: Penguin Books, 1984. 680 pp. Illustrated.**

Provides the final results for all sports from the 1896 through the 1984 Olympic Games. Also tells the stories of individual athletes before and after their Olympic careers, and recounts dramatic contests for medals in all sports.

DEWEY: 796.48 W196 c ISBN 0-14-01-0771-1

♦ 65 ♦

Coubertin's Olympics: How the Games Began. **Davida Kristy. Minneapolis, MN: Lerner Publications, 1995. 128 pp. Illustrated. Index.**

Offers a biography of Baron Pierre de Coubertin, focusing on the central occupation of his adult life, the establishment of the modern Olympic Games. Discusses the events and controversies which marked the early years of the modern Games, 1896 to 1936. Illustrated with black-and-white photos. End-notes. Lists sources.

DEWEY: 338.4 7796 092   LC: GV 721.2 C68 K75   ISBN 0-8225-3327-8

♦ 66 ♦

Easter and Other Spring Holidays. **Gilda Berger. New York: Franklin Watts, 1983. 66 pp. Illustrated. Index.**

Describes past and present springtime celebrations, noting their origins and customs. Treats ancient Greek, Roman, Celtic, and Northern European beliefs and practices, May Day, Walpurgis Night, Holi, Buddha's Birthday (Asia), April Fool's Day, Shumbun-no-hi (Japan), Tu Bishvat, Purim, and Passover. Special emphasis on the Easter season, including Shrove Tuesday, Ash Wednesday, and Holy Week. Also covers Shavuot and Pentecost. Gives Easter crafts, activities, and recipes. For young readers. Black-and-white photos illustrate.

DEWEY: 394.2 68283   LC: GT 4935 B47   ISBN 0-531-04547-1

♦ 67 ♦

The Guinness Book of Olympic Facts and Feats. **Stan Greenberg. Enfield, Middlesex, England: Guinness Superlatives Limited, 1983. 256 pp. Illustrated. Index.**

Briefly reviews the history and athletic highlights of the modern Olympic Games (from 1896 to 1984). Gives brief history of each sporting event, and notes medal winners and record setters in each event from 1896 to 1984. Also lists firsts, mosts, greatests, youngests, oldests, and other superlatives for each sport. Illustrated with color and black-and-white photos.

DEWEY: 796.4 809   LC: GV 721.8   ISBN 0-85112-273-6

♦ 68 ♦

Happy New Year Round the World. **Lois S. Johnson. Illustrated by Lili Cassel Wronker. Rand McNally and Company, 1966. 176 pp. Index.**

Tells how the New Year is celebrated in 26 countries of Europe, Asia, Africa, the Middle East, and Latin America. Includes entry for the United States. Describes customs, foods, festivities, religious observances, and greetings. Each entry gives New Year words in foreign languages. For young readers.

DEWEY: 394.268

♦ 69 ♦

Harvest Festivals Around the World. **Judith Hoffman Corwin. Parsipanny, NJ: Julian Messner, 1995. 48 pp. Illustrated.**

Briefly describes harvest festivals from 14 different cultures: Hopi, French Canadian, Inca, West Indian, Swiss, English, ancient Egyptian, Nigerian, Israeli, Japanese, Chinese, and Indian. Gives craft activity for each holiday. For children.

DEWEY: 394.2 64 LC: GT 4380.C67 ISBN 0-671-87239-7

♦ 70 ♦

Luna: Myth and Mystery. **Kathleen Cain. Boulder, CO: Johnson Publishing Company, 1991. 202 pp. Illustrated. Bibliography. Glossary. Index.**

Presents a wide range of folklore, facts, myths, gods, goddesses, stories, songs, poems, legends, rituals, festivals, beliefs, and customs associated with the moon from past and present cultures around the world. Also treats lunar calendars, plants and animals associated with or affected by the moon, and moon astronomy and space exploration. Gives further readings, moon-related associations, and suppliers of moon paraphernalia. Black-and-white illustrations. Endnotes for each chapter.

DEWEY: 398.362 LC: BL 325.M56 C35 ISBN 1-55566-070-3

♦ 71 ♦

May Day. **Dorothy Les Tina. Illustrated by Hope Meryman. New York: Thomas Y. Crowell, 1967. 34 pp.**

Briefly describes May celebrations from around the world and throughout history. For children.

DEWEY: 394 M466L

♦ 72 ♦

National Holidays Around the World. **Lavinia Dobler. New York: Fleet Press, 1968. 234 pp. Illustrated. Bibliography. Index.**

Depicts national holiday and independence day celebrations for 134 countries. Also describes the nation's flag, its history, and symbolism. Written for older children.

DEWEY: 394.26 ISBN 0-8303-0044-9

♦ 73 ♦

New Year. **Alan Blackwood. Vero Beach, FL: Rourke Enterprises, Inc., 1987. 48 pp. Glossary. Illustrated. Index.**

Discusses ancient celebrations of the New Year in Egypt, Babylonia, Rome, and in Celtic lands. Explanation of the Jewish and Chinese calendars, the Muslim and Hindu New Year, New Year observances throughout Asia, the New Year in the United States and Britain, and some mention of various European customs. Entries on St. Sebastian and St. Basil. Further reading list. For young readers. One volume in a series entitled *Holidays and Festivals.* (NR)

DEWEY: 394.2 683 LC: GT4905. B42 ISBN 0-86592-981-5

♦ 74 ♦

New Year: Its History, Customs, and Superstitions. **Theodor H. Gaster. New York: Abelard-Schuman, 1955. 138 pp. Illustrated. Bibliography. Index.**

Reviews the popular beliefs and practices surrounding New Year's celebrations in many cultures, ancient and contemporary. Covers such widespread practices as noise-making, fortune-telling, feasting, ritual cleansing, exchanging gifts and greetings, and more.

DEWEY: 394 N532 G

♦ 75 ♦

New Year's Day. **Lynn Groh. Illustrated by Leonard Shortall. Champaign, IL: Garrard Publishing Company, 1964. 64 pp.**

Describes New Year's Day celebrations across cultures and throughout history. Treats the ancient Babylonians, Jews, Greeks, and Romans. Also treats old European customs, Native North American celebrations, Chinese New Year, and other contemporary American celebrations. Illustrated with two-tone drawings. For children.

DEWEY: 394.2683

♦ 76 ♦

The Nobel Prize. **Peter Wilhelm. London: Springwood Books, 1983. 111 pp. Illustrated.**

Provides a brief biography of Alfred Nobel, founder of the Nobel Prizes, describes the Nobel Prize nomination procedure and the awards ceremonies, and explains the various undertakings of the Nobel Foundation. Also furnishes interviews with six past winners who discuss how the prize has changed their lives. Gives Nobel Prize statistics, and a listing of past winners in all categories from 1901 to 1982. Illustrated with color and black-and-white photos.

DEWEY: 007.9 W678 ISBN 0-86254-111-5

♦ 77 ♦

The Olympics: A History of the Games. **William Oscar Johnson. Birmingham, AL: Oxmoor House, Inc., 1992. 224 pp. Illustrated. Appendix. Index.**

Gives a history of the modern Olympic Games from 1896 to 1988. Recounts athletic highlights, tells the story of noted Olympic athletes, and traces the development and changing spirit of the Games. Appendix lists gold medal winners and record setters from the 1896 through the 1992 winter Games. More than 180 color photos illustrate.

DEWEY: 796.48 J71 ISBN 0-8487-1115-7

♦ 78 ♦

The Olympics Factbook: A Spectator's Guide to the Winter and Summer Games. **Martin Connors, Diane L. Dupuis, and Brad Morgan. Detroit, MI: Visible Ink Press, 1992. 613 pp. Illustrated.**

Provides background information on the sporting events of the modern Olympics. Furnishes brief history of the sport, including Olympic history; explains event rules and strategies; tells how each Olympic event is won or scored; discusses the achievements of potential 1992 medal winners; lists events schedules for the 1992 games; and furnishes names and scores (or times) of previous medal winners. Illustrated with black-and-white photos.

DEWEY: 796.48 ISBN 0-8103-9417-0

♦ 79 ♦

Rest Days: A Study in Early Law and Morality. **Hutton Webster. 1916. Reprint. Detroit, MI: Omnigraphics, Inc., 1992. 325 pp. Index.**

Recounts customary beliefs and practices associated with culturally designated days of rest. Covers ancient and modern cultures from around the world, with an emphasis on non-Western societies. Discusses taboos in various Pacific island and Asian cultures; holy days in ancient societies of the Old World; Babylonian "evil days"; the Jewish Sabbath; and lunar calendars, festivals, and beliefs; death-related practices; market days; and unlucky days around the world.

DEWEY: 394 W379 LC: GT3930.H87 ISBN 1-55888-919-9

♦ 80 ♦

Seasonal Feasts and Festivals. **E. O. James. 1961. Reprint. Detroit, MI: Omnigraphics, Inc., 1993. 336 pp. Bibliography. Index.**

Learned compilation and analysis of data on more than 100 season-based festivals, rituals, and popular celebrations of Europe and the Near East, from Paleolithic times to the eighteenth century. Notes similarities across cultures and traces historical transformations and continuations of earlier practices and beliefs in folklore, myth, elements of worship, popular celebrations, and customs. Covers Paleolithic hunting rites, the emergence of agriculturally oriented cults, seasonal festivals and calendar systems of ancient Egypt, Mesopotamia, Palestine, Asia Minor, Greece, and Rome. Also treats the development of the Christian liturgical calendar and Christian feasts, medieval liturgical plays, seasonal folk plays, popular dances, and festivals.

DEWEY: 394.2 LC: GT3930.J3 ISBN 0-7808-0001-X

♦ 81 ♦

The Solstice Evergreen: The History, Folklore, and Origins of the Christmas Tree. **Sheryl Ann Karas. Boulder Creek, CA: Aslan Publishing, 1991. 137 pp. Illustrated. Appendix. Bibliography. Index.**

Explores the spiritual symbolism of the tree, with emphasis on the evergreen tree. Discusses folk beliefs and observances connecting trees with spirituality in many religions and cultures, including such world religions as Christianity, but also ancient and indigenous religions. Includes folktales from many lands and times. Appendix lists folktales by theme. Black-and-white drawings illustrate.

DEWEY: 398.2 88282 LC: GT4989 K37 ISBN 0-944031-26-9

♦ 82 ♦

Spring Festivals. **Mike Rosen. New York: The Bookwright Press, 1991. 32 pp. Illustrated. Glossary. Index.** 📖

Introduces children to spring holidays from various countries and religions. Includes April Fool's Day, Purim, Holi (India), Passover, various flower festivals, Easter, Ch'ing Ming, various new year festivals, Baisakhi, Buddhist New Year, and the Apoo festival (Ghana). Color photos illustrate. Further reading list. One book in a series on seasonal festivals.

DEWEY: 394.2 683 LC: GT 4995.V4 R67 ISBN 0-531-18384-X

♦ 83 ♦

The Story of the Olympic Games, 776 B.C. to 1972. **Revised edition. John Kieran and Arthur Daley. Philadelphia, PA: J. B. Lippincott Company, 1973. 542 pp. Index.**

Noted sportswriters recount the athletic achievements and political controversies of the modern Olympiads, from the Athens Games of 1896 to the Munich Games of 1972. Briefly summarizes the history of the ancient Olympics. Includes a list of champions in all events of the modern Olympics.

DEWEY: 796.4 8 09 LC: GV 23. K5 ISBN 0-397-00899-6

♦ 84 ♦

Summer Festivals. **Mike Rosen. New York: The Bookwright Press, 1991. 32 pp. Illustrated. Glossary. Index.**

Introduces children to summer festivals from around the world. Covers traditional May Day in Britain, May Day as a workers' holiday, the Dragon Boat Festival (China), the summer solstice, the Obon Festival (Japan), Festival of the Hungry Ghosts (China), Independence Day (France, Canada, the United States), Australia Day, Eisteddfod (Wales), and the Notting Hill Carnival (England). Describes festival highlights and significance. Illustrated with color photos. Further reading list. One book in a series on seasonal festivals.

DEWEY: 394.2 683 LC: GT 3933.R66 ISBN 0-531-18383-1

♦ 85 ♦

United Nations Day. **Olive Rabe. Illustrated by Aliki. New York: Thomas Y. Crowell Company, 1965. 34 pp.**

Explains the observation of United Nations Day by describing the founding of the United Nations and sketching the programs it sponsors. Illustrated with color drawings. For children.

DEWEY: 394 U58r

♦ 86 ♦

The United Nations 50th Anniversary Book. **Barbara Brenner. New York: Atheneum Books for Young Readers, 1995. 90 pp. Illustrated. Index.**

Gives a history of the first 50 years of the United Nations, tells how it works, and describes its programs around the world. Covers seven areas of U.N. activity: peace, human rights, the environment, health, education, culture and the arts, and space programs. Offers 50-year scorecard of U.N. achievements and remaining challenges. Amply illustrated with color photos. Provides resource list of nongovernmental organizations. For young readers.

DEWEY: 341.23 1 LC: JX1977.B69 ISBN 0-689-31912-6

♦ 87 ♦

We Celebrate New Year. **Bobbie Kalman. Illustrated by Tina Holdcroft. New York: Crabtree Publishing Company, 1985. 56 pp. Index.**

Describes New Year customs, crafts, games, foods, superstitions, and celebrations from around the world. Also covers holidays celebrated near New Year, such as St. Sylvester's Day (Europe), Jonkonoo (the Caribbean), and Diwali (India). Furnishes games and stories based on the materials covered in the book. Illustrated with color drawings. For children. One volume in a series entitled *Holidays and Festivals.*

DEWEY: 398.2 683 LC: GT 4905 K35 ISBN 0-86505-041-4

♦ 88 ♦

Winter Festivals. **Mike Rosen. New York: Bookwright Press, 1990. 32 pp. Illustrated. Glossary. Index.**

Introduces winter festivals from around the world to children. Covers Peruvian and other winter solstice celebrations, Christmas, Pongol (India), Chinese and other New Year festivals, Mardi Gras, Carnival, and various snow festivals. Gives further reading list. Color photos of celebrations illustrate. One book in a series on seasonal festivals.

DEWEY: 394.2 683 LC: GT 3933.R67 ISBN 0-531-18353-X

♦ 89 ♦

The Words of Peace: Selections from the Speeches of the Winners of the Nobel Peace Prize. **Irwin Abrams, ed. Foreword by Jimmy Carter. Introduction by Jakob Sverdrup. New York: Newmarket Press, 1990. 139 pp. Illustrated. Index.**

Excerpts from the speeches of Nobel Peace Prize winners on peace and such related themes as human connectedness, faith, hope, war, violence, nonviolence, human rights, politics, and leadership. Gives chronology of Peace Prize winners from 1901 to 1989. Illustrated with black-and-white photos.

DEWEY: 327.1 72 LC: JX 1963. W713 ISBN 1-55704-060-5

Historic Events Commemorated Around the World

♦ 90 ♦

The Atomic Bomb: Voices from Hiroshima and Nagasaki. **Kyoko Selden and Mark Selden. Armonk, NY: M. E. Sharpe, Inc., 1989. 257 pp. Illustrated. Bibliography.**

An anthology of short stories, poetry, photographs, drawings, and memories of the bombings of Hiroshima and Nagasaki. Contributors include survivors of the blasts as well as Japanese writers and artists. Includes an essay explaining and critiquing the reasons for the bombings.

DEWEY: 940.54 25 LC: D767.25 H6 A87 ISBN 0-87332-556-7

♦ 91 ♦

Christopher Columbus. **Gianni Granzotto. Translated by Stephen Sartarelli. Garden City, New York: Doubleday and Company, Inc., 1985. 300 pp. Maps. Index.**

Offers a biography of Christopher Columbus for the general reader. Describes his achievements and his character.

DEWEY: 970.01 5 LC: E111. G784 ISBN 0-385-19677-6

♦ 92 ♦

Columbus: An Annotated Guide to the Scholarship on His Life and Writings, 1750-1988. **Foster Provost. Detroit, MI: Omnigraphics, Inc., 1991. 225 pp. Indexes.**

Furnishes an annotated bibliography of 780 works concerning Christopher Columbus published between the years 1750 and 1988. Emphasizes works published after 1875; covers works in English, Spanish, Italian, and other languages. Chronologically arranged within the following seven categories: collections of documents and texts, editions and transcriptions of primary documents, studies of primary documents, Columbus's life, Columbiana, bibliographies, and Columbus scholarship. Cross-referenced. Index of authors and editors, persons and places, and topics.

DEWEY: 016.97001 5 LC: Z8187.P76 ISBN 1-55888-157-3

♦ 93 ♦

Columbus Documents: Summaries of Documents in Genoa. **Luciano F. Farina and Robert W. Tolf, eds. Translated by Luciano F. Farina. Detroit, MI: Omnigraphics, Inc., 1992. 166 pp. Appendices. Index.**

Offers an English-language summarized translation of 179 historical documents concerning Christopher Columbus located in Genoan archives. Entries note document number, date of composition or notarization, city and exact location where document was drafted, archive or location where document can currently be found, name of notary who drafted the document, location of the file that contains the document, and summary of the document's contents. Appendix A treats Columbus's *Book of Royal Privileges,* appendix B gives a synopsis of Giovanni Monleone and Giovanni Pessagno's *Christopher Columbus: Documents and Proofs of His Genoese Origins,* and appendix C lists individuals whose names appear in the documents treated in this work.

DEWEY: 016.97001 5 LC: Z6616. C73 C65 ISBN 1-55888-156-5

♦ 94 ♦

The Conquest of Paradise: Christopher Columbus and the Columbian Legacy. **Kirkpatrick Sale. New York: Alfred A. Knopf, 1990. 453 pp. Index.**

Describes the voyages of Columbus, their impact on Europe, Columbus as a product of his age, and the attitudes towards nature and native peoples that Columbus brought with him to the New World. Also documents the continuance of these attitudes by the European colonists who followed Columbus, and the historical development of the myths and legends surrounding Columbus. Source notes and endnotes.

DEWEY: 970.01 5 LC: E112. S16 ISBN 0-394-57429-X

♦ 95 ♦

Conscience and Courage: Rescuers of Jews During the Holocaust. **Eva Fogelman. New York: Anchor Books, 1994. 393 pp. Bibliograpy. Index.**

Documents the stories of many people who acted to save Jews during the Holocaust, from well-known to unknown individuals. Examines the psychological make-up of these people in an attempt to explain their acts of conscience and courage, and to contribute to the psychology of altruism. Endnotes.

DEWEY: 940.53 18 0922 LC: D804.3 F64 ISBN 0-385-42027-7

♦ 96 ♦

The Day the War Ended: May 8, 1945 Victory in Europe. **Martin Gilbert. New York: Henry Holt and Company, 1995. 473 pp. Illustrated. Maps. Bibliography. Index.**

Describes the events of the last days of World War II in Europe, the liberation of the camps, the German surrender, and the celebrations of V-E Day in Europe, Russia, and the U.S. Many first-hand accounts and anecdotes woven into the text. Black-and-white photos illustrate.

DEWEY: 940.54 21 LC: D755.7 G55 ISBN 0-8050-3926-0

♦ 97 ♦

D-Day. **Wallace B. Black and Jean F. Blashfield. New York: Crestwood House, 1992. 48 pp. Illustrated. Glossary. Index.**

Gives historical background and describes D-Day and the liberation of France. Illustrated with black-and-white photos. For young readers. One volume in a series entitled *World War II 50th Anniversary.*

DEWEY: 940.54 2142 LC: D756.5 N6 B5 ISBN 0-89686-566-5

♦ 98 ♦

D-Day. **Marilyn Miller. Morristown, NJ: Silver Burdett Company, 1986. 64 pp. Illustrated. Index.**

Describes the Nazi takeover of Europe and the preparations for and events of D-Day 1944. Also discusses the Allied campaign to liberate Europe. Illustrated with black-and-white drawings and photos. Suggested reading list. For young readers. One volume in a series entitled *Turning Points in American History.*

DEWEY: 940.54 21 LC: D756.5 N6 M48 ISBN 0-382-06825-4

♦ 99 ♦

D-Day June 6, 1944: The Climactic Battle of World War II. **Stephen E. Ambrose. New York: Simon and Schuster, 1994. 655 pp. Illustrated. Appendix. Bibliography. Glossary. Index.**

In-depth historical study of the preparations for and the events of D-Day, 1944. Based on archival research and the testimony of American, Canadian, British, French, and German participants.

DEWEY: 940.54 2142 LC: D756.5 N6 A455 ISBN 0-671-67334-3

♦ 100 ♦

The End of Order: Versailles 1919. **Charles L. Mee, Jr. New York: E. P. Dutton, 1980. 301 pp. Bibliography. Index.**

Describes the people, conversations, attitudes, and events that went into the writing and signing of the Versailles peace treaty in 1919 that ended World War I.

DEWEY: 940.3141 LC: D644. M43 ISBN 0-525-09810-0

♦ 101 ♦

Eye-Witness to D-Day: The Story of the Battle by Those Who Were There. **Jon E. Lewis, ed. Foreword by Field Marshal Lord Carver. New York: Carroll and Graf Publishers, 1994. 314 pp. Illustrated. Appendices.**

The story of D-Day and the Allied liberation of Normandy as told through the first-hand accounts of Allied soldiers and officers, French citizens, and German soldiers. Appendices give the Allied order of the day, the Allied order of battle and map, a military glossary, and sources.

DEWEY: 940.5421 ISBN 0-7867-0090-4

♦ 102 ♦

Hiroshima No Pika. **Toshi Maruki. New York: Lothrop, Lee and Shepard Books, 1980. 44 pp. Illustrated.**

Dramatized retelling of the bombing of Hiroshima from the perspective of a little girl who survived the blast. Briefly describes memorial activities of Peace Day (August 6) in Hiroshima. Color drawings illustrate. For children.

DEWEY: 940.54 26 LC: D767.25 H6 M2913 ISBN 0-688-01297-3

♦ 103 ♦

The Holocaust: A History of the Jews of Europe During the Second World War. **Martin Gilbert. New York: Holt, Rinehart and Winston, 1985. 959 pp. Illustrated. Index.**

A detailed historical account of the Nazi attempt to destroy European Jewry. Covers the years 1933 to 1945, giving a brief history of European anti-Semitism and explaining how Hitler aroused these long-standing hatreds. Describes the programs of mass slaughter, the concentration camps, and resistance efforts. Includes stories of eyewitnesses. References and sources given in endnotes.

DEWEY: 940.53 15 03924 LC: D810 J4 G525 ISBN 0-03-062416-9

♦ 104 ♦

June 6, 1944: The Voices of D-Day. **Gerald Astor. New York: St. Martin's Press, 1994. 370 pp. Illustrated. Bibliography.**

An account of the events of D-Day drawn largely from interviews with veterans. Provides list of veterans interviewed, noting their occupations after the war.

DEWEY: 940.54 2142 LC: D756.5 N6 J86 ISBN 0-312-110140-6

♦ 105 ♦

The Longest Day: June 6, 1944. **Cornelius Ryan. New York: Simon and Schuster, 1959. 350 pp. Illustrated. Maps. Bibliography. Index.**

Detailed retelling of the events of D-Day, June 6, 1944. Based on interviews, questionnaires, letters, and memorabilia from more than 1000 D-Day veterans. Gives partial list of American, British, Canadian, and German D-Day veterans and their current occupations.

DEWEY: 940.542 ISBN 671-20814-1

♦ 106 ♦

Never To Forget: The Jews of the Holocaust. **Milton Meltzer. New York: Harper and Row, Publishers, 1976. 217 pp. Bibliography. Index.**

Explains how Hitler inflamed long-standing anti-Semitic sentiments and describes the Nazi persecution and extermination of six million Jews. Also describes organized and individual acts of resistance. Chronology of important dates in the history of Nazi Germany.

DEWEY: 940.5315 ISBN 0-06-024174-8

♦ 107 ♦

November 1918. **Gordon Brook-Shepherd. Boston, MA: Little, Brown and Company, 1981. 461 pp. Illustrated. Appendices. Bibliography. Index.**

Recounts the history of the last 100 days of World War I. References given in endnotes. Appendix A reprints President Wilson's Peace Program; Appendix B, the Armistice convention with Bulgaria; Appendix C, the Armistice with Austria-Hungary; and Appendix D, the armistice with Germany.

DEWEY: 940.3 B871 ISBN 0-316-10960-6

♦ 108 ♦

On the Wings of Peace. **Sheila Hamanaka, comp. New York: Clarion Books, 1995. 144 pp. Illustrated. Bibliography.**

An international collection of authors and illustrators provides children's stories, poems, and prose on the themes of war and peace between peoples and nations. Special emphasis on the bombings of Hiroshima and Nagasaki. Bibliography of books and videos for adults and children on Hiroshima, Nagasaki, and atomic war. Royalties from sales are donated to Amnesty International U.S.A., For Our Children's Sake Foundation, and Friends of Hibakusha.

DEWEY: 810.8 O58 LC: PZ5. O57 ISBN 0-395-72619-0

♦ 109 ♦

The Other Victims: First-Person Stories of Non-Jews Persecuted by the Nazis. **Ina R. Friedman. Boston, MA: Houghton Mifflin Company, 1990. 214 pp. Index.**

Explains the Nazi policy of exterminating or enslaving dissenters and peoples deemed inferior. Offers first-hand accounts from survivors of groups persecuted by the Nazis, including gypsies, homosexuals, the disabled, Christian clergy and laity, Communists, Blacks, and Slavs. Further reading list. For young readers.

DEWEY: 940.53 161 0922 LC: D811. A2 F74 ISBN 0-395-50212-8

♦ 110 ♦

Sadako and the Thousand Paper Cranes. **Eleanor Coerr. Illustrated by Ronald Himler. New York: G. P. Putnam 's Sons, 1977. 64 pp.**

Describes the life and early death of Sadako, a Japanese girl who survived the atomic bombing of Hiroshima. Notes that a statue of Sadako was placed in Hiroshima Peace Park in 1958, beneath which thousands of folded cranes are placed on Peace Day (August 6) in her memory. For children.

DEWEY: 940.5316 LC: RJ416. L4 C63 ISBN 0-399-20520-9

♦ 111 ♦

Seeds of Change: A Quincentennial Commemoration. **Herman J. Viola and Carolyn Margolis, eds. Washington, DC: Smithsonian Institute Press, 1991. 278 pp. Illustrated. Index.**

A collection of essays by noted authorities on the positive and negative aspects, for various nations and ethnic groups, of Columbus's voyages to the

New World. Covers the decimation of Native American peoples by Old World diseases, the importation of African slaves, the impact of Native American foods on European populations, the transfer of European plants and animals to the New World, and related issues. Companion volume to Smithsonian Quincentenary exhibit. Gives sources and suggested readings.

DEWEY: 970.01 5 LC: E112. S45 ISBN 1-56098-035-4

♦ 112 ♦

Smoke and Ashes: The Story of the Holocaust. **Barbara Rogasky. New York: Holiday House, 1988. 187 pp. Illustrated. Index.**

Tells the story of the Holocaust. Gives short history of anti-Semitism, explains how Hitler came to power, describes the concentration camps, the programs of mass slaughter, the efforts of rescuers, the end of the war, and the war crimes trials. Illustrated with more than eighty black-and-white photos. Suitable for teens.

DEWEY: 940.53 15 03924 LC: D810 J4 R618 ISBN 0-8234-0697-0

♦ 113 ♦

Victory in Europe. **Wallace B. Black and Jean F. Blashfield. New York: Crestwood House, 1993. 48 pp. Illustrated. Glossary. Index.**

Describes the military campaigns which led to the Allied victory in Europe. Illustrated with black-and-white photos. For young readers. One volume in a series entitled *World War II 50th Anniversary.*

DEWEY: 940.54 21 LC: D743. B493 ISBN 0-89686-570-3

♦ 114 ♦

Victory in Europe: D-Day to VE Day in Full Color. **Max Hastings. Photos by George Stevens. Boston, MA: Little, Brown and Company, 1985. 192 pp. Bibliography. Index.**

Tells the story of the liberation of Europe, from D-Day to V-E Day, in text and in 200 rare color photos taken by film director George Stevens.

DEWEY: 940.5421

♦ 115 ♦

Victory in Europe: The Fall of Hitler's Germany. **Edward F. Dolan. New York: Franklin Watts, 1988. 159 pp. Illustrated. Index.**

Summarizes the events of the last months of World War II, ending with the German surrender and V-E Day. Gives further reading list. Illustrated with black-and-white photos. For young readers.

DEWEY: 940.54 21 LC: D755.6 D65 ISBN 0-531-10522-9

♦ 116 ♦

The Voyage of Christopher Columbus: Columbus' Own Journal of Discovery Newly Restored and Translated. **John Cummins. New York: St. Martin's Press, 1992. 241 pp. Illustrated. Appendices. Bibliography. Index.**

Provides a new interpretation and translation of Columbus's shipboard journal. Lengthy introduction provides historical insights into the character of Columbus, the motives for the voyages, shipboard life, and the navigational skills and geographical knowledge of Europeans of that era. Appendix one reproduces testimony from a lawsuit filed against the Spanish crown by Columbus's family. Appendix two reproduces the payroll of the voyage.

DEWEY: 970.01 5 092 LC: E118. C725 ISBN 0-312-07880-3

♦ 117 ♦

"When They Came To Take My Father": Voices of the Holocaust. **Leora Kahn and Rachel Hager, eds. Photographs by Mark Seliger. New York: Arcade Publishing, 1996. 175 pp.**

Holocaust testimony from 46 survivors. Lavishly illustrated with black-and-white portraits of each survivor. Also includes introduction by Robert Jay Lifton and essays on Holocaust themes by Arthur Hertzberg, Eva Fogelman, Yaffa Eliach, Abe Foxman, and Anne Roiphe.

DEWEY: 940. 5318 LC: D804.3 W453 ISBN 1-55970-305-9

♦ 118 ♦

Witnesses to the Holocaust: An Oral History. **Rhoda G. Lewin, ed. Boston, MA: Twayne Publishers, 1990. 240 pp. Illustrated. Appendix. Glossary. Index.**

Presents the testimony of 60 Holocaust survivors. Based on interviews with concentration camp and other Holocaust survivors, as well as Americans who helped to liberate the camps. Appendix gives guide for teachers and discussion leaders. Black-and-white photos illustrate.

DEWEY: 940. 53 18 LC: D804.3 W47 ISBN 0-8057-9100-04

Holiday Preparations, Activities, and Advice

♦ 119 ♦

The Alternate Celebrations Catalogue. **Milo Shannon-Thornberry. New York: The Pilgrim Press, 1982. 192 pp. Illustrated.**

Suggests alternatives to contemporary, highly commercialized holiday and life-cycle celebrations. Life-cycle celebrations covered include births, birthdays, bar and bat mitzvahs, weddings, funerals, tooth rites, graduations, anniversaries, and retirement. Holidays covered include New Year, Emancipation Day, Martin Luther King, Jr.'s birthday, Valentine's Day, St. Patrick's Day, April Fool's Day, Purim, Passover, Lent, Palm Sunday, Easter, Shavuot, Pentecost, Memorial Day, Parent's Day, Independence Day, Hiroshima Day, Women's Equality Day, Labor Day, Rosh Hashanah, Yom Kippur, Sukkot, Halloween, Thanksgiving, Christmas, and Hanukkah. Also discusses the psychology of consumption, gift giving, and voluntary simplicity. Offers suggestions for homemade gifts and craft projects. Illustrated with black-and-white drawings.

DEWEY: 394.2 6973 LC: GT 4803 A64 ISBN 0-8398-0601-6

♦ 120 ♦

Fireworks! Pyrotechnics on Display. **Norman D. Anderson and Walter R. Brown. New York: Dodd, Mead and Company, 1983. 79 pp. Illustrated. Index.**

Tells how fireworks are used in celebrations and festivals of many countries. Reviews their history, explains how they are made, and describes setup of fireworks displays. Recounts stories of several historical fireworks disasters, tells how to photograph fireworks, and notes additional uses. Lists state laws concerning sale and use of fireworks. Illustrated with black-and-white photos. For older children.

DEWEY: 662.1 LC: TP300.A5 ISBN 0-396-08142-8

♦ 121 ♦

Folk and Festival Costume of the World. **R. Turner Wilcox. New York: Charles Scribner's Sons, 1965. Unpaginated. Bibliography. Illustrated. Index.**

More than 600 detailed black-and-white drawings and accompanying text describe folk costumes from 110 nations and regions of the world. Gives several costumes for each country or region, representing variations in local style, profession, or occasion.

DEWEY: 391. W667 f

♦ 122 ♦

Folk Festivals: A Handbook for Organization and Management. **Joe Wilson and Lee Udall. Knoxville, TN: University of Tennessee Press, 1982. 278 pp. Illustrated. Bibliography. Index.**

Thorough guide to planning and running folk festivals. Part one covers administration, programming, publicity, hospitality, and production. Also gives chapter on the nature of folklore and the history and variety of folk festivals in the U.S. Part two tells how several different kinds of successful folk festivals were organized. Prints interviews with folk festival performers. Provides samples of more than forty documents created in the production of a folk festival. Illustrated with black-and-white photos. Bibliography of American folklore.

DEWEY: 907.4 LC: GT 3935. W54 ISBN 0-87049-300-0

♦ 123 ♦

Folk Festivals and the Foreign Community. **Dorothy Gladys Spicer. 1923. Reprint. Detroit, MI: Omnigraphics, Inc., 1990. 152 pp. Bibliography.**

Defines folk festivals, discusses their social significance, and tells how to organize and produce them. Based on experience organizing folk festivals in emigrant communities around 1920. Outlines four festival programs based loosely on May Day, St. John's Eve, the feast of Ingathering, and Yuletide themes, which feature the seasonal folklore, music, and dances of European ethnic groups. Suggests sources for costume ideas, music, and dances.

DEWEY: 394.2 6973 LC: GT 3930. S6 ISBN 1-55888-874-8

♦ 124 ♦

Happy Holidays! Uplifting Advice About How to Avoid the Holiday Blues and Recapture the True Spirit of Christmas, Hanukkah, and New Year's.

Wayne W. Dyer. New York: William Morrow and Company, Inc., 1986. 91 pp. Illustrated.

Suggests attitudes and activities that diminish holiday stress and help one to participate in the true spirit of the holidays. Illustrated with black-and-white drawings.

DEWEY: 616.8527 ISBN 0-688-06466-3

♦ 125 ♦

***Holidays of the World Cookbook for Students.* Lois Sinaiko Webb. Phoenix, AZ: Oryx Press, 1995. 297 pp. Bibliography. Index.**

Offers 388 holiday-related recipes from more than 136 countries. Covers Africa, the Middle East, Europe, Asia and the Pacific, the Caribbean, Latin America, and North America. Gives information about way of life, religions, and holidays observed for each world region. Introduces each country with notes on typical dishes, holiday celebrations, and customs. Summarizes the lunar, Gregorian, Christian, Hebrew, Islamic, Hindu, Buddhist, and Chinese calendars.

DEWEY: 641.5 68 LC: TX 739 W43 ISBN 0-89774-884-0

♦ 126 ♦

***Masks.* Amanda Earl and Danielle Sensier. New York: Thomson Learning, 1995. 48 pp. Illustrated. Glossary. Index.**

Introduces the styles and uses of ceremonial masks from around the world. Provides one chapter each on Europe, North America, Central and South America, Asia, Africa, and the Pacific. Many masks covered are used for festivals or seasonal celebrations. Includes instructions for several mask-making projects. Illustrated with color photos. Further reading list. For children. One volume in a series entitled *Traditions of the World.*

DEWEY: 391 434 LC: GT 1747 E25 ISBN 1-56847-226-9

♦ 127 ♦

***Masks and the Art of Expression.* John Mack, ed. New York: Harry N. Abrams, Inc., Publishers, 1994. 224 pp. Illustrated. Bibliography. Index.**

Presents a collection of essays by noted authorities on masking traditions around the world. Treats Africa, Oceania, Mexico and highland South America, northwest Native America, Japan, ancient Greece, ancient Rome, and Europe. Essays discuss appearance and uses of masks, as well mythological, symbolic, or social themes represented by the masks. Essay on Europe discusses masking in relation to European folk festivals, such as Carnival. Beautifully illustrated with color photos.

DEWEY: 391.434 LC: GT 1747 M369 ISBN 0-8109-3641-0

♦ 128 ♦

Multicultural Projects Index: Things to Make and Do to Celebrate Festivals, Cultures, and Holidays Around the World. **Mary Anne Pilger. Englewood, CO: Libraries Unlimited, Inc., 1992. 200 pp. Bibliography.**

Offers an index to 1,161 books providing information about foods, crafts, and activities associated with festivals, holidays, and cultures of the world. Arranged by subject in dictionary-style entries. Entries give book and page number on which information on the subject is found. Books are numbered in the main text; a bibliography of books indexed, with full citations, appears after the main text.

DEWEY: 016.37019 6 LC: LC1099 P55 ISBN 0-87287-867-8

♦ 129 ♦

The Mystery of Masks. **Christine Price. New York: Charles Scribner's Sons, 1978. 64 pp. Illustrated.**

Discusses the use of masks in folk ceremonies and festivals from ancient to contemporary times. Describes celebrations at which masks are featured. Covers events from Native North and Central America, Africa, the Pacific, and Asia. Illustrated with black-and-white drawings of ritual masks from American museum collections. For young readers.

DEWEY: 392 LC: GN 419.5 P74 ISBN 0-684-15653-9

♦ 130 ♦

National Anthems of the World. **Seventh edition. W. L. Reed and M. J. Bristow, eds. London: Blandford Press, 1987. 513 pp. Appendix.**

Furnishes words and music to the national anthems of 172 countries. Gives verses in original language or languages (in transliteration where necessary) and in English. Appendix lists national days of each country.

DEWEY: 784.71 ISBN 0-7137-1962-1

♦ 131 ♦

New Traditions: Redefining Celebrations for Today's Family. **Susan Abel Lieberman. 1984. Reprint. New York: The Noonday Press, Farrar, Straus and Giroux, 1991. 195 pp.**

Gathers together a collection of alternative celebrations for traditional events which are designed to emphasize the event's meaning, enhance personal relationships, and create warm memories. Also suggests new celebrations which focus on family, friends, and community. Covers Christian and Jewish religious holidays, national holidays, birthdays, bar mitzvahs, confirmations, anniversaries, and other rites of passage. Addresses the special situations of single-parent families and singles. First published in 1984 as *Let's Celebrate.*

DEWEY: 394 L716n LC: GR 105.L495 ISBN 0-374-52262-6

♦ 132 ♦

Parades! Celebrations and Circuses on the March. **Gary Jennings. Philadelphia, PA: J. B. Lippincott Company, 1966. 150 pp. Illustrated. Index.**

Provides an overview of the parade as an activity of celebration, observance, or commemoration throughout history and across cultures. Describes a wide variety of parades and processions associated with holidays and seasonal festivals, the return of victorious armies, military displays, circuses and spectacles, weddings and funerals. Also treats marching music. Illustrated with black-and-white photos. Provides abbreviated bibliography.

DEWEY: 394.5

♦ 133 ♦

Parades: How to Plan, Promote, and Stage Them. **Valerie Lagauskas. New York: Sterling Publishing Company, 1982. 160 pp. Illustrated. Appendix. Index.**

Tells how to design and stage a parade using examples from the author's experience in organizing the Macy's Thanksgiving Day parade in New York. Chapters cover selecting a date and theme, utilizing volunteers, setting up committees and timetables, managing promotion and publicity, deciding on a budget and insurance, determining a route, and choosing parade entrants. Appendices list basic parade regulations, give sample application forms for various parade entrants, and explain how to apply paper maché to chicken wire shapes. Illustrated with color and black-and-white photos.

DEWEY: 791.6 LC: GT 3980. L33 ISBN 0-8069-0237-X

♦ 134 ♦

Special Events: The Art and Science of Celebration. **Joe Jeff Goldblatt. Foreword by Linda Faulkner, Social Secretary to the White House during the Reagan Administration. New York: Van Nostrand Reinhold, 1990. 386 pp. Illustrated. Appendixes. Glossary. Index.**

Guide to the special events industry, including social, retail, corporate and government events, meetings, and conventions. Provides techniques for budgeting, planning, and creating events such as theme parties, awards ceremonies, holidays, fairs, festivals, sporting events, and more. Appendix lists related books and organizations, and reprints the Flag Code. References. (NR)

DEWEY: 394.2 6 068 LC: AS6.G64 ISBN 0-442-22681-0

♦ 135 ♦

To Celebrate: Reshaping Holidays and Rites of Passage. **Alternatives staff members. Ellenwood, GA: Alternatives, 1987. 224 pp. Appendix.**

Provides inspiration and advice on how to decrease consumerism and increase spirituality, ecological responsibility, charity, and community togetherness in holiday and life-cycle celebrations. Treats Christian, Jewish, and Muslim holidays, New Year, Emancipation Day, Martin Luther King, Jr. Day, Day of Remembrance, Presidents' Day, Chinese New Year, International Women's Day, Mother's and Father's Day, Memorial Day, Dominion Day, Independence Day, Hiroshima Day, Women's Equality Day, Labor Day, Columbus Day, United Nations Day, Halloween, Thanksgiving, Festival of Our Lady of Guadalupe, Kwanzaa, and more. Appendix gives addresses of self-help craft groups and indexes the names of non-profit organizations whose advertisements appear in the text.

DEWEY: 394.2 LC: GT3932 T6 ISBN 0-914966-05-7

Anthropological, Historical, Philosophical, and Theological Approaches to Festivity

♦ 136 ♦

The Celebration of Society: Perspectives on Contemporary Cultural Performance. **Frank E. Manning, ed. Bowling Green, OH: Bowling Green University Popular Press, 1983. 208 pp. Bibliography. Indexes.**

Explores the functions and meanings of various genres of cultural performance, including community festivals, sporting events, masquerades, and ethnic festivals. Contents include "Cosmos and Chaos: Celebration in the Modern World" by Frank E. Manning; "High, Healthy, and Happy: Ontario Mythology on Parade" by Carole Farber; "Family and Corporation: Celebration in Central Minnesota" by Robert H. Lavenda; "Will the Sheik Use Up His Blinding Fireball? The Ideology of Professional Wrestling" by Jim Freedman; "Get Some Money for Your Honey: Gambling on the Wages of Sin" by Frank E. Manning; "Carnaval in Rio: Dionysian Drama in an Industrializing Society" by Victor Turner; "The Shit Devil: Pretense and Politics Among West African Urban Children" by Jeanne Cannizzo; "Barren Bulls and Charging Cows: Cowboy Celebrations in Copal and Calgary" by Herman Konrad; "Political Powwow: The Rise and Fall of an Urban Native Festival" by Noel Dyck; and "The Spirit of Celebration" by Victor Turner.

DEWEY: 394　　LC: GT 3930 M36　　ISBN 0-87972-245-2

♦ 137 ♦

Celebration: Studies in Festivity and Ritual. **Victor Turner, ed. Washington, DC: Smithsonian Institution Press, 1982. 320 pp. Index.**

Text designed to accompany *Celebration: A World of Art and Ritual,* an exhibit organized by the Smithsonian Institution in 1982. Contains articles exploring the nature of celebration as a genre of human interaction, and the role of art objects and rituals associated with celebrations of many kinds. Festivals covered include Juneteenth, Holy Week among Southwest Hispanics, Tzotzil (Mayan) Carnival, the Car Festival (India), the Dragon Boat Festival (China), the Ramlila Festival (India), German-American passion plays in the United States, and more.

DEWEY: 394 LC: GT 3930.C44 ISBN 0-87474-920-4

♦ 138 ♦

Celebrations: The Cult of Anniversaries in Europe and the United States Today. **William M. Johnston. New Brunswick, NJ: Transaction Publishers, 1991. 187 pp. Bibliography. Index.**

Analyzes the cult of anniversaries in the United States, Britain, France, Germany, Italy, and Austria since the 1970s. Contrasts the objects, purposes, and organization of European and American anniversary celebrations. Links the rise of the cult of anniversaries with the development of postmodernism. Identifies the human need for long-term calendrical rhythms as well as the utility of anniversaries in sharpening a sense of national identity as factors contributing to their proliferation in the late twentieth century.

DEWEY: 394.2 LC: E169.12.J645 ISBN 0-88738-375-0

♦ 139 ♦

The Cultures of Celebration. **Ray B. Browne and Michael T. Marsden, eds. Bowling Green, OH: Bowling Green State University Popular Press, 1994. 244 pp.**

Essays by scholars of popular culture, theater, English literature, history, and other disciplines explore the forms and social content of a wide range of public celebrations. Emphasis on celebrations of North American popular culture, such as the circus, wild west shows, beauty contests, seasonal festivals, and theme parks. Also contains essays on Shi'ite Muslim rituals, male and female imagery in traditional English festivals, Australian folk festivals, contemporary celebrations at Stonehenge, the Lord Mayor's Procession (Britain), and Columbus centennials.

DEWEY: 394.2 6 LC: GT 3930 C85 ISBN 0-87972-651-2

♦ 140 ♦

The Feast of Fools: A Theological Essay on Festivity and Fantasy. **Harvey Cox. Cambridge, MA: Harvard University Press, 1969. 204 pp. Appendix. Index.**

Explores the social and spiritual dimensions of festivity and fantasy, and argues that contemporary Christianity and secular society need a re-infusion of both. Appendix reviews theological trends which have influenced the author. References given in endnotes.

DEWEY: 230 LC: BT 28 C65 ISBN 674-29525-0

♦ 141 ♦

Festivals and Celebrations. **Roland Auguet. New York: Franklin Watts Publishers, 1975. 128 pp. Illustrated. Index.**

Provides history and description of eight festivals, spectacles, and celebrations of ancient, medieval, and contemporary Europe. Covers the Roman Games, the medieval Feast of Fools, Mountebanks, the Commedia Dell'Arte, Carnivals, the Circus, contemporary horse racing, and television shows. Considers the history of festival and celebration in Europe, the human motivation behind these events, their social causes, effects, and future. Amply illustrated with color and black-and-white photos. Further reading list. For young readers.

DEWEY: 394.2 ISBN 531-02117-3

♦ 142 ♦

Flights of Fancy, Leaps of Faith: Children's Myths in Contemporary America. **Cindy Dell Clark. Chicago: University of Chicago Press, 1995. 158 pp. Illustrated. Appendix. Bibliography. Index.**

Researcher combines psychological and anthropological approaches to investigate children's perceptions of juvenile myths surrounding holidays or life-cycle events. Considers their impact on children's psychological development. Discusses the Tooth Fairy, aspects of Christmas and Easter celebrations, Santa Claus, and the Easter Bunny. Appendix provides a discussion of methodologies for doing anthropology with children.

LC: BF 723.I5C55 ISBN 0-226-10777-9

♦ 143 ♦

Homo Ludens: A Study of the Play-Element in Culture. **J. Huizinga. Boston, MA: Beacon Press, 1955. 220 pp. Index.**

A learned treatise on the nature of play and its role in human culture by the noted Dutch historian. Identifies the play element in ritual, ceremony, and festivity. Examines the role of play in many domains of human activity, arguing for its centrality in the cultural process.

DEWEY: 901 LC: CB 151.H815

♦ 144 ♦

In Tune With the World: A Theory of Festivity. **Josef Pieper. Translated by Richard Winston and Clara Winston. New York: Harcourt, Brace and World, Inc., 1965. 81 pp. Index.**

A philosophical essay on the nature of festivity. Explores the definition of festivity, its roots in the human psyche and spirit, and the Christian theology of festivity. Argues that festivity is the celebration of Creation. Also considers the impact of economic and political forces on festival observance and the relationship between festivity, ritual and artistic expression.

DEWEY: 394P LC: GT 3930 P433

♦ 145 ♦

The Masks of Play. **Brian Sutton-Smith and Diana Kelly-Byrne, eds. New York: Leisure Press, 1984. 200 pp.**

A collection of essays by cultural anthropologists documenting a wide range of human play forms and considering the meaning and function of play in human society. Essays grouped together by the following themes: festival play, adult recreation and games, children's play, animals' play, and theories of play. Festivals addressed include the Sohrae Festival (India), the Alikali Devils of Sierra Leone festivals, Carnival (Canada), and Foley Fun Days (Minnesota). Bibliographies given for each essay.

DEWEY: 306.4819 LC: GN 454 M37 ISBN 0-88011-208-5

♦ 146 ♦

Models and Mirrors: Towards an Anthropology of Public Events. **Don Handelman. Cambridge, England: Cambridge University Press, 1990. 330 pp. Bibliography. Index.**

Develops a theoretical approach to the study of public events, including festivals, ceremonies, and various forms of play. Examines the Palio of Siena (Italy), Christmas mumming in Newfoundland, Holocaust Memorial Day and Israel Independence Day, and various holiday celebrations in Israeli kindergartens. Also discusses the clown as a symbolic character often found at public events, drawing on examples from Pakistani, Hopi, and Tewa cultures.

DEWEY: 394.2 LC: GT 3930.H34 ISBN 0-521-35069-7

♦ 147 ♦

Parades and Power: Street Theatre in Nineteenth-Century Philadelphia. **Susan G. Davis. Philadelphia, PA: Temple University Press, 1986. 235 pp. Illustrated. Index.**

An historical study of parades and other public ceremonies in nineteenth-century Philadelphia. Analyzes the political ramifications of the social relations represented in these and other public ceremonies and celebrations. Discusses various holidays, including the Fourth of July, Christmas, Muster

Day, Washington's Birthday, the festivals of various ethnic groups, and more. Endnotes.

DEWEY: 394.5 0974811 LC: GT 40111 P46 D38 ISBN 0-87722-394-7

♦ 148 ♦

Rite, Drama, Festival, Spectacle: Rehearsals Toward a Theory of Cultural Performance. **John J. MacAloon. Philadelphia, PA: Institute for the Study of Human Issues, 1984. 280 pp.**

A collection of scholarly essays that ponder the social, cultural and individual effects and influences of public performances of many kinds. Includes "Introduction: Cultural Performances, Culture Theory" by John J. MacAloon; "Liminality and the Performative Genres" by Victor Turner; "Charivari, Honor, and Community in Seventeenth-Century Lyon and Geneva" by Natalie Zemon Davis; "'Rough Music' in The Duchess of Malfi: Webster's Dance of Madmen and the Charivari Tradition" by Frank W. Wadsworth; "Borges's 'Immortal': Metaritual, Metaliterature, Metaperformance" by Sophia S. Morgan; "Arrange Me into Disorder: Fragments and Reflections on Ritual Clowning" by Barbara Babcock; "The Diviner and the Detective" by Hilda Kuper; "A Death in Due Time: Construction of Self and Culture in Ritual Drama" by Barbara G. Myerhoff; "The Ritual Process and the Problem of Reflexivity in Sinhalese Demon Exorcisms" by Bruce Kapferer; "Carnival in Multiple Planes" by Roberto Da Matta; and "Olympic Games and the Theory of Spectacle in Modern Societies" by John J. MacAloon.

DEWEY: 790.2 LC: GT 3930.R57 ISBN 0-89727-045-2

♦ 149 ♦

The Rites of Rulers: Ritual in Industrial Society The Soviet Case. **Christel Lane. Cambridge, England: Cambridge University Press, 1981. 308 pp. Appendices. Bibliography. Index.**

A theoretically oriented study of the political uses of ritual and festivity which focuses on the ways in which the Soviet government manipulated various celebrations in order to reflect its official political ideology. Includes discussion of life-cycle rituals, initiation into social and political groups, labor rituals, holidays, and military and patriotic celebrations. Covers many holidays, including Harvest Day, Sabantui, Holiday of the First Sheaf, Holiday of the Hammer and Sickle, Seeing-off of Winter (Maslenitsa), Holiday of the Birch, Ligo, Ivan Kupala, Holiday of Spring (Novruz), New Year, and Victory Day. Analyzes common themes in Soviet rituals, and compares with rituals of other modern societies. Appendix A offers songs and poetry from celebrations; appendix B, the Soviet ritual calendar.

DEWEY: 301.2 1 LC: GT 4856 A2 L36 ISBN 0-521-22608-2

♦ 150 ♦

Time Out of Time: Essays on the Festival. **Alessandro Falassi, ed. Albuquerque, NM: University of New Mexico Press, 1987. 311 pp.**

Presents a collection of theoretical and descriptive essays concerning the concept of festivity and specific festivals from around the world and throughout history. Social scientists and literary figures address Roman Carnival, three festivals of the French Revolution, the 1936 Olympics, the Point Hope Whale Festival (Inuit/Eskimo), the Saba Gêdé festival (Bali), the Olojo Festival (Yoruba, Africa), the Palio of Siena (Italy), the Rabb pilgrimage (Algeria), the Guéré Excision Festival (Ivory Coast), Carnival in Rio de Janeiro, and various Spanish, American, Pacific, Japanese, Chinese, Russian, and Azorean festivals. References and suggestions for further reading given in endnotes.

DEWEY: 394.2 6 LC: GT 3930. T56 ISBN 0-8263-0932-1

CHAPTER TWO

Holidays of Religious Traditions

General Works

♦ 151 ♦

Archeological Encyclopedia of the Holy Land. **Avraham Negev, ed. 1972. Reprint. New York: Prentice Hall General Reference and Travel, 1990. 354 pp. Illustrated. Maps. Glossary. Tables.**

Gives location, historical remarks, and notes on archeological excavations for most place names occurring in the Bible. Dictionary-style entries give Bible chapters and verses mentioning location. Contains overview articles on the archeology of the Holy Land and on various aspects of life in biblical times. Cross-referenced.

DEWEY: 913.330303 LC: DS 11 A2 ISBN 0-13-044090-6

♦ 152 ♦

A Dictionary of Non-Christian Religions. **Geoffrey Parrinder. 1971. Reprint. New York: State Mutual Book and Periodical Service, Ltd., 1981. 320 pp. Illustrated. Bibliography. Tables.**

Covers non-Christian, non-biblical religions from around the world, ancient and contemporary. Lists people, deities, rites, locations, festivals, texts, philosophies, etc. Special focus on Hinduism, Buddhism, and Islam. More than 2,400 concise, informative entries. Amply cross-referenced. Contains 242 drawings and 94 photographs. Further reading list.

DEWEY: 290.3 LC: BL 31 P36 ISBN 0-7175-0972-9

♦ 153 ♦

A Dictionary of Traditional Symbols. **Second edition. J. E. Cirlot. Translated by Jack Sage. New York: Barnes and Noble Books, 1993. 419 pp. Illustrated. Bibliography. Index.**

Provides encyclopedia-style explanations of the symbolic significance of a wide variety of images, objects, and activities found in Western and Eastern mythology and art. Entries range from one sentence to several pages of text. Offers introductory essay on the interpretation of symbols. Black-and-white illustrations. First edition published in 1962.

DEWEY: 398.303 ISBN 0-88029-702-6

♦ 154 ♦

Eastern Religions. **Elizabeth Seeger. New York: Thomas Crowell and Company, 1973. 213 pp. Illustrated. Bibliography. Index.**

An introduction to the five major religions of Asia: Hinduism, Buddhism, Confucianism, Taoism, and Shinto. Explains the founding, historical development, and central teachings of each tradition. Summarizes sacred writings and lives of important religious figures, and recounts important parables and stories associated with each tradition. Briefly addresses the impact that contact with the West has made on the practice of these religions in the East. Occasional description of rites, practices, and festivals. Suitable for teens.

DEWEY: J 294 LC: BL 92. S43 ISBN 0-690-25342-7

♦ 155 ♦

The Encyclopedia of Religion. **Mircea Eliade, ed. New York: Macmillan, 1987. 16 volumes. About 8,000 pages. Index in volume 16.**

A comprehensive collection of articles by leading scholars and religious figures touching on all aspects of religion. Reflects the significant increase in knowledge and changing interpretive frameworks which have marked the study of religion in the last sixty years. Treats religious ideologies and practices, as well as sociological aspects of religions from Paleolithic times to the present. Generates broad view of topics through composite entries joining several articles under a common heading. Articles list works cited and give suggestions for further reading. Ample coverage of non-Western religions. Extensively cross-referenced.

DEWEY: 200.321 LC: BL 31. E46 ISBN 0-02-909480-1

♦ 156 ♦

The Encyclopaedia of Religion and Ethics. **James Hastings, ed. Herndon, VA: Books International Inc., 1926. 13 volumes. Index in volume 13.**

Covers ideas, practices, people, places, movements, and systems of thought associated with the world's religions and major ethical systems. Bibliographic references provided with articles.

LC: BL 31 E4 ISBN 0-567-09489-8

♦ 157 ♦

Fasting: The Phenomenon of Self-Denial. **Eric N. Rogers. Nashville, TN: Thomas Nelson Inc., Publishers, 1976. 160 pp. Index.**

Offers an introduction to biological, psychological, and sociological aspects of fasting, and describes religious and political fasting traditions. Treats Jewish, Christian, Muslim, Hindu, and Buddhist fasting practices, many of which mark the observance of special days or times of year.

DEWEY: 248.273 LC: BV 5055. R63 ISBN 0-8407-6462-6

♦ 158 ♦

Great Religions of the World. **Merle Severy, ed. Washington, DC: National Geographic Book Service, 1971. 420 pp. Illustrated. Index.**

Offers articles by various authorities on the history, spirit and observances of five world religions: Hinduism, Buddhism, Judaism, Islam, and Christianity. Gives excerpts from the sacred writings of each religion. Some coverage of festivals and ceremonies. Beautifully illustrated with 350 color photos. Lists reference works consulted. For the general reader.

ISBN 87044-103-5

♦ 159 ♦

How to Be a Perfect Stranger: A Guide to Etiquette in Other People's Religious Ceremonies. **Arthur J. Magida, ed. Woodstock, VT: Jewish Lights Publishing, 1996. 417 pp. Glossary.**

Provides an overview of the content of, and the expected dress and behavior at, the services of 20 religious and denominational groups. Covers the Assemblies of God, Baptist, Buddhist, Christian Scientist, Disciples of Christ, Episcopalian, Greek Orthodox, Hindu, Islamic, Jehovah's Witnesses, Jewish, Lutheran, Methodist, Mormon, Presbyterian, Quaker, Roman Catholic, Seventh-day Adventist, and United Church of Christ ceremonies. Lists each group's major religious holidays and their significance. Reviews the various calendar systems of the major religions and furnishes a calendar listing of their holidays for the years 1996 to 1998.

DEWEY: 291.3 8 LC: BJ 2010.M34 ISBN 1-879045-39-7

♦ 160 ♦

An Illustrated Encyclopaedia of Traditional Symbols. **J. C. Cooper. London: Thames and Hudson, 1978. 207 pp. Illustrated. Bibliography. Glossary.**

Offers close to 1500 entries explaining the symbolism of natural and man-made objects, plants, animals, shapes, stones, numbers, actions, and parts of the body in a wide variety of ancient and contemporary cultural and religious traditions. Many references to non-Western and indigenous cultures. Entries first list widely occurring interpretation of each symbol, if applicable, then address culturally specific variations. More than 200 black-and-white illustrations.

DEWEY: 398.303 ISBN 0-5000-27125-9

♦ 161 ♦

Oriental Philosophies. **John M. Koller. New York: Charles Scribner's Sons, 1970. 303 pp. Glossary. Index.**

Learned, readable account of Eastern philosophical traditions. Introduces Eastern ways of life and thought through presenting central issues and problems in Hinduism, Buddhism, and Chinese philosophy. Covers the history of these traditions, their central tenets, divisions within them, and important figures associated with their founding and development. Footnotes give bibliographic references. Further reading list.

DEWEY: 181 K LC: B 121. K 56

♦ 162 ♦

The Penguin Dictionary of Religions. **John R. Hinnells, ed. London: Penguin Books, Ltd., 1984. 550 pp. Maps. Bibliography. Indexes.**

Compilation of wide-ranging and substantial entries by 29 scholars from various disciplines. Covers beliefs, practices, places, people, writings, customs, institutions, and more. Emphasis on living religions, especially Christianity, Islam, Buddhism, Judaism, and Hinduism, but some coverage of primal religions, new religions and philosophies, and ancient religions as well. Extensive bibliography cross-referenced with entries. General index. Synoptic index.

DEWEY: 200.3 21 LC: BL 31 ISBN 0-7139-1514-5

♦ 163 ♦

Perennial Dictionary of World Religions. **Keith Crim, ed. San Francisco, CA: Harper and Row, 1989. 830 pp. Illustrated. Maps.**

Originally published as *Abingdon Dictionary of World Religions.* Collaborative effort of more than 150 scholars representing the major religious traditions as well as the disciplines of sociology, anthropology, and history. Entries explain doctrines, sects, sacred writings, religious practices, and significance of holy sites, objects, and important personalities. Includes comprehensive articles on each religious tradition. Many entries include bibliographies. Cross-referenced.

DEWEY: 291.0321 LC: BL 31. A24 ISBN 0-06-061613-X

♦ 164 ♦

Pilgrimages. **Richard Barber. Woodbridge, Suffolk, England: Boydell Press, 1991. 159 pp. Illustrated. Bibliography.**

Provides an historical overview of pilgrimage traditions in the world's major religions. Describes beliefs and practices entailed in various pilgrimages, and draws out common themes. Gives a chapter on pilgrimages to Jerusalem, Mecca, Rome and the European shrines, Benares and the Indian shrines, and Buddhist pilgrimages. Endnotes give sources of quotations. Select bibliography.

DEWEY: 291.3 5 LC: BL 619.P5 B37 ISBN 0-85115-519-7

♦ 165 ♦

Religious Holidays and Calendars: An Encyclopedic Handbook. **Second edition. Karen Bellenir, ed. Detroit, MI: Omnigraphics, Inc., 1998. 316 pp. Bibliography. Indexes.**

Explains the relationship between religious holidays and calendars, and describes more than 450 religious holidays. Part one gives four chapters on the history of calendars. Summarizes the historical development and workings of various calendar traditions from ancient to present times, including the Babylonian, Hebrew, Greek, Egyptian, Roman, Julian, Gregorian, Islamic, Indian, Buddhist, Chinese, Mayan, Aztec, and French Revolutionary calendars. Part two addresses 14 religious traditions, offering a chapter each on Judaism, Zoroastrianism, Christianity, Islam, Baha'i, Hinduism, Jainism, Sikhism, Buddhism, Chinese religions (including Taoism, Confucianism and folk religion), Shinto, Native American religions, Paganism, and West African religions. Summarizes each religion's beliefs, treats the relationship of the holidays to the calendar system, and describes holiday significance and customs. Bibliography arranged by topic. General index, calendars index, and alphabetical as well as chronological holiday indexes. Lists Internet sources.

DEWEY: 529.3 LC: CE 6. K45 ISBN 0-7808-0258-6

♦ 166 ♦

Religions. **James Haskins. Philadelphia, PA: J. B. Lippincott, 1973. 157 pp. Index.**

Explains central beliefs, practices, and origins of the five predominant world religions: Hinduism, Buddhism, Judaism, Christianity, and Islam. Comments on religious trends in North America during the 1960s. Written for older children.

DEWEY: J 291 LC: BL 92. H ISBN 0-397-31212-1

♦ 167 ♦

Religions East and West. **Larry Kettelkamp. New York: William Morrow and Company, 1972. 128 pp. Illustrated. Index.**

Presents origins, basic beliefs, and important stories from six Eastern and four Western religions. Covers ancient Egyptian beliefs, Hinduism, Buddhism, Taoism, Confucianism, Shinto, Zoroastrianism, Judaism, Christianity, and Islam. Written for children.

DEWEY: J 200.9 LC: BL 92.K45 ISBN 0-688-20030-3

♦ 168 ♦

Sacred Dance: Encounter with the Gods. **Maria-Gabriele Wosien. New York: Avon Books, 1974. 128 pp. Illustrated.**

Documents the wide variety of sacred dance traditions and ceremonies, and considers the special contribution of dance to religious worship and celebration. Beautifully illustrated with 30 color and 112 black-and-white plates and photos depicting sacred dances throughout history and from a wide variety of cultural and religious traditions. Many dances covered form part of observance or celebration at feasts or festivals.

DEWEY: 291.3 7 LC: BL 605 W67

♦ 169 ♦

Sacred Journeys: The Anthropology of Pilgrimage. **Alan Morinis, ed. Foreword by Victor Turner. Westport, CT: Greenwood Press, 1992. 325 pp. Bibliography. Index.**

A collection of essays and articles on the concept of pilgrimage and on specific pilgrimages of various religions. Essays include: "Spiritual Magnetism: An Organizing Principle for the Study of Pilgrimage" by James J. Preston; "Pilgrimage and Tourism: Convergence and Divergence" by Erik Cohen; "The Great Maharashtrian Pilgrimage: Pandharpur and Alandi" by John M. Staley; "Velankanni Calling: Hindu Patterns of Pilgrimage at a Christian Shrine" by Paul Younger; "Persistent Peregrination: From Sun Dance to Catholic Pilgrimage Among Canadian Prairie Indians" by Alan Morinis; "Pilgrimage and Heresy: The Transformation of Faith at a Shrine in Wisconsin" by Peter W. Wood; "Pilgrimages in the Caribbean: A Comparison of Cases from Haiti and Trinidad" by Stephen D. Glazier; "Pilgrim Narratives of Jerusalem and the Holy Land: A Study in Ideological Distortion" by Glenn Bowman; "Pilgrimage and Its Influence on West African Islam" by James Steel Thayer; "Specialists in Miraculous Action: Some Shrines in Shiraz" by Anne H. Betteridge; "Sanctification Overland: The Creation of a Thai Buddhist

Pilgrimage Center" by James B. Pruess; "Mission to Waitangi: A Maori Pilgrimage" by Karen P. Sinclair; and "Postscript: Anthropology as Pilgrimage, Anthropologist as Pilgrim" by Colin Turnbull.

DEWEY: 306.6 91446 LC: BL 619.P5 S23 ISBN 0-313-27879-2

♦ 170 ♦

Sacred Place. **Jean Holm, ed., with John Bowker. London: Pinter Publishers Ltd., 1994. 206 pp. Index.**

A collection of essays by various authorities outlining the concept of sacred place in eight religious traditions. Treats Buddhism, Christianity, Hinduism, Islam, Judaism, Sikhism, Chinese, and Japanese religion. Most essays touch on ceremonies and pilgrimages. Each essay lists suggestions for further reading. For the general reader. One volume in a series entitled *Themes in Religious Studies.*

DEWEY: 291.3 5 LC: BL 580. S2297 ISBN 1-85567-104-2

♦ 171 ♦

Sacrifice and Sacrament. **E. O. James. New York: Barnes and Noble, Inc., 1962. 319 pp. Bibliography. Index.**

Systematic examination and comparison of the rites of, and beliefs surrounding, sacrifice and sacrament in ancient religions as well as Judaism and Christianity. Treats ancient Egypt, India, Mesopotamia, Babylon, Israel, Greece, Rome, and Native North and South America. Much coverage of Christian rituals, such as baptism, penance, marriage, and those rituals surrounding the Eucharist and the expiation of sins. Numerous festivals of the ancient world considered throughout.

LC: BL 570 J32

♦ 172 ♦

Ten Religions of the East. **Edward Rice. New York: Four Winds Press, 1978. 154 pp. Illustrated. Index.**

Explains the origins, development, beliefs, and practices of 10 lesser-known Eastern religions. Treats founders and other important figures. Covers Jainism, Zoroastrianism, Sikhism, Taoism, Confucianism, Bon, Shinto, Cao Dai, Baha'i, and Theosophy. Written for teens.

DEWEY: J 294 R LC: BL 92 ISBN 0-590-07473-3

♦ 173 ♦

This Day in Religion. **Ernie Gross. New York: Neal-Schuman Publisher, Inc., 1990. 294 pp. Bibliography. Glossary. Index.**

Offers a day-by-day listing of significant events in the world of religion from biblical times to the present. Focuses on Christianity, but some coverage of Judaism and Eastern religions. Includes saints' days, the birth or death of religious leaders or notable figures in the world of religion, appointments, canonizations, feast days, founding dates of organizations and associations, and other important events.

DEWEY: 270.0202 ISBN 1-55570-045-4

♦ 174 ♦

The World's Religions. **Revised and updated edition. Huston Smith. San Francisco, CA: HarperSanFrancisco, a division of HarperCollins, 1991. 399 pp. Index.**

Noted scholar of comparative religion provides a comprehensive overview of the teachings of Hinduism, Buddhism, Confucianism, Taoism, Islam, Judaism, Christianity, and the primal religions for the general reader. Includes suggestions for further reading.

DEWEY: 291 LC: BL 80.2.S645 ISBN 0-06-250799-0

♦ 175 ♦

Worship. **Jean Holm, ed., with John Bowker. London: Pinter Publishers, Ltd., 1994. 187 pp. Index.**

Offers a collection of essays by various authorities outlining the nature of worship in eight religious traditions. Treats Buddhism, Christianity, Hinduism, Islam, Judaism, Sikhism, Chinese, and Japanese religion. Explains communal and individual beliefs and practices, including prayer, offerings, chanting, music, art, dance, and various rituals. Offers description of Buddhist and Jewish festivals and some coverage of Sikh festivals. For the general reader. Gives further reading list. One volume in a series entitled *Themes in Religious Studies.*

DEWEY: 291.4 3 LC: BL 550 W66 ISBN 1-85567-110-7

♦ 176 ♦

Worship in the World's Religions. **Geoffrey Parrinder. Second edition. London: Sheldon Press, 1974. 239 pp. Bibliographies. Index.**

Summarizes practices of worship in 10 religious traditions: Hinduism, Buddhism (Theraveda and Mahayana), Sikhism, Zoroastrianism, Jainism, Chinese cults and Taoism, Shinto, Judaism, Islam, and Christianity. Also briefly treats pre-literary religions. Covers congregational worship, prayer and personal worship, festivals, beliefs, sanctuaries, shrines, and pilgrimages. Furnishes bibliography for each religion discussed.

DEWEY: 291.3 LC: BL 550 P3 ISBN 0-85969-035-0

Baha'i

♦ 177 ♦

The Baha'i Faith: Dawn of a New Day. **Jessyca Russell Gaver. New York: Hawthorn Books, 1967. Index.**

Presents an introduction to Baha'i beliefs, way of life, and the lives and achievements of some Baha'i leaders. Some discussion of the Baha'i calendar as well as the observation of the Nineteen-Day Feast, New Year, and the Ridvan Festival.

DEWEY: 297.89

♦ 178 ♦

Bahá'u'lláh and the New Era: An Introduction to the Bahá'í Faith. **Fourth edition, revised. J. E. Esslemont. 1923. Reprint. Wilmette, IL: Bahá'í Publishing Trust, 1980. 300 pp. Index.**

An overview of the history and teachings of the Baha'i faith. Gives biography of the founder and early leaders of Baha'i, explains basic principles and precepts of the faith. Also lists holidays and presents the Baha'i calendar. Further reading list.

DEWEY: 297.89 LC: BP 365. E8 ISBN 0-87743-136-1

Buddhism

♦ 179 ♦

The Beginnings of Buddhism. **Kogen Mizuno. Translated by Richard Gage. Boston, MA: Charles E. Tuttle Co., 1980. 220 pp. Illustrated. Map. Glossary. Index.**

An account of the founding of the Buddhist religion, with emphasis on the life and teachings of the Buddha. Written for the general reader.

DEWEY: 294.3 63　　LC: BQ 4115 M　　ISBN 4-333-00383-0

♦ 180 ♦

The Buddha's Way. **H. Saddhatissa. New York: George Allen and Unwin, 1971. 139 pp. Illustrated. Appendices. Bibliography. Glossary. Index.**

Lucid, simple explanation of the Buddhist way of life and its philosophical underpinnings. Part one introduces basic tenets. Part two explores the "Four Noble Truths" of Buddhism, outlining the philosophical basis of Buddhist beliefs as well as their practice in daily life. Part three teaches basic meditation techniques and summarizes various levels of meditative control and awareness. Numerous appendices include additional Buddhist teachings in the form of excerpts from various Buddhist scriptures, a list of major Buddhist festivals, a listing of Buddhist sacred sites in India, and a chronology of important events in the history of Buddhism in the East and the West.

DEWEY: 294.3 S124　　ISBN 0-8076-0635-9

♦ 181 ♦

Buddhism. **Catherine Hewitt. New York: Thomas Learning, 1995. 48 pp. Illustrated. Glossary. Index.**

Introduces Buddhism to young readers. Covers the life of the Buddha, the historical spread of Buddhism, the Buddhist world today, Buddhist scriptures and practices, home and family life, monasteries, life-cycle rituals, and festivals. Notes the main festivals of Theraveda, Tibetan, and Zen Buddhism. Special attention to Vesak and other celebrations of the Buddha's Birthday. Gives further reading list. Illustrated with color photos.

DEWEY: 294.3 LC: BQ4032. H49 ISBN 1-56847-375-3

♦ 182 ♦

Buddhist Festivals. **John Snelling. Vero Beach, FL: Rourke Enterprises, Inc., 1987. 48 pp. Illustrated. Maps. Glossary. Index.**

For young readers. Provides historical background on Buddha and discusses Buddhist festivals in Thailand, Sri Lanka, Tibet, and Japan, as well as brief notes on Buddhist observances in Asia, the United States, and Britain. Further reading list. One volume in a series entitled *Holidays and Festivals.* (NR)

DEWEY: 294.3 436 LC: BQ570.S64

♦ 183 ♦

The Buddhist World. **Anne Bancroft. Morristown, NJ: Silver Burdett Company, 1985. 45 pp. Illustrated. Glossary. Index.**

Provides an overview of Buddhist belief and practice, including festivals, for young readers. Describes the celebration of the Festival of the Tooth (Sri Lanka), and Vesak (or Buddha's Birthday). Offers briefer descriptions of the following Thai Buddhist festivals: Songkran, the Water Festival, Fighting Kites, Plowing Festival, Loy Krathong, Kathin, and the Elephant Festival. Further reading and resource list. Illustrated with color photos.

DEWEY: 294.3 ISBN 0-382-06747-9

♦ 184 ♦

Ten Lives of the Buddha: Siamese Temple Paintings and Jataka Tales. **Elizabeth Wray, Clare Rosenfield, and Dorothy Bailey. Photographs by Joe D. Wray. New York: Weatherhill, 1972. 154 pp. Bibliography. Glossary.**

Retells the last 10 Jataka tales—legends concerning the previous incarnations of the Buddha and representing the 10 cardinal virtues to which Buddhists aspire. Accompanying photographs illustrate depictions of these legends in the art of Thai Buddhist temples.

DEWEY: 294.382 LC: BL 1411 J32W7 ISBN 0-8348-0067-5

Christianity

General Works

♦ 185 ♦

Catholic Almanac. **Annual. Felician A. Foy, ed. Huntington, IN: Our Sunday Visitor, Inc. 600 pp. Glossary. Index.**

A collection of dates, facts, doctrines, and occurrences pertaining to current events in the Catholic Church. Contains calendar of important events within the Catholic Church for the preceding year as well as chronology of important historical events. Summarizes significant proclamations and statements, furnishes data on important institutions and personnel, and provides articles summarizing the Catholic viewpoint on many religious issues. Glossary illuminates numerous Christian terms, phrases, and concepts in terms of Catholic teachings.

DEWEY: 282 ISBN 0-87973-265-2

♦ 186 ♦

Christ and the Fine Arts: An Anthology of Pictures, Poetry, Music, and Stories Centering in the Life of Christ. **Cynthia Pearl Maus. Revised and enlarged edition. New York: Harper and Row, 1959. 813 pp. Illustrated. Indexes.**

Brings together 100 pieces of art (with accompanying interpretations), 117 hymns, 256 poems, and 76 stories depicting the life of Jesus Christ. Also features essays on the use of art, poetry, music, and story in the teaching of the Christian religion to young people. Materials grouped around seven themes: the nativity and childhood of Jesus, Jesus as a youth, characteristics of the adult Jesus, the crucifixion, the resurrection, and Jesus' presence among Christians today.

DEWEY: 232.9 M459 LC: BT 199.M3

♦ 187 ♦

The Christian Calendar. **Volume 113 of** ***Twentieth Century Encyclopedia of Catholicism.*** **Noële M. Denis-Boulet. Translated by P. Hepburne-Scott. New York: Hawthorn Books, 1960. 126 pp. Bibliography.**

Tells how the Christian calendar evolved from earlier calendars, describes the early observance of Christian holidays, and explains their placement in the Christian year. Treats Sunday, Easter, Lent, Epiphany, Advent, the Ember days, the Feast of Our Lady, and saints' days. History of martyrologies. Also discusses calendar reforms through history and contemporary reform proposal of a world calendar.

DEWEY: 264. 021 LC: BV 30 D443

♦ 188 ♦

The Christian Calendar: A Complete Guide to the Seasons of the Christian Year Telling the Story of Christ and the Saints from Advent to Pentecost. **Leonard W. Cowie and John Selwyn Gummer. Springfield, MA: C. and G. Merriam Co., 1974. 256 pp. Illustrated. Glossarial Index.**

Explains the significance of eight liturgical seasons of the Christian year: Advent, Christmas, Epiphany, Septuagesima, Lent, Easter, and Pentecost. Discusses scripture and festival associated with each Sunday of the liturgical year. Describes how these seasons and their feast days were incorporated into Christian worship and identifies Bible passages associated with them. Part two provides a chronologically organized calendar of saints' days and a list of patron saints. Follows the lectionary of the English Book of Common Prayer and the Roman Missal. Amply illustrated with European art.

DEWEY: 263.9 LC: BV 30. C7 ISBN 0-87779-040-X

♦ 189 ♦

Christian Myth and Ritual: An Historical Study. **E. O. James. London: John Murray, 1933. 345 pp. Bibliography. Index.**

Traces the historical development of common thematic elements in the prebiblical religions of the Old World and in Christian rituals, folk beliefs, and practices. Chapters cover divine kingship, the coronation ceremony, ordination rites, initiation ceremonies, altar rituals, marriage, last rites, processions, mystery plays, seasonal festivities, and the Christian ritual pattern. Treatment of festivals, feasts and fasts, both ancient and Christian, interspersed throughout. Particular attention given to Candlemas, the Christmas season, Easter and Holy Week, Shrovetide, the Feast of St. Mark, and Rogationtide.

DEWEY: 264 J

♦ 190 ♦

Christian Symbols Ancient and Modern: A Handbook for Students. **Heather Child and Dorothy Colles. New York: Charles Scribner's Sons, 1971. 270 pp. Illustrated. Bibliography. Index.**

Reviews the origin, meaning, and history of Christian symbols used in the decorative arts of the Church, such as stained glass windows, carvings, ritual objects, ecclesiastical robes, etc. Treats common Christian symbols, such as the cross, as well as the lesser-known symbolism of animals, numbers, the months, the calendar, and more. Generously illustrated with 33 black-and-white plates and 114 line drawings.

DEWEY: 246.55 LC: BV 150 C53 ISBN 684-13093-9

♦ 191 ♦

Christian Symbols, Ancient Roots. **Elizabeth Rees. London: Jessica Kingsley Publishers, Ltd., 1992. 165 pp. Illustrated. Appendix. Bibliography. Index.**

Explores the meaning of common Christian symbols to the ancient cultures of biblical times with the goal of restoring their original power and evocativeness. Covers symbols commonly used in worship and in some holiday celebrations, such as bread, water, and the tree or cross. Combines the perspectives of theology, drama, psychology, and anthropology. Appendices include exercises in use and appreciation of Christian symbols.

DEWEY: 246 LC: BV 150 ISBN 1-85302-046-X

♦ 192 ♦

Christian Symbols and How to Use Them. **Sr. M. A. Justina Knapp. 1935. Reprint. Detroit, MI: Omnigraphics, Inc., 1974. 164 pp. Illustrated. Bibliography. Index.**

Explains more than 100 symbols commonly used in the ceremonial art and architecture of the Catholic Church. Also covers symbolic use of color in rites and worship. Text accompanied by easily reproducible line drawings.

DEWEY: 246 LC: BV 150 K62 ISBN 0-8103-4050-X

♦ 193 ♦

The Christian Year: Its Purpose and Its History. **Walker Gwynne. 1917. Reprint. Detroit, MI: Omnigraphics, Inc., 1990. 143 pp. Appendix. Index.**

Reviews the history of the Christian year and explains the significance of the major feasts and fasts. Discusses the reasons for the Christian year and Puritan objections to it, the Jewish ritual year, festivals of the early Christians, the value of custom and tradition in worship, the Church calendar, and technical words used in the Church calendar. Specific festivals covered include Advent, Christmas, Circumcision, Epiphany, Presentation in the Temple, Annunciation, Transfiguration, Easter, Ascension, Whitsunday, Trinity, the Feast of St. Michael and All Angels, the Feast of All Saints, various saints' days, Black-Letter Days, Lent and other fast days, Good Friday, and Easter. Gives chapter on revisions to and variations of Church calendars. Appendix lists liturgical colors and provides questions for examination or review.

DEWEY: 263. 9 LC: BV 30. G85 ISBN 1-55888-870-5

♦ 194 ♦

Church Festival Decorations: Being Full Directions for Garnishing Churches for Christmas, Easter, Whitsuntide and Harvest. **Ernest R. Suffling. 1907. Reprint. Detroit, MI: Omnigraphics, Inc., 1990. 156 pp. Illustrated. Index.**

Tells how to decorate churches for festival days and seasons. Focuses on Christmas, Easter, Whitsuntide, and Harvest. Reviews meaning of liturgical colors and Christian symbols, including various forms of the cross and saints' emblems. Explains how to make wreaths, emblems, scrolls, banners, trellises and other decorations; discusses the decoration of existing architectural features; describes materials; and suggests appropriate texts.

DEWEY: 745.92 6 LC: SB 449.5 C43 S93 ISBN 1-55888-871-3

♦ 195 ♦

Dictionary of Christian Lore and Legend. **J.C.J. Metford. New York: Thames and Hudson, Ltd., 1991. 272 pp. Illustrated.**

A guide to the meaning of symbols, sayings, stories, and concepts of Christian origin which are commonly represented in literature and the arts, or which have become part of popular culture. More than 1,700 articles and 283 illustrations. Much cross-referencing.

DEWEY: 203 LC: BR 95.M396 ISBN 0-500-27373-1

♦ 196 ♦

The Evolution of the Christian Year. **A. Allan McArthur. Greenwich, CT: Seabury Press, 1953. 192 pp. Index.**

Learned treatise on the historical development of the Christian year. Chapters covers Sunday, Christmas and Epiphany, Good Friday and Easter, Ascension and Pentecost. Endnotes. Biblical references.

LC: BV 30 M23

♦ 197 ♦

A Feast of Festivals: Celebrating the Spiritual Seasons of the Year. **Hugo Slim. London: Marshall Pickering, an imprint of HarperCollins Publishers, 1996. 197 pp. Appendices.**

Reviews the spiritual themes, observance, and significance of the festivals of the Christian year. Also gives liturgical colors, Bible readings, and prayers. Covers the Sundays before Advent, Advent, the Christmas season, the Feast of the Holy Innocents, Epiphany, Candlemas, Shrovetide, Lent, Ash Wednesday, Mothering Sunday, the Annunciation, Passiontide, the days of Holy Week, Easter, Ascension Day, Pentecost, Trinity Sunday, Corpus Christi, Nativity of the Blessed Virgin, Harvest Festival and Thanksgiving, All Hallows Eve, All Saints' Day, and All Souls' Day. Appendix one notes Sunday reflection themes for the entire year (from the Church of England Alternative Service Book); appendix two lists saints' days.

ISBN 0-551-02850-5

♦ 198 ♦

The Festivals and Their Meaning: Christmas, Easter, Ascension and Pentecost, Michaelmas. **Rudolf Steiner. London: Rudolf Steiner Press, 1981. 399 pp.**

Reprints a number of lectures given by Steiner in the early twentieth century on the meaning of the great Christian festivals from an anthroposophical perspective. Covers Christmas, Easter, Ascension and Pentecost (including Whitsuntide), and Michaelmas. Theological emphasis, but some consideration of the origins and historical development of the festivals.

LC: GT 3930 S74 ISBN 0-85440-370-1

♦ 199 ♦

Festivals, Holy Days and Saints' Days: A Study in Origins and Survivals in Church Ceremonies and Popular Customs. **Ethel L. Urlin. 1915. Reprint. Detroit, MI: Omnigraphics, Inc., 1990. 272 pp. Illustrated. Bibliography. Index.**

Detailed account of the folklore, history and legends surrounding 52 Christian saints' days, holy days, and festivals. Emphasizes history and lore of practices found in Great Britain.

DEWEY: 263.9 LC: BV 35. U ISBN 1-55888-873

♦ 200 ♦

Great Catholic Festivals. **James L. Monk. New York: Henry Schuman, 1951. 110 pp. Illustrated. Index.**

Discusses origins and Catholic observance of Christmas, Epiphany, Easter, Pentecost, Corpus Christi, and Assumption. One volume in a series entitled *Great Religious Festivals.* (NR)

♦ 201 ♦

The Great Church Year: The Best of Karl Rahner's Homilies, Sermons, and Meditations. **Karl Rahner. Albert Raffelt and Harvey D. Egan, eds. New York: Crossroads Publishing Company, 1995. 396 pp. Index.**

Furnishes a collection of 120 sermons, homilies, and meditations on the festivals, observances, and themes of the Christian year by Karl Rahner. Covers Advent, Christmas, St. Sylvester's Day, New Year, Epiphany, Lent (including Mardi Gras, Ash Wednesday, and the days of Holy Week), Easter, Pentecost, Corpus Christi, the feast days of many saints, and more. Accessible to the general reader. Index of biblical passages.

DEWEY: 252.6 LC: BX1756 R25 G7613 ISBN 0-8245-1228-6

♦ 202 ♦

Handbook of Christian Feasts and Customs. **Francis X. Weiser. New York: Harcourt, Brace, and World, Inc., 1958. 366 pp. Glossary. Index.**

Discusses the history and manner of observance of Christian feasts. Addresses liturgical and popular aspects of celebrations, including folklore, foods, symbols, and customs. Part one covers feasts marking the seasons or units of time, part two covers celebrations relating to the life of Jesus Christ, and part three presents the veneration of the saints and of Mary.

DEWEY: 264

♦ 203 ♦

Holidays of the Church. **Martin Winkler. Translated by Marguérite Buchloh and Igor Rosimirow. Recklinghausen, Germany: Aurel Bongers Publishers, 1958. U.S. distributors, Taplinger Publishing Co. 80 pp. Illustrated.**

Presents 16 Russian paintings which represent themes from the major festivals of the Eastern Orthodox church. Gives commentary on the paintings, notes the feast date, describes the celebrated event, and mentions devotional practices. Color plates.

LC: N8050.W5313

♦ 204 ♦

The Holyday Book. **Francis X. Weiser. Illustrated by Robert Frankenberg. New York: Harcourt, Brace and Company, 1956. 217 pp. Index.**

Presents the religious customs associated with the feasts of the Pentecost season and saints' days throughout the year, tracing their origins. Covers the feast of Pentecost, Trinity Sunday, Corpus Christi and Thanksgiving. Also discusses Sunday observances, Candlemas, the Annunciation, the Assumption, the Nativity of Mary, the Immaculate Conception, All Saints' and All Souls' Day. Reviews the life and lore of the major saints.

DEWEY: 394 W443h LC: GT3930.W44

♦ 205 ♦

Holy Days in the United States: History, Theology, Celebration. **Secretariat, Bishops' Committee on the Liturgy, National Conference of Catholic Bishops. Washington, DC: United States Catholic Conference, 1984. 100 pp. Illustrated.**

Explains the history of Catholic Holy Days of Obligation, their theology and liturgy. Covers the Nativity of the Lord Jesus Christ, the Solemnity of Mary, the Solemnity of the Ascension of the Lord, the Solemnity of the Assumption of the Blessed Virgin Mary, the Solemnity of All Saints, and the Solemnity of the Immaculate Conception of the Blessed Virgin Mary. Discusses American history of observance of these days, offers pastoral-liturgical suggestions, furnishes discussion questions, and gives further reading list.

DEWEY: 263.97 LC: BX1977.U6 H65

♦ 206 ♦

Holy Places of Christendom. **Stewart Perowne. New York: Oxford University Press, 1976. 160 pp. Illustrated. Index.**

Describes historic and contemporary sites of Christian pilgrimage and the events or people associated with them. Covers sites associated with the birth, life, death, and resurrection of Jesus Christ, and sites associated with the saints and the spread of Christianity. Generously illustrated with color photos of shrines and artwork.

DEWEY: 263. 042 ISBN 0-19-519878-6

♦ 207 ♦

An Illustrated History of the Popes. **Michael Walsh. New York: St. Martin's Press, 1980. 256 pp. Illustrated. Tables. Bibliography.**

Discusses the lives of the popes and the changing nature of the papacy since its inception to present times. Considers the character, career, and legacy of the popes who most affected the role and scope of the papacy. Also provides a chronology of all 263 popes, from St. Peter to John Paul II. Amply illustrated.

DEWEY: 262.1309 LC: BX 955.2 ISBN 0-312-40817-X

♦ 208 ♦

Image and Pilgrimage in Christian Culture: Anthropological Perspectives. **Victor Turner and Edith Turner. New York: Columbia University Press, 1978. 281 pp. Illustrated. Appendices. Bibliography. Index.**

Provides an overview of the popular beliefs and theological concepts which have given rise to Christian pilgrimage and analyzes the images and symbols around which these pilgrimages are often focused. Also reviews the history and myths associated with Mexican pilgrimages, describes the Irish Lough Dergh pilgrimage, considers the conflict between iconophily and iconoclasm in Marian pilgrimage, and contrasts medieval and post-industrial pilgrimage patterns. Appendices provide notes on processual symbolic analysis, including the definition of many terms, and a chronology of the Lough Dergh pilgrimage.

DEWEY: 248.29 LC: BX 2323. T87 ISBN 0-231-04286-8

♦ 209 ♦

Mormonism and the American Experience. **Klaus J. Hansen. Chicago: University of Chicago Press, 1981. 257 pp. Index.**

A history of the origin and development of the Church of Jesus Christ of the Latter-day Saints (Mormons) from its founding in nineteenth-century America to present times. Discusses the changing relationship between Mormonism and mainstream American culture, as well as the change and development in Mormon beliefs and practices over time.

DEWEY: 289.373 LC: BX 8635.2 ISBN 0-226-31552-5

♦ 210 ♦

The Music of the English Church. **Kenneth R. Long. 1972. Reprint. Forestburgh, NY: Lubrecht and Cramer, Ltd., 1991. 480 pp. Bibliography. Index of musical examples. General Index.**

Documents the evolution of English Church music from the time of the English Reformation to the present day and relates it to developments within the wider tradition of Western European music. Covers musical styles and composers who exemplify musical styles or who sponsored significant innovations. Provides excerpts from musical scores.

DEWEY: 783.026342 LC: ML 3131 L 848 ISBN 0-340-14962-0

♦ 211 ♦

Names and Name-Days. **Donald Attwater. 1939. Reprint. Detroit, MI: Omnigraphics, Inc., 1991. 124 pp.**

Lists first names, their meaning, saints associated with them, and their feast days. Also gives a calendar of saints with a saint for every day of the year, and identifies patron saints of trades, professions, undertakings, illnesses, emergencies, nations, and English and Irish dioceses.

DEWEY: 929.4 LC: CS 2367 A8 ISBN 1-55888-877-2

♦ 212 ♦

Pilgrimage: An Image of Medieval Religion. **Jonathan Sumpton. Totowa, NJ: Rowman and Littlefield, 1975. 391 pp. Illustrated. Bibliography. Index.**

Examines pilgrimage as an important component of popular, Christian religious devotion in the Middle Ages. Discusses the cult of the saints and their relics, and other beliefs which inspired pilgrimage, such as those related to the forgiveness of sins, miraculous healings, and other interventions. Describes the experience of pilgrimage and considers changing patterns of pilgrimage, the impact of the Crusades, and the relationship between the masses of pilgrims and the official Church hierarchy.

DEWEY: 270.2 S956p ISBN 0-87471-677-2

♦ 213 ♦

Pilgrimages: A Guide to the Holy Places of Europe for Today's Traveler. **Paul Lambourne Higgins. Englewood Cliffs, NJ: Steeple Books, 1984. 146 pp. Index.**

Retells the legends, lore, and history associated with 34 sites of Christian pilgrimage in northern Europe. Also gives tips on transportation to these sites and suggests places to stay. Covers important pilgrimage sites in the British Isles, northern France, the Teutonic countries, Switzerland, the Lowlands, and Scandinavia.

DEWEY: 263. 042 4 LC: BX 2320.5 E85H53 ISBN 0-13-676163-1

♦ 214 ♦

Saints and Festivals of the Christian Church. **H. Pomeroy Brewster. 1904. Reprint. Detroit, MI: Omnigraphics, Inc., 1990. 558 pp. Appendices. Index.**

Over 450 entries relating the history and lore of Christian saints and celebrations associated with certain calendar dates or times of year. Arranged by calendar date.

DEWEY: 299.932 LC: BR 1710 B7 ISBN 1-55888-878-0

♦ 215 ♦

Seasons of Celebration. **Thomas Merton. New York: Farrar, Straus and Giroux, 1965. 248 pp.**

Thoughtful consideration of the deeper spiritual meaning of the cycle of liturgical feasts by the well-known Catholic monk and writer. Discusses Advent, Christmas, Ash Wednesday, Lent, and Easter. Also addresses liturgical renewal within the Catholic Church.

DEWEY: 264.02

♦ 216 ♦

Stories for the Christian Year. **Eugene H. Peterson, ed. New York: Macmillan Publishing Company, 1992. 214 pp.**

A collection of 23 short stories written by the members of the Chrysostom Society, a group of Christian writers. Stories address the spiritual themes of Christian fasts and festivals, including Advent, Christmas, St. Stephen's Day, Holy Innocents' Day, Epiphany, Shrove Tuesday, Ash Wednesday, Lent, the days of Holy Week, Easter, Ascension, Pentecost, Trinity Sunday, All Saints' and All Souls' Day.

DEWEY: 813. 0108382 LC: PS 648. C43 S74 ISBN 0-02-525430-8

♦ 217 ♦

The World of Icons. **H. P. Gerhard. New York: Harper and Row, 1971. 232 pp. Illustrated. Maps. Tables. Bibliography. Catalogues. Indexes.**

Surveys the history of icons in Eastern Christianity from biblical times to the seventeenth century. Addresses styles, artists, and uses.

DEWEY: 755.2 LC: N 8187 S5313 ISBN 06-433258-6

♦ 218 ♦

Worship Resources for the Christian Year. **Charles L. Wallis, ed. New York: Harper and Row, Publishers, 1954. 483 pp. Indexes.**

Suggests a wide variety of materials for use in the preparation of worship services for holidays and other special days of the Christian year (with a focus on those of most concern to evangelical Protestantism). Covers Advent, Christmas, Lent, Palm Sunday, Maundy Thursday, Good Friday, Easter, Universal Week of Prayer, Universal Bible Sunday, Reformation Sunday, Missionary Sunday, World Wide Communion Sunday, World Order Day, World Temperance Day, Stewardship Sunday, Mother's Day, Children's Day, Youth Sunday, Christian Education Week, Commencement Sunday, and Sundays related to American national holidays, such as Memorial Day, Labor Sunday, and Race Relations Sunday. Furnishes calls to worship and opening scriptural sentences, invocations, prayers, litanies, brief poems, topics, texts, and homiletic suggestions. Indexes for authors and sources, texts, poetry, special days and occasions, and general topics.

DEWEY: 264 W214

Christmas

♦ 219 ♦

The Big Book of Christmas Plays: 21 Modern and Traditional One-Act Plays for the Celebration of Christmas. **Sylvia E. Kamerman, ed. Boston, MA: Plays, Inc., 1988. 357 pp. Production notes.**

A collection of one-act plays about Christmas grouped according to suitability for elementary school, middle school, and high school productions. Plays range from dramas to comedies to fantasies. Also includes a puppet play and four Christmas plays adapted from classic literature, including Charles Dickens's *A Christmas Carol,* Victor Hugo's *Les Misérables,* Louisa May Alcott's *Little Women,* and a Sherlock Holmes story by Arthur Conan Doyle. Plays feature simple sets and props and adaptable casting requirements. Production notes describe sex and age of characters, playing time, costumes, props, sets, and lighting for each play.

DEWEY: 808. 8241   LC: PN 6120. C5C5143   ISBN 0-8238-0288-4

♦ 220 ♦

A Book of Christmas. **William Sansom. New York: McGraw-Hill Book Company, 1968. 256 pp. Illustrated. Bibliography.**

Weaves together a wealth of information and anecdote concerning the celebration of Christmas. Includes a discussion of the origins of Christmas celebrations and their associations with pagan rites, medieval and later European Christmas practices, nineteenth-century British and American customs and celebrations, contemporary issues of Christmas commercialism and charity, and a review of Christmas literature. Amply illustrated with a wide range of color photos depicting the Christmas story as told by artists, from medieval stained glass windows to contemporary advertisements.

DEWEY: 394.268

♦ 221 ♦

The Book of Christmas. **Reader's Digest Association. Montreal, Canada: Reader's Digest Association, 1979. 303. Illustrated.**

Part anthology, part picture book—this Christmas collection is divided into four sections. Part one reprints Bible passages foretelling and describing the birth of Christ. Richly illustrated with color plates of European paintings depicting these passages. Part two presents an essay entitled "The History of Christmas," by Rummer Godden. Part three brings together well-known and lesser-known Christmas literature, from Dickens's *A Christmas Carol* to poems by e. e. cummings and Langston Hughes, and an early letter of Pope John XXIII. Part four describes Christmas celebrations in nine, mostly European, countries and is illustrated with color photos of these events.

DEWEY: 394.268 ISBN 0-89577-013-X

♦ 222 ♦

The Book of Christmas. **Brendan Lehane. Alexandria, VA: Time-Life Books, 1986. 141 pp. Bibliography. Illustrated.**

Recounts myths, legends, folklore, and scripture surrounding Christmas, focusing on ancient and medieval Europe. Covers important saints of the winter season, their feats and folklore; legends, spirits and gods of winter darkness; feasts, games, rites and rituals associated with the return of the light, noting where these traditions have been maintained and incorporated into Christmas celebrations; words to 10 Christmas carols; and the story of Christ's birth, in scripture and in legend. Part of a series on folk tales, myths, and legends entitled "The Enchanted World."

DEWEY: 394.268282 LC: GT 4985 L44 ISBN 0-8094-5261-8

♦ 223 ♦

The Book of Christmas Folklore. **Tristram Potter Coffin. New York: Seabury Press, 1973. 192 pp. Indexes.**

Folklore scholar Tristram Potter Coffin surveys popular beliefs and practices surrounding the celebration of Christmas. Discusses the origins and history of European Christmas celebrations and the development of traditional Christmas practices, such as decorating Christmas trees, hanging greenery, lighting candles, feasting, and gift giving. Also reviews the legends surrounding the birth, life, and death of Jesus Christ, the historical development of such Christmas customs as caroling, mumming, and the performing of nativity plays, and the evolution of Christmas literature. Focuses on Anglo-American traditions.

DEWEY: 394.268282 LC: GT 4985. C546 ISBN 0-8164-9158-5

♦ 224 ♦

The Christmas Almanack. **Gerard and Patricia Del Re. Illustrations by Doug Jamieson. Garden City, NY: Doubleday and Company, 1979. 402 pp. Illustrated. Index.**

A wide-ranging collection of information about Christmas and things associated with Christmas. Presents gospel passages concerning the birth of Christ; synopses of books, movies, and television productions about Christmas; facts concerning the place of Christmas on the calendar; description of past and present Christmas customs and festivities from around the world; translations of "Merry Christmas" into foreign languages; Christmas recipes and craft ideas; and an assortment of Christmas facts and anecdotes. Also describes music written for Christmas and prints Christmas poems and carol lyrics.

DEWEY: 394 C555 LC: GT 4985. D47 ISBN 0-385-13353-7

♦ 225 ♦

Christmas: An Annotated Bibliography. **Sue Samuelson. New York: Garland Publishing, Inc., 1982. 96 pp. Index.**

Presents an annotated bibliography of historical, folkloristic, sociological, and psychological works on Christmas. Introduction discusses the development of Christmas literature in each of the four disciplines, noting important publications. Bibliography covers over 425 articles and books. Volume four in the Garland Folklore Bibliographies series.

DEWEY: 016. 3942 68282 LC: Z5711. C5S25 ISBN 0-8240-9263-5

♦ 226 ♦

Christmas and Christmas Lore. **Thomas G. Crippen. 1923. Reprint. Detroit, MI: Omnigraphics, Inc., 1990. 223 pp. Illustrated.**

Collection of customs, traditions, and legends relating to Christmas, drawn from chapbooks and pamphlets of the seventeenth and eighteenth centuries and from various books dealing with antiquities and legends.

DEWEY: 394.2 68282 LC: GT4985.C7 ISBN 1-55888-860-8

♦ 227 ♦

Christmas and its Customs: A Brief Study. **Christina Hole. Illustrated by T. Every-Clayton. New York: M. Barrows and Company, Inc., 1957. 95 pp. Bibliography. Index.**

Discusses origins of the holiday and its traditions, including garlands, gift-giving, carols, foods, legends, and superstitions. Also covers Twelfth Night and New Year. (NR)

♦ 228 ♦

Christmas: A Pictorial Pilgrimage. **Pierre Benoit. Nashville, TN: Abingdon Press, 1969. 124 pp. Illustrated.**

Offers an armchair tour of pilgrimage sites in Nazareth and Bethlehem associated with the birth of Jesus. Summarizes the history of early Christian Christmas observances, reprints gospel excerpts and retells the story of Jesus' birth, comments on the archeological evidence for sites of Christian pilgrimage, and describes the sites, their shrines, and artwork in words and in color and black-and-white photographs.

DEWEY: 394 C555 ISBN 687-07751-6

♦ 229 ♦

Christmas Around the World. **Mary D. Lankford. Illustrated by Karen Dugan. New York: Morrow Junior Books, 1995. 47 pp. Bibliography. Glossary. Index.** 📖

Tells how Christmas is celebrated in 12 countries: Australia, Canada, Ethiopia, Germany, Great Britain, Greece, Guatemala, Italy, Mexico, the Philippines, Sweden, and the United States (Alaska). Describes festivities, customs, symbols. Also gives chronology of important dates in the history of Christmas, instructions for Christmas craft projects, and a selection of Christmas facts and sayings. Illustrated with color drawings. For children.

DEWEY: 394.2 663 LC: GT 4985.5 L36 ISBN 0-688-12167-5

♦ 230 ♦

Christmas Book. **Harry Ballam and Phyllis Digby Morton, eds. 1947. Reprint. Detroit, MI: Omnigraphics, Inc., 1990. 260 pp. Illustrated. Appendix.**

An anthology of articles and stories by Charles Dickens, Aldous Huxley, Washington Irving, Bram Stoker, and others on the subject of Christmas, its spirit and celebration. Black-and-white drawings illustrate. Includes several holiday quizzes; answers given in appendix.

DEWEY: 820.8 033 LC: PN 6071. C6 B28 ISBN 1-55888-854-3

♦ 231 ♦

Christmas Book. **Francis X. Weiser. 1952. Reprint. Detroit, MI: Omnigraphics, Inc., 1990. 188 pp. Illustrated. Index.**

Relates the story of the celebration of Christmas, from its beginnings in the Gospels through the festivities of the Middle Ages, and on to the decline and eventual revival of Christmas customs in Europe and the United States. Ancient and familiar hymns are included, as well as a section on holiday breads and pastries.

DEWEY: 394.2 68268 LC: GT 4985. W42 ISBN 1-55888-855-1

♦ 232 ♦

Christmas Crafts and Customs Around the World. **Virginie Fowler. Englewood, NJ: Prentice-Hall, Inc., 1984. 174 pp. Illustrated. Index.**

Offers a collection of Christmas season foods and crafts from around the world. Describes customs and gives instructions for related craft project or recipe. Includes crafts and customs from England, France, Germany, Greece, Holland, Italy, Scandinavia, Thailand, China, the Philippines, Latin America, the Caribbean, and the United States. One chapter explains craft processes.

DEWEY: 394.2 68282 LC: TT900 C4 E43 ISBN 0-13-133661-4

♦ 233 ♦

Christmas Customs Around the World. **Herbert H. Wernecke. Philadelphia, PA: Westminster Press, 1979. 188 pp. Bibliography. Index.**

Describes Christmas celebrations in 60 countries of North, South, and Central America, Europe, Africa, the Middle East, and East Asia. Offers Christmas recipes from around the world and suggestions for incorporating customs from other lands into church and school Christmas programs.

DEWEY: 394 C555 ISBN 0-664-24258-8

♦ 234 ♦

Christmas Everywhere: A Book of Christmas Customs of Many Lands. **New revised and enlarged edition. Elizabeth Hough Sechrist. 1962. Reprint. Detroit, MI: Omnigraphics, Inc., 1997. 186 pp. Illustrated.**

Describes how Christmas is celebrated in 20 countries and regions of the world. Tells Christmas stories, relates customs. For young readers.

DEWEY: 394.2 ISBN 0-7808-0267-5

♦ 235 ♦

Christmas Gifts That Always Fit. **James W. Moore. Nashville, TN: Dimensions For Living, 1996. 126 pp.**

Anecdotes and advice on how to enrich oneself and others with the gifts most in keeping with the spirit of Christmas: kindness, faith, acceptance, love, friendship, time, forgiveness, encouragement, contemplation, and worship.

DEWEY: 263.91 LC: BV45 M64 ISBN 0-687-06148-2

♦ 236 ♦

The Christmas Holiday Book. **Henderson Yorke, et al. New York: Parents' Magazine Press, 1972. 320 pp. Illustrated. Indexes.**

A collection of Christmas lore and activities. Reprints gospel passages touching on the birth of Jesus; recounts Christmas history, traditions, and festivities; describes Christmas celebrations from other lands; and suggests Christmas activities for families. Also gives words and music to 21 Christmas carols, 14 stories and poems, and 57 Christmas recipes. Illustrated throughout with drawings, color photos, and lithographs.

DEWEY: 394. 2682 ISBN 0-8193-0557-X

♦ 237 ♦

Christmas in Ritual and Tradition: Christian and Pagan. **Clement A. Miles. 1912. Reprint. Detroit, MI: Omnigraphics, Inc., 1990. 400 pp. Illustrated. Bibliography. Index.**

Describes the religious observance and folk celebration of Christmas. Part I deals with forms of Christian observance, examining Latin and European hymns and poetry, liturgy, popular customs, and dramas, pageants, and plays. Part II covers pre-Christian winter festivals and their surviving customs. Includes discussion of the Christmas tree, gifts, cards, and mumming, as well as more than 20 saints' days and other holidays and festivals observed throughout the year in Europe. Bibliographical references given in endnotes.

DEWEY: 394 M LC: GT 4985. M5 ISBN 1-55888-896-9

♦ 238 ♦

Christmas in the Good Old Days: A Victorian Album of Stories, Poems, and Pictures of the Personalities Who Rediscovered Christmas. **Daniel J. Foley, ed. 1961. Reprint. Detroit, MI: Omnigraphics, Inc., 1993. 224 pp. Illustrated. Bibliography. Index.**

A collection of nineteenth-century Christmas stories and poems written by such authors as Louisa May Alcott, Washington Irving, Bret Harte, O. Henry, Charles Dickens, Hans Christian Andersen, Herman Melville, and others. Includes brief sketches of the authors.

DEWEY: 394 C555 cf LC: PN 6071 C6 C527 ISBN 0-7808-0003-6

♦ 239 ♦

Christmas: Its Origins and Associations. **W. F. Dawson. 1902. Reprint. Detroit, MI: Omnigraphics, Inc., 1990. 366 pp. Illustrated. Index.**

Detailed study of the origins, history, and celebration of Christmas across nineteen centuries. Also describes British Christmas customs and festivities, and includes information on Christmas in various lands. Arranged chronologically. Illustrated with black-and-white drawings.

DEWEY: 394.268 LC: GT 4985 D45 ISBN 1-55888-842-X

♦ 240 ♦

Christmas: Its Origins, Celebration and Significance as Related in Prose and Verse. **Robert Haven Schauffler. 1912. Reprint. New Introduction by Tristram Potter Coffin. Detroit, MI: Omnigraphics, Inc., 1990. 354 pp. Index.**

A collection of stories, song lyrics, poems, and letters describing the origins of Christmas, its spirit and meaning, and the manner in which it is celebrated. Includes selections by William Shakespeare, Charles Dickens, Washington Irving, William Wordsworth, and other noted and less-known writers. One volume in a series entitled *Our American Holidays.*

DEWEY: 394 C555 LC: PN 6071. C6C54 ISBN 1-55888-824-1

♦ 241 ♦

Christmas Plays and Programs: A Collection of Royalty-free Plays, Playlets, Choral Readings, Poems, Songs, and Games for Young People. **Aileen Fisher. Boston, MA: Plays, Inc., 1970. 344 pp.**

Furnishes 12 plays, 12 playlets and spelldowns, 14 group and choral readings, six recitations, thirty poems, 19 songs, and 16 games for Christmas.

Production notes list characters, playing time, costumes, props, setting, and lighting for plays.

DEWEY: 394.2 ISBN 0-8238-0017-2

♦ 242 ♦

Christmas Tidings. **William Muir Auld. 1933. Reprint. Detroit, MI: Omnigraphics, Inc., 1990. 156 pp. Index.**

Conveys the spiritual meaning and mystery of the Christmas season, with reference to legends, verse, devotional writings, various liturgies, and the Bible. References given in endnotes.

DEWEY: 263.91 LC: BT 315. A8 ISBN 1-55888-862-4

♦ 243 ♦

Christmas Traditions. **William Muir Auld. 1931. Reprint. Detroit, MI: Omnigraphics, Inc., 1992. 179 pp. Index.**

Descriptive account of European Christmas lore and customs, with a British emphasis. Describes the origins and spread of the Christmas holiday, its appropriation of pagan festivities, the rise of caroling, and the origins and meaning of such Christmas customs as decorating with greenery, lighting a Yule log, adorning Christmas trees, ringing bells, and gift giving.

DEWEY: 394.268 LC: GT4985.A8 ISBN 0-55888-895-0

♦ 244 ♦

The Christmas Tree Book: The History of the Christmas Tree and Antique Christmas Tree Ornaments. **Phillip V. Snyder. New York: Viking Press, 1976. 176 pp. Illustrated. Bibliography. Index.**

Covers the history of the Christmas tree and its decorations, from its German origins to its adoption as an American Christmas custom in the nineteenth century and its continuing popularity in the twentieth century. Describes early, homemade ornaments (often made of foodstuffs) and the shift to manufactured ornaments, noting changing designs and materials (tin, wax, paper maché, glass), and ends with shift from candles to electric Christmas tree lights. Photos of antique ornaments and nineteenth-century engravings of Christmas scenes serve as illustrations.

DEWEY: 394.268282. 028 LC: GT 4985. S59 ISBN 0-670-22115-5

♦ 245 ♦

Christmas: Why We Celebrate It the Way We Do. **Martin Hintz and Kate Hintz. Mankato, MN: Capstone Press, 1996. 48 pp. Illustrated. Glossary. Index.**

Explains the origins of Christmas and describes Christmas customs of many lands. Also treats Christmas symbols such as Santa Claus and Christmas trees. Gives further reading and resource list. For children.

DEWEY: 394.2663 LC: GT4985. 5 H55 ISBN 1-56065-327-2

♦ 246 ♦

Creative Christmas Crafts. **Alison Wormleigh, ed. Philadelphia, PA: Running Press, 1993. 144 pp. Illustrated. Glossary. Index.**

Presents a variety of home craft projects for Christmas, including cards, gift wraps, ornaments for tree and table, needlework projects, mobiles, candles, and more. Wide range of materials used, for example, metal foil, bread dough, pine cones, and other natural items. Beautifully illustrated with color photos of every craft project. Provides patterns to transfer. Glossary teaches some basic craft techniques and terms.

DEWEY: 394 C555 cg ISBN 1-56138-294-9

♦ 247 ♦

The Everything Christmas Book. **Expanded edition. Michelle Bevilacqua and Brandon Toropov, eds. Illustrated by Barry Littmann. Holbrook, MA: Adams Media Corporation, 1996. 470 pp. Bibliography. Index.**

A compendium of Christmas lore, literature, crafts, customs, foods, and history. Covers origins and historical development of Christmas and its customs, Christmas customs and observances around the world, the history of Santa Claus, and the celebration of Hanukkah and Kwanzaa. Reprints numerous Christmas stories and poems, gives words and music to 35 Christmas carols, and provides instructions for craft projects, homemade gifts, and home decorations. Offers collection of facts and anecdotes about twentieth-century American Christmas celebrations and gift-giving practices. Furnishes Christmas recipes, lists Christmas festivals and fairs in major population centers throughout the U.S., and suggests Christmas party ideas and games.

DEWEY: 394.2 663 0973 LC: GT 4986.A1 E94 ISBN 1-55850-697-7

♦ 248 ♦

The Family Read-Aloud Christmas Treasury. **Alice Low, ed. Illustrated by Marc Brown. Boston, MA: Little, Brown and Company, 1989. 136 pp.**

Gathers together 54 varied stories, poems, carols and rhymes for children. Poems by well-known authors, such as John Updike, A. A. Milne, e. e. cummings, and Langston Hughes. Color illustrations on nearly every page.

DEWEY: J394 C55 LC: PZ5.F2144 ISBN 0-316-53371-8

♦ 249 ♦

The Father Christmas Letters. **J.R.R. Tolkien. Boston, MA: Houghton Mifflin Company, 1976. 43 pp. Illustrated. Appendix.**

Presents 16 Christmas letters from famous fantasy writer J.R.R. Tolkien, writing as Father Christmas (the British equivalent of Santa Claus), to his children. Letters describe the fantasy world of Father Christmas and other members of the North Pole community, including Father Christmas's bumbling assistant—the North Polar Bear—as well as snow elves, red gnomes, snow men, cave bears, and Father Christmas's principal adversaries, the goblins. Several letters have been reproduced to show Tolkien's own, creative calligraphy. Color illustrations reproduce most of his original drawings, stamps, and postmarks. Appendix gives letter written with the polar bear alphabet alongside a key to that alphabet.

DEWEY: 394.2682 ISBN 0-395-24981-3

♦ 250 ♦

46 Days of Christmas: A Cycle of Old World Songs, Legends and Customs. **Dorothy Gladys Spicer. Illustrated by Anne Marie Jauss. New York: Coward-McCann, Inc., 1960. 96 pp. Indexes.**

Offers a collection of Christmas season celebrations from around the world beginning with the celebration of St. Barbara's Day (December 4) and ending with Old Twelfth Night (January 18). Introduces young readers to the legends, customs, and songs which accompany celebrations in Syria, the Netherlands, France, Luxembourg, Sweden, England, Poland, Czechoslovakia, Germany, Italy, Spain, Portugal, Romania, Ireland, Bulgaria, Belgium, and Armenia. Illustrated with black-and-white drawings. Country index, song title index, and special days index.

DEWEY: 394.2

♦ 251 ♦

4000 Years of Christmas. **Earl W. Count. New York: Henry Schuman, 1948. 95 pp. Index.**

Recounts Christmas lore and legends, and identifies the origins of Christmas customs. Describes the Babylonian New Year Festival and Roman Saturnalia, reviews the lore and legend of St. Nicholas, and discusses such Christmas symbols as greenery and Christmas trees. Prints words to many Christmas songs. One volume in a series entitled *Great Religious Festivals.*

DEWEY: 394.2 C832f LC: GT4985.C65 ISBN 1-55888-279-0

♦ 252 ♦

***The Guinness Book of Christmas.* Tom Hartman, ed. Cartoons by Wonk and Peter Harris. Enfield, Middlesex, England: Guinness Books, 1984. 144 pp.**

From the publishers of *The Guinness Book of World Records* comes this book of facts about Christmas. Covers words, customs, music, weather, food, coins, stamps, sports, and anniversaries associated with Christmas. Content has British emphasis. Photos, cartoons, poems, quizzes, recipes, and anecdotes dispersed throughout.

DEWEY: 394.2 68282 LC: GT 4985 ISBN 0-85112-404-6

♦ 253 ♦

***The History of the Christmas Card.* George Buday. 1954. Reprint. Detroit, MI: Omnigraphics, Inc., 1992. 304 pp. Appendices. Bibliography. Index.**

Details the origins and development of the Christmas card in Britain during the Victorian and Edwardian periods. Discusses manufacturers and artists, production techniques, genres of sentiment and design, modes of delivery, and popular attitudes and customs around giving and receiving cards. Numerous black-and-white photos of Victorian Christmas cards.

DEWEY: 741.68 LC: NC1866.C5B8 ISBN 1-55888-909-4

♦ 254 ♦

***Holly, Reindeer, and Colored Lights: The Story of Christmas Symbols.* Edna Barth. Illustrated by Ursula Arndt. New York: Seabury Press, 1971. 96 pp. Illustrated. Index.**

Explains the origins of 17 symbols of Christmas and describes historical and contemporary customs surrounding them from around the world. Symbols include the Christmas tree, the Yule log, Christmas colors, bells, cards, and more. Includes a further reading list of stories and poems about Christmas for young readers. Written for children.

DEWEY: J 394 C555

♦ 255 ♦

Ho Ho Ho: The Complete Book of Christmas Words. **Lynda Graham-Barber. New York: Bradbury Press, 1993. 119 pp. Illustrated. Bibliography. Index.**

Discusses the meaning and history of words and customs associated with Christmas. Briefly outlines Christmas customs in 11 different countries. Includes a timeline of important events in Christmas history and a further reading list. Black-and-white illustrations. For children.

DEWEY: 394.2 68282 014 LC: GT4985.5 G72 ISBN 0-02-736933-1

♦ 256 ♦

Merry Christmas: A History of the Holiday. **Patricia Bunning Stevens. New York: Macmillan, 1979. 158 pp. Illustrated. Bibliography. Index.**

Discusses the origins and history of European Christmas celebrations and customs. Offers chapters on Christmas in the Gospels, ancient midwinter festivals, the beginnings of Christmas, medieval European Christmas customs, mythical bringers of gifts (such as Santa Claus), Christmas decorations, and Christmas from the seventeenth to the twentieth centuries. Black-and-white illustrations.

DEWEY: 394.2682 LC: GT4985.S76 ISBN 0-02-788210-1

♦ 257 ♦

An Old-Fashioned Christmas. **Country Home Magazine. Des Moines, IA: Meredith Books, 1992. 192 pp. Index.**

Presents a collection of materials concerning Christmas preparations, decorations, and celebrations in the United States. Describes Christmas decorations and celebrations in eight homes across the U.S., with accompanying photographs. Relates Christmas lore and history of Christmas customs. Introduces the work of a number of folk artists working with the theme of Christmas, as well as a variety of Christmas collector's items, including ornaments, toys, and cards. Gives Christmas recipes. Describes Christmas celebrations in six historic villages, such as colonial Williamsburg. Features 174 color photos plus 108 illustrations.

DEWEY: 394.2682 ISBN 0-696-01965

♦ 258 ♦

1001 Christmas Facts and Fancies. **Alfred Carl Hottes. 1946. Reprint. Detroit, MI: Omnigraphics, Inc., 1990. 308 pp. Illustrated. Index.**

Presents the lore and customs of Christmas. Gives legends, stories, songs, foods, symbols, folklore, toasts, crafts, and decorations. Discusses ancient midwinter celebrations and reprints the gospel story of Christmas. Describes Christmas customs, lore, and foods from other countries.

DEWEY: 394 C555 ISBN 1-55888-858-6

♦ 259 ♦

Origami for Christmas. **Chiyo Araki. New York: Kodansha America, 1983. 148 pp. Illustrated.**

Shows how to make Christmas decorations from origami, the traditional Japanese craft of folding paper. Part one explains how to fold 33 basic shapes, from the typical crane shape to doves, Christmas trees, flowers, stars, Santas, baskets, and more. Part two describes how to combine these shapes into larger arrangements, such as wreaths, nativity scenes, gift wrappings, and bouquets. Features step-by-step instructions with accompanying diagrams. Color photos illustrate finished arrangements.

DEWEY: 736. 982 LC: TT 900. C4A7 ISBN 0-87011-528-6

♦ 260 ♦

Story of Santa Klaus, Told for Children of all Ages, From Six to Sixty. **William S. Walsh. 1909. Reprint. Detroit, MI: Omnigraphics, Inc., 1991. 231 pp. Illustrated.**

Discusses the origin and development of the Klaus legend, mythological concepts absorbed by Christianity, the Three Kings, Twelfth Night customs, Father Christmas, and Christmas traditions and observances in various countries. Illustrations by artists of all times from Fra Angelico to Henry Hutt.

DEWEY: 394.268 LC: GT4985.W3 ISBN 1-55888-922-1

♦ 261 ♦

Story of the Carol. **Edmondstoune Duncan. 1911. Reprint. Detroit, MI: Omnigraphics, Inc., 1992. 253 pp. Illustrated. Appendices. Bibliography.**

Surveys development of the forms and purposes of carols, as well as the days, feasts, pageants, and religious rites associated with them. Includes words and music to traditional carols. Appendices cover brief biographical notes on relevant individuals, glossary, chronological table of development of carols, and list of manuscript carols held in the British museum.

DEWEY: 782.28 09 LC: ML 2880.D911 ISBN 1-55888-921-3

♦ 262 ♦

Take Joy! The Tasha Tudor Christmas Book. **Tasha Tudor. Cleveland, OH: World Publishing Co., 1966. 157 pp. Illustrated. Index.**

A collection of stories, poems, carols, customs, legends, and sentiments concerning Christmas. Illustrated with color drawings. Both words and music given for carols. Also includes description of preparations for and celebrations of the author's own Christmas on a New England farm. Written for children.

DEWEY: J 394 C555

♦ 263 ♦

The 365 Days of Christmas: Keeping the Wonder of It All Ever Green. **William J. Byron. Mahwah, NJ: Paulist Press, 1996. 96 pp. Illustrated.**

Provides 14 short essays which consider the spiritual meaning of Christmas and tell how to keep the spirit of Christmas alive all year long.

DEWEY: 242.33 LC: BT 315.2 B97 ISBN 0-8091-0481-4

♦ 264 ♦

The Trees of Christmas. **Edna Metcalfe. Nashville, TN: Abingdon Press, 1979. 188 pp. Illustrated. Index.**

Full-page color photos depict 23 Christmas trees from around the world. Accompanying text provides instructions for making ornaments and other depicted decorations and describes how Christmas is celebrated in these lands. European emphasis. Provides a list of books for further reading on Christmas crafts and customs.

DEWEY: 394. C555 LC: GT 4989. M47 ISBN 0-687-42591-3

♦ 265 ♦

The Twelve Days of Christmas. **Miles Hadfield and John Hadfield. Boston, MA: Little, Brown and Company, 1961. 176 pp. Illustrated. Index.**

Recounts the customs of the Twelve Days of Christmas, including Christmas Eve, Christmas, Boxing Day, New Year's Eve, New Year, the Eve of Epiphany, and Epiphany (or Twelfth Day). Traces the history and meaning of various customs, legends, and symbols from pagan through Victorian times, including the use of holly and mistletoe as Christmas decorations, gift giving, Christmas cards, feasting and merry-making, St. Nicholas and Santa Claus, Christmas carols, first footing, the hunting of the wren, and various Christmas season entertainments, superstitions, and legends. Illustrated with color and black-and-white photos. British emphasis.

DEWEY: 394.2

♦ 266 ♦

Unplug the Christmas Machine: How to Have the Christmas You've Always Wanted. **Jo Robinson and Jean Coppock Staeheli. New York: William Morrow and Company, 1982. 239 pp. Appendices. Bibliography. Index.**

A guide to reducing materialism and fostering simplicity in Christmas celebrations. Reviews sources of holiday stress for women and for men, suggests ways of increasing communication between family members about holiday expectations, ways to reduce childrens' material expectations of Christmas and increase their participation in other aspects of celebration, and ways to arrange a more spiritual and personally meaningful celebration of Christmas. Appendices include recommendations for easy and inexpensive Christmas decorations, foods, and gifts; a Christmas budget planner; and ideas for alternative Christmas activities. Bibliography gives suggestions for further reading.

DEWEY: 394.2 68282 LC: GT 4985. R62 ISBN 0-688-01319-8

♦ 267 ♦

Unwrapping Christmas. **Daniel Miller, ed. Oxford, England: Clarendon Press, 1993. 239 pp. Index.**

Ten anthropological essays describe and interpret contemporary Christmas celebrations in many nations, including the United States, Trinidad, Sweden, Great Britain, and among the Iñupiat (Eskimo) of Alaska. Includes "A Theory of Christmas" and "Christmas against Materialism in Thailand" by Daniel Miller; "Father Christmas Executed" by Claude Lévi-Strauss; "The Rituals of Christmas Giving" by James Carrier; "Materialism and the Making of the Modern American Christmas" by Russell Belk; "Cinderella Christmas: Kitsch, Consumerism, and Youth in Japan" by Brian Moeran and Lisa Skov; "The English Christmas and the Family: Time Out and Alternative Realities" by Adam Kuper; "Christmas Cards and the Construction of Social Realities in Britain Today" by Mary Searle-Chatterjee; "Christmas Present; Christmas Public" by Barbara Bodernhorn; and "The Great Christmas Quarrel and Other Swedish Traditions" by Orvar Lögren.

DEWEY: 394.2 68282 LC: GT 4985.U55 ISBN 0-19-827903-5

♦ 268 ♦

Victorian Christmas Crafts: A Treasury of Gifts, Ornaments, and Other Holiday Specialties to Prepare. **Barbara Bruno. New York: Van Nostrand Reinhold Company, 1984. 114 pp. Illustrated. Index.**

Describes home preparations for Christmas in the Victorian age and introduces 48 Victorian Christmas craft projects with instructions on how to make them. Features ornaments for home and tree, trinkets and simple gifts, recipes for Christmas sweets, and more. Many unusual project ideas. Crafts use inexpensive, easily obtainable materials. Generously illustrated with author's own drawings.

DEWEY: 745.5941 LC: TT 900. C4B78 ISBN 0-442-21384-0

♦ 269 ♦

The Whole Christmas Catalogue: The Complete Compendium of Christmas Traditions, Recipes, Crafts, Carols, Lore, and More. **Meg Crager and Margaret Grace. Photos by Jack Deutsch. Philadelphia, PA: Courage Books, 1994. 179 pp. Illustrated. Index.**

Explains the origins of Christmas customs and traditions, provides more than 50 Christmas recipes, suggests craft and party ideas, prints 19 Christmas stories, songs, and poems, and tells how to improve home snapshots. Further reading list.

DEWEY: 394.2663 LC: TT900.C4 W48 ISBN 1-56138-438-0

Easter and Lent

♦ 270 ♦

Book of Easter. **Introduction by William C. Doane. 1910. Reprint. Detroit, MI: Omnigraphics, Inc., 1990. 246 pp. Illustrated.**

A collection of Easter poems, stories, hymns, and essays along with reproductions of famous paintings relating to Easter by Rembrandt, Rubens, Fra Angelico, Breton, Veronese, and others. Compiles historical information, myths, and legends concerning the people and events associated with Good Friday, Easter, and the Ascension.

DEWEY: 808.8 033 LC: PN6071.E2B6 ISBN 1-55888-868-3

♦ 271 ♦

A Book of Lent: With Daily Devotions. **Victor E. Beck and Paul M. Lindberg. Illustrations by Don Wallerstedt. Philadelphia, PA: Fortress Press, 1963. 197 pp.**

Explains the symbols, customs, and spiritual significance of Lent, and offers daily meditations for the Lenten season, beginning with Septuagesima Sunday and ending with Holy Saturday. Meditations give scripture reading, interpretive commentary, and a prayer.

DEWEY: 242.3

♦ 272 ♦

Easter. **Cass R. Sandak. New York: Crestwood House, 1990. 48 pp. Illustrated. Index.**

Reviews the events of the first Easter and describes the religious beliefs, folklore, and customs which characterize the celebration of the Easter season (including Carnival, Lent, and Holy Week) in many countries. Offers Easter trivia and further reading list. Illustrated with color photos. For children.

DEWEY: 394.2 68283 LC: GT4935. S3 ISBN 0-89686-499-5

♦ 273 ♦

Easter and Its Customs. **Christina Hole. M. Barrows and Company, Inc., 1961. 96 pp. Illustrated. Index.**

Describes the folklore and festivities of the Easter season, with particular emphasis on British traditions. Covers Shrovetide, Mothering Sunday, Good Friday, Easter, Easter Monday, and Hocktide. Uncovers origins of customs and symbols.

DEWEY: 394.26

♦ 274 ♦

Easter: A Pictorial Pilgrimage. **Pierre Benoit. Nashville, TN: Abingdon Press, 1969. 154 pp. Illustrated.**

Bible excerpts tell the story of the first Easter, from Jesus' entry into Jerusalem to his Resurrection. Illustrated with photos of sites in Jerusalem where the events of Holy Week are thought to have taken place. Also includes photos of famous artwork. Brief discussion of archeological evidence.

DEWEY: 242.36 ISBN 687-11495-0

♦ 275 ♦

The Easter Book. **Jenny Vaughan. New York: Grosset and Dunlap, 1981. 47 pp. Illustrated. Index.**

Relates a selection of Easter customs, celebrations, legends, and lore from many lands. Also gives craft activities, games, recipes, songs, and poems. Illustrated with colorful drawings. For children.

DEWEY: 394 E13v ISBN 0-448-13492-6

♦ 276 ♦

The Easter Book. **Francis X. Weiser. New York: Harcourt, Brace and Company, 1954. 224 pp. Illustrated. Index.**

Acquaints the reader with the forms of observance, customs, and folklore of the Easter season, with an emphasis on European traditions. Discusses pre-Lent and Carnival, Lent, Palm Sunday, Maundy Thursday, Good Friday, Holy Saturday, Easter, and Easter foods, music, and symbols. Traces history of various practices, gives references cited in endnotes.

DEWEY: 394.26

♦ 277 ♦

The Easter Book of Legends and Stories. **Alice Isabel Hazeltine and Elva Sophronia Smith. Illustrated by Pamela Bianco. 1947. Reprint. Detroit, MI: Omnigraphics, Inc., 1992. 392 pp. Indexes.**

An anthology of stories, poems, and plays about Easter, its legends, symbols, and celebration. Includes selections by Emily Dickinson, A. E. Housman, Robert Frost, and many more. For children.

DEWEY: 394 E13 h LC: PN6071.E2H3 ISBN 1-55888-857-8

♦ 278 ♦

An Easter Celebration: Traditions and Customs from Around the World. **Pamela Kennedy. Nashville, TN: Ideals Children's Books, 1990. 32 pp. Illustrated.**

Explains the origins, meaning, and relationship between folk and religious Easter customs. Treats ancient spring festivals, the relationship of Easter to Passover, Easter legends, and Easter symbols, such as decorated eggs, lilies, palm leaves, bonfires, the cross, rabbits, and lambs. Also describes Easter customs, such as foot washing and egg rolling. Discusses the popular celebration and religious observance of Carnival, Lent, and Holy Week. Gives several recipes.

DEWEY: 394.2 68283 LC: GT 4935 K46 ISBN 0-8249-8506-0

♦ 279 ♦

Easter Chimes: Stories for Easter and the Spring Season. **New, revised edition. Wilhelmina Harper. Illustrated by Hoot von Zitzewitz. New York: E. P. Dutton and Co., Inc., 1965. 253 pp.**

A collection of 38 Easter stories and poems. Includes selections by Hans Christian Andersen, Padraic Colum, Carol Ryrie Brink, and others. Black-and-white drawings illustrate. For children.

DEWEY: J 394 E13H

♦ 280 ♦

Easter Eggs for Everyone. **Evelyn Coskey. Illustrated by Giorgetta Bell. Nashville, TN: Abingdon Press, 1973. 191 pp. Bibliography. Index.**

Teaches a variety of techniques for decorating Easter eggs, including traditional Ukrainian and Slavic egg-dyeing processes as well as contemporary American designs and ideas. Includes chapters on the legends, customs, and folklore surrounding eggs and Easter eggs.

DEWEY: 394 E13 c LC: TT 896.7.C67 ISBN 0-0687-11492-6

♦ 281 ♦

Easter Garland: A Vivid Tapestry of Customs, Traditions, Symbolism, Folklore, History, Legend, and Story. **Priscilla Sawyer Lord and Daniel J. Foley. Drawings by Charlotte Edmands Bowden. Philadelphia, PA: ChiltonBooks, 1963. 141 pp. Bibliography. Index.**

Reviews the folklore of Easter. Covers the customs, stories, and beliefs surrounding the flowers, trees, birds, animals, and foods symbolic of Easter or represented in Easter lore. Prints the Easter story as told in the Gospels, and various short stories featuring Easter. Also discusses legend of the Holy Grail, Mardi Gras, Easter seals, and the Lenten season with its foods and practices. Gives recipes.

DEWEY: 394.26

♦ 282 ♦

Easter: Its History, Celebration, Spirit, and Significance as Related in Prose and Verse. **Susan Tracy Rice, comp. Robert Haven Schauffler, ed. New York: Dodd, Mead and Company, 1916. 261 pp.**

An anthology of poems, essays, quotations, and songs touching on the meaning and celebration of Easter. Some discussion of Easter customs in various cultures. Includes selections by Christina Rossetti, Oscar Wilde, Edmund

Spenser, Robert Browning, George Herbert, Lewis Carroll, Emily Dickinson, and many others. One volume in a series entitled *Our American Holidays.*

LC: GT 4935 R5 ISBN 1-55888-863-2

♦ 283 ♦

Easter: Its Story and Meaning. **Alan Watts. New York: Henry Schuman, 1950. 128 pp. Illustrated. Index.**

Noted philosopher of religion draws out the universal meaning of the Easter festival by comparing it to similar spring festivals of ancient peoples. Chapters address the following mythological themes and symbols: the cycle of death and rebirth, death and resurrection of a god, spring, the sun, eggs, and mystery. Also retells the biblical Easter story, explains Christian Easter symbols, relates Easter folklore, and describes Easter ceremonies of the medieval church. One volume in a series entitled *Great Religious Festivals.*

DEWEY: 394.2 W349e

♦ 284 ♦

The Easter Mysteries. **Beatrice Bruteau. New York: Crossroad Publishing Company, 1995. 190 pp.**

Discusses the rites and spiritual themes of Lent and Easter, including prayer, fasting, foot washing, communion, baptism, resurrection, and more. Guides the reader towards a deeper spiritual experience of the Easter season and a more profound understanding of Christianity. Gives suggested exercises. Endnotes.

DEWEY: 242. 34 LC: BX 2170 I4 B78 ISBN 0-8245-1493-9

♦ 285 ♦

The Easter Story. **New York: The Metropolitan Museum of Art, 1967. 40 pp. Illustrated.**

Tells the story of the first Easter in images and in text. Reproduces artwork in the collection of the Metropolitan Museum alongside excerpts from the Gospels of the King James Bible.

DEWEY: 232.96

♦ 286 ♦

Easter: The Legends and the Facts. **Eleanor C. Merry. London: New Knowledge Books, 1967. 153 pp. Index.**

Draws links between the religious message of Easter and the deeper meanings of ancient and medieval European legends, affirming the truth of various aspects of the Christian faith. Discusses symbolism of the sun, moon, and earth in the ancient religions of the Mediterranean, the legend of Parsifal, the ancient Celtic legend of Conchubar, and the legend of Faust.

LC: BP 595 M4

♦ 287 ♦

Easter the World Over. **Priscilla Sawyer Lord and Daniel J. Foley. Philadelphia, PA: Chilton Book Company, 1971. 289 pp. Illustrated. Bibliography. Index.**

Presents the folklore and folk festivities of the Easter season (including Lent and Carnival). Covers more than 40 countries in Europe, Latin America, the Caribbean, Asia, North America, and the Middle East. Also describes non-Christian holidays occurring in these countries during the Easter season. Features the lore of Easter eggs. Reprints Bible excerpts telling the story of the death and Resurrection of Christ. Briefly reviews Easter music and representations of Easter in the arts.

DEWEY: 394 E13 Le ISBN 0-8019-5542-4

♦ 288 ♦

An Egg at Easter. **Venetia Newall. Bloomington, IN: Indiana University Press, 1971. 423 pp. Illustrated. Appendices. Bibliography. Index.**

A comprehensive study of the world folklore of eggs from ancient to modern times. Covers creation myths, sacrificial practices, magic, witchcraft, and beliefs linking eggs with fertility, purity, the spirit, and rebirth. Also examines Christian beliefs and practices surrounding eggs, with a special emphasis on the meanings, uses, designs, and various techniques involved in decorating Easter eggs. Appendices list various substances used to dye eggs and beliefs surrounding the early Germanic goddess, Eastre.

DEWEY: 394.269 ISBN 253-31942-0

♦ 289 ♦

First Easter: The True and Unfamiliar Story. **Paul L. Maier. New York: Harper and Row, 1973. 128 pp. Illustrated.**

Reconstructs the events of the first Easter from a careful reading of biblical texts and other primary sources. Illustrated with photos of Jerusalem sites where the events are thought to have taken place.

DEWEY: 232.96 M 217 f ISBN 06-065397

♦ 290 ♦

It's Time for Easter. **Elizabeth Hough Sechrist and Janette Woolsey. Illustrations by Elsie Jane McCorkell. Philadelphia, PA: Macrae Smith Company, 1961. 255 pp. Index.**

An Easter anthology. Describes Easter season customs from Europe and around the world, examines Easter symbols and legends, and explores Easter music. Also gives a brief history of Easter, and reprints the Easter story as it is told in the Gospels, along with 16 Easter poems and 12 Easter stories. Appropriate for older children.

DEWEY: 394.26

♦ 291 ♦

The Joys of Easter. **Rachel Hartman. Illustrated by Ragna Tischler. New York: Meredith Press, 1967. 113 pp. Index.**

Identifies six joys inherent in the celebration of Easter: the joys of anticipation, continuity, new beginnings, celebration, communication, and happiness amidst suffering. Chapters show how each joy is embodied in the religious and popular customs, legends, symbols, and music of the Easter season. Also gives recipes.

DEWEY: 394 E13 ha

♦ 292 ♦

Lilies, Rabbits, and Painted Eggs: The Story of Easter Symbols. **Edna Barth. Illustrated by Ursula Arndt. New York: Seabury Press, 1970. 64 pp. Index.**

Introduces children to Easter customs by way of explaining the meaning and origins of Easter symbols. Outlines the story of Christ's resurrection, discusses animals, foods, plants, and other items associated with Easter. Includes further reading list.

DEWEY: 394.268

♦ 293 ♦

Meditations for Lent. **James G. Kirk. Philadelphia, PA: Westminster Press, 1988. 174 pp. Illustrated. Index.**

Offers a scripture reading, meditation, and prayer for each day of Lent and Holy Week. Meditation themes are based on the daily Bible passage from the lectionary.

DEWEY: 242.34 LC: BV 85. K55 ISBN 0-664-25038-6

♦ 294 ♦

Pancakes and Painted Eggs: A Book for Easter and All the Days of the Year. **Jean Chapman. Illustrated by Kilmeny Niland. Chicago, IL: Children's Press International, 1981. 176 pp. Index.**

A children's anthology for the Easter season. Provides stories, legends, songs, poems, and descriptions of Easter season customs and beliefs from many countries. Treats Carnival (Shrove Tuesday), Ash Wednesday, Lent, Mothering Sunday, Palm Sunday, Holy Thursday, Good Friday, and Easter. Includes selections by William Blake, Leo Tolstoy, Oscar Wilde, and many others. Illustrated with color and black-and-white drawings.

DEWEY: 394.2682

♦ 295 ♦

Passion for Pilgrimage. **Alan Jones. San Francisco, CA: Harper and Row, 1988. 187 pp. Bibliography.**

Meditations on the spiritual themes of Lent, Holy Week, and Easter and the broader message they carry about human relationships and relationship with God. References given in endnotes. Select bibliography.

DEWEY: 242.34   LC: BV 85 J62   ISBN 0-06-064180-0

♦ 296 ♦

A Season With the Savior: Meditations on Mark. **Edward R. Sims. New York: Seabury Press, 1978. Unpaginated.**

Offers meditations on and readings from the Gospel according to Mark for the observance of Lent. Morning and evening entries for every day of the seven weeks of Lent. Includes weekly summary and questions for review and reflection.

DEWEY: 225.3 06   LC: BS 2585.4 S57   ISBN 0-8164-0413-5

♦ 297 ♦

Wilderness Wanderings: A Lenten Pilgrimage. **Marilyn Brown Oden. Nashville, TN: Upper Room, 1995. 143 pp. Bibliography.**

Supplies spiritual themes, inspirational prose, meditations, and prayers to aid in the observance of the seven weeks of Lent. Also provides questions for weekly review and suggested activities for study groups.

DEWEY: 263.92   ISBN 0-8358-0743-6

The Saints

GENERAL WORKS

♦ 298 ♦

A Biographical Dictionary of the Saints, with a General Introduction to Hagiology. **George Frederick Holweck. 1924. Reprint. Detroit, MI: Omnigraphics, Inc., 1990. 1053 pp.**

Covers thousands of saints—all those venerated in any Christian church, including those not officially canonized but with popular cult following. Brief bibliographical notices. (NR)

DEWEY: 270.092 LC: BX4655.H6 ISBN 1-55888-846-2

♦ 299 ♦

The Book of Saints: A Dictionary of Servants of God. **Sixth edition, entirely revised and reset. Compiled by the Benedictine monks of St. Augustine's Abbey, Ramsgate. Wilton, CT: Morehouse Publishing, 1993. 606 pp. Illustrated. Bibliography.**

Gives brief, dictionary-style entries for more than 10,000 Catholic and Orthodox saints. Gives name, dates, feast day, and significant, verifiable life events; legends, if given, are so noted. Notes changes in status of certain Catholic saints since 1969 General Calendar reforms. Provides list of emblems associated with saints, a list of saints' patronages, and a list of ancient sibyls, their emblems, and prophecies.

DEWEY: 282. 092 2 LC: BX 4655.2 B66 ISBN 0-8192-1611-9

♦ 300 ♦

A Calendar of Saints: The Lives of the Principal Saints. **James Bentley. New York: Facts on File, 1986. 256 pp. Illustrated. Index.**

Gives a brief biography of one saint for every day of the year. Includes famous and relatively unknown saints. Arranged by day of veneration. Beautifully illustrated with color and black-and-white photos of European artwork depicting the lives of the saints. Appropriate for teens.

DEWEY: 270. 092 2 LC: BX 4651.2 B46 ISBN 0-8160-1682-8

♦ 301 ♦

The Cult of the Saints: Its Rise and Its Function in Latin Christianity. **Peter Brown. Chicago, IL: University of Chicago Press, 1981. 187 pp. Index.**

Considers the historical development of the cult of the saints, from early Christian times to the Middle Ages. Describes the practices and beliefs which grew up around the cult of the saints and explores its meaning to ordinary people as well as to the Church hierarchy. Citations given in endnotes.

DEWEY: 270.2 LC: BX 2333. B74 ISBN 0-226-07621-0

♦ 302 ♦

Dictionary of Saints. **John J. Delaney. Garden City, NY: Doubleday and Company, Inc., 1980. 647 pp.**

Contains 5,000 succinct, dictionary-style entries. Organized alphabetically by name. Includes both the Roman Catholic and Byzantine ecclesiastical calendars, a chronology of popes and world rulers, and a list patron saints and their symbols.

DEWEY: 252.2 D337 LC: BX 4655.8 D44 ISBN 0-385-13594-7

♦ 303 ♦

The Encyclopedia of Saints. **Clemens Jöckle. London: Alpine Fine Arts Collection (U.K.) Ltd., 1995. 480 pp. Illustrated.**

Covers all saints in the Roman Catholic General Calendar of 1969, as well as a number of saints from regional churches, especially those with a rich iconographic tradition, a notable history of veneration, or other remarkable features. Arranged in alphabetical order by saint's name, each entry gives the saint's name, feast day, legends and/or major life events, a list of their patronages (of places, people, or situations), places where they are venerated, superstitions attached to them, and notes about the location of their relics or other cult sites. Also provides commentary on their representation in works of art, including a list of paintings in which they are represented. Many entries are illustrated with color or black-and-white reproductions of European paintings.

LC: BX 4655.8 J6213 ISBN 0-88168-226-8

♦ 304 ♦

Lives and Legends of the Georgian Saints. **David Marshall Lang. London: George Allen and Unwin, 1956. 180 pp. Bibliography. Index.**

Presents the biographies and legends of 10 Georgian saints. Includes St. Nino, the Nine Martyred Children of Kola, St. Shushanik, Peter the Iberian, St. David of Garesja, St. Eustace, St. Abo of Baghdad, St. Gregory of Khandzta, the Georgian Anthonites, and Queen Ketevan.

DEWEY: 235.2 L269L

♦ 305 ♦

Lives of the Saints. **Four volumes. Complete edition. Alban Butler. Edited, revised, and supplemented by Herbert Thurston and Donald Attwater. New York: P. J. Kennedy and Sons, 1956. Volume one, 720 pp. Volume two, 692 pp. Volume three, 705 pp. Volume four, 707 pp. Index in volume four.**

A revision and expansion of Butler's classic work, written over 200 years ago, with the purpose of providing short, accurate, and readable accounts of the lives of the saints familiar to English-speaking Catholics. Entries expanded to 2,565. Organized by calendar date. Appendices include a memoir of Alban Butler, an account of the processes of beatification and sanctification, and a list of recent beatifications.

DEWEY: 235.2 B LC: BX 4654. B8

♦ 306 ♦

The Oxford Dictionary of Saints. **David Hugh Farmer. 1978. Reprint. New York: Oxford University Press, 1993. 440 pp. Appendix. Geographical Index.**

Brief, scholarly accounts of the lives of about 1,000 saints associated with Great Britain by birth, death, or tradition of veneration. Entries accompanied by bibliographic references. Appendices includes a list of English people who have been candidates for canonization and are associated with a popular cult; a list of patronages of saints; emblems of saints; places in Great Britain and Ireland associated with saints; and a calendar of saints' days.

DEWEY: 270 LC: BR 1710 ISBN 0-19-283069-4

♦ 307 ♦

The Penguin Dictionary of Saints. **Donald Attwater. Baltimore, MD: Penguin Books, 1965. Second edition revised and updated by Catherine Rachel Johnson, 1983. Bibliography. Glossary.**

Summarizes the lives of hundreds of saints, with a special emphasis on British and Irish saints. Entries tell where the saints were born, lived, died; major events in their lives; personal characteristics; and any writings or legends attributed to them. Includes some Orthodox saints. Arranged in calendar order, all dates have at least one saint, while some have two or more. Provides a glossary of Christian terms. Lists emblems of some saints and feast days of all saints covered in the book.

DEWEY: 235.2029 ISBN 0-14-051123-7

♦ 308 ♦

The Saint Book, for Parents, Teachers, Homilists, Storytellers, and Children. **Mary Reed Newland. New York: Seabury Press, 1979. 194 pp. Illustrated.**

Furnishes biographies for more than 50 saints. Gives day of veneration, and dates of birth and death (when known). Appropriate for children.

DEWEY: 282.09 LC: BX 4655.2 N48 ISBN 0-8164-0210-8

♦ 309 ♦

Saints in Folklore. **Christina Hole. Illustrated by T. Every-Clayton. New York: M. Barrows and Company, Inc., 1965. 159 pp. Bibliography. Index.**

Retells the legends associated with early saints, gives what is known about their actual lives, and describes devotions, customs, or celebrations associated with them from medieval to present times. Covers St. Nicholas of Myra, St. George of England, St. Joseph of Arimathea, St. Christopher, St. Blaise, St. Catherine of Alexandria, St. Oswald of Northumbria, the Seven Sleepers of Ephesus, St. Lucy, St. Thomas the Apostle, and St. John the Baptist. Also gives the lore and legends of saints associated with holy wells.

DEWEY: 398.22

♦ 310 ♦

Saints of Russia. **Constantin De Grunwald. Translated by Roger Capel. New York: Macmillan Company, 1960. 180 pp. Index.**

Recounts the life and deeds of 10 Russian saints: St. Vladamir, the Holy Brothers Boris and Gleb, St. Theodosius, St. Alexander Nevski, St. Sergius of Radonezh, St. Nil Sorski, St. Philip (Primate of Moscow), St. Tikhon of Zadonsk, and St. Seraphin of Sarov. Briefly describes popular devotions associated with these saints.

DEWEY: 235.2 G891 s

♦ 311 ♦

Saints: The Chosen Few. **Manuela Dunn-Mascetti. New York: Ballantine Books, 1994. 255 pp. Illustrated. Index.**

Provides an overview of sainthood in the Christian, Jewish, Islamic, Hindu, and Buddhist religious traditions. Discusses the meaning of sainthood, the qualities of saints, and the official as well as popular recognition of saints. Profiles the lives of numerous saints. Considers the divine intervention of saints, miracles, and pilgrimages. Gives a list of patronages, along with prayers and offerings, for 21 Christian saints. Beautifully illustrated with color photos and reproductions of artworks.

DEWEY: 235.2092 ISBN 0-345-38382-6

ST. FRANCIS OF ASSISI

♦ 312 ♦

Francis of Assisi. **John Holland Smith. New York: Charles Scribner's Sons, 1972. 210 pp. Bibliography. Index.**

A standard biography of the saint and his times. Concludes with his canonization.

DEWEY: 271.3 F818 sm ISBN 684-12985-X

♦ 313 ♦

God's Fool: The Life and Times of Francis of Assisi. **Julien Green. Translated by Peter Heinegg. San Francisco, CA: Harper and Row, 1985. 273 pp.**

Presents a series of short vignettes conveying both the human and the saintly episodes in the life of Francis of Assisi. Also provides background information on the social and religious mores of the time.

DEWEY: 271.3 024 LC: BX 4700. F6 G6913 ISBN 0-06-063462-6

ST. MARTIN

♦ 314 ♦

Saint Martin. **Edith Delamare. Translated by Rosemary Sheed. New York: Macmillan Company, 1962. 116 pp. Appendices. Bibliography.**

Tells the story of the life of St. Martin of Tours. Appendices briefly describe his cult in Tours, Paris, and in Hungary.

DEWEY: 921

ST. MARY MAGDALEN

♦ 315 ♦

Mary Magdalen: Myth and Metaphor. **Susan Haskins. New York: Harcourt Brace and Company, 1993. 518 pp. Illustrated. Bibliography. Index.**

Gives a detailed history of the image and the cult of Mary Magdalen, from the time of Christ to the late twentieth century. Explores the relationship between the changing images of Mary Magdalen, and Church and social views about the nature of women and their role in society.

DEWEY: 261.834 H351M LC: BS 2485.H27 ISBN 0-15-157765-X

ST. NICHOLAS

♦ 316 ♦

Saint Nicholas. **Jeanne Ancelet-Hustache. Translated by Rosemary Sheed. New York: Macmillan Company, 1962. 96 pp.**

Reviews the history, legends, devotion to, and popular celebration of St. Nicholas. Discusses the historical process by which this saint of Asia Minor became popular in Europe, the legends and facts of his life, his role as a patron saint, and his association with children and scholars. Part of a series entitled "Your Name—Your Saint."

DEWEY: 921

♦ 317 ♦

St. Nicholas: His Legend and His Role in the Christmas Celebration and Other Popular Customs. **George H. McKnight. 1917. Reprint. Williamstown, MA: Corner House Publisher, 1974. 153 pp. Illustrated.**

Gives a brief biography of St. Nicholas's life. Discusses the major legends associated with St. Nicholas, their historical development, and the popular customs and devotions that have grown up around them. Reviews the patronages of St. Nicholas and pagan elements within the saint's folklore. Describes the St. Nicholas plays of the medieval Church and the celebration of St. Nicholas's Day in many European countries. Citations given in endnotes.

DEWEY: 282.0924

♦ 318 ♦

Saint Nicholas: Life and Legend. **Martin Ebon. San Francisco, CA: Harper and Row, 1975. 119 pp. Illustrated. Bibliography.**

Recounts the history and lore surrounding the life and deeds of St. Nicholas, the third-century Byzantine saint whom legend transformed into Santa Claus. Traces historical changes in the image of the saint and in beliefs about his miraculous feats and powers of intervention, as legends concerning St. Nicholas migrated from the Mediterranean world to western Europe, and then to the United States.

DEWEY: 282. 0924 LC: BX 4700. N55E26 ISBN 0-06-062113-3

♦ 319 ♦

Saint Nicholas of Myra, Bari, and Manhattan: Biography of a Legend. **Charles W. Jones. Chicago: University of Chicago Press, 1978. 558 pp. Bibliography. Indexes.**

A scholarly investigation of the historical development of the legends surrounding St. Nicholas. Gives index of manuscripts cited, index of historic writings concerning Nicholas and his deeds, and a general index.

DEWEY: 282.092 4 LC: BX 4700. N55 J63 ISBN 0-226-40699-7

ST. PATRICK

♦ 320 ♦

The Living Legend of St. Patrick. **Alannah Hopkin. New York: St. Martin's Press, 1990. 191 pp. Illustrated. Appendices. Index.**

Reviews the life and lore of St. Patrick, with particular attention to the historical development of legends, beliefs, and practices associated with the saint from the early Middle Ages to modern times. Recounts experiences and observations gleaned from visits to Irish sacred sites and participation in devotional practices associated with St. Patrick. Examines the history of symbols associated with St. Patrick and the rise of contemporary St. Patrick's Day observances. Appendix reprints translation of two texts written by Patrick.

DEWEY: 270.2 092 LC: BR 1720. P26 H66 ISBN 0-312-03859-3

♦ 321 ♦

Who Was Saint Patrick? **E. A. Thompson. New York: St. Martin's Press, 1985. 190 pp. Appendix. Bibliography. Index.**

Sifts through the historical evidence in order to provide an accurate biography of St. Patrick's life and deeds, and to draw a picture of his true character. Appendix summarizes debates over the dates of Patrick's birth and death. Further reading list.

DEWEY: 270.2 092 4 LC: BR 1720. P 26 T48 ISBN 0-312-87084

ST. PETER

♦ 322 ♦

The Bones of St. Peter: The First Full Account of the Search for the Apostle's Body. **John Evangelist Walsh. Garden City, NY: Doubleday and Company, Inc., 1982. 195 pp. Illustrated. Appendices. Bibliography. Index.**

Tells the story of the discovery, excavation, and study of the bones said to be St. Peter's from their traditionally ascribed resting place beneath St. Peter's Basilica in Rome.

DEWEY: 225.924 LC: BS 2515. W28 ISBN 0-385-15038-5

♦ 323 ♦

Saint Peter: A Biography. **Michael Grant. New York: Scribner, 1994. 212 pp. Illustrated. Bibliography. Index.**

Composes a biography of St. Peter from a careful review of New Testament and other ancient accounts of his actions and from scholarly knowledge of life in the ancient Mediterranean world. Attempts to distinguish the historical from the legendary Peter. References given in endnotes.

DEWEY: 225.9 2 LC: BS 2515 G65 ISBN 0-684-19354-X

VIRGIN MARY

♦ 324 ♦

Alone of All Her Sex: The Myth and the Cult of the Virgin Mary. **Marina Warner. New York: Alfred A. Knopf, 1976. 400 pp. Illustrated. Appendices. Bibliography. Index.**

A comprehensive examination of the historical development of beliefs and cults surrounding the Virgin Mary, as represented in theological writings, popular practices, and other historical evidence. Identifies changing images of Mary and the ways in which they both reflected and reinforced attitudes about the spiritual nature of women and the position of women in society. Includes a chronology of important events in the development of Marian worship from 100 A.D. to 1974. Color and black-and-white plates of European artwork depicting the Virgin.

DEWEY: 232.91 LC: BT 602.W37 ISBN 0-394-49913-1

♦ 325 ♦

Legends of the Madonna, As Represented in the Fine Arts. **Anna Jameson. 1890. Reprint. Detroit, MI: Omnigraphics, Inc., 1990. 344 pp. Illustrated. Indexes.**

Tells how the Madonna has been portrayed in Western art and describes associated legends. Organized by painting subjects. Covers Mary without a child, Mary and child, the life of Mary from birth to marriage, from the Annunciation to the return from Egypt, from the sojourn in Egypt to the Crucifixion, and from the Resurrection to the Assumption. Black-and-white etchings and woodcuts illustrate. General index, index of artists, and index of churches, galleries, museums, and collections.

DEWEY: 704.9 4855 LC: N8070. J36 ISBN 1-55888-274-4

♦ 326 ♦

The Mary Myth: On the Femininity of God. **Andrew M. Greeley. New York: Seabury Press, 1977. 229 pp. Illustrated.**

Reviews the traditional Catholic symbolism of Mary and argues that this symbolic tradition offers insight into the feminine aspects of God. Considers four aspects of Mary's image—mother, virgin, lover, and griever—and shows how these reflect a divine, feminine archtype present in many eras and many religions.

DEWEY: 232.91 LC: BT 613. G73 ISBN 0-8164-0333-3

♦ 327 ♦

The World's Great Madonnas: An Anthology of Pictures, Poetry, Music, and Stories Centering in the Life of the Madonna and her Son. **Cynthia Pearl Maus. New York: Harper and Row, 1947. 789 pp. Indexes.**

A fine arts anthology of works featuring the Virgin Mary. Reproduces 114 paintings, along with interpretive commentary, and prints 239 poems, 60 stories, and 62 songs. Materials collected from Europe (including Russia), India, China, Japan, Central and West Africa, South Africa, Australia, Canada, the United States, Mexico, Argentina, Brazil, Peru, Ecuador, Colombia, and Paraguay. Covers many centuries. Lists symbols of the Virgin commonly used in Western art. Gives art and art interpretation index, poetry index, story index, and music index.

DEWEY: 232.93

Hinduism

General Works

♦ 328 ♦

Hindu Fasts and Festivals and Their Philosophy. **Swami Sivananda. Rikhikesh, India: Sivananda Publication League, 1947. 161 pp. Appendix.**

Describes 35 Hindu festivals, their origins, their devotional practices, and their religious meaning and purpose. Also describes 32 other special observances and ritual devotions associated with dates, days of the month, or astronomical occurrences. Gives dates according to the traditional Indian calendar.

DEWEY: 294.5 S624

♦ 329 ♦

Hindu Festivals. **Swasti Mitter. Vero Beach, FL: Rourke Enterprises, Inc., 1989. 48 pp. Illustrated. Glossary. Index.**

Background for young readers on Hindu beliefs, history, and festivals in and outside India. Note on the Hindu calendar and chronological table of Hindu holidays by month. One volume in a series entitled *Holidays and Festivals.* (NR)

DEWEY: 294.5 36 LC: BL1239.72.M58 ISBN 0-86592-986-6

♦ 330 ♦

Hindu Holidays and Ceremonials with Dissertations on Origin, Folklore and Symbols. **Rai Bahadur B. A. Gupte. Calcutta and Simla, India: Thacker, Spink and Co., 1919. 285 pp. Illustrated.**

The main text contains dictionary-style entries on Hindu festivals, days and places of worship and ceremony, and mythological and historical persons along with constellations associated with them. Brief glossary precedes main text with entries on animals and plants with folkloric significance. (NR)

♦ 331 ♦

Hindu Religion, Customs, and Manners: Describing the Customs and Manners, Religious, Social and Domestic Life, Arts and Sciences of the Hindus. **Fourth revised edition. P. Thomas. Bombay, India: D. B. Taraporevala Sons and Co., 1960. 139 pp. Illustrated. Index.**

Provides information and opinion on the mythology, history, caste system, religion, philosophy, social and domestic life, customs, manners, dress, superstitions, ceremonies, literature, languages, music, dancing, arts, and eroticism of the Hindus. Also gives chapter on related religions (Buddhism, Jainism, and Sikhism) as well as chapter on the Hindu calendar and holidays. Explains Hindu eras, beliefs associated with the days of the week and Vratas (special days of religious observance). Describes the origin and celebration of 12 Hindu festivals, including Divali, Dasara, Mahashivaratri, Ganesh Chaturti, and Narali Purnima (or Coconut Day).

DEWEY: 294 T461

♦ 332 ♦

The Hindu Religious Year. **M. M. Underhill. London: Oxford University Press, 1921. 194 pp. Index.**

Catalogues more than 200 Hindu feasts and fasts, identifying celebrated deity or event, describing associated folkloric practices, and tracing the festival's origins. Festivals grouped according to origins: solar and seasonal festivals, lunar and planetary festivals, festivals dedicated to Vishnu and Shiva, and festivals with animistic origins. Also explains the Hindu calendar system—from days to eras—and notes auspicious and inauspicious times of year. Includes a chart of festivals arranged according to the Hindu calendar, and a listing of the main religious festivals of the state of Maharashtra.

DEWEY: 294.5 U55

Diwali

♦ 333 ♦

Sweet-Tooth Sunil. **Joan Solomon. London, England: Evans Brothers Limited, 1984. 31 pp. Illustrated.**

Shows how a Hindu family in Great Britain celebrates Diwali. Explains holiday's significance, describes religious observance, customs, and foods. Color photos illustrate. For children. One book in a series entitled *The Way We Live.*

DEWEY: 294.536 ISBN 0-237-60120-6

Holi

♦ 334 ♦

Holi. **Dilip Kadodwala. Austin, TX: Raintree Steck-Vaughn Publishers, 1997. 31 pp. Illustrated. Glossary. Index.**

Tells how Hindus celebrate Holi. Relates holiday's significance, describes customs and foods, and retells holiday stories. Explains some basic tenets and practices of Hinduism. Gives craft and recipe. Color photos depict celebrations in India and Nepal. For children. One book in a series entitled *A World of Holidays.*

DEWEY: 294.5 36 LC: BL1239.82H65D55 ISBN 0-8172-4610-X

♦ 335 ♦

Holi; Hindu Festival of Spring. **Olivia Bennet. London, England: Evans Brothers Limited, 1987. 25 pp. Illustrated.**

Tells how Hindus in Great Britain celebrate the festival of Holi. Explains origins and significance of holiday, describes religious and folk celebrations. Color photos illustrate. For children. One book in a series entitled *The Way We Live.*

DEWEY: 294.536 ISBN 0-237-60135-4

Islam

General Works

♦ 336 ♦

The Concise Encyclopedia of Islam. **Cyril Glassé. Introduction by Huston Smith. San Francisco, CA: Harper and Row, 1989. 472 pp. Illustrated. Appendices. Bibliography.**

More than 1,100 entries cover people, places, texts, beliefs, rituals, festivals, prayer, sects, law, the calendar, institutions, history, culture, languages, medicine, and sciences. Cross-referenced. Appendices include historical maps of the Islamic world, facts about Mecca and the Hajj, schematic representation of the branches of Islam, geneological tables, and a chronology of important historical events in the Islamic world.

DEWEY: 297 G464c   ISBN 0-06-063123-6

♦ 337 ♦

Islam. **Alan Brine. Essex, England: Longman Group UK Limited, 1991. 63 pp. Illustrated. Glossary. Index.**

Provides an introduction to the practices and beliefs of the Islamic faith. Amply illustrated. Gives assignments and suggestions for further reading. For children.

DEWEY: J297   ISBN 0-582-02967-8

♦ 338 ♦

Islam: A Primer. **Revised edition. John Sabini. Washington, DC: Middle East Editorial Associates, 1990. 122 pp. Maps. Glossary.**

Brief introduction to Islamic faith and civilization. Explains basic religious tenets; Islamic law; origins of Islam; Islamic sects; the historical development and spread of Islam; the relationship between Judaism, Christianity and Islam; the achievements of Islamic civilization; and everyday Muslim customs and beliefs. Includes further reading list.

DEWEY: 297   LC: BP 161.2 S18   ISBN 0-918992-08-7

♦ 339 ♦

Islam in East Africa. **J. Spencer Trimingham. Oxford, England: Clarendon Press, 1964. 198 pp. Maps. Glossary. Index.**

Furnishes an overview of Islamic beliefs and practices in East Africa. Chapters on the history of Islam in East Africa, distinctive features of East African Islam, Islamic beliefs, organizations, and practices, folk religion, life-cycle ceremonies, Islam in society, and the effects of modernization and social change on Islam. Some description of the celebration of Islamic festivals, including New Year, the Tenth of Muharram, the birth of the Prophet (Mulud al-Nabi), the Ascension of the Prophet (27th of Rajab), Ramadan, the Night of Destiny (Lailat al-Qadr), and various celebrations in honor of the saints. References given in footnotes.

DEWEY: 297.0967 LC: BP 64 A4 E27

♦ 340 ♦

Islam in West Africa. **J. Spencer Trimingham. London: Oxford University Press, 1959. 262 pp. Map. Appendices. Glossary. Indexes.**

Discusses the practice of Islam in West Africa with special attention to the interaction of Islamic and pre-Islamic religious beliefs, social structure, and economy. Covers history of West African Islam, beliefs, practices, and observances. Explanation of Islamic cults and clerics, festivals, life-cycle rituals, and social customs. Briefly describes the celebration of the Tenth of Muharram, the Birthday of the Prophet (Mulud al-Nabi), the Hajj, and Ramadan. Glossary-index of Arabic and African terms. General index.

DEWEY: 297 LC: BP 64 A4 W4

♦ 341 ♦

The Life and Times of Muhammad. **Sir John Glubb. Lanham, MD: Madison Books, 1970. 416 pp. Maps. Bibliography. Index.**

Biography of Muhammad, the founder of Islam, including description of the social and religious climate of the era and the establishment of the Islamic religion. Compiled for the general reader from the Muslim traditional teachings, early biographies, and the Qur'an, with added commentary stemming from the author's experience of daily life among Arabic peoples.

DEWEY: 297.63 LC: BP 75.G58 ISBN 0-8128-1393-6

♦ 342 ♦

Mecca the Blessed, Madinah the Radiant. **Emel Esin. New York: Crown Publishers, 1963. 222 pp. Illustrated. Index.**

Furnishes a history of the Muslim holy cities of Mecca and Medina, from ancient times to the early twentieth century. Gives biblical texts concerning the Hijaz, tells the story of Muhammad's life and the founding of Islam. Amply illustrated with black-and-white and color photos of places, people, and artwork. Endnotes. Oversize.

DEWEY: 297 E74m

♦ 343 ♦

The Message of the Qur'an. **Translated and supplemented by Muhammad Asad. Ann Arbor, MI: New Era Publications, 1980. 998 pp. Appendices.**

Presents the Qur'an, the holy book of Islam, to English-speaking readers. Each chapter prints Arabic original alongside English translation, and is accompanied by introductory commentary and footnotes. Translator provides general introduction.

DEWEY: 297.1227 LC: BP 130.4 ISBN 0-317-52456-9

♦ 344 ♦

Muhammad: A Biography of the Prophet. **Karen Armstrong. San Francisco, CA: HarperSanFrancisco, a division of HarperCollins, 1992. 290 pp. Maps. Bibliography. Index.**

A biography of Muhammad, the founder of Islam, which addresses a number of common Western stereotypes about the religion. Includes genealogical charts.

DEWEY: 297.63 LC: BP 75. A76 ISBN 0-06-250014-7

♦ 345 ♦

Muhammadan Festivals. **G. E. Von Grunebaum. New York: Henry Schuman, 1951. 107 pp. Illustrated. Bibliography. Index.**

Provides a general overview of Muslim festivals. Treats the Hajj (Pilgrimage to Mecca), Ramadan, the Tenth of Muharram, and various practices concerning saints. Discusses festival origins, historical development, devotional practices, and the religious doctrines which underlay them. Summarizes the founding and basic tenets of Islam.

DEWEY: 297V946

♦ 346 ♦

Muslim Festivals. **M. M. Ahsan. Vero Beach, FL: Rourke Enterprises, Inc., 1987. 48 pp. Illustrated. Glossary. Index.**

Provides a general introduction to the Islamic religion and its holidays. Covers Ramadan, Id al-Fitr, the Hajj, and Id al-Adha, describing celebratory and devotional practices and explaining their meaning. Briefer coverage given to Mulud-al-Nabi, Lailatul Bara'at (Lailat al Bara'at), Lailatul Mi'raj (Lailat al-Miraj), Ashura, and Muharram. Explains the Islamic calendar and tells how holiday dates are determined. Further reading list. Amply illustrated with color photos of Muslim families and celebrations in many countries. Written for children.

DEWEY: 297.36 LC: BP 186. A47 ISBN 0-86592-979-3

♦ 347 ♦

Muslim Holidays. **Faith Winchester. Mankato, MN: Bridgestone Books, 1996. 24 pp. Illustrated. Index.**

Outlines the celebration of seven Muslim holidays: Muharram, Ashura, Birthday of the Prophet (Mulud-al-Nabi), Ramadan, Id al-Fitr, Id al-Adha, and the Hajj. Gives a craft project, pronunciation guide, and further reading and resource list. Color photos illustrate. For children. One book in a series entitled *Ethnic Holidays.*

DEWEY: 394.2 6917671 LC: GT4887.A2W55 ISBN 1-56065-459-7

♦ 348 ♦

Muslim Saints and Mystics. **Farid Al-Din Attar. Translated by A. J. Arberry. 1966. Reprint. New York: Viking Press, 1988. 287 pp.**

Excerpts from the classic work, *Memorial of the Saints,* by the medieval Persian poet Farid Al-Din Attar. Covers 38 saints and sages from the seventh to tenth centuries belonging to the Sufi, or mystical, movement within Islam. Entries recount significant sayings, teachings, actions, and events in their lives. Translator provides a brief biography and bibliography for each saint.

DEWEY: 297.6 LC: BP 189.4 F 323 ISBN 0-14-019114-3

♦ 349 ♦

The Qur'an: The First American Version. **Translated and supplemented by T. B. Irving. Brattleboro, VT: Amana Books, 1985. 401 pp.**

Translation of the Qur'an, the sacred book of the Islamic religion, into contemporary American English. Translator provides general introduction as well as brief introductions to each chapter.

DEWEY: 297.122521 LC: BP 130.4 ISBN 0-915597-08-X

♦ 350 ♦

Religious Performance in Contemporary Islam: Shi'i Devotional Rituals in South Asia. **Vernon James Schubel. Columbia, SC: University of South Carolina, 1993. 198 pp. Illustrated. Appendix. Bibliography. Glossary. Index.**

In-depth study of the observances of Muharram in Karachi, Pakistan. Covers private devotions and public events. Analysis of the function of ritual and performance in the religious experience of South Asian Shi'ite Muslims.

DEWEY: 297.302 09549183 LC: BP 194.5 T4 S38 ISBN 0-87249-859-X

♦ 351 ♦

Ritual and Religion Among the Muslims in India. **Imtiaz Ahmad, ed. New Delhi, India: Manohar, 1981. 246 pp. Glossary. Index.**

Offers a collection of essays on popular religious rituals of India's Muslim communities. Treats a number of festivals, including the celebration of Muharram, the Festival of Salar Masud, the Urs (death or memorial festival) for Amir Khusro, the Basant Festival, the Bara Wafat Festival (or the Id-al-Mulud-al-Nabi), and the Urs of Hazrat Nizamuddin. Includes "Religious Ideology and Social Structure: The Muslims and Hindus of Kashmir" by T. N. Madan; "Islamization and Muslim Ethnicity in South India" by Mattison Mines; "Muslim Rituals: The Household Rites vs. the Public Festivals in Rural India" by Lina M. Fruzzetti; "Ideal and Reality in Observance of Moharram: A Behavioral Interpretation" by A. R. Saiyid; "Saint Worship in Indian Islam: The Legend of the Martyr Salar Masud Ghazi" by Kerrin Graefin V. Schwerin; "Creating a Scene: The Disruption of Ceremonial in a Sufi Shrine" by Patricia Jeffery; and "Mira Datar Dargah: The Psychiatry of a Muslim Shrine" by Beatrix Pfleiderer.

DEWEY: 297. R615

Hajj

♦ 352 ♦

The Hadj: An American's Pilgrimage to Mecca. **Michael Wolfe. New York: Atlantic Monthly Press, 1993. 331 pp. Appendix. Bibliography.**

Traveler's account of the Hajj Pilgrimage written by an American Muslim convert. Some discussion of Ramadan and exploration of Islamic spirituality.

DEWEY: 297.55 LC: BP 187.3 W65 ISBN 0-87113-518-3

♦ 353 ♦

Hajj Paintings: Folk Art of the Great Pilgrimage. **Ann Parker and Avon Neal. Washington, DC: Smithsonian Institution Press, 1995. 164 pp. Illustrated. Glossary.**

Documents the Egyptian folk art tradition of Hajj paintings, made to commemorate one's completion of the Hajj pilgrimage. Numerous color photos of paintings are accompanied by text explaining the history of the Hajj, its sites, rituals, customs, and symbols. Discusses composition, aesthetic, and techniques of the paintings, and provides other commentary on daily life and holidays in Egypt.

DEWEY: 755. 9755 LC: ND 2863. N33 ISBN 1-56098-546-1

♦ 354 ♦

The Hajj: The Muslim Pilgrimage to Mecca and the Holy Places. **F. E. Peters. Princeton, NJ: Princeton University Press, 1994. 399 pp. Illustrated. Bibliography. Index.**

Gives a detailed history of the Hajj from pre-Islamic times to 1926. Illustrated with black-and-white photos.

DEWEY: 297.55 LC: BP 187.3.P475 ISBN 0-691-02120-1

♦ 355 ♦

The Hajj Today: A Survey of the Contemporary Makkah Pilgrimage. **David Edwin Long. Albany, NY: State University of New York Press, 1979. Maps. Appendices. Bibliography. Glossary. Index.**

A study of the religious, economic, and administrative aspects of the Hajj. Reviews the history and rites of the pilgrimage. Examines the service industry which has grown up around it, the public administration of the many foreign visitors, public health issues, and the social, political, and economic impact of the Hajj on Saudi Arabia. Appendices give statistics on Hajj pilgrims for the nineteenth and twentieth centuries, a glossary, and maps.

DEWEY: 297.38 LC: BP187.3 L66 ISBN 0-87395-382-7

Ramadan and Id

♦ 356 ♦

Id-ul-Fitr. **Rosalind Kerven. Austin, TX: Raintree Steck-Vaughn Publishers, 1997. 31 pp. Illustrated. Glossary. Index.**

Tells how Muslims from many countries celebrate Id al-Fitr. Explains the founding and basic tenets of Islam, the fast of Ramadan, and some common Muslim customs. Shows worship and feasting that take place on Id al-Fitr. Color photos depict celebrations and customs from many lands. Gives recipe and craft project. For children. One book in a series entitled *A World of Holidays.*

DEWEY: 297.36 LC: BP186.45. K47 ISBN 0-8172-4609-6

♦ 357 ♦

Ramadan. **Suhaib Hamid Ghazi. New York: Holiday House, 1996. Unpaginated. Illustrated. Glossary.**

Explains the customs and significance of Ramadan. Offers some background information on Islam. Introduces words related to Ramadan. Color illustrations. For children.

DEWEY: 297.36 LC: BP186.4 G43 ISBN 0-8234-1254-7

♦ 358 ♦

Ramadan and Id al-Fitr. **Dianne M. MacMillan. Hillside, NJ: Enslow Publishers, Inc., 1994. 48 pp. Illustrated. Glossary. Index.**

Presents the Islamic religion and its most important holiday, Ramadan, to children, explaining many common words, concepts, and customs. Introduces basic facts about the life of Muhammad, the founding of the Islamic religion, the Qur'an, and Islamic prayer practices. Describes Ramadan and Id al-Fitr observance and celebrations. Illustrated with color and black-and-white photos. One book in a series entitled *Best Holiday Books.*

DEWEY: 297.36 LC: BP 186.4 M27 ISBN 0-89490-502-3

Judaism

General Works

♦ 359 ♦

The Biblical and Historical Background of the Jewish Holy Days. **Abraham P. Bloch. New York: Ktav Publishing House, 1978. 281 pp. Bibliography. Index.**

Discusses origins and traces development of Jewish Holy Days using scripture and historical records, noting changes in meaning, emphasis, and manner of celebration. Addresses the Sabbath, Rosh Hashanah, Yom Kippur, Sukkot, Hanukkah, Purim, Passover, Lag ba-Omer, Shavuot, Second Festival Days of the Diaspora, Festival of the Fifteenth Day of Av, Fast of Esther, Fast of the Seventeenth of Tammuz, Fast of Tisha be-Av, and Holocaust Memorial Day.

DEWEY: 296.43 LC: BM 690. B ISBN 0-87068-338-1

♦ 360 ♦

The Book of Our Heritage. **Eliyahu Kitov. Three volumes. Translated by Nathan Bulman. 1968. Reprint. Spring Valley, NY: Phillip Feldheim, Inc., 1978. 1155 pp. Glossary. Index.**

Detailed coverage of the significance and origins of the Jewish calendar and practices associated with holy days. Recounts Jewish lore and scripture associated with months, seasons, and holy days. Teaches rituals associated with religious observance. Written in a traditional style with the purpose of educating Jews about their religious heritage.

DEWEY: 296.43 LC: BM 690 K 5313 ISBN 0-87306-151-9

♦ 361 ♦

Celebration: The Book of Jewish Festivals. **Naomi Black, ed. Middle Village, NY: Jonathan David Publishers, 1989. 159 pp. Illustrated. Index.**

An aid to the celebration of seven Jewish holidays: Rosh Hashanah, Yom Kippur, Sukkot, Hanukkah, Purim, Passover, and Shavuot. Presents history and significance of holiday, gives holiday stories for adults and children to enjoy, and suggests menus, recipes, and craft ideas. Beautifully illustrated with more than 200 color photos of artwork depicting holiday themes, ceremonial objects, holiday preparations, celebrations, foods, and table settings.

DEWEY: 296. 43 LC: BM 690. C44 ISBN 0-8246-0340-0

♦ 362 ♦

The Complete Book of Jewish Observance. **Leo Trepp. New York: Behrman House, Inc., 1980. 370 pp. Bibliography. Index.**

An introduction to Jewish practices and observances shaping the yearly cycle and the life cycle. Interprets prayers, symbols, and dietary laws; discusses the origins, meaning, and observance of holidays, festivals, and the Sabbath; defines circumcision, bar and bat mitzvah and other rituals of the life cycle; and explains the Jewish lunar calendar. Includes Orthodox, Conservative, Reform, and Reconstructionist views on customs and practices.

DEWEY: 296.4 LC: BM 690. T73 ISBN 0-671-41797-5

♦ 363 ♦

The Complete Family Guide to the Jewish Holidays. **Dahlia Hardof Renberg. New York: Adama Books, 1985. 255 pp. Illustrated. Indexes.**

Designed to help parents make the celebration of Jewish holidays more meaningful and exciting for children ages five through nine. Tells the story of the holiday in simple words, provides additional information for parents, suggests craft projects and ideas for children's holiday parties, gives words and music to songs, and provides recipes. The first chapter explains Rosh Hodesh (the first day of the lunar month) and the Jewish calendar for adults. Covers 14 holidays: Rosh Hodesh, Rosh Hashanah, Yom Kippur, Sukkot, Simhat Torah, Hanukkah, Tu Bishvat, Purim, Passover, Israel Independence Day, Lag ba-Omer, Shavuot, Tisha be-Av, and the Sabbath.

DEWEY: 296.4 LC: BM 690. R44 ISBN 0-915361-09-4

♦ 364 ♦

Days of Awe: A Treasury of Jewish Wisdom for Reflection, Repentance, and Renewal on the High Holy Days. **S. Y. Agnon, ed. Foreword by Arthur Green. Introduction by Judah Goldin. New York: Schocken Books, 1995. 296 pp. Bibliography.**

Nobel-Prize winning author offers a collection of prayers, customs, devotional practices, and inspirational prose from the Bible, the Talmud, the Midrash, and the Zohar for Rosh Hashanah, Yom Kippur, and the days in between. First published in English in 1948.

DEWEY: 296.4 31 LC: BM 693.H5Y32313 ISBN 0-8052-1048-2

♦ 365 ♦

The Family Treasury of the Jewish Holidays. **Malka Drucker. Illustrated by Nancy Patz. Boston, MA: Little, Brown, and Company, 1994. 180 pp. Glossary. Index.**

Introduces 12 Jewish holidays, including the Sabbath, to children. Describes holiday celebrations and their meaning, and gives stories from Jewish scripture and folklore which illustrate the principles of the holiday. Also gives recipes, crafts, songs, and activities.

DEWEY: 296.43 LC: BM 690. D77 ISBN 0-316-19343-7

♦ 366 ♦

Festival Days: A History of Jewish Celebrations. **Chaim Raphael. New York: Grove Weidenfield, 1990. 144 pp. Bibliography. Index.**

An historical essay on the role and meaning of festivity and of the major festivals in Judaism. Considers the yearly round of festivals, the three main festival groups (the pilgrim festivals, the Days of Awe, and the patriotic festivals), and individual festivals. Covers Passover, Shavuot, Sukkot, Rosh Hashanah, Yom Kippur, Hanukkah, Purim, and Tisha be-Av.

DEWEY: 296.43 LC: BM 690.R39 ISBN 0-8021-1147-5

♦ 367 ♦

Festivals of the Jewish Year. **Theodor Gaster. New York: William Sloane Associates, 1953. 308 pp. Bibliography. Indexes.**

Applies a comparative approach to the study of Jewish holidays. Reviews the devotional and celebratory practices of the major Jewish festivals, outlines their historical development, identifies comparable practices among other peoples, and summarizes their spiritual significance. Covers Passover, Shavuot, Sukkot, the Feast of Azereth, Simhat Torah, Rosh Hashanah, Yom Kippur, the four fasts (of Tevet, Tammuz, Av, and Gedalia), Purim, Hanukkah, Tu Bishvat, and the Sabbath. Index of poems translated and index of first lines.

LC: BM 690 G33

♦ 368 ♦

Gates of the Seasons: A Guide to the Jewish Year. **Peter S. Knobel, ed. New York: Central Conference of American Rabbis, 1983. 208 pp. Appendices. Index.**

Provides a guide to the *mitzvot,* or religious precepts, associated with Jewish holidays, presenting those which might deepen and enrich one's participation in Judaism. Lists and explains mitzvot for more than 10 holidays, including Rosh Hashanah, Yom Kippur, Passover, Shavuot, Sukkot (including Atzeret and Simhat Torah), Hanukkah, Purim, Rosh Hodesh, Israel Independence Day, Holocaust Memorial Day, Tisha be-Av, and more. Appendices include eight brief essays on various issues associated with the holidays, a glossary, calendar dates for the major Jewish holidays from 1983 to 2008, and suggestions for further reading. Author's perspective is that of Reform Judaism.

DEWEY: 296.43 LC: BM 700 G 35 ISBN 0-916694-92-5

♦ 369 ♦

The Glory of the Jewish Holidays. **Hillel Seidman. New York: Shengold Publishers, 1969. 239 pp. Illustrated.**

Tells the story of 14 Jewish holidays, including the Sabbath. Gives the origins, history, and religious significance of each holiday, notes important texts associated with it, and describes contemporary and past celebrations throughout the Jewish diaspora. Illustrated with photos of religious objects, art, and celebrations.

DEWEY: 296. 43

♦ 370 ♦

Heritage of Music: The Music of the Jewish People. **Judith Eisenstein. 1972. Reprint. Wyncote, PA: Reconstructionist Press, 1981. 339 pp. Illustrated. Tables. Bibliography. Discography. Index.**

A collection of more than 100 Jewish songs from around the world, with emphasis on selections suitable for holidays, celebrations, and worship. Includes musical score of songs as well as historical and cultural commentary. Suggests suitable pieces for a variety of occasions, appropriate performance style, and instrumentation.

DEWEY: 781.72924 LC: ML 3776 E 48 ISBN 0-685-56531-9

♦ 371 ♦

A History of Judaism. Volume One, From Abraham to Maimonides. **Daniel Jeremy Silver. Basic Books: New York, 1974. 476 pp. Illustrated. Appendices. Bibliography. Glossary. Index.**

A far-reaching study of Jewish history, religion, thought, and culture from its beginnings in the ancient Middle East through the flowering of Jewish culture in the medieval Muslim world. Ends with discussion of Maimonides, a Jewish philosopher of twelfth-century Spain. Endnotes list works cited, and the bibliography provides suggestions for further study.

DEWEY: 296 H 673 LC: BM 155.2 H57 ISBN 465-030006-8

♦ 372 ♦

A History of Judaism. Volume Two, Europe and the New World. **Bernard Martin. New York: Basic Books, 1974. 527 pp. Illustrated. Appendices. Bibliography. Glossary. Index.**

Continues the study of Jewish history begun in volume one, starting with the thirteenth century and the blossoming contributions of European Jews. Continues through the establishment of American Jewish communities, the Holocaust, and the founding of the state of Israel. Endnotes list works cited, and the bibliography provides suggestions for further study.

DEWEY: 296 LC: BM 155.2 H57 ISBN 465-03007-6

♦ 373 ♦

In the Jewish Tradition: A Year of Food and Festivities. **Judith B. Fellner. New York: Smithmark Publishers, Inc., 1995. 128 pp. Illustrated. Index.**

Celebrates the spirit of the major Jewish holidays. Summarizes festival origins, history, and customs; describes religious rituals; provides many recipes; and offers insights into the festival's deeper meaning. Covers Rosh Hashanah, Yom Kippur, Sukkot, Shemini Atzeret, Simhat Torah, Hannukah, Purim, Passover, and Shavuot. Beautifully illustrated with color photos. Gives further reading list for children and adults and words and music to Jewish holiday songs. Lists Judaica shops, Jewish bookstores, and other Jewish resources throughout the United States.

DEWEY: 296.4 3 LC: BM 690.F418 ISBN 0-8317-5268-8

♦ 374 ♦

The Jewish Catalog. **Richard Seigel, Michael Strassfeld, and Sharon Strassfeld, comps. and eds. Philadelphia, PA: Jewish Publication Society of America, 1973. 320 pp. Illustrated. Bibliography.**

Provides a wide variety of information about Jewish life, lore, and observance. Divided into four chapters: space, time, word, and man/woman. Describes customs, symbols, objects, arts, devotional practices, foods, writings, and public worship. Oriented towards home life and personal observance, but includes sections on the Jewish calendar, holidays, and life-cycle rituals; much appropriate background to these subjects throughout the book. Lists many additional resources, including Jewish Studies programs, Jewish political and service organizations, and more. Bibliography lists books on many aspects of Jewish life, thought, and history.

DEWEY: 296.4 S571j ISBN 0-8276-0042-9

♦ 375 ♦

***Jewish Ceremonial Art.* Joseph Gutman. New York: Thomas Yoseloff, 1964. 37 pp. Illustrated. Bibliography.**

Addresses the use of art objects in Jewish synagogue ceremonies, holiday-related ceremonies, and life-cycle ceremonies. Sixty-one color and black-and-white plates illustrate.

DEWEY: 704.94896

♦ 376 ♦

***Jewish Ceremonial Art and Religious Observance.* Abram Kanof. 1970. Reprint. Hewlett, NY: Gefen Books, 1992. 253 pp. Illustrated. Glossary-Index.**

Discusses the expression of Jewish religious symbols, concepts, and rituals in architecture and art objects connected with religious observance. Also addresses the role of ceremonial art and art objects in worship. Richly illustrated.

DEWEY: 704. 9489 LC: NK 1672.K32 ISBN 965-229-055-6

♦ 377 ♦

***Jewish Ceremonial Institutions and Customs.* Third and revised edition. William Rosenau. 1925. Reprint. Detroit, MI: Omnigraphics, Inc., 1992. 190 pp. Illustrated. Index.**

Describes Jewish home and synagogue customs. Covers the synagogue and its ceremonial objects, weekday services, Sabbath services, worshippers, Yom Kippur, Rosh Hashanah, the Days of Awe, Passover, Pentecost, the fasts and minor holidays, customs observed in Jewish homes, home celebration of religious holidays, circumcision, redemption of the first born, bar mitzvah, marriage, divorce, chalitzah, mourning, and kosher slaughter. Illustrated with black-and-white photos.

DEWEY: 296.4 LC: BM 700. R58 ISBN 1-55888-912-4

♦ 378 ♦

Jewish Customs and Ceremonies. **Ben M. Edidin. Illustrated by H. Norman Tress. New York: Hebrew Publishing Company, 1941. 178 pp. Bibliography. Glossary. Index.**

A supplemental text for *Jewish Holidays and Festivals* (by the same author; see entry ♦ 387 ♦). Describes everyday customs as well as those associated with holidays and other important events, such as birth, bar and bat mitzvah, marriage, burial, and worship.

DEWEY: 296.4 E23j

♦ 379 ♦

Jewish Days: A Book of Jewish Life and Culture Around the Year. **Francine Klagsbrun. Illustrated by Mark Podwal. New York: Farrar Straus Giroux, 1996. 232 pp. Index.**

Describes the observance of Jewish holidays and commemorations, and offers insights into Jewish spirituality and culture. Holidays covered include the Sabbath, Rosh Hodesh, Rosh Hashanah, the Days of Awe, the Ten Days of Repentance, the Fast of Gedaliah, Yom Kippur, Sukkot, Shemini Atzeret, Simhat Torah, Hanukkah, Tu Bishvat, Ta'anit Esther, Purim, Passover, Yom ha-Shoah (Holocaust Memorial Day), Israel Independence Day, Shavuot, and Tisha be-Av. Also covers many days and times of year associated with important events in Jewish history from ancient to contemporary times. Organized by Jewish month. Illustrated with color and black-and-white drawings.

DEWEY: 296.4 3 LC: BM 690. K57 ISBN 0-374-17923-9

♦ 380 ♦

Jewish Days and Holidays. **Greer Fay Cashman. Illustrated by Alona Frankel. 1976. Reprint. New York: Adama Books, 1986. 64 pp.**

Introduces children to the stories behind and celebrations of 11 Jewish holidays. Covers Rosh Hashanah, Yom Kippur, Sukkot, Simhat Torah, Hanukkah, Purim, Passover, Israel Independence Day, Shavuot, Tisha be-Av and the Sabbath.

DEWEY: J 296. 43 ISBN 0-915361-58-2

♦ 381 ♦

Jewish Family Celebrations: The Sabbath, Festivals, and Ceremonies. **Arlene Rossen Cardozo. New York: St. Martin's Press, 1982. 268 pp. Bibliography. Glossary. Indexes.**

Covers home celebration of Jewish holy days and life-cycle ceremonies. Treats the Sabbath, Rosh Hashanah, Yom Kippur, Sukkot, Simhat Torah, Hanukkah, Purim, Passover, Shavuot, Yom ha-Shoah, Israel Independence Day, birth, death, bar and bat mitzvah, and weddings. Gives brief history of each festival, discusses preparations, and offers recipes, songs, blessings, and suggested activities of observance or celebration. Further reading list. General index and indexes of songs, recipes, and blessings.

DEWEY: 296.4 LC: BM 700 C37 ISBN 0-312-44231-9

♦ 382 ♦

Jewish Festivals. **Reuben Turner. Vero Beach, FL: Rourke Enterprises, Inc., 1987. 48 pp. Glossary. Illustrated. Map. Index.**

Present scriptural background for young readers on the Jewish feasts, along with customs and traditions, recipes and food, and activities associated with them. Sections explaining the Jewish calendar, including a calendar of festivals, and the Hebrew alphabet. Further reading list. (NR)

DEWEY: 296.4 3 LC: BM690.T87 ISBN 0-86592-977-7

♦ 383 ♦

The Jewish Festivals: From Their Beginnings to Our Own Day. **Hayyim Schauss. Translated by Samuel Jaffe. Cincinnati, OH: Union of American Hebrew Congregations, 1938. 320 pp. Illustrated. Bibliography. Index.**

Discusses the religious significance and observance of the major Jewish festivals from biblical to modern times. Also gives a history of festival customs and ceremonies. Attention to home and synagogue observances. Treats the Sabbath, Passover, Shavuot, Tisha be-Av, Rosh Hashanah, Yom Kippur, the Days of Awe, Sukkot, Hannukah, and Purim. Chapter on the minor festivals. Black-and-white photos illustrate. Endnotes.

DEWEY: 296 S313j

♦ 384 ♦

The Jewish Holiday Cookbook: An International Collection of Recipes and Customs. **Gloria Kaufer Greene. New York: Times Books, 1985. 399 pp. Index.**

Presents 250 recipes for 14 Jewish holidays: Shabbat (the Sabbath), Rosh Hashanah, Yom Kippur, Sukkot, Shemini Atzeret, Simhat Torah, Hanukkah, Tu Bishvat, Purim, Passover, Israel Independence Day, Jerusalem Day, Lag ba-Omer, and Shavuot. Introduces each holiday by reviewing its traditions and customs, including those that are food-related.

DEWEY: 641.59 2 924 LC: TX 724 K392 ISBN 0-8129-1224-1

♦ 385 ♦

Jewish Holidays. **Mary Turck. New York: Crestwood House, 1990. 48 pp. Illustrated. Index.**

Tells how Jewish holidays and life-cycle events are celebrated. Covers the Sabbath, Rosh Hashanah, Yom Kippur, Sukkot, Hanukkah, Purim, Passover, Shavuot, Tisha be-Av, Yom ha-Shoah (Holocaust Memorial Day), and ceremonies surrounding birth, coming of age, marriage, and death. Relates holiday origins, legends, and customs. Explains ethnic and religious components of Jewish identity, noting diverse ways of being Jewish. Illustrated with color photos. Further reading list. For children.

DEWEY: 296.4 3 LC: BM 690.T86 ISBN 0-89686-502-9

♦ 386 ♦

The Jewish Holidays: A Guide and Commentary. **Michael Strassfeld. New York: Harper Collins, 1993. 248 pp. Illustrated. Appendices. Index.**

A practical and thought-provoking guide to 10 Jewish festivals: the Omer (including Holocaust Memorial Day, Israel Independence Day, and Jerusalem Day), Shavuot, the Three Weeks (including Tisha be-Av and Tu be-Av), Rosh Hashanah, Yom Kippur, Sukkot, Shemini Atzeret and Simhat Torah, Hanukkah, Tu Bishvat, and Purim. Gives the origins and ideas associated with each festival, its traditional rituals and practices, suggestions for contemporary or special focus observance, and ways of interpreting its significance. Comments from five other experts of varied viewpoints are printed in margins of main text. Appendices include guides to the Jewish calendar, Jewish law and customs, Torah readings for the holidays, a list of customary Hebrew blessings, and the calendar dates for important Jewish holidays from 1985 to 2000.

DEWEY: 296.43 ISBN 0-685-72282-1

♦ 387 ♦

Jewish Holidays and Festivals. **Ben M. Edidin. Illustrated by Kyra Markham. 1940. Reprint. Detroit, MI: Omnigraphics, Inc., 1993. 66 pp. Bibliography. Glossary. Index.**

Discusses history, significance, and customs associated with Jewish holidays and anniversaries. Covers the Sabbath, Rosh Hodesh, Yom Kippur, Rosh

Hashanah, Sukkot, Simhat Torah, Hanukkah, Tu Bishvat, Purim, Passover, Lag ba-Omer, Shavuot, Tisha be-Av, and more.

DEWEY: 296.4 3 LC: BM 690 E3 ISBN 0-7808-0000-1

♦ 388 ♦

Jewish Holidays in the Spring. **Dianne M. MacMillan. Hillside, NJ: Enslow Publishers, 1994. 48 pp. Illustrated. Glossary. Index.**

Explains the meaning of Jewish holidays occurring in the spring to small children. Covers Purim, Passover, Lag ba-Omer, and Shavuot. Includes glossary and index. One book in a series entitled *Best Holiday Books.*

DEWEY: 296.43 LC: BM 690. M23 ISBN 0-89490-503-1

♦ 389 ♦

The Jewish Holy Days: Their Spiritual Significance. **Moshe A. Braun. Northvale, NJ: Jason Aronson, Inc., 1996. 429 pp. Glossary. Index.**

Presents the teachings of the *Sfas Emes,* Hasidic Rabbi Yehudah Aryeh Leib Alter's classic work on Jewish spirituality, for the general reader. Discusses the deeper spiritual significance of the Jewish holidays, their laws and customs. Covers the Days of Awe (the month of Elul, Rosh Hashanah, the Ten Days of Repentance, the Sabbath of Repentance, and Yom Kippur), Sukkot, Hanukkah, Purim, Passover, and Shavuot. Lists laws and customs, prayers and blessings for each holiday. Abbreviated history for some holidays.

DEWEY: 296.4 3 LC: BM 690.B76 ISBN 1-56821-553-3

♦ 390 ♦

The Jewish Party Book: A Contemporary Guide to Customs, Crafts, and Foods. **Mae Shafter Rockland. New York: Schocken Books, 1978. 264 pp. Illustrated. Appendix. Index.**

Gives recipes, crafts, customs, and suggestions for holiday entertaining and home observance. Holidays covered include Rosh Hashanah, Yom Kippur, Sukkot, Simhat Torah, Hanukkah, Tu Bishvat, Purim, Passover, Israeli Independence Day, Lag ba-Omer, Shavuot, Rosh Hodesh, and Sabbath. Also covers life-cycle events, such as birth, bar and bat mitzvah, weddings, family reunions, and housewarmings. Appendix gives dates for the Jewish holidays from 1978 to 2000.

DEWEY: 392 LC: BM 700. R53 ISBN 0-8052-3689-9

♦ 391 ♦

The Meaning of Judaism. **Roland B. Gittelsohn. New York: World Publishing Co., 1970. 221 pp. Index.**

An introduction to the basic elements of Judaism, including religious beliefs, cultural outlook, and various ways of construing a Jewish identity. Includes some contrast of Jewish with Christian perspectives.

DEWEY: 296 LC: BM 561

♦ 392 ♦

Menorahs, Mezuzas, and Other Jewish Symbols. **Miriam Chaikin. Illustrated by Erika Weihs. New York: Clarion Books, 1990. 102 pp. Bibliography. Index.**

Identifies and explains the significance of a wide range of Jewish symbols. Treats the symbol of the Sabbath; symbolic ideas, acts, garments, and styles of dress; symbols used in Jewish worship; symbols of the Jewish home; symbols of the Jewish holidays; and symbols of the state of Israel. Illustrated with black-and-white drawings. Endnotes give sources. For children.

DEWEY: 296.4 LC: BM657.2 C45 ISBN 0-89919-856-2

♦ 393 ♦

My First Book of Jewish Holidays. **Maida Silverman. Illustrated by Barbara Garrison. New York: Dial Books for Young Readers, a Division of Penguin Books, 1994. 32 pp. Glossary.**

Introduces the celebrations surrounding 10 Jewish holidays, including the Sabbath, to young children.

DEWEY: 296.4 3 LC: BM 690. S497 ISBN 0-8037-1427-0

♦ 394 ♦

One People: The Story of the Eastern Jews. **Devorah Hacohen and Menahem Hacohen. Translated by Israel I. Taslitt. Introduction by Yigal Allon. New York: Sabra Books/Funk and Wagnalls, 1969. 195 pp. Illustrated. Bibliography. Glossary.**

Provides a summary of the history, religious observances, folk beliefs, and home life of the Eastern Jews. Covers the Jewish communities of Iraq, Kurdistan, Persia, the Caucasus, Bukhara, North Africa, Morocco, Algeria, Tunisia and Jerba, Libya, Cyrenaica, Egypt, Syria, Yemen, Hadramaut, Aden, Turkey, Salonika, Bulgaria, and India. Some coverage of Jewish holiday observances and other Jewish ceremonies. Illustrated with black-and-white photos.

DEWEY: 956.93 H124o ISBN 87631-009

♦ 395 ♦

Preparing Your Heart for the High Holy Days: A Guided Journal. **Kerry M. Olitzky and Rachel T. Sabath. Philadelphia, PA: Jewish Publication Society, 1996. 100 pp. Glossary.**

Offers daily meditations and commentary for each day of Elul and the first 10 days of Tishri, from Rosh Hashanah to Yom Kippur. Meditations and commentary reflect the themes of the 27th psalm and come from a wide variety of sources, including the prayer book of the High Holy Days, the Bible, hasidic tales, rabbinic writings, and the work of contemporary spiritual teachers. Blank page included with each entry encourages the reader to reflect on her or his moral and spiritual state in preparation for the High Holy Days.

DEWEY: 296.431 LC: BM693.E48 O43 ISBN 0-8276-0578-1

♦ 396 ♦

Rosh Hashanah and Yom Kippur: Sweet Beginnings. **Malka Drucker. Illustrated by Brom Hoban. New York: Holiday House, 1981. 95 pp. Appendix. Glossary. Index.**

Explains the observance and meaning of Rosh Hashanah and Yom Kippur to young readers. Covers home and synagogue customs and rituals. Gives recipes, crafts, and games. Appendix prints prayers for the High Holy Days. Black-and-white drawings and photos illustrate.

DEWEY: 296.4 31 LC: BM 693 H5 D78 ISBN 0-8234-0427-7

♦ 397 ♦

Seasons of Our Joy: A Handbook of Jewish Festivals. **Arthur Waskow. Illustrated by Martin Farren and Joan Benjamin-Farren. Toronto, Canada: Bantam Books, 1982. 240 pp. Appendices.**

Proponent of the movement for Jewish renewal discusses 16 Jewish holidays in relationship to the yearly cycle of seasons: Rosh Hashanah, Yom Kippur, Sukkot, Shemini Atzeret, Simhat Torah, Hanukkah, Tu Bishvat, Purim, Passover, the Omer (including Lag ba-Omer, Holocaust Memorial Day, Israel Independence Day, and Jerusalem Day), Shavuot, and Tisha be-Av. Gives origins of each festival, notes traditional modes of religious and secular celebration, and suggests new approaches to understanding and celebrating each festival. Also gives recipes, songs, and suggestions for further reading.

Appendices include glossary, discussions of the second day of festivals and the importance of the lunar cycle, and a list of calendar dates for the major Jewish festivals from 1980 to 2009.

DEWEY: 296.43 LC: BM 690. W28 ISBN 0-553-01369-6

♦ 398 ♦

Seasons for Celebration: A Contemporary Guide to the Joys, Practices, and Traditions of the Jewish Holidays. **Karen L. Fox and Phyllis Zimbler Miller. Illustrations by Vicki Reikes Fox. New York: Perigree Books, 1992. 159 pp. Appendix. Index.**

A guide to celebrating the Jewish holidays. Covers the Sabbath (Shabbat), Rosh Hashanah, Yom Kippur, Sukkot, Simhat Torah, Hanukkah, Tu Bishvat, Purim, Passover (Pesach), and Shavuot. For each holiday discusses home traditions, synagogue traditions, theological or philosophical issues, gives recipes and blessings, and suggests activities. Notes differences between Conservative, Orthodox, Reform, and Reconstructionist views and observances. Appendix gives dates for holidays covered from 1992 to 2005 and gives brief explanation of the Jewish calendar system. Also lists Jewish holidays not covered in the book and gives addresses of Jewish organizations.

DEWEY: 296.4 LC: BM 690.F69 ISBN 0-339-51764-2

♦ 399 ♦

Symbols of Judaism. **Marc-Alain Ouaknin. Paris, France: Editions Assouline, n.d. 128 pp. Illustrated.**

Explains the uses and significance of 30 symbols central to Jewish worship and celebration. Covers everyday and ceremonial objects, such as the Mezuzah and the Shofar, as well as customs and objects associated with specific festivals (Sabbath, Rosh Hashanah, Sukkot, Hanukkah, Tu Bishvat, Passover, and Lag ba-Omer). Includes brief explanation of the Jewish calendar. Beautiful color photos of each symbol. Oversize.

DEWEY: 296.46 ISBN 2-908228-35-1

♦ 400 ♦

To Be a Jew: A Guide to Jewish Observance in Contemporary Life. **Hayim Donin. 1972. Reprint. New York: Basic Books, 1991. 336 pp. Index.**

An authoritative handbook of Jewish beliefs and practices compiled for those who would like practical guidance in the hows and whys of contemporary Jewish observance. Covers daily and Sabbath practices, prayer and public worship, dietary laws, observance of holy days and special occasions, and basic beliefs. Supplies further reading list.

DEWEY: 296.4 LC: BM 700.D58 ISBN 465-08639-X

♦ 401 ♦

To Life: A Celebration of Jewish Being and Thinking. **Harold Kushner. Boston: Little, Brown and Company, 1993. 304 pp.**

Best-selling author's explanation of Jewish spirituality. Provides thoughtful discussion of Jewish perspectives on social relationships and responsibilities, prayer, holy day and Sabbath observances, dietary laws, and Jewish identity.

DEWEY: 296 K LC: BM 45. K 87 ISBN 0-316-50735-0

♦ 402 ♦

A Treasury of Jewish Holidays: History, Legends, Traditions. **Hyman E. Goldin. Illustrated by Resko. 1952. Reprint. Detroit, MI: Omnigraphics, Inc., 1997. 308 pp. Index.**

Recounts the scriptural origins, history, lore, and customary forms of synagogue and home observance for more than 14 Jewish holidays. Covers the Sabbath, Rosh Hashanah, Rosh Hodesh, the Fast of Gedaliah, Yom Kippur, Sukkot, Hanukkah, Tu Bishvat, Purim, Passover, Lag ba-Omer, Shavuot, the Seventeenth of Tammuz, Tisha be-Av, and more. Includes brief history of the founding of the state of Israel. Also gives twenty-year calendar of Jewish feasts and fasts, covering the years 1951 to 1971.

DEWEY: 296 G61 ISBN 0-7808-0266-7

Hanukkah

♦ 403 ♦

All About Hanukkah. **Judye Groner and Madeline Wikler. Illustrated by Rosalyn Schanzer. Rockville, MD: Kar-Ben Copies, 1988. 32 pp.**

Explains the origin and meaning of Hanukkah. Describes Hanukkah celebrations, customs, and games, and includes a recipe and a song. Written for young children.

DEWEY: 296.4 35 LC: BM 695 H3 G68 ISBN 0-930494-81-4

♦ 404 ♦

A Blazing Fountain: A Book for Hanukkah. **David Rosenberg. New York: Schocken Books, 1978. 179 pp.**

Offers a selection of sacred and devotional texts concerning Hanukkah translated into contemporary English. Includes selections from the Book of Judith, the First and Second Book of Maccabees, the Book of Daniel, the Torah, Zechariah, Kings, Ezra, the Hallel, Shehecheyanu, Hanerot Hallalu, Maoz Tzur, and Al Hanissim.

DEWEY: 296.4 35 LC: BM 695. H3B55 ISBN 0-8052-3690-2

♦ 405 ♦

A Great Miracle Happened There: A Chanukah Story. **Karla Kuskin. Illustrated by Robert Andrew Parker. Willa Perlman Books, a division of Harper Collins, 1993. 29 pp.**

On the first night of Hanukkah, a mother tells her son and her son's non-Jewish friend the story behind the holiday. Adults in the Jewish family express a variety of opinions about the holiday. Written for small children.

DEWEY: 296.4 35 LC: BM 695. H3 K 87 ISBN 0-06-023617-5

♦ 406 ♦

The Hanukkah Anthology. **Philip Goodman. Philadelphia, PA: Jewish Publication Society of America, 1981. 465 pp. Illustrated. Bibliography. Glossary.**

A collection of texts concerning Hanukkah, or the Feast of Lights, which commemorates the Maccabean revolt that freed the Jewish people from foreign domination and persecution. A wide variety of articles and essays cover the origins and history of Hanukkah. Provides excerpts from post-biblical writings, the Talmud, Midrash, and Jewish law concerning Hanukkah; modern prose and poetry about Hanukkah; a discussion of the representation of Hanukkah in the arts; descriptions of Hanukkah celebrations around the world; and odd facts about the holiday. Also gives children's stories and poems about Hanukkah, examples of Hanukkah services, ideas for programs and activities, and Hanukkah dances, games, and songs.

DEWEY: 296.435 LC: BM 695. H3 H37 ISBN 0-8276-0080-1

♦ 407 ♦

The Hanukkah Book. **Mae Shafter Rockland. New York: Schocken Books, 1975. 174 pp. Illustrated. Appendix. Index.**

A guide to celebrating Hanukkah. Discusses the origins, history, significance, and observance of Hanukkah. Suggests party ideas, foods, decorations, and children's games, gifts, and crafts. Appendix suggests ways of using the Hebrew alphabet in crafts.

DEWEY: 296.435 R683h LC: TT900.H34 R6 ISBN 0-8052-3590-6

♦ 408 ♦

Hanukkah: The Festival of Lights. **Jenny Koralek. Illustrated by Juan Wijngaard. New York: Lothrop, Lee and Shepard Books, 1990. 29 pp.**

Retells the story of Hanukkah for young children.

DEWEY: 296.4 35 LC: BM 695. H3 K67 ISBN 0-888-09329-9

♦ 409 ♦

The Maccabees. **Moshe Pearlman. New York: Macmillan Publishing Co., 1973. 272 pp. Illustrated. Bibliography. Index.**

Provides a dramatized history of the Maccabee revolt for the general reader. Based on ancient Hebrew, Greek, and Roman sources. Illustrated with color and black-and-white photos of ancient art and artifacts. Gives chronology and genealogical tables.

DEWEY: 933

Passover

♦ 410 ♦

Ask Another Question. **Miriam Chaikin. Illustrated by Marvin Friedman. New York: Clarion Books, 1985. 89 pp. Glossary. Index.**

Provides a general introduction to Passover for children. Retells the Exodus story; explains how the holiday, its traditional practices, and the Haggadah developed; depicts a typical Seder celebration in the U.S; gives examples of differing Passover customs in other lands; and describes Passover foods and songs. Suggests books for further reading.

DEWEY: 296.4 37 LC: BM 695. P3 C46 ISBN 0-89919-281-5

♦ 411 ♦

A Feast of History: Passover Through the Ages as a Key to Jewish Experience, with a New Translation of the Haggadah for Use at the Seder. **Chaim Raphael. New York: Simon and Schuster, 1972. 250 pp. Illustrated.**

Two texts in one volume. From the front of the book forward, is a discussion of the history of Passover, treating it as a window on Jewish identity. Covers earliest origins of the holiday and its development over time, with particular emphasis on Seder celebrations and the development of the Haggadah (ritual texts describing the Jewish Exodus from Egypt). From the back of the book backwards, is a discussion of the Haggadah, in Hebrew and in English, for use in Seder celebrations. Richly illustrated with color photos of Passover preparations, celebrations and ritual objects, as well as artwork depicting the Exodus story.

DEWEY: 296.437 ISBN 671-21175-7

♦ 412 ♦

Keeping Passover: Everything You Need to Know to Bring the Ancient Tradition to Life and to Create Your Own Passover Celebration. **Ira Steingroot. San Francisco, CA: HarperSanFrancisco, 1995. 338 pp. Glossary.**

A comprehensive guide to developing a personally meaningful celebration of Passover. Teaches and explains meaning of Seder preparations, rituals, symbols, and blessings. Gives excellent annotated bibliography of more than 120 Haggadot, grouped according to philosophical orientation (Orthodox, Conservative, Reform, Feminist, Renewal, and more). Also gives discography of Passover music, list of Passover cookbooks, recipes, and hints on preparing Passover dishes. Suggests ways to involve children and provides bibliography of children's books on Passover. Also gives calendar dates for Passover through 2010.

DEWEY: 296.4 37 LC: BM 695 P35 S73 ISBN 0-06-067553-5

♦ 413 ♦

The Passover Anthology. **Philip Goodman. Philadelphia, PA: The Jewish Publication Society of America, 1961. 496 pp. Illustrated. Bibliography. Glossary.**

Presents a collection of texts concerning Passover. Offers a selection of articles and essays describing the origins and history of Passover, the Haggadah, and Passover celebrations and customs around the world. Also gives excerpts from the Bible, post-biblical writings, the Talmud, Midrash, and Jewish law concerning Passover. Provides selections from medieval and modern prose, contemporary poetry and short stories, articles about Passover as represented in music and art, and children's stories and poems about Passover. Also gives Passover recipes, dances, ideas for crafts and programs, and an outline of practices entailed in the observance of Passover.

DEWEY: 296.4 37 LC: BM 695. P3 G6 ISBN 0-8276-0019-4

♦ 414 ♦

Passover: A Season of Freedom. **Malka Drucker. Illustrated by Brom Hoban. New York: Holiday House, 1981. 95 pp. Appendix. Glossary. Index.**

Retells the story of the Israelite escape from slavery in Egypt and discusses Passover preparations and celebrations. Detailed description of the Seder meal and rituals. Depicts Passover foods and gives recipes. Suggests Passover crafts and games. Illustrated with black-and-white photos. Appendix prints Passover blessings, further reading list. For young readers.

DEWEY: 296.4 37 LC: BM 695 P3 D78 ISBN 0-8234-0389-0

♦ 415 ♦

Passover: Its History and Traditions. **Theodor H. Gaster. Boston, MA: Beacon Press, 1949. 102 pp. Illustrated. Bibliography. Index.**

Explores Passover rites and legends from the perspective of comparative religion. Identifies origins of the holiday, points out parallels in other cultural traditions, explains its symbols, and discusses its spiritual significance. One volume in a series entitled *Great Religious Festivals.*

DEWEY: 296.4 37 LC: BM 695. P3 G36

♦ 416 ♦

The Passover Journey: A Seder Companion. **Barbara Diamond Goldin. Illustrated by Neil Waldman. New York: Viking Press, 1994. 56 pp. Glossary.**

Retells the story of Moses and the Israelite escape from Egypt. Explains the Passover Seder as a commemoration of the escape, describing the foods, blessings, and other Seder customs and relating their significance. Illustrated with color drawings. Gives notes on sources. For children.

DEWEY: 269.4 37 LC: BM 695. P3 G58 ISBN 0-670-82421-6

♦ 417 ♦

The Passover Seder. **Ron Wolfson, with Joel Lurie Grishaver. New York: Federation of Jewish Men's Clubs, 1988. 332 pp. Bibliography.**

Practical guide for celebrating the Passover Seder, written especially for those without much exposure to Jewish religious observance. Part one introduces the Passover Haggadah (the text which guides the celebration) in sections, teaching the rituals and explaining their meaning. Also answers practical questions and lists ceremonial objects needed. Part two provides a thorough guide to Seder preparations, including tips on how to organize a Seder service, choose a Haggadah, select kosher foods, and how to kosher utensils and make other kitchen preparations. Furnishes a selected bibliography of Haggadot, children's books on Passover, and other resource books on Jewish holidays. A workbook, audiotape, and teacher's guide are available from the publisher. One volume in a series entitled "The Art of Jewish Living."

DEWEY: 296.437 ISBN 0-935665-01-7

♦ 418 ♦

The Passover Seder: Afikomen in Exile. **Ruth Gruber Fredman. Philadelphia, PA: University of Pennsylvania Press, 1981. 168 pp. Bibliography. Index.**

A cultural anthropologist analyzes the Passover Seder and its symbols as a key to understanding Jewish concepts, values, and world views, and the tensions that exist between them. Part of a series entitled "Symbol and Culture."

DEWEY: 296.4 37 LC: BM 695. P35 F73 ISBN 0-8122-7788-0

Purim

♦ 419 ♦

Esther. **Miriam Chaikin. Illustrated by Vera Rosenberry. Philadelphia, PA: Jewish Publication Society, 1987. 28 pp.**

Retells the biblical story of Esther. Illustrated with black-and-white drawings. For children.

DEWEY: 222.909505 LC: BS 580. E8 C48 ISBN 0-8276-0272-3

♦ 420 ♦

The Purim Anthology. **Philip Goodman. Philadelphia, PA: The Jewish Publication Society of America, 1980. 525 pp. Illustrated. Bibliography. Glossary.**

A collection of texts concerning Purim. Recounts origins of Purim, reprints the Book of Esther, and describes Purim celebrations around the world, including special Purims. Gives excerpts from post-biblical religious writings, the Talmud, Midrash, and Jewish law concerning Purim; provides selections from contemporary prose and poetry about Purim; essays on Purim in music and art; and Purim pranks, plays, jokes, and children's stories and poems. Describes Purim services, gives ideas for Purim parties, and furnishes words and music to Hebrew, Yiddish, and English Purim songs and liturgical music.

DEWEY: 296.436 LC: BM 695. P8 P63 ISBN 0-8276-0022-4

Rosh Hashanah

♦ 421 ♦

The Rosh Hashanah Anthology. **Philip Goodman. Philadelphia, PA: The Jewish Publication Society of America, 1973. Illustrated. Bibliography. Glossary.**

Furnishes a collection of texts on Rosh Hashanah, or the Jewish New Year. Gives excerpts from the Bible, post-biblical writings, the Talmud, Midrash, Jewish law, and medieval Jewish literature concerning Rosh Hashanah. Offers scriptural readings, prayers, and parables for Rosh Hashanah, and essays concerning the Shofar, the ceremony of Tashlikh, the representation of Rosh Hashanah in music and art, and descriptions of Rosh Hashanah celebrations from around the world. Also provides Hasidic lore and teachings, poetry, short stories, and recipes for the holiday, along with children's stories and poems, suggestions for Rosh Hashanah programs, and a collection of interesting facts about the holiday. Bibliography includes listings of Hasidic tales, sermons, liturgy, music, sound recordings, children's stories, and audio-visual materials.

DEWEY: 394.2682 ISBN 0-8276-0023-2

Rosh Hodesh

♦ 422 ♦

Celebrating the New Moon: A Rosh Chodesh Anthology. **Susan Berrin, ed. Northvale, NJ: Jason Aronson, Inc., 1996. 331 pp. Appendices. Bibliography. Glossary. Index.**

Offers a collection of texts concerning Rosh Hodesh, the celebration of the first day of the Jewish month, marked by the appearance of a new moon. Presents the history of Rosh Hodesh, modes of celebration, analysis of its social and spiritual importance, and consideration of the role of feminism in its increasing observance. Also gives ways of celebrating the holiday, reflections of the moon as a spiritual symbol within Judaism and as a symbol of particular importance to women, as well as meditative writings, songs, poetry, and prayers relating to Rosh Hodesh. Numerous appendices include a calendar of Rosh Hodesh observances, a directory of groups observing Rosh Hodesh, a model ceremony, and more.

DEWEY: 296.4 39 LC: BM 695. N4 C45 ISBN 1-56821-459-6

♦ 423 ♦

The Rosh Hodesh Table: Foods at the New Moon. **Judith Solomon. New York: Biblio Press, 1995. 138 pp. Illustrated. Bibliography.**

Gives foods associated with the 13 months of the Jewish calendar. Also provides information about the role of food in Jewish rituals, recipes for Jewish holidays, and Jewish history and lore, with an emphasis on women and their role in Judaism. Further reading list.

DEWEY: 641. 5676 ISBN 0-930395-23-9

Sabbath

♦ 424 ♦

The Jewish Sabbath: A Renewed Encounter. **Pinchas H. Peli. New York: Schocken Books, 1991. 173 pp. Appendices.**

Originally published with the title *Shabbat Shalom.* A noted professor of Jewish thought reflects on the meaning and observance of the Jewish Sabbath. Reviews wide range of Jewish literature on the Sabbath, with special attention to biblical texts. References cited given in endnotes. Appendices include biblical texts referring to the Sabbath, description of conflicts over Sabbath observances in Israel, and notes on Hasidic approaches to the Sabbath.

DEWEY: 296.4 1 LC: BM 685. P36 ISBN 0-8052-0998-0

♦ 425 ♦

The Sabbath: Its Meaning for Modern Man. **Expanded edition. Abraham Joshua Heschel. Illustrated by Ilya Schor. New York: Farrar, Strauss and Company, 1951. 136 pp.**

Renowned Jewish theologian's thoughtful and simply written essay on the spiritual meaning of the Sabbath. Contrasts Sabbath emphasis on the sanctification of time with weekday obsessions with the world of space and things. Concludes that the association of the holy and of God with time and historical events was a uniquely Jewish contribution to the religious development of humanity. Illustrated with artist's woodcuts.

DEWEY: 296.4 LC: BM 685. H4 ISBN 0-374-51267-1

♦ 426 ♦

Shabbat: A Peaceful Island. **Malka Drucker. Illustrated by Brom Hoban. New York: Holiday House, 1983. 95 pp. Appendix. Glossary. Index.**

Teaches the history, meaning, customs, rituals, and legends of the Jewish Sabbath to young readers. Covers home and synagogue observance. Also treats the special Sabbaths. Discusses Sabbath foods and gives recipes, crafts, and games. Appendix lists the 39 forbidden acts of the Sabbath. Further reading list. Black-and-white photos and drawings illustrate.

DEWEY: 296.4 1 LC: BM 685. D78 ISBN 0-8234-0500-1

Shavuot

♦ 427 ♦

The Shavuot Anthology. **Philip Goodman. Philadelphia, PA: The Jewish Publication Society of America, 1974. 369 pp. Illustrated. Bibliography. Glossary. Index.**

Presents a wide variety of texts concerning Shavuot, or the Feast of Weeks, which commemorates the giving of the Ten Commandments to Moses on Mount Sinai. Gives Bible excerpts, post-biblical and medieval religious texts, selections from the Talmud, Midrash, and medieval Jewish literature; Jewish laws and practices concerning Shavuot; brief descriptions of Shavuot celebrations from around the world; excerpts from contemporary writers on the meaning of Shavuot; poetry, short stories, jokes, and children's stories about Shavuot; recipes; music and lyrics to songs; and celebratory projects for families and congregations.

DEWEY: 296.438 LC: BM 695. S5 S5 ISBN 0-8276-0057-7

Sukkot and Simhat Torah

♦ 428 ♦

Shake a Palm Branch. **Miriam Chaikin. Illustrated by Marvin Friedman. New York: Clarion Books, 1984. 88 pp. Glossary. Index.**

Discusses the origins, historical development, and significance of Sukkot. Explains how the holiday is celebrated today, in the United States and abroad, and reviews Sukkot blessings, prayers, foods, and customs. Also covers Shemini Atzeret. Gives holiday songs and explains Jewish terms used throughout. Two-tone drawings illustrate. Further reading list. For young readers.

DEWEY: 296.433 LC: BM 695 S8 C53 ISBN 0-89919-254-8

♦ 429 ♦

The Sukkot and Simhat Torah Anthology. **Philip Goodman. Philadelphia, PA: The Jewish Publication Society of America, 1973. 475 pp. Illustrated. Bibliography. Glossary.**

A collection of texts concerning Sukkot and Simhat Torah. Gives excerpts from the Bible, post-biblical writings, the Talmud, Midrash, Jewish law, and liturgy concerning the holidays. Also supplies selections from medieval Jewish literature, Hasidic lore, contemporary prose, poetry, and short stories featuring the holidays; holiday humor; articles concerning the historical development of the festivals and their customary practices; the holidays' representation in the arts; and descriptions of celebrations around the world. Provides children's stories and poems about the holidays, recipes, activities and programs, holiday dances, and words and music to holiday songs.

DEWEY: 296.433 LC: BM 695 S8. G66 ISBN 0-8276-0010-0

♦ 430 ♦

Sukkot: A Time to Rejoice. **Malka Drucker. Illustrated by Brom Hoban. New York: Holiday House, 1982. 96 pp. Appendix. Glossary. Index.**

Explains the history, lore, customs, and religious rituals of Sukkot to young readers. Covers home and synagogue observances. Also discusses Simhat Torah and Shemini Atzeret. Gives crafts, recipes, and games. Appendix prints Sukkot prayers. Illustrated with black-and-white photos and drawings.

DEWEY: 296.4 33 LC: BM 695 S8 D78 ISBN 0-8234-0466-8

Yom Kippur

♦ 431 ♦

Kol Nidrei: Its Origin, Development, and Significance. **Stuart Weinberg Gershon. Northvale, NJ: Jason Aronson, Inc., 1994. 175 pp. Appendices. Bibliography. Index.**

Examines the sources and history of *Kol Nidrei,* a central text in the liturgy of Yom Kippur, analyzing its relationship to the holiday and offering an explanation for its potency. Appendices give various musical and textual versions of *Kol Nidrei.*

DEWEY: 296. 4 32 LC: BM 670. K6 G47 ISBN 1-56821-200-3

♦ 432 ♦

The Yom Kippur Anthology. **Philip Goodman. Philadelphia, PA: The Jewish Publication Society of America, 1971. 399 pp. Illustrated. Bibliography. Glossary.**

Presents a collection of texts concerning Yom Kippur. Gives selections from the Bible, post-biblical writings, the Talmud, Midrash, Jewish law, and medieval Jewish literature. Also gives prayers, Hasidic stories and teachings, articles and essays on *Kol Nidrei,* and on Yom Kippur as represented in music and art. Provides selections from contemporary prose, poetry, short stories, and children's stories and poems about Yom Kippur. Also offers descriptions of Yom Kippur celebrations around the world, as well as a collection of interesting facts and ideas about Yom Kippur.

DEWEY: 296.432 LC: BM 695. A8 G66

Neopaganism

♦ 433 ♦

Casting the Circle: A Women's Book of Ritual. **Diane Stein. Freedom, CA: The Crossing Press, 1990. 260 pp. Appendix. Bibliography.**

Presents a collection of rituals and lore for contemporary Goddess worshippers. Tells how to set up an altar; when, why and how to do various rituals; explains the meaning of the rituals; and lists associated symbols. Offers rituals to celebrate the waxing and waning moon and the eight Sabbats (Winter Solstice, Candlemas, Spring Equinox, Beltane, Summer Solstice, Lammas, Autumn Equinox, and Halloween). Also offers rituals for female life-cycle events and personal needs. Appendix gives essay on history of the contemporary Women's Spirituality movement and its similarities to and differences from traditional Wicca, or witchcraft.

DEWEY: 291.3 8 082 LC: BF 1623. R6 S74 ISBN 0-89594-411-1

♦ 434 ♦

Celebrate the Earth: A Year of Holidays in the Pagan Tradition. **Laurie Cabot and Jean Mills. New York: Delta Books, 1994. 272 pp. Appendix.**

Furnishes rituals, spells, meditations, symbols, ceremonial objects, activities, lore, and recipes for the celebration of eight Pagan (Celtic) holidays: Samhain, Yule, Imbolc, Spring Equinox, Beltane, Midsummer, Lughnasadh, and Mabon. Appendix explains basic elements of witchcraft, lists the year's moons and their correspondences, identifies the sacred trees of the Celts, and gives resource and further reading list.

DEWEY: 299 LC: BF 1572 F37 C32 ISBN 0-385-30920-1

♦ 435 ♦

Drawing Down the Moon: Witches, Druids, Goddess-Worshippers, and Other Pagans in America Today. **Margot Adler. New York: Viking Press, 1979. 455 pp. Appendices. Index.**

A survey of the contemporary Neopagan movement. Introduces outlooks, beliefs, sects, their history, and the influence of the feminist movement and ancient mythologies on various Neopagan groups. Author discusses own experiences as a participant observer among many of these groups, illustrates common attitudes of Neopagans towards contemporary social concerns, and presents a critical review of the scholarly literature on Neopagans. Appendices present selected rituals, reprint various proclamations, and provide a resource list.

DEWEY: 133.4 0973 LC: BF1573. A34 ISBN 0-670-28342-8

♦ 436 ♦

Eight Sabbats for Witches, and Rites for Birth, Marriage and Death. **Janet and Stewart Farrar. Custer, WA: Phoenix Publishing, Inc., 1981. 192 pp. Illustrated. Bibliography. Index.**

Provides rituals, legends, customs, and lore for the observance of eight witches' Sabbats: Imbolc, Spring Equinox, Beltane, Midsummer, Lughnasadh, Autumn Equinox, Samhain, and Yule. Also describes the Opening Ritual, the Great Rite, and the Closing Ritual. Furnishes witches' rituals for birth (wiccaning), marriage (handfasting),and death (requiem). Includes some description of folk customs of the British Isles.

DEWEY: 299 LC: BF1571.F34 ISBN 0-919345-26-3

♦ 437 ♦

Grandmother Moon: Lunar Magic in Our Lives: Spells, Rituals, Goddesses, Legends, and Emotions Under the Moon. **Zsuzsanna E. Budapest. San Francisco, CA: HarperSanFrancisco, 1991. 288 pp. Illustrated. Bibliography. Index.**

A founder of the Goddess movement presents a goddess, an emotion, a story, astrological insights, spells, and moon festivals for each of the 13 lunar months. Emphasizes festivals from those cultures with lunar calendars, such as those of Asia, the Middle East, ancient Egypt, Greece, and Rome, and Native America. Festival entries explain significance and describe celebrations. Black-and-white drawings illustrate.

DEWEY: 133.5 3 LC: BF1723.B83 ISBN 0-06-250114-3

♦ 438 ♦

The Grandmother of Time: A Woman's Book of Celebrations, Spells, and Sacred Objects for Every Month of the Year. **Zsuzsanna E. Budapest. San**

Francisco, CA: Harper and Row, 1989. 261 pp. Illustrated. Bibliography. Index.

A collection of holidays, spells, stories, and lore for the seasons, months, and days of the year from a founder of the contemporary Goddess movement. Offers a celebratory theme for each month, naming an ancient goddess, activities, events, principles, ideas, spells, colors, plants, animals, and gems which highlight the spirit of the month. Also gives dates and brief descriptions of ancient (mostly European) festivals honoring goddesses, with suggestions on how to revive their commemoration.

DEWEY: 291.4 46 024042 LC: BL 625.7 B83 ISBN 0-06-250109-7

♦ 439 ♦

Seasonal Dance: How to Celebrate the Pagan Year. **Janice Broch and Veronica MacLer. York Beach, ME: Samuel Weiser, Inc., 1993. 171 pp. Illustrated. Appendices. Bibliography. Index.**

Provides rituals for the observance of the eight seasonal festivals of the Pagan year: Samhain, Yule, Imbolc, Ostara, Beltane, Litha, Lammas, and the autumn equinox. Also discusses lore and customs of Celtic and other ancient northern European observances, and gives chapter on creating rituals. Appendices present songs, chants, dances, symbols, games, recipes, gods, goddesses, further reading list, and research tips. Black-and-white drawings illustrate. Resource list.

DEWEY: 299 LC: BF1566 B743 ISBN 0-87728-774-0

♦ 440 ♦

The Spiral Dance: A Rebirth of the Ancient Religion of the Great Goddess. **Tenth anniversary edition, revised and updated. Starhawk. San Francisco, CA: HarperSanFrancisco, 1989. 288 pp. Bibliography. Index.**

Foundational text in the revival of Goddess worship, or witchcraft. Presents an introduction to the outlook, lore, and practices of contemporary witchcraft or Goddess worship. Introduces exercises, invocations, chants, blessings, spells, charms, lunar celebrations, holidays, and myths. Also includes a resource list as well as a table of correspondences for the elements and the sun, moon, and stars. This edition offers author's comments on, and minor revisions of, the first edition as well as an updated bibliography.

DEWEY: 299 LC: BF 1566.S77 ISBN 0-06-250815-6

♦ 441 ♦

The Wicca Book of Days: Legend and Lore for Every Day of the Year. **Gerina Dunwich. New York: Citadel Press, 1995. 168 pp. Illustrated. Bibliography. Index.**

Gives a holiday, festival, or important event from Wiccan history for every day of the year. Includes religious and folk holidays from Asia, Africa, North and South America, and Europe, as well as festivals from ancient Rome, Greece, Egypt, the Americas and the Middle East. Black-and-white drawings illustrate.

DEWEY: 291.3 6 LC: BF1572. F37 D86 ISBN 0-8065-1685-2

♦ 442 ♦

Wheel of the Year: Living the Magical Life. **Pauline Campanelli and Dan Campanelli. St. Paul, MN: Llewellyn Publications, 1989. 159 pp. Illustrated.**

Offers lore, legends, rituals, symbols, spells, crafts, ornaments, ceremonial objects, and customs associated with the month, seasons, and Pagan holidays. Organized by month.

DEWEY: 291.3 6 LC: BF 1623 R6 C36 ISBN 0-87542-091-5

♦ 443 ♦

A Woman's Book of Rituals and Celebrations. **Barbara Ardinger. San Rafael, CA: New World Library, 1992. 212 pp. Appendix. Bibliography. Discography.**

A manual and spiritual guide for those interested in contemporary Neopagan Goddess worship and witchcraft. Part one introduces spiritual principles and beliefs. Part two teaches home-based rites and practices. Part three introduces 12 seasonal festivals and their celebration. Includes a resource guide.

DEWEY: 291.3 8 082 LC: BL 625.7 A55 ISBN 0-931432-90-1

Shinto

♦ 444 ♦

Matsuri: Festivals of a Japanese Town. **Michael Ashkenazi. Honolulu, HI: University of Hawaii Press, 1993. 192 pp. Bibliography. Glossary. Index.**

An anthropological study of the Shinto festival cycle in a Japanese town. Addresses the structure, activities, and organization of festivals; presents the perspectives of the laity and clergy; and analyzes the reasons for their survival in spite of the dramatic social and economic changes which have characterized twentieth-century Japan.

DEWEY: 394.2 68299561 LC: BL 2224.7 A84 ISBN 0-8248-1385-5

♦ 445 ♦

Shinto: Japan's Spiritual Roots. **Stuart D. B. Picken. Introduction by Edwin O. Reischauer. Tokyo, Japan: Kodansha International Ltd., 1980. 80 pp. Illustrated. Maps. Glossary.**

Provides an introduction to the spirit and the practices of Shinto, including festivals, prayer, and ceremonies. Also discusses Shinto deities, architecture, aesthetics, and philosophy. Festivals covered include the Autumn Festival, Obon, and New Year. Beautifully illustrated with color photographs. Gives map of Japan with important shrines marked and their major festival dates noted. Offers map of the Tsurugaoka Hachiman Shrine complex.

DEWEY: 299.561 LC: BL 2220 P5 ISBN 0-87011-410-7

♦ 446 ♦

Shinto: The Kami Way. **Motonori Ono. Rutland, VT: Bridgeway Press, 1962. 116 pp. Illustrated. Index.**

Simple introduction to the beliefs, practices, and history of Shinto. Covers Shinto mythology, scripture, spirits, shrines, customs, philosophy, priests, parishes, and relationship with other religions. Outlines basic elements of

Shinto worship, including home, shrine, and festival practices. Black-and-white photos illustrate.

DEWEY: 299.56

♦ 447 ♦

A Year in the Life of a Shinto Shrine. **John K. Nelson. Seattle, WA: University of Washington Press, 1996. 286 pp. Illustrated. Appendices. Bibliography. Glossary. Index.**

A descriptive account of more than 50 Shinto festivals and ceremonies. Based on the author's participation in and observation of the yearly ritual cycle at Suwa Shrine in Nagasaki, Japan. Elucidates fundamental spiritual concepts of Shinto and conveys contemporary relevance of its ancient rites to worshippers and priests. Appendices provide a festival and ritual calendar and offer a map and guide to Suwa Shrine. References cited in endnotes.

DEWEY: 299.56135 LC: BL 2225.N2552 S883 ISBN 0-295-97499-0

Sikhism

General Works

♦ 448 ♦

Sikh Festivals. **Sukhbir Singh Kapoor. Vero Beach, FL: Rourke Enterprises, Inc., 1989. 48 pp. Illustrated. Glossary. Index.**

Background for young readers on Sikh religious beliefs, history, and ceremonies and festivals. Chronological table of holidays by Hindu month. List of Sikh gurus. Further reading list. One volume in a series entitled *Holidays and Festivals.* (NR)

DEWEY: 294.6 36 LC: BL2018.37.K37 ISBN 0-86592-984-X

♦ 449 ♦

The Sikh World. **Daljit Singh and Angela Smith. Morristown, NJ: Silver Burdett Company, 1985. 45 pp. Illustrated. Glossary. Index.**

Introduces young readers to the beliefs and practices of the Sikhs. Describes the celebration of the three major festivals: Baisakhi, Diwali, and Hola Mohalla. Also tells how the gurpub festivals, which celebrate the lives of Sikh gurus, are observed. Includes calendar of the Sikh year, further reading list, and suggestions for appropriate dress and behavior when visiting a gurdwara. Illustrated with color photos.

DEWEY: 296.4 LC: BL 2018 D336 ISBN 0-382-09159-0

Baisakhi

♦ 450 ♦

Bobbi's New Year. **Joan Solomon. London, England: Evans Brothers Limited, 1980. Unpaginated. Illustrated.**

Follows the experiences of a young boy as his family observes the Sikh New Year festival, Baisakhi. Color photos illustrate. For children. One book in a series entitled *The Way We Live.*

DEWEY: 294.536 ISBN 0-237-60114-1

Zoroastrianism

♦ 451 ♦

Zoroastrianism: A Beleaguered Faith. **Cyrus R. Pangborn. New York: Advent Books, 1983. 162 pp. Illustrated. Bibliography. Index.**

An introduction to Zoroastrianism for the general reader. Discusses its founder, the prophet Zoroaster (or Zarathushtra); development as a faith tradition; holy writings; central beliefs; social teachings; religious institutions; and rituals, holy days, and ceremonies.

DEWEY: 295 P LC: BL 1571 P3 ISBN 0-89891-006-4

CHAPTER THREE

Holidays of World Regions, Nations, and Ethnic Groups

Africa

General Works

♦ 452 ♦

Africa Adorned. **Angela Fisher. New York: Harry N. Abrams, Inc., 1984. 304 pp. Illustrated. Bibliography. Index.**

Photo essay and text on the art of personal adornment among the diverse peoples of Africa. Some coverage of festivals, including the Eunoto Ceremony of the Maasai (East Africa), the Geerewol Festival of the Wodaabe nomads, the Cure Salee Festival of the Tuareg and Wodaabe (West African savannah), and the Imilchil Fair of the Berbers (North Africa). Describes celebrations and ceremonies in words and pictures. Lavishly illustrated with more than 400 color photos and over 40 black-and-white photos. Oversize.

DEWEY: 391. 7 096 LC: GT 1580. F57 ISBN 0-8109-1823-4

♦ 453 ♦

Africa's Ogun: Old World and New. **Sandra T. Barnes, ed. Bloomington, IN: Indiana University Press, 1989. 274 pp. Illustrated. Index.**

Presents a collection of articles concerning the African god Ogun, and the history, myth, devotions, rituals, and art associated with him in West Africa and the New World."The Dreadful God and the Divine King,"by John Pemberton III, describes many rituals of the Odun Ogun and Odun Oba festivals of the Yoruba people of Nigeria. References given in endnotes. Illustrated with black-and-white photos and diagrams.

DEWEY: 299.63 LC: BL 2480.Y6 A46 ISBN 0-253-30282-X

♦ 454 ♦

I Am Not Myself: The Art of African Masquerade. **Herbert M. Cole, ed. Los Angeles, CA: Museum of Cultural History, University of California, 1985. Monograph series, number 26. 111 pp. Illustrated. Bibliography.**

Brings together a collection of essays by noted authorities on the art of African masks and masquerading. Festivals and ceremonies mentioned throughout, including the Egungun, Gelede, Efe, and Epa Festivals of the Yoruba people, and the Aminague, Okakagbe, and Olimi Festivals of the Northern Edo. Black-and-white photos illustrate. Endnotes.

LC: GN 645 I2 ISBN 0-930741-02-1

♦ 455 ♦

Introduction to African Religion. **Second edition, revised. John S. Mbiti. Portsmouth, NH: Heinemann Educational Books, Inc., 1991. 216 pp. Illustrated. Appendices. Index.**

Furnishes an overview of the beliefs and practices of Africa's indigenous religions. Touches on all aspects of African religions, including view of the universe and God; modes of worship; spirits; creation beliefs; rituals of birth, youth, marriage and death; festivals; religious leaders; religious objects and places; and more. Appendices provide questions to test comprehension, further reading list, and examples of African sayings and proverbs. Appropriate as high school or college introductory text, or for the general reader.

DEWEY: 299.6 ISBN 0435-94002-3

♦ 456 ♦

Religions of Africa. **Noel Q. King. New York: Harper and Row, 1970. 116 pp. Glossary. Index.**

An introduction to the indigenous religions of equatorial Africa. Discusses Ashanti, Yoruba, and others' religious festivals, ceremonies, and customs, such as the Egungun Festival and ceremonies for Yoruba deities. Also covers birth, initiation, marriage, and death customs, concepts of the divine, and the role of religious leaders among various African ethnic groups. Further reading list.

DEWEY: 299.6 LC: BL 24000 K5

♦ 457 ♦

Religions of Africa: Traditions in Transformation. **E. Thomas Lawson. San Francisco, CA: Harper and Row, 1984. 106 pp. Illustrated. Glossary.**

Surveys history and religious traditions of the Zulu and Yoruba people. Covers customs, legends, and ceremonies associated with birth, puberty, marriage, and death. Festivals described include Zulu/Shembe Festival, New Year, and the New Yam Festival. Further reading list. Notes. (NR)

DEWEY: 299.683 LC: BL2480.Z8 L39 ISBN 0-06-065211-X

♦ 458 ♦

The Travelers' Guide to African Customs and Manners. **Elizabeth Devine and Nancy L. Braganti. New York: St. Martin's Press, 1995. 223 pp.**

Alerts travelers to everyday social customs in African countries. Covers Botswana, Cameroon, Ivory Coast, Ghana, Kenya, Mali, Namibia, Nigeria, Senegal, South Africa, Tanzania, Uganda, and Zimbabwe. Lists national holidays for all countries. Other topics covered include greetings, conversation, telephones, public behavior, dress, meals, hotels, tipping, visits to private homes, business practices, transportation, legal issues, safety, and health. Gives useful phrases in French and in several African languages.

DEWEY: 967 D495T LC: DT 349.8 D48 ISBN 0-312-11909-7

♦ 459 ♦

Working the Spirit: Ceremonies of the African Diaspora. **Joseph M. Murphy. Boston, MA: Beacon Press, 1994. 263 pp. Bibliography. Glossary. Index.**

Traces the African roots of ritual practices in five religions of the African diaspora: Haitian Vodou, Brazilian Candomblé, Cuban and Cuban-American Santería, Revival Zion in Jamaica, and the Black Church in the United States. Also analyzes the concept of spirit in these traditions.

DEWEY: 200.89 96 LC: BL 2490 M87 ISBN 0-8070-1220-3

Dogon

♦ 460 ♦

Masked Dancers of West Africa: The Dogon. **Stephen Pern and the Editors of Time-Life Books. Amsterdam, Netherlands: Time-Life Books, 1982. 168 pp. Illustrated. Bibliography. Index.**

Describes in words and photos the everyday and ceremonial life of the Dogon people of West Africa. Covers many aspects of the six-day Buro Festival (a spring fertility festival), including popular customs, ceremonies, festivities, dances, and costumes. Also covers funerals and other ceremonies involving masked dancing, including a memorial ceremony for the dead held every 10 to 15 years. Describes festive atmosphere of the weekly open-air market. Beautifully illustrated with many color photos.

DEWEY: 966.23 ISBN 7054-0706-3

Ethiopia

♦ 461 ♦

Wax and Gold: Tradition and Innovation in Ethiopian Culture. **Donald N. Levine. Chicago: University of Chicago Press, 1965. 315 pp. Illustrated. Map. Glossary. Index.**

Provides an overview of the social and cultural life of the Amhara, Ethiopia's predominant ethnic group. Discusses history, the peasant way of life and world view, adolescence and coming of age, social stratification, the effects of modernization, religion, and values. Brief coverage given to a number of festivals, including St. John's Day (or New Year's Day), Masqal, St. Michael's Day, Christmas, Timqat (or Epiphany), and the Assumption of Mary. Illustrated with black-and-white photos and tables. References given in endnotes.

DEWEY: 963 L665w

Ghana

♦ 462 ♦

Festivals of Ghana. **A. A. Opoku. Accra, Ghana: Ghana Publishing Corporation, 1970. 79 pp. Illustrated.**

Describes 12 major festivals of the Akan, Akwamu, Effutu, Fante, Gomua, Agona, Ashanti, Ga, Ewe, and Brong peoples of Ghana. Covers Adae, Odwira, the Yam Festival, the Deer Catching Festival, Akwambo, Ayerye, the Papa Festival, Homowo, the Damba, the Kwafie Festival, and others. Describes ceremonies and festive activities, retells associated stories and myths. Provides list of 26 additional Ghanaian festivals not covered in the book. Illustrated with black-and-white photos of festival activities.

DEWEY: 394.2 69667 LC: GT 4889 G5 O6

♦ 463 ♦

Homowo and Other Ga-Adangme Festivals. **Charles Nii Ammah. Accra, Ghana: Sedco Publishing Limited, 1982. 66 pp. Illustrated. Bibliography. Glossary.**

Describes the dances, feasting, ceremonies, and other customs through which the Ga-Adangme people of Ghana celebrate the festival of Homowo.

Reviews the celebration of the festival in 12 different areas, noting differences in dates, duration, personnel, and customs. Other festivals, such as the Wo Domi festival, mentioned briefly.

LC: DT 510.43 G3 A46

Maasai

♦ 464 ♦

The Maasai of Mataporo: A Study of the Rituals of Rebellion. **Paul Spencer. Bloomington, IN: Indiana University Press, 1988. 297 pp. Glossary. Indexes.**

Furnishes a scholarly study of rituals of the Maasai of Mataporo, Kenya. Detailed description of the Eunoto festival. Some coverage of other situational or life-cycle festivals, such as the Women's Festival and the Boys' Dancing Festival.

DEWEY: 306.08996 LC: DT 433.545. M33 S64 ISBN 0-253-33625-2

Yoruba

♦ 465 ♦

Yoruba Myths. **Ulli Beier. Cambridge, England: Cambridge University Press, 1980. 82 pp. Illustrated.**

The author and contributors present 41 myths from Nigeria about Yoruba deities, including Ogun and Oranmiyan. (NR)

DEWEY: 398.2 09668 LC: GR351.32.Y56Y67 ISBN 0-521-22995-2

Ancient

General Works

♦ 466 ♦

Cybele and Attis: The Myth and the Cult. **Maarten J. Vermaseren. Translated by A.M.H. Lemmers. London: Thames and Hudson, 1977. 224 pp. Illustrated. Bibliography. Glossary. Index.**

Explores the cult of the goddess Cybele in the ancient Mediterranean world, from early worship in Asia Minor and Greece, through adoption by the Romans and spread throughout the Roman Empire. Examines range of myths associated with Cybele and with her consort, Attis. Describes modes of worship, including festivals. Illustrated with black-and-white plates of ancient artwork depicting Cybele and Attis.

LC: BL 820 C8.V4513

♦ 467 ♦

The Dionysiac Mysteries of the Hellenistic and Roman Age. **Martin P. Nilsson. 1957. Reprint. New York: Arno Press, 1975. 150 pp. Illustrated. Index.**

Treats the cult of Dionysus (or Bacchus) in ancient Greece and Rome. Discusses the celebration of the Mysteries, dances, festivals, and initiation ceremonies; the organization, character and functionaries of the Dionysian associations; beliefs in the afterlife; symbols; attitudes towards children; and Orphic and Pythagorean influences. Scholarly.

DEWEY: 292.9 LC: BL 820.B2 N5 ISBN 0-405-07261-9

♦ 468 ♦

The Gods of Mexico. **C. A. Burland. New York: G. P. Putnam's Sons, 1967. 219 pp. Illustrated. Maps. Appendices. Bibliography. Index.**

Alphabetical listing of Aztec gods. Guide to pronunciation. Covers Aztec, Mayan, Toltec, and Olmec cultures, cities, calendar systems, deities, and religions. Aztec ceremonies and festivals described. Appendices discuss Mayan, Aztec, and other Mexican codices and Tlachtli, a ball game. (NR)

DEWEY: 299.7 LC: F1219.3.R38 B8

♦ 469 ♦

The Golden Bough: The Roots of Religion and Folklore. **James G. Frazer. 1890. Reprint. New York: Avenal Books, 1981. 407 pp. Illustrated. Index.**

Recounts myths, legends, superstitions, celebrations, religious beliefs, and folkloric practices of the world, contemporary and ancient. Identifies common themes, uncovers common assumptions about the relationship between the spiritual and material worlds, and retraces the outlines of prehistoric religious beliefs. Emphasis on folklore of rural Europe. Considered a classic work.

DEWEY: 291 LC: BL 310. F7 ISBN 0-517-336332

♦ 470 ♦

Holidays of Legend, From New Years to Christmas. **Mildred H. Arthur. Illustrated by Sofia. New York: Harvey House, 1971. 124 pp. Index.**

Recounts the folklore, legend, and myth of ancient celebrations associated with contemporary popular holidays. Covers New Year's Day, Valentine's Day, St. Patrick's Day, April Fool's Day, Easter, May Day, Halloween, Thanksgiving, and Christmas. Written for children.

DEWEY: 394.26

♦ 471 ♦

The Magickal Year. **Diana Ferguson. New York: Quality Paperback Book Club, 1996. 224 pp. Illustrated. Bibliography. Index.**

Presents a collection of lore, legends, customs, and deities associated with ancient seasonal celebrations. Emphasis on ancient Europe. Covers Christmas, New Year, Imbolc, May Day, midsummer, Lughnasadh, Halloween, Samhain, and other ancient festivals held around the time of the solstices, equinoxes, and quarter days. Numerous color and black-and-white illustrations. Pronunciation guide.

DEWEY: 133.4 3 LC: BF1623.R6 F47

♦ 472 ♦

The Oxford Classical Dictionary. **Second edition. N.G.L. Hammond and H. H. Scullard. Oxford, England: Clarendon Press, 1970. 1176 pp. Bibliography. Index.**

Covers the ancient Greek and Roman worlds. Treats place names, mythological figures, legends, notable individuals, institutions, customs, natural features, political and administrative units, festivals, cults, and more. Entries are substantial and most list sources. Offers bibliography of books in many languages. Index of people, places, and things mentioned throughout that are not titles of entries.

DEWEY: 913. 38003 LC: DE5. 09

♦ 473 ♦

Religions of the Ancient Near East. **Helmer Ringgren. Translated by John Sturdy. Philadelphia, PA: Westminster Press, 1973. 198 pp. Bibliography. Index.**

Provides an overview of ancient Sumerian, Babylonian, Assyrian, and West Semitic religions. Covers gods, mythology, cult, kingship, divine-human relationship, morality, and the afterlife. Some description of festivals including the Sumerian New Year Festival and the Babylonian and Assyrian Evil Days and New Year (Akitu) Festival.

DEWEY: 299.9 LC: BL 1600.R513 ISBN 0-664-20953-X

♦ 474 ♦

The White Goddess: A Historical Grammar of Poetic Myth. **Amended and enlarged edition. Robert Graves. New York: Farrar, Straus and Giroux, 1966. 511 pp. Index.**

Exploration of the early European Goddess religions. Identifies archetypes of the White Goddess and her son as they appear in the guises of different cultural traditions, and argues that these mythic themes continued to inspire poets of the West long after the religious cults became extinct. Special emphasis on Celtic and Welsh mythology and lore.

DEWEY: 809.1 LC: PN 1077 G7 ISBN 0-374-28932-8

♦ 475 ♦

The Winter Solstice. **Ellen Jackson. Illustrated by Jan Davey Ellis. Brookfield, CT: Millbrook Press, 1994. 28 pp.**

Tells how ancient people celebrated the winter solstice. Introduces Celtic, Roman, Scandinavian, Incan, Hopi and Pueblo beliefs and practices. Retells Cherokee creation story. For young children.

DEWEY: 394. 2 683 LC: GT 4995. W55J33 ISBN 1-56294-400-2

Aztec

♦ 476 ♦

Book of the Gods and Rites and the Ancient Calendar. **Diego Durán. Translated and edited by Fernando Horcasitas and Doris Heyden. Foreword by Miguel León-Portilla. Norman, OK: University of Oklahoma Press, 1971. 502 pp. Illustrated. Bibliography. Glossary.**

Presents a detailed recording of Aztec religious life written in the sixteenth century by Fray Diego Durán, an early Spanish colonizer and missionary. Covers the numerous Aztec gods, their characteristics, powers, idols, ceremonies, and devotees; also describes feast day games and activities. Furnishes detailed account of the Aztec calendar, including descriptions of numerous festivals. Glossary of Nahuatl (Aztec) words.

DEWEY: 299.792 LC: F1219.D9513 ISBN 0-8061-0889-4

♦ 477 ♦

The Jade Steps: A Ritual Life of the Aztecs. **Burr Cartwright Brundage. Foreword by Arthur J. O. Anderson. Salt Lake City, UT: University of Utah Press, 1985. 280 pp. Illustrated. Appendices. Bibliography. Index.**

Professor of history unravels the complex lore connecting the Aztec gods, rituals, festivals, and calendar. Explains the Aztec calendar and almanac and the cycles of time they created. Describes places of worship and sacrifice, ceremonies, images of the gods and their function, priests and their roles, festivals and their themes. Appendices provide a synopsis of 14 fixed-day and 14 movable-day festivals.

DEWEY: 299.78 LC: F1219.76 R45 B77 ISBN 0-87480-247-4

Celtic and Northern European

♦ 478 ♦

The Avebury Cycle. **Michael Dames. Second edition. London: Thames and Hudson, Ltd., 1996. 240 pp. Illustrated. Bibliography. Index.**

Argues that the Neolithic stone monuments at Avebury, England, formed a complex of ceremonial settings. Proposes that Neolithic peoples used these monuments to stage a year-long series of celebrations of the agricultural cycle and the human life cycle, symbolized in images of the Goddess. Some reference to modern British folk customs and celebrations. Illustrated with many black-and-white photos and diagrams.

ISBN 0-500-27886-5

♦ 479 ♦

The Celtic Book of Days: A Guide to Celtic Wisdom and Spirituality. **Caitlín Matthews. Rochester, VT: Destiny Books, 1995. 128 pp. Illustrated. Bibliography. Index.**

Gives a Celtic holiday, saint's day, legend, mythic character, belief, custom, prophecy, riddle, blessing, prayer, or invocation for every day of the year. Uses Pagan and Christian materials. The four Celtic quarterly festivals, Samhain, Imbolc, Beltane, and Lughnasadh, provide themes for the four seasons. Beautifully illustrated with color reproductions of Celtic drawings, motifs, and designs, as well as more recent artwork depicting Celtic themes.

DEWEY: 299.16 LC: BL 900 M464 ISBN 0-82981-604-X

♦ 480 ♦

The Celtic Druid's Year: Seasonal Cycles of the Ancient Celts. **John King. London: Blandford, 1994. 240 pp. Illustrated. Bibliography. Index.**

Gives an overview about what is known of Celtic society and its Druidic religion. Summarizes history of the Celts from ancient to medieval times, notes similarities with and differences from other ancient peoples, describes the roles and functions of the Druids, and recounts Celtic mythology. Reconstructs the annual ceremonies associated with the eight major seasonal festivals: Beltane, midsummer solstice, Lughnasa (Lughnasadh), autumn equinox, Samhain, midwinter solstice, Imbolc, and vernal equinox. Describes what is known of the astronomy, mathematics, and calendar calculations of the Druids, linking them to Pythagorean mathematics, astronomy, and philosophy, and explaining their central role in determining the timing and meaning of the eight major festivals.

LC: DA 141 K55 ISBN 0-7137-2461-7

♦ 481 ♦

The Celtic Year: A Month-by-Month Celebration of Celtic Christian Festivals and Sites. **Shirley Toulson. Shaftesbury, Dorset, England: Element Books, 1993. 259 pp. Illustrated. Maps. Bibliography. Indexes.**

Introduces the reader to more than 200 Celtic saints from the first millennium. Book divided into the four Celtic seasons and the twelve Gregorian months. Presents an apostle for each season and elements of Celtic belief and practice for each month. Saints and other holy figures listed by date of veneration. Entries describe their life and legends and identify churches, shrines and other places of worship associated with them. Poems, blessings, maps showing locations of sites, Celtic designs and drawings interspersed throughout.

LC: BR754 A1T68 ISBN 1-85230-361

♦ 482 ♦

Earth Rites: Fertility Practices in Pre-Industrial Britain. **Janet Bord and Colin Bord. London: Granada Publishing Ltd., 1982. 273 pp. Illustrated. Bibliography. Index.**

Documents ancient fertility rites and celebrations in the British Isles, many of which continued until Industrial times. Includes description of traditional seasonal rituals and festivals, linking them in theme to ancient fertility practices.

DEWEY: 392. 0942 LC: BL 600 ISBN 0-246-11431-2

♦ 483 ♦

The Festival of Lughnasa: A Study of the Survival of the Celtic Festival of the Beginning of the Harvest. **Máire MacNeill. London: Oxford University Press, 1962. 697 pp. Illustrated. Appendices. Indexes.**

Comprehensive study of the surviving folklore of the ancient Celtic festival of Lughnasa (Lughnasadh). Author sifts through responses to a 1942 survey by the Irish Folklore Commission, identifying and explaining themes. Covers names, dates, and legends associated with the festival, as well as manner and sites of observance. Concludes with a summary of the probable rites and beliefs of the ancient festival. Focus is on Ireland, but a chapter is devoted to similar beliefs and practices in Great Britain and France. Appendices provide the texts of the Lughnasadh legends, a list and brief description of the Holy Well Assemblies, a list of local Lughnasadh and Lammas Fairs, a list of festival names, and the text of the original questionnaire. Separate indexes for days and seasons; beliefs, customs, and legends; characters in legends; places; historical references; and texts and authorities cited.

DEWEY: 398.30415 M169

Chinese

♦ 484 ♦

Festivals and Songs of Ancient China. **Marcel Granet. London: George Routledge and Sons, Ltd., 1932. 281 pp. Appendices.**

Analyzes the poetry of the ancient Chinese *Shih Ching,* or *The Book of Odes,* as a window on popular beliefs and rituals of ancient China. Describes four festivals of ancient China, discusses celebratory practices and locations, and argues that they were essentially seasonal celebrations. Concludes with observations on the expression of deeply rooted elements of Chinese philosophy in festival celebrations.

DEWEY: 915.1G756 fa

♦ 485 ♦

Festivals in Classical China: New Year and Other Annual Observances During the Han Dynasty 206 B.C.-A.D. 220. **Derk Bodde. Princeton, NJ: Princeton University Press, 1975. 439 pp. Illustrated. Bibliography. Index.**

Scholarly study of the festivals of ancient China during the time of the Han Dynasty, with a special emphasis on New Year celebrations. Discusses celebrations, ceremonies, and underlying beliefs, and sheds light on the life of ordinary people in ancient China. Festivals covered include the La Festival (or People's New Year), the Great Exorcism, the Lunar New Year (or Official New Year), the Winter Solstice (or Solar New Year), Spring's Beginning (or the Seasonal New Year), Plowing, the Supreme Intermediary, the First Sericulturalist, the Lustration Festival, various summer festivals, the Day of Concealment, the Ch'u-Liu Sacrifice, the Registration of Households, the Grand Military Review, Entertaining the Aged, and Competitive Hunting.

DEWEY: 394.2 6921 LC: GT4883 A2 B63 ISBN 0-621-03098-7

♦ 486 ♦

The Ghost Festival in Medieval China. **Stephen F. Teiser. Princeton, NJ: Princeton University Press, 1988. 275 pp. Bibliography. Glossary. Index.**

Scholarly analysis of the religious and social importance of the Ghost Festival in medieval China (approximately fifth through tenth centuries). Discusses the ways in which various medieval texts portray the Ghost Festival and analyzes its founding legend. Explores cosmology, ancient history and precedents, and social functions served by the festival. Provides a character glossary of Japanese, Korean, and Chinese words.

LC: BQ 5720 U6 T45 ISBN 0-691-05525-4

Egyptian

♦ 487 ♦

Egyptian Festivals: Enactments of Religious Renewal. **C. J. Bleeker. Leiden, Netherlands: E. J. Brill, 1967. 158 pp. Bibliography. Index.**

A scholarly analysis of ancient Egyptian religiosity as it is revealed in their festivals. Partially reconstructs festivals using ancient texts and inscriptions. Special emphasis on the festival of Sokaris, the festivals of the king, and the festivals of the dead.

LC: BL1 N972

Greek

♦ 488 ♦

The Attic Festivals of Demeter and Their Relation to the Agricultural Year. **Allaire Chandor Brumfield. Salem, NH: Ayer Company, 1981. 257 pp. Appendix. Bibliography. Indexes.**

Scholarly investigation of the various Attic (ancient Greek) festivals of Demeter. Covers Proerosia, Thesmophoria, Haloa, Cloaia, the Lesser Mysteries, various harvest festivals, Skira, and the Eleusinian Mysteries. Argues that these festivals attempted to ritually ensure a good harvest and consolidate community attention on important moments of the agricultural cycle. Appendix provides a glossary of Greek agricultural words. Gives general index and index of Greek words.

DEWEY: 292.38 LC: BL 820. C5 B8 ISBN 0-881443-030-7

♦ 489 ♦

Cretan Cults and Festivals. **R. F. Willetts. London: Routledge and Kegan Paul, 1962. 362 pp. Appendix. Bibliography. Indexes.**

Scholarly summation of what is known about the history and significance of the religious cults of ancient Crete, including their festivals. Provides background information on Cretan society, economy, and relations with other ancient civilizations, including those of the Greek mainland. Emphasis is on exploring the religious cults, although some information on religious festivals and the Cretan calendar is also provided.

LC: BL 793 C7W5

♦ 490 ♦

Dance in Ancient Greece. **Lillian B. Lawler. Middletown, CT: Wesleyan University Press, 1964. 160 pp. Illustrated. Index.**

Furnishes an overview of dance in ancient Greece. Discusses its historical development as well as social and cultural functions, and describes the movements, the dancers, and dance events. Includes a chapter on dance at shrines and festivals, but much information on ritual and ceremonial dances, such as those performed during the Eleusinian Mysteries and those connected with the worship of Dionysus, scattered throughout. References given in endnotes. Illustrated with black-and-white photos of ancient artwork depicting dancers.

LC: GV 1611 L37

♦ 491 ♦

Eleusis and the Eleusinian Mysteries. **George E. Mylonas. Princeton, NJ: Princeton University Press, 1961. 346 pp. Illustrated. Appendix. Bibliography. Glossary. Index.**

Offers a history and description of the Eleusinian Mystery cult, their temple, their sacred stories, and their celebrations. Reconstructs what is known of these secret rites from historical and archeological record. Emphasizes history and archeology of the temple compound, covering period from about 1500 B.C. to about 400 A.D. Appendix reviews writings of early Christian Fathers on the Mysteries. Illustrations include a general plan of the temple compound, plus black-and-white photos of artifacts, sculpture, and the remains of buildings.

DEWEY: 292.65

♦ 492 ♦

Festivals of the Athenians. **H. W. Parke. Ithaca, NY: Cornell University Press, 1977. 208 pp. Illustrated. Map. Bibliography. Index.**

Describes festivals celebrated in ancient Athens. Part one presents, in chronological order, the festivals associated with a specific calendar date. Part two covers local and movable festivals. Gives background information on Athenian religion and daily life. Includes a calendar of Athenian festivals and a map of Athens showing principal sanctuaries.

DEWEY: 949.5 P 237f ISBN 0-8014-1054-1

♦ 493 ♦

Greek Folk Religion. **Martin P. Nilsson. Foreword by Arthur Darby Nock. 1940. Reprint. Philadelphia, PA: University of Pennsylvania Press, 1987. 166 pp. Illustrated. Index.**

Gives an overview of the folk religious beliefs and practices of ancient Greece. Describes rural customs and festivals, including Thesmophoria, Thalysia, Kalamaia, Thargelia, Anthesteria, Haloa, Athenian All Souls' Day, vintage festivals, the panegyreis, and more. Chapter devoted to the Eleusinian Mysteries. Contrasts rural and urban life and religion. Discusses the role of seers and oracles, the gods and rites of home and hearth, various religious movements, and beliefs regarding the afterlife.

DEWEY: 292 ISBN 0-8122-1034-4

♦ 494 ♦

Olympic Games in Ancient Greece. **Shirley Glubok and Alfred Tamarin. New York: Harper and Row Publishers, 1976. 116 pp. Illustrated. Index.**

Portrays the daily sequence of events which characterized the Olympic Games of ancient Greece, from the journey to Olympia to the victors' banquet on the final day of the Games. Describes athletic events and competitions. Illustrated with black-and-white photos of ancient Greek artworks depicting athletes, athletic events, and the remains of the Olympic compound. Gives chronology of important events in the history of the ancient and modern Olympics. Suitable for older children.

DEWEY: 796.4 8 LC: GV 23.G55 ISBN 0-06-022047-3

♦ 495 ♦

The Olympic Games: The First Thousand Years. **M. I. Finley and H. W. Pleket. New York: The Viking Press, 1976. 140 pp. Illustrated. Index.**

A many-faceted account of the Olympic Games of ancient Greece. Describes political, social, and religious aspects of the Games, sporting events, facilities, rules, judging, athletes and their preparations, patrons, and spectators. Illustrations show the Olympic compound and reproduce Greek artwork depicting the Games or other Greek athletic events.

DEWEY: 796.4 8 LC: GV 23.F56 ISBN 0-670-52406-9

♦ 496 ♦

The Thread of Ariadne: The Labyrinth of the Calendar of Minos. **Charles F. Herberger. New York: Philosophical Library, 1972. 158 pp. Appendix. Bibliography.**

Author uses analysis of myth, symbols, his knowledge of ancient Cretan society, and his interpretation of an ancient fresco to recreate the ritual calendar of ancient Crete.

DEWEY: 292 H414t ISBN 8022-2089-4

Incan

♦ 497 ♦

Astronomy and Empire in the Ancient Andes: The Cultural Origins of Inca Skywatching. **Brian S. Bauer and David S. P. Dearborn. Austin, TX: University of Texas Press, 1995. 220 pp. Illustrated. Tables. Appendix. Bibliography. Glossary. Index.**

An archeologist and an astronomer team up to discuss the relationship between Inca astronomy, their calendar and ceremonial systems, and the expansion of the Inca empire. Summarizes Inca astronomy and the Inca calendar. Explores the connection between the use of the sun as a symbol of Inca rule and the development of Inca skywatching.

DEWEY: 520.98 09024 LC: F 3429.3 CI4B38 ISBN 0-292-70829-7

Japanese

♦ 498 ♦

Five Sacred Festivals of Ancient Japan: Their Symbolism and Historical Development. **U. A. Casal. Rutland, VT: Charles E. Tuttle Company, 1967. 114 pp. Illustrated. Index.**

Describes five Japanese festivals, traces the history of their celebrations and symbols as far back as ancient times, and offers explanations of their cultural significance. Covers the New Year Festival, the Girls' Festival, the Boys' Festival, the Star Festival, and the Chrysanthemum Festival.

LC: GT 4884 A2C3

Near Eastern

♦ 499 ♦

Babylonian and Assyrian Religion. **S. H. Hooke. Norman, OK: University of Oklahoma Press, 1963. 131 pp. Illustrated. Appendix. Bibliography. Index.**

Summarizes what is known about the religion of ancient Babylon and Assyria. Describes Babylonian and Assyrian gods, their myths, cults, and rituals, as well as the duties of priests, divination, astrology, and everyday religious practice. Information on religious festivals threaded throughout, with particular emphasis on the Babylonian New Year Festival. Appendix reproduces texts of religious rituals, including the ritual texts for the Babylonian New Year Festival.

DEWEY: 299.2

♦ 500 ♦

Myth and Ritual in the Ancient Near East: An Archeological and Documentary Study. **E. O. James. London: Thames and Hudson, 1958. 352 pp. Bibliography. Index.**

Examines the function of and relationship between myth and ritual in many regions and cultures of the ancient Near East. Treats Egypt, Mesopotamia, Anatolia, Greece, Israel, Syria, and Palestine. Reviews principal myths and rituals, including many performed for festivals. Includes chart summarizing the chronological sequence of various civilizations and historical periods, their central myths, and rituals. References cited in endnotes.

DEWEY: 290 J27m

♦ 501 ♦

Thespis: Ritual, Myth, and Drama in the Ancient Near East. **Theodor H. Gaster. Second edition, revised. Foreword by Gilbert Murray. Garden City, NY: Anchor Books, 1961. 515 pp. Bibliography. Indexes.**

Explores the connection between surviving mythological texts of ancient Near Eastern cultures and their seasonal rituals and festivals. Particular attention given to the ancient Egyptians, Hittites, and Canaanites. Also examines writings of the biblical Jews and ancient Greeks. Identifies basic pattern of seasonal celebration common to many times and cultures and discusses its meaning. Provides index of motifs and index of subjects and authors.

LC: BL 96. G3

Roman

♦ 502 ♦

Festivals and Ceremonies of the Roman Republic. **H. H. Scullard. Ithaca, NY: Cornell University Press, 1981. 288 pp. Illustrated. Index.**

Describes numerous holidays and ceremonies of the Republic. Part one provides introduction to Roman religion. Part two gives historical background of festivals and identifies (when possible) deity or event celebrated, manner of observance, legends and temple sites associated with the celebration, and references made to the festival in ancient texts. Part three covers other ceremonies, such as those connected with triumphs, ovations, and meetings of the Senate. Provides a map of Rome identifying sites of temples and buildings, a further reading list, a list of Roman calendars and festivals, a complete Roman calendar, and a list of temples and their dates of construction.

LC: GT 4852. R6. S35 ISBN 0-8014-1402-4

♦ 503 ♦

The Roman Festivals of the Period of the Republic: An Introduction to the Study of the Religion of the Romans. **W. Warde Fowler. London: Macmillan and Company, 1899. 373 pp. Indexes.**

Reports information on Roman holidays derived from a study of Roman calendar fragments and Latin and ancient Greek texts. Gives dates of festivals, deity or event honored, popular festivities, manner of religious observance, and history of the holiday, when known. Also introduces Roman calendar and its history. Separate indexes provided for subjects, Latin words, Latin authors quoted, and Greek authors quoted.

LC: DG 125 F 78

♦ 504 ♦

The Romans and Their Gods in the Age of Augustus. **R. M. Ogilvie. New York: W. W. Norton and Company, 1969. 135 pp. Bibliography. Index.**

Provides an introduction to religious belief and practice in ancient Rome. Chapters cover the gods, prayer, sacrifice, festivals, private devotions, priests, and religion during the reign of Augustus. Gives list of classical authors cited in text, their dates, and works.

LC: BL 802 O36 ISBN 393-05399-7

Asia

General Works

♦ 505 ♦

Celebrate! In Southeast Asia. **Joe Viesti and Diane Hall. New York: Lothrop, Lee and Shepard Books, 1996. 30 pp. Illustrated.**

Describes the celebration of 11 Southeast Asian festivals in words and in many color photos. Covers Songkran, or the New Year Festival, and Surin, or Elephant Round-up (from Thailand); Thaipusam, or Hindu Day of Atonement (from Malaysia); the Mooncake, or Mid-Autumn, Festival (from Singapore); the Kesada Offering and cremation ceremonies (from Indonesia); Ati-Atihan and the Apalit River Festival, or the Feast of St. Peter and St. Paul (from the Philippines); Tet, or Vietnamese New Year (from Vietnam); the That Luang Festival (from Laos); and Chaul Chhnaim, or Khmer New Year (from Cambodia). For children.

DEWEY: 394.2 6959 LC: GT 4876.5 V54 ISBN 0-688-13488-2

♦ 506 ♦

Festivals in Asia. **Asian Copublication Programme Series Two, Sponsored by the Asian Cultural Centre for Unesco. Tokyo, Japan: Kodansha International, Ltd. 1975. Distributed in the United States by Harper and Row Publishers, New York. 66 pp. Illustrated.**

Presents 10 children's stories about 10 Asian festivals. Covers Chinese New Year in Singapore, the Girls' Festival and the Boys' Festival in Japan, New Year in Bangladesh, the Water Festival in Burma, New Year in Cambodia, New Year in Laos, New Year in Sri Lanka, and May celebrations in the Philippines. Stories describe children's participation in festival celebrations. Illustrated with color drawings.

DEWEY: 394.26 ISBN 0-87011-265-1

♦ 507 ♦

More Festivals in Asia. **Asian Copublication Programme Series Two, Sponsored by the Asian Cultural Centre for Unesco. Tokyo, Japan: Kodansha International, Ltd. 1975. Distributed in the United States by Harper and Row Publishers, New York. 66 pp. Illustrated.**

Presents 10 children's stories about 10 Asian festivals. Includes Tan-O Day in Korea, Id-al-Fitr in Pakistan, Lebaran in Indonesia, Hari Raya Puasa in Malaysia, the Mid-Autumn Festival in Vietnam, Dasain in Nepal, Diwali in India, Loy Krathong in Thailand, and the Buzkashi Game in Afghanistan. Stories describe children's participation in festival celebrations. Illustrated with color drawings.

DEWEY: 394.26 ISBN 0-87011-273-2

China

♦ 508 ♦

Annual Customs and Festivals in Peking. **Second edition, revised. Tun Li-Ch'en. Translated by Derk Bodde. Hong Kong: Hong Kong University Press, 1965. 147 pp. Appendices. Bibliography. Index.**

Describes more than 100 customs, festivals, seasonal occurrences and events, civic and religious rites, and items of folklore associated with dates or months of the year. Arranged in calendar order by Chinese month. Written around 1900. Appendices introduce the Chinese calendar and traditional Chinese weights and measures, list major Chinese festivals, give chronology of Chinese dynasties, concordances of Chinese and Gregorian calendars for 1957-1984, and English translations of Chinese terms appearing in the text.

LC: GT4883 P4 T8

♦ 509 ♦

A Book of Chinese Festivals. **Judith Karen Gee. Illustrated by Chen Zhi Huang. Manitoba, Canada: Steam RR Publications and Chingee Publications, 1989. 27 pp. Glossary.**

Describes the festivities, foods, and legends associated with four Chinese festivals. Covers the Spring Festival (or Chinese New Year), the Lantern Festival, the Dragon Boat Festival, and the Mid-Autumn Festival. Gives glossary of Chinese and English words. Colorful paintings illustrate. For young children.

DEWEY: 394.26951 LC: GT 4883.A2 G43 ISBN 0-9692499-4-2

♦ 510 ♦

Chinese Creeds and Customs. **V. R. Burkhardt. Three volumes in one. Tapei, Taiwan: Book World Co., 1958. Volume one, 181 pp., index i-v. Appendices. Bibliography. Illustrated. Volume two, 201 pp., index i-ix. Appendices. Bibliography. Illustrated. Volume three, 164 pp., index i-vii. Appendices. Bibliography. Illustrated.**

A comprehensive collection of Chinese folk practices and beliefs, including a consideration of the Chinese calendar, religious beliefs and customs, symbols, legends, the folklore of animals, spirits, foods, places, and much more. Covers festivals and other celebrations. Appendices include a list of the 24 segments of the Chinese year, the 10 celestial stems and 12 earthly branches, and a table of Chinese temples that lists each temple's locale, god(s) worshipped, and date founded.

LC: DS721 B8

♦ 511 ♦

Chinese Festivals. **Wolfram Eberhard. Taipei, Taiwan: Orient Cultural Service, 1972. 137 pp. Illustrated.**

Offers description and analysis of seven popular Chinese festivals: the New Year's festival, Ch'ing Ming, the Dragon Boat Festival, the Weaving Maid and the Cowherd, the Feast of the Souls, the Mid-Autumn Festival, and Sending the Winter Dress. Outlines the main features of each festival, reviews its history and folklore, discusses cultural themes celebrated, identifies religious and mythological aspects of the festival, and considers festival's meaning in the context of Chinese culture.

DEWEY: 398.33 E16

♦ 512 ♦

Chinese Festivals in Hong Kong. **Joan Law and Barbara E. Ward. Hong Kong: South China Morning Post Ltd., 1982. 95 pp. Illustrated. Glossary. Index.**

Provides an overview of 27 traditional Chinese festivals celebrated in Hong Kong. Entries explain the festival's significance, retell associated legends, and describe important customs, foods, and festivities; entries also indicate locations of festivals celebrated in Hong Kong and give transportation tips. Furnishes festival calendar, map of Hong Kong with festival locations marked, and further reading list. Illustrated with 85 color plates.

DEWEY: 394.2 L412c ISBN 962-10-0002-5

♦ 513 ♦

Chinese Festivals in Malaya. **Dorothy Lo and Leon Comber. Singapore: Eastern Universities Press Ltd., 1958. 66 pp. Illustrated. Bibliography. Indexes.**

Reviews the customs, legends, and foods of the major Chinese festivals celebrated in Malaya. Covers Chinese New Year, Ch'ing Ming, the Dragon Boat Festival, the Feast of the Seven Sisters (the Weaving Maid and the Cowherd), the Feast of the Hungry Ghosts, the Mid-Autumn Festival, the Double Ninth Festival, and the Winter Solstice Festival. Gives Chinese character index and general index.

LC: GT 4879 L6

♦ 514 ♦

The Chinese New Year. **Cheng Hou-Tien. New York: Holt, Rinehart and Winston, 1976. 29 pp. Illustrated.**

Tells how the Chinese New Year is celebrated. Describes preparations, observances, customs, foods, festivities, and lore. Includes description of the Lantern Festival. Gives Chinese zodiac signs for the years 1977 to 1988. Scissor-cut illustrations. For children.

DEWEY: 394.2 683 LC: GT 4905.C45 ISBN 0-03-017511-9

♦ 515 ♦

Chinese New Year: Fact and Folklore. **William C. Hu. Foreword by Leonard Woodcock. Ann Arbor, MI: Ars Ceramica, Ltd., 1991. 400 pp. Illustrated. Appendix.**

Detailed coverage of the history, folklore, foods, and customs of the Chinese New Year season. Explains the traditional Chinese calendar and the 12-year zodiac cycle, describes celebratory foods and activities, gives recipes, discusses holiday customs in historical perspective, relates holiday folklore, depicts holiday preparations, interprets holiday symbols, and portrays holiday decorations for home and street. Appendix lists holiday superstitions, couplets, and epigrams and provides a calendar of Gregorian and Chinese dates for Chinese New Year from 1900 to 2050. Also gives Chinese zodiac signs for those years.

DEWEY: 641.3 H8 LC: DS 727. H8 ISBN 0-89344-037-X

♦ 516 ♦

Chinese Traditional Festivals. **Marie-Luise Latsch. Singapore, Malaysia: Graham Brash, 1985. 103 pp. Appendix.**

Describes seven traditional Chinese festivals, discussing their history and portraying their customs and celebrations in ancient and modern times. Covers the Spring Festival (or Lunar New Year Festival), the Lantern Festival, the Pure Brightness Festival (Ch'ing Ming), the Dragon Boat Festival, the Mid-Autumn Festival, the Kitchen God Festival, and Lunar New Year's Eve celebrations. Also reviews historical development of the traditional Chinese calendar. Appendix gives brief descriptions of 15 festivals of China's minority ethnic groups.

DEWEY: 394.2 L355c LC: GT 4883 A2L38 ISBN 9971-947-80-3

♦ 517 ♦

Folk Customs at Traditional Chinese Festivals. **Qi Xing. Translated by Ren Jiazhen. Illustrated by Yang Guanghua. Beijing, China: Foreign Languages Press, 1988. 125 pp. Appendices.**

Describes customary festivities for 13 traditional Chinese festivals, including the Spring Festival (Chinese New Year), the Lantern Festival, Spring Dragon Day, Clear and Bright Festival (Ch'ing Ming), Dragon Boat Festival, Heaven's Gift Day, Double Seventh Night (the Weaving Maid and the Cowherd), Middle of the Year Festival, Mid-Autumn Festival, Double Ninth Day, Eighth Day of the Twelfth Month, Kitchen God's Day, and New Year's Eve. Also gives brief descriptions of 10 minor festivals. Covers major festivals of 15 ethnic minority groups, for example Tibetans and Mongolians, as well as 20 minor ethnic festivals. Appendices explain various elements of the traditional Chinese calendar systems, including the Twenty-four Solar Terms, the Ten Heavenly Stems and Twelve Earthly Branches, list modern China's commemorative days, and provide a brief chronology of periods in Chinese history.

LC: GT 4883 H74 ISBN 0-8351-1593-3

♦ 518 ♦

Folkways in China. **Lewis Hodous. London: Arthur Probsthain, 1929. 248 pp. Illustrated. Bibliography. Index.**

Author relates his travels to more than 20 festivals in China, covering history, lore, superstitions, customs, and foods. List of Chinese names. (NR)

DEWEY: 394.2 6951 LC: DS721.H55 ISBN 0-404-56935-8

♦ 519 ♦

Mooncakes and Hungry Ghosts: Festivals of China. **Carol Stepanchuk and Charles Wong. San Francisco, CA: China Books and Periodicals, 1991. 146 pp. Illustrated. Appendices. Bibliography.**

Offers a wealth of information on the celebration of nine major Chinese festivals: New Year; Dragon Boat Festival; Mid-Autumn Festival; Clear Brightness Festival (Ch'ing Ming); Feast of the Hungry Ghosts; the Weaving Maid and the Cowherd; Tian Hou, Protectress of Seafarers; and Double Yang Day. Describes foods, festivities, folklore, poetry, deities, beliefs, and common practices. Also gives brief descriptions of 12 festivals celebrated by China's ethnic minorities. Appendices explain the Chinese calendar, list birthdays and festivals in chronological order, introduce Chinese symbols of celebration, describe decorated altars, present glossary of Chinese characters and chronology of Chinese dynasties. Illustrated with color and black-and-white photos.

DEWEY: 394.2695 ISBN 0-8351-7481-9

♦ 520 ♦

The Moon Year: A Record of Chinese Customs and Festivals. **Juliet Bredon and Igor Mitrophanow. Shanghai, China: Kelly and Walsh, Ltd., 1927. 522 pp. Illustrated. Bibliography. Index.**

Describes a multitude of practices, beliefs, and legends associated with Chinese festivals, calendar dates, or times of year. Explains the Chinese calendar, characterizes important deities, spirits, and religious beliefs, and reviews imperial ceremonies. Devotes one chapter to each month, its festivals, lore, and customs. Includes astronomical chart of the Chinese year.

DEWEY: 915.1 B831

♦ 521 ♦

Red Eggs and Dragon Boats: Celebrating Chinese Festivals. **Carol Stepanchuk. Berkeley, CA: Pacific View Press, 1994. 48 pp. Illustrated.**

Describes the celebration of six Chinese festivals: the New Year Festival, the Lantern Festival, Clear Brightness Festival (Ch'ing Ming), Dragon Boat Festival, the Moon Festival (the Mid-Autumn Festival), and One Month celebrations for new babies. Describes customs, beliefs, foods, and entertainments; retells legends; introduces elements of Chinese culture; gives recipes. Illustrated with color photos of Chinese folk art.

DEWEY: 394.2683 ISBN 1-881896-08-0

India

♦ 522 ♦

Festivals, Fairs and Customs of Himachal Pradesh. **Mian Goverdhan Singh. New Delhi, India: Indus Publishing Company, 1992. 128 pp. Illustrated. Appendices. Bibliography. Glossary. Index.**

Gives an overview of the history, culture, and festive occasions of Himachal Pradesh, a Himalayan state in northern India. Covers more than 22 festivals and 16 fairs, reviewing celebrated beliefs and customary practices. Also provides information on birth and marriage customs. Appendices give a calendar of festivals and a calendar of fairs, with both Indian and Gregorian dates. Black-and-white photos illustrate.

LC: GT 4876 A3 H547 ISBN 81-85182-64-7

♦ 523 ♦

Festivals of India. **Brijendra Nath Sharma. New Delhi, India: Abhinav Publications, 1978. 156 pp. Illustrated. Bibliography. Index.**

Provides brief descriptions of 185 modern and 44 ancient and medieval festivals of India. Covers local and nationally celebrated holidays. Includes festivals of minority religious groups, such as Christians, Sikhs, Buddhists, and Jews. Gives dates according to the traditional Indian calendar. Amply illustrated with black-and-white plates of Indian works of art depicting gods, myths, and celebrations, as well as photos of contemporary festivals.

LC: GT 4876 A2 S5

♦ 524 ♦

Festive India. **Photographs by Gurmeet Thukral, text by Arun Sanon. New Delhi, India: Frank Brothers and Company, 1987. 126 pp. Appendix.**

Portrays the celebration of 26 Indian festivals in words and color photos. Emphasizes Hindu holidays, but also covers some Buddhist, Sikh, Jain, Muslim and Christian holidays, as well as seasonal festivals. Explains festivals' origin and meaning, describes celebrations, customs, and rituals, retells legends and stories. Appendix gives calendar of 49 Indian festivals, listing festival name and when and where celebrated.

LC: GT 4876 A2 T491

♦ 525 ♦

India Celebrates! **Jane Werner Watson. Illustrated by Susan Andersen. Champaign, IL: Garrard Publishing Company 1974. 96 pp. Index.**

Describes how people in India celebrate eight Hindu holidays and five seasonal ones. Covers Shivaratri, Holi, the Marriage of Meenakshi, Rath Yatra, the Sun Festival (at Konarak), Janmastami, Dussehra, Durga Puja, Diwali, Republic Day, Pongal, spring celebrations, rain celebrations, and Onam (in

Kerala). Mentions minority faiths and their major holidays. Gives pronunciation guide. For children.

DEWEY: 394.2 6954 LC: GT 4876.A2 W37 ISBN 0-8116-4950-4

♦ 526 ♦

Religious Festivals in South India and Sri Lanka. **Guy R. Welbon and Glenn E. Yocum, eds. New Delhi, India: Manohar, 1982. 341 pp. Index.**

Presents a collection of scholarly articles by various authorities on Hindu festivals of south India and Sri Lanka. First article, "The Hindu Religious Calendar" by Karen L. Merrey, gives explanation of the Hindu calendar. Also includes "Festivals in Pancaratra Literature" by H. Daniel Smith; "The Cycle of Festivals at Parthasarathi Temple" by James L. Martin; "The Candala's Song" by Guy R. Welbon; "Two Citra Festivals in Madurai" by D. Dennis Hudson; "Chronometry, Cosmology, and the Festival Calendar of the Murukan Cult" by Fred W. Clothey; "Mahasivaratri: The Saiva Festival of Repentance" by J. Bruce Long; "The Festival Interlude: Some Anthropological Observations" by Suzanne Hanchett; "The End Is the Beginning: A Festival Chain in Andhra Pradesh" by Jane M. Christian; "Kalam Eluttu: Art and Ritual in Kerala" by Clifford R. Jones; "The Kataragama and Kandy Asala Peraharas: Juxtaposing Religious Elements in Sri Lanka" by Donald K. Swearer; and "An-keliya: A Literary-Historical Approach" by Glenn E. Yocum. References cited in endnotes.

LC: BL 1239.72 R441

♦ 527 ♦

Through the Year in India. **Carol Ogle and John Ogle. London: Batsford Academic and Educational Ltd., 1983. 72 pp. Illustrated. Index.**

Supplies an overview of life in India. For each month, provides information on the history, economy, politics, family life, holidays, and religious diversity of India. Illustrated with black-and-white photos. Gives further reading list. For young teens.

DEWEY: 954 ISBN 0-7134-1227-5

♦ 528 ♦

Traditions of Indian Folk Dance. **Kapila Vatsyayan. New Delhi, India: Indian Book Company, 1976. 280 pp. Illustrated.**

Outlines the many local folk dance traditions of India. Tells when, how, and by whom dance is performed, describes motions, music, costumes, and settings, sometimes mentions related ceremonies. Many dances are seasonal or performed for festivals. Illustrated with black-and-white photos and diagrams. Further reading list.

LC: GV 1693V39

Indonesia

♦ 529 ♦

Dance and Drama in Bali. **Beryl De Zoete and Walter Spies. Preface by Arthur Waley. 1938. Reprint. London: Oxford University Press, 1973. 343 pp. Illustrated. Index.**

Detailed description of the costumes, movements, and stories told by the numerous dramatic dances of Bali, many of which are performed in religious or festival contexts. Includes a chapter on ceremonial dances. Illustrated with black-and-white photos.

LC: GV 1703. B3 D4

♦ 530 ♦

Ring of Fire. **Lawrence Blair and Lorne Blair. Toronto, Canada: Bantam Books, 1988. 272 pp. Illustrated. Bibliography. Index.**

Companion volume to documentary film on the diverse peoples and wildlife of Indonesia. Describes and photographs the Pasola rite of Sumba Island.

DEWEY: 306. 09598 LC: GN 635. I65 B65 ISBN 0-553-05232-2

Japan

♦ 531 ♦

Ainu Creed and Cult. **Neil Gordon Munro. Additional chapter, preface, and editing by B. Z. Seligman. Introduction by H. Watanabe. New York: Columbia University Press, 1963. 182 pp. Illustrated. Appendices. Bibliography. Glossary. Index.**

Describes the religious beliefs and practices of the Ainu, a culturally distinct minority group of northern Japan. Covers a variety of customs and beliefs, including those associated with spirits, inau (wooden wands), effigies, and the home. Describes the Feast of All Souls (or the Feast of Falling Tears), and many rituals associated with house building, house warming, exorcism, hunting, fishing, death, and burial. Also give chapter on social organization. Appendix two summarizes the Bear Ceremony. Illustrated with black-and-white photos.

LC: BL 2370 A5 M8

♦ 532 ♦

Calendar of Annual Events in Japan. **S. Uenoda. Tokyo, Japan: Tokyo News Service, Ltd., 1954. 293 pp. Illustrated.**

Lists more than 100 annually occurring holidays, festivals, customs, commemorations, ceremonies, and seasonal events in Japan. Gives brief description, often including history of the celebration. Black-and-white photos illustrate.

LC: GT 4884 A2 U3

♦ 533 ♦

Celebrate Japan. **Roxsane Tiernan. Illustrated by Kuniko Iyama. Vancouver, Canada: Maple Leaf Publishing, 1990. 59 pp.**

Tells how Japan's major festivals are celebrated. Covers New Year, Setsubun, the Doll Festival (Girls' Festival), Boys' Festivals (Children's Day, Kodomo-No-Hi), the Star Festival (Tanabata), the Morning Glory Fair (Asagao-Ichi), Obon, the Moon Viewing Ceremony (O-Tsukimi or the Mid-Autumn Festival), the Equinox (O-Higan), Shichi-go-san (the 7-5-3 Festival), and Kariire (the Rice Harvest). Gives foods, customs, lore, and legends. Includes crafts and other activities of celebration. Illustrated with color drawings. Gives listing of annual events in Japan. For children.

DEWEY: 394.2695 ISBN 1-55056-016-6

♦ 534 ♦

Customs and Culture of Okinawa. **Second edition, revised. Gladys Zabilka. Rutland, VT: Bridgeway Press, 1959. 200 pp.**

Provides an overview of Okinawan society and culture. Chapters provide brief introductions to geography, natural environment, history, the people, education, the arts, the economy, indigenous religions, Christianity, festivals, customs, health, places of interest, tales and songs. Festivals covered include New Year, Juriuma, Roundup of the Porpoises, the Doll Festival (or Girls' Festival), the Boys' Festival, Dragon-Boat Races, the Obon Festival, the August Moon Festival (the Mid-Autumn Festival), the Tsunahiki Festival, and the Field Days Festival.

DEWEY: 915.281

♦ 535 ♦

Dolls on Display: Japan in Miniature, Being an Illustrated Commentary on the Girls' Festival and the Boys' Festival. **G. Caiger. Tokyo, Japan: Hokuseido Press, 1934. 141 pp. Illustrated. Appendices.**

Provides detailed descriptions of the dolls, or festival figures, featured in the Girls' Festival and the Boys' Festival. Notes the ways in which they are displayed, their varied costumes, and the sentiments they represent. Black-and-white photos illustrate. Appendices provide additional commentary on Japanese festivals, history, and theater.

DEWEY: 394.3

♦ 536 ♦

Festivals of Japan. **Hal Buell. New York: Dodd, Mead and Company, 1965. 79 pp. Illustrated. Index.**

Describes and photographs customs, ceremonies, costumes, and decorations at Japanese festivals. Covers the Neighborhood Festival, the Buddha's Birthday, Japanese Rodeos, the Dance of the Golden Dragon, the March of the Samurai, the Gion Festival, the Aoi Festivals, various festivals celebrating children, Harvest festivals, the Setsubun Festival, the Snow Festival, the Fireman's Parade, the Hari-Kuyo Festival, and the Tanabata Festival (Star Festival). Generously illustrated with black-and-white photos. For children.

DEWEY: 394.2 6952 LC: GT4884.A2 B8

♦ 537 ♦

Folk Religion in Japan: Continuity and Change. **Ichiro Hori. Joseph M. Kitagawa and Alan L. Miller, eds. Chicago: University of Chicago Press, 1968. 278 pp. Bibliography. Index.**

Outlines Japan's folk religious beliefs and practices, identifying Shinto, Buddhist, Confucian, Taoist, shamanic, and other ancient elements. Special emphasis on Pure Land Buddhist (or Nembutsu) practices, shamanism, and belief in sacred mountains. Festival practices mentioned throughout.

LC: BL 2202 H58

♦ 538 ♦

Japanese Festivals. **Helen Bauer and Sherwin Carlquist. Garden City, NY: Doubleday and Company, Inc., 1965. 224 pp. Illustrated. Map. Index.**

Describes the ceremonies and celebrations of 355 Japanese festivals. Detailed coverage given to the Tenjin Festival, the Aoi Festival (the Hollyhock Festival), the Toshogu Festival (or Sennin-Gyoretsu), the Jidai Festival, the Gion Festival, the Obon Festival, Buddha's Birthday, the Boys' Festival (Children's Day, Tango-no-sekku), the Girls' Festival (Doll Festival), the Tanabata (Star, or Hoshi) Festival, and New Year celebrations. Others listed in calendar order with one-sentence or one-paragraph description. All entries give dates and locations. Also tells the best times and places to view Japanese blossoms. Amply illustrated with black-and-white, as well as some color, photos. Gives pronunciation guide, map showing Japanese prefectures and their capitals, and synopsis of periods in Japanese history.

DEWEY: 915.2

♦ 539 ♦

Japanese Folk Festivals Illustrated. **Hideo Haga. Translated by Fanny Hagin Mayer. Tokyo, Japan: Miura Printing Company, 1970. 223 pp. Illustrated. Map.**

Conveys the spirit of Japan's festivals in words and images. Separate chapters cover folk beliefs and practices, ceremonies, atmosphere, and performances found at festivals. Gives brief description of seasonal festivals, including New Year celebrations, the Flower Festival, the Summer Festival, Obon, and the Harvest Festival. Amply illustrated with color photos. Includes fold-out calendar of 47 Japanese festivals and map of Japan with festival locations marked.

DEWEY: 394.2095 LC: GT 4884 A2 H2813

♦ 540 ♦

Matsuri: World of Japanese Festivals. **Gorazd Vilhar and Charlotte Anderson. Tokyo, Japan: Shufunotomo Co., Ltd., 1994. 160 pp. Illustrated.**

Furnishes a collection of color photos documenting the costumes, decorations, ceremonial objects, makeup, processions, and other activities associated with Japanese festivals. Introductory chapter traces the origins, history, and meaning of Japanese seasonal celebrations and festivals, noting associated legends and beliefs.

DEWEY: 394.2695 V711m ISBN 4-07-976066-3

♦ 541 ♦

The Namahage: A Festival in the Northeast of Japan. **Yoshiko Yamamoto. Foreword by Robert J. Smith. Philadelphia, PA: Institute for the Study of Human Issues, Inc., 1978. 169 pp. Illustrated. Appendices. Bibliography. Index.**

An in-depth study of a single festival, the Namahage (New Year Festival), as it is observed in a village in northeast Japan. Relates festival customs and history, investigates the organization of and attitudes towards the Namahage, and describes similar festivals throughout Japan. Also discusses the social and economic life of the villagers. Foreword considers the decline in communal ritual throughout Japan. Appendices give descriptions of Namahage festival customs and similar customs found in the Ryukyu Islands, the author's questionnaire, genealogical charts of festival maskers, and other annual events in the village.

DEWEY: 394.2 683 LC: GT 4884.034Y35 ISBN 0-915980-66-5

♦ 542 ♦

Spirit and Symbol: The Japanese New Year. **Reiko Mochinaga Brandon and Barbara B. Stephan. Honolulu, HI: Honolulu Academy of Arts, 1994. 144 pp. Illustrated. Bibliography. Index.**

Describes many aspects of New Year celebrations in Japan, including religious practices and observances, popular customs, symbols, decorations, folk arts, food, and clothing. Special attention to sacred symbols; also covers distinct rural celebrations and customs. Profusely illustrated with more than 170 color photographs.

DEWEY: 394.2 614 0952 LC: GT 4905 S65 ISBN 0-937426-24-5

♦ 543 ♦

Through the Year in Japan. **Elizabeth Fusae Thurley. London: Batsford Academic and Educational, 1985. 72 pp. Illustrated. Index.**

Describes Japanese holiday celebrations and gives facts about life in contemporary Japan. Covers New Year, Adults' Day, Risshun (First Day of Spring, Setsubun), National Foundation Day, the Snow Festival, the Girls' Festival, Vernal Equinox Day, Constitution Day, Boys' Day, the Star Festival, the Obon Festival, Respect-for-the-Aged Day, Moon Viewing Night (Mid-Autumn Festival), Autumn Equinox Day, Health and Sport Day, Culture Day, Seven-Five-Three Festival (Shichi-go-san), and Labor Thanksgiving Day. Discusses many aspects of everyday life, such as education, housing, work, food, farming, and the position of women. For older children.

DEWEY: 952. 048 ISBN 0-7134-4819-9

♦ 544 ♦

We Japanese: Being Descriptions of the Customs, Manners, Ceremonies, Festivals, Arts and Crafts of the Japanese Besides Numerous Other Subjects. **Combined edition, three volumes. Volume one written for H. S. K. Yamaguchi by Frederic de Garis, volume two written for H.S.K. Yamaguchi by Atsuharu Sakai, volume three written for K. M.**

Yamaguchi by Atsuharu Sakai. Miyanoshita, Hakone, Japan: Fujiya Hotel, Ltd., 1964. 591 pp. Illustrated. Index.

A compilation of descriptive information concerning Japanese customary practices, manners, festivals, ceremonies, arts, crafts, the calendar system, deities, shrines, legends, symbols, plants, games, foods, religious practices, folk beliefs, and related topics. Illustrated with black-and-white drawings. Festivals covered include New Year, the Girls' Festival, Buddha's Birthday (or Hanamatsuri, the Flower Festival), the Boys' Festival, the Star Festival, the Obon Festival, the Bon-Odori Festival, Shichi-go-san (the 7-5-3 Festival), Miyamairi, Ebisu-ko, Nanakusa (Festival of the Seven Plants), the Tori-no-ichi (or Rake Fair), the Hatsu-uma Festival, O-Eshiki Festival, the Spear Festival, and more.

DEWEY: 952.033

Korea

♦ 545 ♦

Annual Customs of Korea: Notes on the Rites and Ceremonies of the Year. **Choe Saug-su. Seoul, Korea: Seomun-dang Publishing Company, 1983. 168 pp. Illustrated. Indexes.**

Treats nearly 200 annual customs of Korea. Describes practices, explains beliefs, retells legends. Covers seasonal celebrations, and festivals as well as foods, clothing, superstitions, games, ceremonies, divination practices, and various customs associated with certain days or times of year. Organized by lunar month and date. Indexes customs by Korean and English names. Many color photos illustrate.

LC: DS 904 C5413

♦ 546 ♦

Customs and Manners in Korea. **Chun Shin-yong, ed. Seoul, Korea: Si-sa-yong-o-sa, Inc, 1982. 132 pp. Illustrated.**

Offers a collection of essays on aspects of Korean society and culture. Includes "Tradition and Modern Values" by Chun Shin-yong; "Korean Culture and Mental Health" by Lee Boo-young; "Annual Ceremonies and Rituals" by Choi Gil-sung; "Korean Mudang Rites for the Dead and Traditional Catholic Requiem" by D. Kiester; "Several Forms of Korean Folk Rituals" by Kim Yel-kyu; "Humanism in Traditional Korean Culture" by Kang Shin-pyo; "A Study of Footman Characters in Pansori Novels" by Kwon Du-whan and Suh Jong-moon; "Shaman's Spiritual Value Judgement" by Kim Tae-gwon; "Psychic Values of Korean Mythology" by Kim Yeol-kyu; and "Dialogue: Traditional

Thoughts and Manners" by Soh Kwang-hee and Kim Yeol-kyu. Illustrated with color and black-and-white photos.

DEWEY: 951.9

♦ 547 ♦

Korean Holidays and Festivals. **Frances M. Koh. Illustrated by Liz B. Dodson. Minneapolis, MN: EastWest Press, 1990. 31 pp.**

Describes the customs, foods, games, and folk beliefs of nine Korean holidays. Covers Sol-Nal (Lunar New Year's Day), Tae-Bo-Rum (the Great Moon Festival), the Cherry Blossom Festival, Buddha's Birthday, Children's Day, Tan-O Day (Swing Day), Chu-Sok (the Harvest Moon Festival), Winter Solstice Day, and Christmas. Illustrated with color drawings. For children.

DEWEY: 394.2695 ISBN 0-9606090-5-9

♦ 548 ♦

The Moons of Korea. **Kim Yong-ik. Seoul, Korea: Korea Information Service, 1959. 103 pp. Illustrated.**

Presents the holidays, folklore, legends, and folk customs associated with the lunar months of the Korean calendar. Also gives a short story for each month, which centers around the activities, foods, and natural events associated with that time of year. Covers New Year, Cold Food Day, Buddha's Birthday, Tan-O Day, the Seventh Day of the Seventh Month (the Weaving Maid and the Cowherd), the Fifteenth Day of the Eighth Month (Mid-Autumn Festival), and Tong Ji Day (winter solstice). Illustrated with black-and-white drawings.

LC: GR 342 K55

Malaysia

♦ 549 ♦

A Cycle of Chinese Festivities. **C. S. Wong. Singapore: Malaysia Publishing House, Ltd., 1967. 204 pp. Illustrated. Bibliography. Index.**

Examines the historical development of eight Malaysian festivals of Chinese origin. Also discusses the workings and evolution of the Chinese calendar, the uses to which it is put in Malaysia, and the folklore associated with the animal symbols of the twelve-year cycle. Much space devoted to the customs, symbols, festivities, folklore, and religious observances associated with the two-week celebration around Chinese New Year. Also covers Ch'ing Ming, Han Shih, Tung Chih (Winter Solstice), Fifth Moon Festival (the Dragon Boat

Festival), the Weaving Maid and the Cowherd (seventh day of the seventh moon), the Festival of the Hungry Ghosts, the Magnolia Festival, the Moon Festival (Mid-Autumn Festival), the Pilgrimage of the Nine Venerable Sovereigns, and the Kitchen God Festival. Describes associated legends, folk beliefs and practices, religious observances, and celebration. Considers reasons for their historical survival. Offers both Chinese and English bibliographies.

LC: GT 4883 A2 W6

Mauritius

♦ 550 ♦

Festivals of Mauritius. **Ramesh Ramdoyal. Stanley, Rose-Hill, Mauritius: Editions de l'Océan Indien, 1990. 171 pp. Illustrated. Bibliography.**

Introduces the reader to the major religious and ethnic festivals of Mauritius, their celebrations, devotions, legends, and meaning. Presents 25 festivals reflecting the African, Chinese, European, and Indian influences on Mauritian culture. Treat 15 Hindu festivals: Shivaratri (the Great Night of Shiva), Holi, Raksha Bandhan (Rakhi), Ganesh Chaturthi, Diwali, Ganga Snaan, Kavadee (Thai Poosam), Kathi Poosai (Sword Climbing), Theemithi, (fire-walking), Navratri (Durga Puja), Ugadi, Ramabhajanamu, Ammoru Panduga, and Simhadree Appannah (Narasimha Jayanti). Covers three Muslim festivals: Id-al-Fitr, Id al-Adha, and Ghoon (Yamseh or Tazia); three Chinese festivals: New Year (the Spring Festival), the Lantern Festival, and the Mid-Autumn Festival (Moon Festival); and four Christian festivals: Easter, Corpus Christi (Fête Dieu), Sainte-Croix Pilgrimage, and Christmas. Beautifully illustrated with many color photos.

LC: GT 4889 M45

Nepal

♦ 551 ♦

The Festivals of Nepal. **Mary M. Anderson. London: George Allen and Unwin Ltd., 1971. 288 pp. Illustrated. Bibliography. Index.**

Author describes, in chronological order of occurrence, more than 30 Hindu, Buddhist, and Nepalese festivals attended in Nepal, as well as legends and customs associated with them. (NR)

DEWEY: 394.2 09549 6 LC: GT4876.A3N42 ISBN 0043940013

♦ 552 ♦

Nepal, the Land of Festivals. **Trilok Chandra Majupuria and S. P. Gupta. New Delhi, India: S. Chand and Company, Ltd., 1981. Distributed by Asia Book Corporation of America, New York. 152 pp. Illustrated. Bibliography. Glossary.**

Presents 40 festivals of Nepal's various religious and ethnic groups, including Buddhists, Hindus, Sherpas, Tibetans, Nepalis, and others. Entries describe festival origins, celebrations, devotions, customs, and legends. Also provides chapters explaining the Hindu calendar, describing common festival activities and devotional practices, and exploring the history of ritual sacrifice. Illustrated with black-and-white drawings.

DEWEY: 394.269

Philippines

♦ 553 ♦

Christmas in the Philippines. **Editorial and art departments of World Book, Inc. Chicago, IL: World Book, Inc., 1990. 80 pp. Illustrated.**

Describes Christmas season celebrations in the Philippines. Covers preparations, decorations, foods, songs, religious observances, and popular customs. Notes regional variation in festivities. Introduces elements of Filipino history and culture. Gives recipes, crafts, and words and music to Filipino Christmas songs. For older children. One book in a series entitled *Christmas Around the World.*

DEWEY: 394.2663 ISBN 0-7166-0890-1

♦ 554 ♦

Customs and Culture of the Philippines. **Gladys Zabilka. Illustrated by M. Kuwata. Tokyo, Japan: Charles E. Tuttle Co., 1963. 196 pp.**

An introduction to Filipino culture and society. Chapters covers geography, history, ethnic groups, language, education, crafts, industries, festivals, popular customs and attitudes, food, recreation, music and dance. Describes popular customs, decorations, activities of celebration and religious observance for 12 Filipino festivals: town fiestas, All Saints' Day, Christmas, May festivals, St. John the Baptist's Day, Ash Wednesday, Palm Sunday, Good Friday, Holy Saturday, Easter, the Carabao Festival, and the Obando Fiesta. Offers words and music to Filipino folk songs.

DEWEY: 991.4 Z12c

Thailand

♦ 555 ♦

Lahu Nyi (Red Lahu) New Year Celebrations: Ethnographic and Textual Materials. **Anthony J. Walker. Taipei, Taiwan: The Orient Cultural Service, 1983. 175 pp. Illustrated. Bibliography.**

In-depth study of the New Year festival of one of Thailand's ethnic minorities, the Red Lahu (a Tibeto-Burmese people). Describes festival preparations, beliefs, religious observance, and popular customs and celebration. Also translates and presents a number of Lahu prayer texts from the New Year festival. Volume 107 in the Asian Folklore and Social Life Monographs series.

LC: GT 4878 T3 W17

Vietnam

♦ 556 ♦

Customs and Culture of Vietnam. **Ann Caddell Crawford. Illustrated by Hau Dinh Cam. Foreword by Henry Cabot Lodge. Rutland, VT: Charles E. Tuttle Co., 1966. 259 pp. Appendices. Bibliography.**

A compilation of facts about and description of Vietnam, its customs and culture, written by the wife of a U.S. Army officer stationed in the country during the Vietnam War. Topics include the land, history, religions, ethnic minorities, education, social customs and welfare, arts and handicrafts, health, the economy, festivals and holidays, legends, and places of interest. Festivals covered include Tet (or New Year), Hai-Ba-Trung Day, Thanh Minh, Doan Ngu, the Whale Festival, Trung Nguyen, and Trung Thu (the Mid-Autumn Festival). Appendices give South Vietnamese national slogans, coat of arms, and national colors, facts about Vietnam's tribal groups and missionary activity among them, useful Vietnamese words and phrases, South Vietnamese military rank and insignia, a chronology of important events in Vietnamese history, and more.

DEWEY: 915.97

Europe

General Works

♦ 557 ♦

City and Spectacle in Medieval Europe. **Barbara A. Hanawalt and Kathryn L. Reyerson, eds. Minneapolis, MN: University of Minnesota Press, 1994. 331 pp. Index.**

Twelve papers from a conference at the University of Minnesota in 1991 explore various kinds of ritual and ceremony observed in medieval Europe, including liturgical rites in France, Holy Thursday in Spain, Midsummer in London, accounts of several festivals in medieval Castile, and more. (NR)

DEWEY: 394.2 694 LC: GT4842.C58 ISBN 0-8166-2359-7

♦ 558 ♦

Discussion of Holidays in the Later Middle Ages. **Edith Cooperrider Rodgers. New York: Columbia University Press, 1940. 147 pp. Bibliography. Index.**

Examines the celebration of religious holidays in the Middle Ages. Discusses the problem of the proliferation of holidays, regional diversity in saints celebrated, the forms of observance prescribed by the Church, the festivities preferred by the common people, and various ecclesiastical concerns about popular religiosity and campaigns for holiday reform.

DEWEY: 394.26 R691

♦ 559 ♦

European Folk Festivals. **Sam Epstein and Beryl Epstein. Champaign, IL: Garrard Publishing Company, 1968. 64 pp. Illustrated.**

Describes celebrations at traditional European festivals. Covers May Day, Whitsuntide Festivals, Midsummer festivals, and harvest festivals in many west European countries. Also describes festivals featuring sports contests, such as the Italian Palio, and representations of giants. Written for children.

DEWEY: 394.2

♦ 560 ♦

Fast and Feast: Food in Medieval Society. **Bridget Ann Henisch. University Park, PA: Pennsylvania State University, 1976. 279 pp. Illustrated. Index.**

Considers the effect of Church doctrines concerning food and spirituality on the practices of feasting and fasting in medieval Europe. Gives a chapter on religious feasts and fasts. Describes many aspects of medieval feasts, including cooking methods, types of dishes, table manners, decorations, and entertainments. References cited in endnotes. Further reading list.

DEWEY: 394.1 094 LC: GT 2853.E8 H46 ISBN 0-271-01230-7

♦ 561 ♦

Festival Europe: Fairs and Celebrations Throughout Europe. **Margaret M. Johnson. Memphis, TN: Mustang Publishing Co., 1992. 236 pp. Maps.**

Provides a travel guide for more than 700 European festivals. Covers festivals in Ireland, England, Scotland, Wales, the Netherlands, Luxembourg, Belgium, France, Italy, Malta, Austria, Switzerland, Germany, Spain, Portugal, Denmark, Finland, Norway, Sweden, and Greece. Lists each country's festivals by month, with brief descriptions giving location, calendar dates, and activities. Furnishes map of country with festival locations marked. Also names each country's national holidays and lists organizations to contact for more information.

DEWEY: 394.2 694 LC: GT 4842.J64 ISBN 0-914457-41-1

♦ 562 ♦

Festivals Europe. **Robert Meyer, Jr. 1954. Reprint. Detroit, MI: Omnigraphics, Inc., 1993. 328 pp. Index.**

Provides information about more than 600 festivals in 21 European countries: Austria, Belgium, Denmark, Finland, France, Germany, Great Britain, Greece, Holland, Iceland, Ireland, Italy, Luxembourg, Monaco, Norway, Portugal, Spain, Sweden, Switzerland, Turkey, and Yugoslavia. Covers religious, folk, seasonal, harvest, sporting, and cultural celebrations. Detail given varies from page-long descriptive entries to brief listings of date, time, and major attraction. Describes each country's major holidays and celebrated events, and closes with a month-by-month calendar of festivals and a list of bank holidays. Addresses of tourist offices given for those wishing specific dates and further information.

DEWEY: 394.26 ISBN 1-55888-173-5

♦ 563 ♦

Festivals of Europe. **Gordon Cooper. 1961. Reprint. Detroit, MI: Omnigraphics, Inc., 1993. 172 pp. Illustrated. Index.**

Offers brief descriptions of more than 1,200 European festivals. Covers traditional, cultural, religious, and sporting events in 25 European countries (including Iceland and Turkey). Gives travel hints. Furnishes a directory of tourist information centers in 24 countries.

DEWEY: 398.33 LC: GT4842.A2C66 ISBN 0-7808-0005-2

♦ 564 ♦

Festivals of Western Europe. **Dorothy Gladys Spicer. 1958. Reprint. Detroit, MI: Omnigraphics, Inc., 1994. 275 pp. Bibliography. Indexes.**

Describes principal religious, folkloric or peasant festivals in 12 western European countries: Belgium, Denmark, France, Germany, Italy, Luxembourg, the Netherlands, Norway, Portugal, Spain, Sweden, and Switzerland.

DEWEY: 394.26 LC: GT 4842 S6 ISBN 0-7808-0006-0

♦ 565 ♦

Foods and Festivals of the Danube Lands: Germany, Austria, Czechoslovakia, Hungary, Yugoslavia, Bulgaria, Romania, Russia. **Lila Perl. Illustrated by Leo Glueckselig. Cleveland, OH: World Publishing Company, 1969. 287 pp. Index.**

Presents the history and cuisine of the countries linked by the Danube River. Gives synopsis of each country's history, with an emphasis on foods and food customs. Describes typical foods and major festivals, their special dishes and activities. Gives recipes.

DEWEY: 394.2094

♦ 566 ♦

Medieval Holidays and Festivals: A Calendar of Celebrations. **Madeleine Pelner Cosman. New York: Charles Scribner's Sons, 1981. 136 pp. Illustrated. Index.**

Professor of medieval studies describes one medieval holiday for each month of the year: Twelfth Night, St. Valentine's Day, Easter, All Fool's Day, Mayday, Midsummer Eve, St. Swithin's Day, Lammas, Michaelmas, Halloween, St. Catherine's Day, and Christmas. Depicts foods, songs, entertainments, games, customs, and folklore. Separate chapter describes the ceremonies and foods of medieval feasts. Final chapters tell how to recreate your own medieval feast, providing recipes and tips on making costumes and props. Further reading list. Illustrated with black-and-white photos of medieval art.

DEWEY: 394.2 69 02 LC: GT 3933. C67 ISBN 0-684-17172-4

♦ 567 ♦

Music Festivals in Europe and Britain. **Carol Price Rabin. Revised and enlarged edition. Stockbridge, MA: Berkshire Traveller Press, 1984. 191 pp. Illustrations. Index.**

Describes programs, artists, and locations for 110 festivals in 27 countries, including Israel, Russia, Turkey, and Japan. Provides information on ticket reservations and prices, dress codes, local accommodations, and other sight-seeing opportunities. Organized by country.

DEWEY: 780.79 ISBN 0-912944-81-1

♦ 568 ♦

Sword Dance and Drama. **Violet Alford. London: Merlin Press, 1962. 222 pp. Illustrated. Bibliography. Index.**

Reviews the various sword dances and related folk dramas which occur throughout Europe on celebrated days, making the argument that they represent the survival of ancient agricultural and metal-working rites. Covers the dances of Great Britain, the Germanic countries, southern France, islands of the Mediterranean and Adriatic, Czechoslovakia, Hungary, Romania, Spain, and Portugal. Describes the dances, costumes, related festivals and ceremonies, and what is known of their history. For each region of Europe gives references cited and tables listing mining sites and sites of historic or current sword dances and dramas. Summary given in final chapter. Illustrated with black-and-white photos.

LC: GV 1796 S9 A4

♦ 569 ♦

A Religious Guide to Europe. **Daniel M. Madden. New York: Macmillan Publishing Company, Inc., 1975. 529 pp. Index.**

Describes making pilgrimages to hundreds of shrines, sanctuaries, and other holy places in more than 15 European countries, from Ireland to Turkey. Travel and accommodation information, as well as descriptions of secular points of interest are provided.

DEWEY: 914.0455 LC: BR 735. M23 ISBN 0-02-579150

♦ 570 ♦

Revitalizing European Rituals. **Jeremy Boissevain, ed. London: Routledge, 1992. 204 pp. Indexes.**

A collection of scholarly essays examining the recent revival of many local European festivals. Includes "'Heritage' and Critical History in the Reinvention of Mining Festivals in North-east England" by Susan Wright; "Continuity and Change in Political Ritual: May Day in Poland" by Zdzislaw Mach; "Public Celebrations in a Spanish Valley" by Francisco Cruces and Angel Díaz de Rada; "Celebration at Daybreak in Southern Spain" by Henk Driessen; "Pilgrims, 'Yuppies', and Media Men: The Transformation of an Andalusian Pilgrimage" by Mary Crain; "Building Difference: The Political Economy of Tradition in the Ladin Carnival of Val di Fassa" by Cesare Poppi; "Play and Identity: Ritual Change in a Maltese Village" by Jeremy Boissevain; "Mattresses and Migrants: A Patron Saint's Festival on a Small Greek Island Over Two Decades" by Margaret E. Kenna; and "Japanese Ladies and Mexican Hats: Contested Symbols and the Politics of Tradition in a Northern Greek Carnival Celebration" by Jane K. Cowan. Bibliographic references given at the end of each article. Name and subject indexes.

DEWEY: 394.2 6 094 LC: GT 4842. R48 ISBN 0-415-07957-8

♦ 571 ♦

Rice, Spice and Bitter Oranges: Mediterranean Foods and Festivals. **Lila Perl. Illustrated by Stanislao Dino Rigolo. Cleveland, OH: World Publishing Co., 1967. 272 pp. Index.**

Reports on the cuisines and celebrations of the countries of southern Europe, the Levant, and North Africa. Traces the history of foods and their preparation, describes major festivals and their special dishes, gives recipes. Treats Portugal, Spain, Italy, Greece, Turkey, Syria, Israel, and Egypt, with briefer coverage of the countries of North Africa.

DEWEY: 641.59

♦ 572 ♦

Rites and Riots: Folk Customs of Britain and Europe. **Bob Pegg. Poole, Dorset, England: Blandford Press, 1981. 144 pp. Illustrated. Bibliography. Index.**

Provides an overview of some of the seasonal customs of Europe, emphasizing Great Britain, and critically reviews the way in which they have been explained by folklorists and antiquarians. Chapters cover the seasons, folk dances and dramas, and the life cycle. Emphasizes social conflict or disharmony expressed in folk customs and discusses the recent origin of some customs thought to be ancient. Illustrated with black-and-white photos.

DEWEY: 398. 094 LC: GR 135 ISBN 0-7137-0997-9

France

♦ 573 ♦

Blood of the Bastille, 1787-1789, From Calonne 's Dismissal to the Uprising of Paris. **Claude Manceron. Translated by Nancy Amphoux. New York: Simon and Schuster, 1989. 559 pp. Index.**

Describes the events of the two years preceding the uprising of Paris and the beginning of the French Revolution. Narrative culminates in the events of the first Bastille Day on July 14, 1789. References given in endnotes. Fifth volume in a series by the same author on the French Revolution.

DEWEY: 944.04 092 2 S LC: DC 145 M3513 ISBN 0-671-67848-5

♦ 574 ♦

Carnival in Romans. **Emmanuel Le Roy Ladurie. Translated by Mary Feeney. New York: George Braziller, Inc., 1979. 426 pp. Appendix. Bibliography.**

Detailed historical study of a political uprising that occurred during the 1580 Carnival celebrations in the town of Romans. Weaves together description of Carnival festivities, analysis of the growing tension between social and economic classes, and the outbreak of political violence. Considers the relationship between these events and the Carnival celebrations during which they took place. Gives a chapter on the social functions and cultural meanings of the Carnival festival in sixteenth-century France. Citations given in endnotes.

DEWEY: 944. 98 LC: DC 801. R75 L4713 ISBN 0-8076-0928-5

♦ 575 ♦

Christmas in France. **Corinne Madden Ross. 1980. Reprint. Lincolnwood, IL: Passport Books, 1991. 80 pp. Illustrated.**

Conveys the spirit of the Christmas season in France. Describes Christmas decorations, such as Christmas trees, ornaments, flowers, and nativity scenes, and Christmas activities, such as shopping and caroling. Retells Christmas legends. Also describes Christmas foods, the Reveillon feast of Christmas Eve, Christmas Eve church services, and regional Christmas celebrations. Recounts events from past Christmases and old Christmas customs. Gives recipes, craft activities, and words and music to French Christmas carols. Illustrated with color photos. For older children.

DEWEY: 394.2682 LC: GT4987.42.C48

♦ 576 ♦

Christmas Kalends of Provence and Some Other Provençal Festivals. **Thomas Janvier. 1902. Reprint. Detroit, MI: Omnigraphics, Inc., 1990. 262 pp. Illustrated.**

Relates customs and beliefs of the Christmas season in Provence, attributing their origins to ancient times. Also gives author's travel experiences and descriptions. Some coverage of other festivals in the region.

DEWEY: 394.2 6 09449 LC: GT 4849.A3 P755 ISBN 1-55888-823-3

♦ 577 ♦

Festivals and the French Revolution. **Mona Ozouf. Translated by Alan Sheridan. Cambridge, MA: Harvard University Press, 1988. 378 pp. Illustrated. Bibliography. Index.**

Scholarly historical study of the attempt to institutionalize the political and philosophical values of the French Revolution in a series of newly created festivals. Includes discussion of the French Revolutionary calendar. Covers the years 1789 to 1799. Much historical detail and theoretical analysis of the relationship between festivity and society. References cited in endnotes.

DEWEY: 944.04 LC: DC 159.09613 ISBN 0-674-29883-7

♦ 578 ♦

Hollywood on the Riviera: The Inside Story of the Cannes Film Festival. **Cari Beauchamp and Henri Béhar. New York: William Morrow and Company, Inc., 1992. 491 pp. Illustrated. Appendices. Bibliography. Index.**

Provides behind-the-scenes glimpses of the producers, directors, actors, screenings, gossip, career moves, business deals, and intrigues of the Cannes Film Festival. Many anecdotes concerning the film stars of yesterday and today. Treats the history of the festival and the growth of its prestige within the film industry. Appendices include the festival's rules and regulations for film entries, a list of the Cannes Jury members since 1946, and a list of the awards winners in all categories since 1946.

DEWEY: 971.43 079 44941 LC: PN 1993.4 B36 ISBN 0-688-11007-X

♦ 579 ♦

The Taking of the Bastille, July 14th, 1789. **Jacques Godechot. Translated by Jean Stewart. Preface by Charles Tilly. New York: Charles Scribner's Sons, 1970. 368 pp. Appendices. Bibliography. Index.**

Places an account of the events of the first Bastille Day and the beginnings of the French Revolution within the wider context of eighteenth-century political, economic, and social change. Appendices reprint firsthand accounts of the taking of the Bastille.

DEWEY: 944.041

Germany

♦ 580 ♦

A Calendar of German Customs. **Richard Thonger. London: Oswald Wolff, 1966. 126 pp. Illustrated.**

Presents, in calendar order, a collection of German folk customs and celebrations. Covers holidays and fairs, describing traditional activities and practices. Illustrated with reproductions of drawings and other artwork by German artists.

LC: GT 4850 A2 T5

♦ 581 ♦

Christmas in Today's Germany. **Staff of World Book, Inc. Chicago: World Book, Inc., 1993. 80 pp. Illustrated. Map.**

Portrays Christmas season celebrations in Germany. Describes preparations, decorations, foods, music, and popular customs; retells legends; and traces the history of German Christmas symbols and customs, such as the Christmas tree and Advent calendars. Treats six holidays of the Christmas season: St. Martin's Day, St. Nicholas's Day, Christmas, St. Stephen's Day, New Year's Eve (or St. Sylvester's Day), and Epiphany. Gives recipes, crafts, and words and music to German Christmas songs. Also introduces elements of recent German history. Illustrated with color photos and map of Germany showing states and their capitals. For older children. One book in a series entitled *Christmas Around the World.*

DEWEY: 394.2663 ISBN 0-7166-0893-6

♦ 582 ♦

German Festivals and Customs. **Jennifer M. Russ. London: Oswald Wolff, 1982. 166 pp. Illustrated. Appendix. Bibliography. Indexes.**

Describes customs, legends, stories, rhymes, foods, and folk art associated with traditional German festivals, holidays, and fairs, with special emphasis on those associated with the Christian year. Notes regional variation. Also covers daily customs and family celebrations, such as christenings. Provides geographical and subject index. Illustrated with black-and-white photos of customary practices and celebrations.

DEWEY: 394.2 0943 LC: GT 4850 ISBN 0-85496-365-0

Greece

♦ 583 ♦

Greek Calendar Customs. **George Megas. Athens, Greece: Press and Information Department, Prime Minister's Office, 1958. 159 pp. Illustrated.**

Describes the folk beliefs, customs, foods, religious observances, celebrations, sayings, and symbols associated with numerous Greek festivals and other Greek calendar customs. Emphasis is on religious festivals; many Orthodox saints' days covered. Arranged in calendar order. Illustrated with black-and-white photos.

DEWEY: 292 M496

♦ 584 ♦

Greek Saints and Their Festivals. **Mary Hamilton. Edinburgh, Scotland: William Blackwood and Sons, 1910. 211 pp. Index.**

Discusses the Greek saints, their legends, attributes, patronages, and festivals. Relates the customs and folklore of Greek holidays and describes their popular celebration and religious observance. Covers the Festival of the Annunciation (at Tinos), Christmas, New Year, the Twelve Days, Epiphany, Carnival, Palm Sunday, Easter, Ascension, Pentecost, St. John the Baptist's Day, flower festivals, and the Panagia.

♦ 585 ♦

Meet the Greeks. **Anne Anthony. Athens, Greece: Icaros, 1950. 141 pp. Illustrated.**

Presents a brief introduction to Greek social customs, religion, language, and festivals. Covers Independence Day, the Feast of the Annunciation, Carnival, Lent, Holy Week and Easter, May Day, the Feast of St. Constantine and St. Helena, the Feast of John the Baptist, the Feast of Peter and Paul, the Assumption of the Virgin, the Exaltation of the Cross, the Feast of St. Dionysus the Areopagite, the Feast of St. Demetrius, October 28 ("Ohi" Day, or No Day), the Feast of St. Andrew, Christmas, New Year, and Epiphany.

Gives history and describes religious devotions, foods, legends, and popular customs.

LC: DF 741 A5

Hungary

♦ 586 ♦

Hungarian Folk Customs. **Tekla Dömötör. Gyoma, Hungary: Corvina Press, 1972. 86 pp. + plates. Illustrated. Maps. Bibliography.**

Describes Hungarian folk customs related to the celebration of holidays, saints' days, other special days, and seasons. Also covers customs related to life-cycle events, morality, and the law. Some discussion of history of customs and their present-day study in Hungary. Color and black-and-white photos illustrate.

LC: DB9205.5 D6

Ireland

♦ 587 ♦

All Silver and No Brass: An Irish Christmas Mumming. **Henry Glassie. Illustrated by the author. Bloomington, IN: Indiana University Press, 1975. 192 pp. Bibliography. Glossary. Index.**

A study of the now-extinct practice of Christmas-season mumming in a rural region of Northern Ireland. Transcribes interviews with former mummers and their audience. Interprets the cultural meaning and social function of mumming. Also reviews other rural seasonal celebrations, including those around Halloween, St. Brighid's Day (St. Bridget's Day), May Day, Lammas, Bonfire Night, midsummer, and Easter. Endnotes.

DEWEY: 398.2 36 LC: PR 8793. F6 G6 ISBN 0-253-30470-9

♦ 588 ♦

Christmas in Ireland. **Editorial and art departments of World Book, Inc. Chicago: World Book Inc., 1985. 80 pp. Illustrated.**

Portrays the celebrations of the Christmas season in Ireland. Describes popular customs, religious observances, foods, preparations, Nativity scenes and other Christmas decorations. Reprints an Irish Christmas story. Covers Advent, Christmas, St. Stephen's Day, Holy Innocents' Day, New Year, and Epiphany. Gives Christmas recipes, crafts, and words and music to Irish

Christmas songs. Illustrated with color photos. For older children. One book in a series entitled *Christmas Around the World.*

DEWEY: 394.2663 ISBN 0-7166-0885-5

♦ 589 ♦

A Handbook of Irish Folklore. **Seán Ó Súilleabháin. 1942. Reprint. Hatboro, PA: Folklore Associates, Inc., 1963. 699 pp.**

A comprehensive collection of Irish folklore and a guide to further folklore collections. Chapters cover lore of dwellings and towns, household and livelihood, trade and travel, community life, the body and the life cycle, the natural environment, folk medicine, festivals and the calendar, popular beliefs, mythology, history, religion, pastimes, and tales. Each chapter also gives series of questions to guide in the further collection of Irish folklore. Much information pertinent to holidays, festivals, and fairs interspersed throughout.

DEWEY: 398.21

♦ 590 ♦

Irish Folk Ways. **E. Estyn Evans. New York: The Devin-Adair Company, 1957. 324 pp. Illustrated. Bibliography. Index.**

Presents a collection of Irish folk ways, with a particular emphasis on the material culture of home life and farming. Also offers a chapter on fairs and gatherings, a chapter on festivals, and a chapter on pishrogues, or folk beliefs relating to the supernatural. Illustrated with black-and-white drawings and photos.

DEWEY: 398.8415 E92

♦ 591 ♦

The Year in Ireland. **Kevin Danaher. Cork, Ireland: Mercier Press, 1972. 274 pp. Illustrated. Appendix. Bibliography. Index.**

Offers a comprehensive collection of the folklore and folk practices associated with celebrated days. Covers St. Brighid's Day (St. Bridget's Day), Candlemas, Shrove Tuesday, Ash Wednesday, Lent, St. Patrick's Day, Lady Day, Palm Sunday, Easter, April Fools' Day, May Day, Ascension Thursday, Whitsuntide, Corpus Christi, Midsummer, St. Peter and St. Paul's Day, July 12, St. Swithin's Day, the First of the Harvest, Lugnasadh and other harvest customs, the Assumption, St. Bartholomew's Day, Pattern Day, Michaelmas, the End of the Harvest, Samhain, All Soul's Day, Martinmas, and the Christmas season. Notes regional variation and gives historical background for many practices. Appendix lists Church feasts and fasts.

LC: DA 925. D33 ISBN 85342-280-X

Italy

♦ 592 ♦

Celebrating Italy. **Carol Field. New York: William Morrow and Company, 1990. 530 pp. Illustrated. Bibliography. Index.**

Describes 37 traditional Italian festivals and provides 175 recipes for festival foods. Offers detailed travelogue description of festival activities along with information concerning the festival's origins, history, legends, and lore. Includes national festivals, such as Holy Week and Easter, and local festivals, such as the Strawberry Festival in Nemi. Also gives festival calendar listing hundreds of Italian festivals, noting location, date, and chief attractions.

DEWEY: 394.2 6 0945 LC: GT 4852.A2F54 ISBN 0-688-07093-0

♦ 593 ♦

Christmas in Italy. **Chicago: World Book-Childcraft International, Inc., 1979. 80 pp. Illustrated.**

Describes celebrations of the Christmas season in Italy. Explains the diversity of Italian regional celebrations and tells how St. Nicholas's Day, St. Lucia's Day, Christmas Eve, Christmas, New Year, and Epiphany are observed and celebrated. Depicts the goods and atmosphere of Italian markets, retells the legend of La Befana, shows how many Italians—from famous artists to children—have depicted scenes from the story of Christ's birth in paintings and Nativity scenes (*presepi*). Also describes Italian folk music for Christmas, Christmas observances at the Vatican, and Italian Christmas foods. Gives craft activities, recipes, and words and music to Italian Christmas songs. Amply illustrated with color photos. For older children. One book in a series entitled *Christmas Around the World.*

DEWEY: 394.2682 ISBN 0-7166-2008-1

♦ 594 ♦

Festa: Recipes and Recollections of Italian Holidays. **Helen Barolini. Illustrations by Karen Barbour. San Diego, CA: Harcourt Brace Jovanovich, 1988. 366 pp. Illustrated. Index.**

Combines holiday legends and customs, stories of life in Italy, and holiday recipes to convey the spirit and flavor of Italy's holidays. Each month covered in a separate chapter.

DEWEY: 641.5945 LC: TX 723. B245 ISBN 0-15-145771-9

♦ 595 ♦

The Festival of San Giovanni: Imagery and Political Power in Renaissance Florence. **Heidi L. Chrétien. New York: Peter Lang, 1994. 172 pp. Illustrated. Bibliography.**

Shows how the powerful Medici family of Renaissance Florence used the city's annual celebration of its patron saint (John the Baptist) to bolster its political domination of the city. Discusses festival celebrations before and after Medici alterations. Highlights these changes through comparison with nearby Pistoia's patron saint festival, dedicated to San Jacopo (St. James).

DEWEY: 394.2 694551 LC: GT 4995. J6 C47 ISBN 0-8204-2143-X

♦ 596 ♦

Festivals and Folkways of Italy. **Frances Toor. New York: Crown Publishers, Inc., 1953. 312 pp. Illustrated. Appendix. Bibliography. Index.**

An Italian travelogue, featuring descriptions of the ambience, folk customs, and festivals of Italian cities and regions, with special emphasis on Sicily, Rome, Sardinia and southern Italy. Appendix gives notes on festival seasons, folk arts, and folk beliefs.

DEWEY: 398.33 T672 f

♦ 597 ♦

La Terra in Piazza: An Interpretation of the Palio of Siena. **Alan Dundes and Alessandro Falassi. Berkeley, CA: University of California Press, 1975. 265 pp. Illustrated. Bibliography. Glossary. Index.**

Offers an in-depth study of the most important festival in Siena, the Palio. Reviews the history of the Palio, the organization of the groups that sponsor and participate in it, and the events, activities, and sentiments that make up the festival. Considers its social implications and deeper meanings. Provides a glossary of Italian words associated with the Palio. Illustrated with color photos.

LC: DG 975 S5 D8 ISBN 0-520-02681-0

♦ 598 ♦

Palio and Ponte: An Account of the Sports of Central Italy from the Age of Dante to the XXth Century. **William Heywood. London: Methuen and Company, 1904. 268 pp. Index.**

Provides a history of the Palio of Siena and other chivalric, festival games of central Italy, from the Middle Ages to the turn of the twentieth century. Describes these sporting events, as well as the festivals of which they were the main feature. Discusses the organization, preparations, purpose, prizes, and meaning of the various Palii. Much detail, including historical background of Italian city-states and descriptions of actual events in the history of these festivals.

DEWEY: 914.5 H 619

♦ 599 ♦

Some Italian Scenes and Festivals. **Thomas Ashby. London: Methuen and Co. Ltd., 1929. 179 pp. Illustrated. Index.**

Combines description of Italian towns and scenery with descriptions of local festivals. Covers five regions: the Alban Hills, Tivoli and the Inchinata, the Upper Valley of the Anio, the Abruzzi, Viterbo and Lake Bolsena, and Sardinia. Also provides some historical background. Illustrated with black-and-white photos.

DEWEY: 914.5 A823

♦ 600 ♦

The Two Madonnas: The Politics of Festival in a Sardinian Community. **Sabina Magliocco. New York: Peter Lang, 1993. 158 pp. Illustrated. Bibliography. Glossary.**

Documents the effects of economic development and social change on the two festivals of Monteruju, Sardinia. Treats the Feast of the Assumption and the Nativity of the Virgin. Relates festival history and legends, describes preparations, organization, devotions, public and home celebrations. Gives chapter on history and organization of Sardinian festivals.

DEWEY: 394.2 69459 LC: GT 4852. M67 M34 ISBN 0-8204-1896-X

Poland

♦ 601 ♦

Journeys to Glory. **Adam Bujak, photographer. Text by Marjorie B. Young. New York: Harper and Row, 1976. 203 pp.**

Photojournalist captures the spirit of seven traditional Polish pilgrimages and processions which are made in observance of Catholic and Orthodox feast days. Accompanying text describes events, explains their significance, and summarizes their history. Covers the Celebration of the Baptism of Jesus in the River Jordan (on January 19th), the ceremonies of the Archbrotherhood of the Sufferings of the Lord (every Friday of Lent), the Celebration of the Sufferings of the Lord (Holy Week), the Procession of One Hundred Horses (Easter Monday), the Green Holidays as celebrated by the Marjawici Felicjanowcy (May or early June), two processions celebrating Assumption Day (August 11-19), and the pilgrimage of the Transfiguration of Jesus Christ (August 18). Black-and-white photos.

DEWEY: 394.2 6828 09438 LC: BR 953. B84 ISBN 0-06-069732-6

Portugal

♦ 602 ♦

Portugal: A Book of Folk Ways. **Rodney Gallop. Illustrated by Rodney Gallop and Marjorie Gallop. Cambridge, England: Cambridge University Press, 1936. 291 pp. Illustrated. Bibliography. Index.**

Covers landscape and folk costumes of the North and South, popular beliefs and customs, and folk music and literature. Section on customs describes beliefs, practices, sayings, superstitions, and festival celebrations associated with the seasons, as well popular notions and practices concerning witchcraft, magic, superstition, birth, marriage, and death.

LC: GR235 G17

Russia

♦ 603 ♦

Christmas in Russia. **Editorial and art departments of World Book Publishing. Chicago: World Book, Inc., 1992. 80 pp. Illustrated. Glossary.** 📖

Describes Christmas season celebrations in Old Russia, Soviet Russia, and post-Soviet Russia. Depicts Church services, processions, foods, legends, superstitions, decorations, Christmas mumming, and other customs. Provides background information about the several political upheavals the country has undergone in the last hundred years. Also covers New Year's Eve and Day. Gives Russian crafts, recipes, and words and music to Christmas songs. Illustrated with color photos and drawings. For older children. One book in a series entitled *Christmas Around the World.*

DEWEY: 394.2682 ISBN 0-7166-0892-8

♦ 604 ♦

A Parade of Soviet Holidays. **Jane Werner Watson. Illustrated by Ben Stahl. Champaign, IL: Garrard Publishing Company, 1974. 96 pp. Index.**

Portrays the celebration of 16 Russian and Soviet holidays and eight holidays of the Republics. Covers New Year's Day, Army Day and Boys' Day, Women's Day, Pancake Day, Easter, Children's Book Holiday, Subbotnik (Lenin's Birthday), Cosmonauts' Day, May Day, the Anniversary of Victory, Young Pioneers' Holiday, Midsummer's Eve, Harvest Day celebrations, National Sports Day, the Anniversary of the Revolution, and Christmas in Russia. Also covers the Tartar Festival of the Plow, the Siberian Ysyakh holiday, Sports Day in the Central Asian Republics, Bairam (a Muslim holiday), the Estonian Ligo Festival, the Cotton Harvest in Uzbekistan, the Grape Harvest in the Caucasus, and the Mushroom Harvest in Byelorussia. Gives pronunciation guide. For children.

DEWEY: 394.2 6947 LC: GT 4856.A2 W37 ISBN 0-8116-4951-2

♦ 605 ♦

A Russian Folk Calendar: Rites, Customs, and Popular Beliefs. **Polina Rozhnova. Moscow, Russia: Novosti, 1992. 164 pp.**

Describes the many Russian folk practices, beliefs, sayings, superstitions, and festivities associated with the seasons, the months, and specific days. Covers saints' days, holidays, and days associated with legend, folklore, and agricultural practices. Arranged in calendar order.

LC: GR 930 R69

Scandinavia

♦ 606 ♦

Christmas in Denmark. **Staff of World Book Encyclopedia, Inc. Chicago: World Book Encyclopedia, Inc., 1986. 80 pp. Illustrated.**

Tells how the Christmas season is celebrated in Denmark. Describes preparations, decorations, symbols, foods, customs, and religious observances. Gives history of Christmas in Denmark, summarizes the life of Hans Christian Andersen, and prints two of his stories. Provides Danish Christmas recipes, crafts, and songs. For older children. One volume in a series entitled *Christmas Around the World.*

DEWEY: 394.2663 ISBN 0-7166-0886-3

♦ 607 ♦

Christmas in Norway: Past and Present. **Vera Henriksen. Oslo, Norway: Johan Grundt Tanum Forlag, 1970. 63 pp. Illustrated.**

Describes the folk customs and beliefs of the Norwegian Christmas season, from pagan times to the present. Covers the Viking Feast of "Jol," St. Lucy's Eve (St. Lucia's Day), St. Thomas's Day, Christmas Eve, Christmas, St. Stephen's Day, and St. Knut's Day. Retells legends, traces the history of customary practices and beliefs, describes special foods and drinks, and examines the history of Christmas symbols, such as yule fires, candles, goats, pageants, straw figures, Christmas trees, St. Nicholas, and gift giving. Gives several Norwegian Christmas recipes.

LC: GT 4987.59 H4

♦ 608 ♦

Christmas in Scandinavia. **Staff of World Book, Inc. Chicago: World Book, Inc., 1977. 80 pp. Illustrated.**

Tells how the Christmas season is celebrated in Scandinavia. Describes preparations, decorations, foods, mythological creatures, and customs, including Danish Christmas plates and Christmas seals. Also covers St. Lucia's Day, St. Stephen's Day, New Year, St. Knut's Day, and Twelfth Night (Epiphany). Gives recipes, crafts, and words and music to Christmas songs. Illustrated with color photos. For children. One volume in a series entitled *Christmas Around the World.*

DEWEY: 394.2682 ISBN 0-7166-2003-0

♦ 609 ♦

Holidays in Scandinavia. **Lee Wyndham. Illustrated by Gordon Laite. Champaign, IL: Garrard Publishing Company, 1975. 95 pp. Illustrated. Index.**

Describes the foods, festivities, and folklore of 10 Scandinavian holidays. Covers the Swedish Vasalopp Festival (a ski festival), Norway's Holmenkollen Day, a Norwegian Sun Pageant, the Lenten season in Scandinavia, Walpurgis Eve in Sweden, Norway's Constitution Day, the Birthday of the Danish Flag, various Scandinavian midsummer festivals, Christmas in Scandinavia, and New Year in Scandinavia. Offers pronunciation guide.

DEWEY: 394.2 6948 LC: DL 11. W9 ISBN 0-8116-4955-5

♦ 610 ♦

Lucia, Child of Light: The History and Tradition of Sweden's Lucia Celebration. **Florence Ekstrand. Seattle, WA: Welcome Press, 1989. 61 pp. Illustrated.**

Recounts the life of St. Lucia and describes how St. Lucia Day is celebrated in Sweden. Discusses how the cult of this southern European saint was established in Sweden and tells how to start a St. Lucia Day celebration in your home, church or community. Gives activities, songs, verse, and recipes.

DEWEY: 394.2682 ISBN 0-916871-12-6

♦ 611 ♦

Swedish Christmas. **Ewert Cagner, Göran Axel-Nilsson, and Henrik Sandblad, comps. Translated by Yvonne Aboav-Elmquist. New York: Henry Holt and Company, 1959. 259 pp. Illustrated.**

A compilation of essays on the spirit, meaning, customs, foods, and festivities of the Christmas season in Sweden. Includes"The Miracle"by Ebba Lindquist; "Lighting a Candle" by Gunnar Edman;"Swedish Christmas" by Helge Åkerhielm;"Fifty Years with Father Christmas" by Erik Lundegård;"The Lapps and Their Christmas" by Ernst Manker; a Swedish Christmas and Advent calendar; description of Swedish Christmas foods, recipes, decorations, games, and words and music to Swedish Christmas songs. Illustrated with black-and-white drawings and color photos.

DEWEY: 394 C555sw

Spain

♦ 612 ♦

Christmas in Spain. **Editorial and art departments of World Book, Inc. Chicago: World Book, Inc., 1983. Illustrated. Glossary.**

Describes Christmas season celebrations in Spain. Treats Christmas Eve, Christmas, Holy Innocents' Day (December 28), New Year, and Epiphany (or Three Kings Day). Depicts preparations, decorations, foods, music, religious observances, popular customs, Nativity scenes, and legends. Notes regional variation in festivities. Illustrated with color photos. Gives recipes, crafts, and words and music to Spanish Christmas songs. For older children. One volume in a series entitled *Christmas Around the World.*

DEWEY: 394.2663 ISBN 0-7166-0882-0

♦ 613 ♦

Festivals and Rituals of Spain. **Christina García Rodero. Text by J. M. Caballero Bonald. Foreword by William A. Christian. New York: Harry N. Abrams, Inc., 1994. 398 pp. Illustrated. Index.**

Photojournalist compiles 187 large color photographs of a variety of local and national celebrations throughout Spain. Covers saints' days, folk festivals, pilgrimages, Carnival, Holy Week, and more. Text by Cabellero Bonald introduces the Spanish fiesta cycle, placing the festivals photographed in a wider, seasonal context and explaining the meaning of devotional and festival activities. Photographer's endnotes tell when and where photos were taken. Oversize.

DEWEY: 394.2 6946 LC: GT 4862. A2 G37 ISBN 0-8109-3839-1

♦ 614 ♦

Fiesta in Pamplona. Dominique Aubier and Inge Morath. Translated by Deirdre Butler. Paris, France: Robert Delpire, 1956. 146 pp. Illustrated.

Furnishes a collection of black-and-white photographs of the Running of the Bulls, or the San Fermín festival, in Pamplona, Spain. Also provides the author's commentary on Spanish values and lifestyle, as well as her experiences at the festival.

DEWEY: 914.6 A89

♦ 615 ♦

Santa Eulalia's People: Ritual Structure and Process in an Andalusian Multicommunity. Francisco Enrique Aguilera. Prospect Heights, IL: Waveland Press, 1990. 188 pp. Illustrated. Appendices. Bibliography. Glossary. Index.

A social study of ritual and festival in a Spanish town. Treats life-cycle rituals as well as three major festivals: Holy Week, the Crosses of May, and the Pilgrimage of St. Eulalia of Merida. Describes and analyzes rituals and celebrations. Glossary of local Spanish words. Appendices include notes on population figures, song types, and marriage patterns, as well as a festival calendar for the town and surrounding area.

ISBN 0-88133-551-7

♦ 616 ♦

Spanish Fiestas (Including Romerias, Excluding Bull-Fights). Nina Epton. New York: A. S. Barnes and Company, 1969. 250 pp. Illustrated. Index.

Covers 105 religious and folk festivals of Spain. Generous entries describe the ceremonies, customs, legends, beliefs, and festivities of these local, regional, and national celebrations. Gives dates and locations. Entries arranged by theme and calendar order.

DEWEY: 394.2094

United Kingdom

GENERAL WORKS

♦ 617 ♦

Bonfires and Bells: National Memory and the Protestant Calendar in Elizabethan and Stuart England. **David Cressy. London: Weidenfeld and Nicolson, 1989. 271 pp. Bibliography. Index.**

Scholarly study of the relationship between popular celebration and political rule in late sixteenth- and seventeenth-century England. Examines decreasing frequency of religious and seasonal festivals and the institution of new political and civic holidays. Includes chapter on the transference of the English calendar to the American colonies.

DEWEY: 390.0942 LC: DA 566.4 C74 ISBN 0-297-79343-8

♦ 618 ♦

British Calendar Customs—England. **Three volumes. A. R. Wright. T. E. Jones, ed. Preface by S. H. Hooke. London: William Glaisher, Ltd., 1936-1940. Volume one, 212 pp. Index. Volume two, 272 pp. Volume three, 333 pp., including index to volumes two and three.**

Encyclopedic coverage of British calendar customs, such as those related to religious feasts and fasts, folk and political holidays, fairs, the seasons, harvest time, and other noted days and times of year. Based on firsthand accounts of popular customs, many from the period of 1840-1880. Gives wide range of folk practices and also folk beliefs, superstitions, and sayings. Notes local and regional variation. Volume one addresses the customs surrounding movable feasts; volume two, those associated with fixed festivals from January to May; and volume three, customs associated with fixed festivals from June to December. Volumes published in 1936, 1938, and 1940, respectively.

DEWEY: 398.842 W947 LC: GT 4843 W7

♦ 619 ♦

British Folk Customs. **Christina Hole. London: Hutchinson and Co., Publishers Ltd., 1976. 232 pp. Illustrated. Map. Bibliography. Index.**

Offers a collection of British folk customs with a particular emphasis on those related to the calendar, time of year, festivals, religious observances, fairs, and doles. Encyclopedia-style entries describe customs, trace their history, and consider their significance. Arranged in alphabetical order. Provides a calendar of selected customs, listing the practice, its location, and date. Provides a map of England with festival locations and counties marked. Illustrated with black-and-white drawings.

DEWEY: 390.0941 ISBN 0-09-127340-4

♦ 620 ♦

British Popular Customs, Past and Present: Illustrating the Social and Domestic Manners of the People. **T. F. Thiselton Dyer. London: George Bell and Sons, 1900. 520 pp. Index.**

Presents, in calendar order, a collection of British popular customs associated with religious and folk festivals, saints' days, and other celebrated days. Emphasis is on England, but also covers Scotland, Wales, and Ireland. Records regional variations. Includes past and present customs, gives description, and notes sources under each entry.

LC: DA 110 T448

♦ 621 ♦

Cakes and Characters: An English Christmas Tradition. **Bridget Ann Henisch. London: Prospect Books, 1984. 236 pp. Illustrated. Appendix. Index.**

Traces the history of English Twelfth Day (or Epiphany) celebrations, from their origins in ancient Rome to the end of the nineteenth century. Focuses on two customs: Twelfth Night cakes and characters. Appendices give various recipes for Twelfth Night cakes. References given in endnotes.

LC: GT 4985 H45 ISBN 0-907325-21-1

♦ 622 ♦

Christmas Customs and Traditions. **Frank Muir. New York: Taplinger Publishing Company, 1975. 111 pp. Illustrated. Index.**

Presents the customs, lore, history, decorations, foods, and festivities of the traditional English Christmas season. Covers traditions associated with specific days, such as All Hallows Eve, Stir Up Sunday, St. Nicholas's Day, St. Thomas's Day, Christmas, Boxing Day, Holy Innocents' Day, New Year, Epiphany (Twelfth Night), Distaff Day, and Plough Monday. Also treats past and present customs of the season, such as the Lords of Misrule, wassailing, mummer's plays, and the Kissing Bough.

DEWEY: 394.2 68282 0941 LC: GT 4987.43.M84 ISBN 0-8008-1552-1

♦ 623 ♦

Christmas in Britain. **Staff of World Book, Inc. Chicago: World Book, Inc., 1978. 80 pp. Illustrated.**

Tells how the Christmas season is celebrated in Britain. Describes the decorations, preparations, foods, lore, history, and customs of Christmas in Britain as seen through the eyes of three children. Also describes the celebration of Boxing Day, Hogmany, Twelfth Night (Epiphany), and local festivals such as the Haxley Hood Game and Burning the Clavie. Explains the history of British Christmas traditions such as mumming, sending Christmas cards, bell ringing, and singing carols. Gives recipes, crafts, and words and music to Christmas songs. Illustrated with color photos. For children. One volume in a series entitled *Christmas Around the World.*

DEWEY: 394.2663 ISBN 0-7166-2007-3

♦ 624 ♦

The Customs and Ceremonies of Great Britain: An Encyclopedia of Living Traditions. **Charles Kightly. London: Thames and Hudson, 1986. 248 pp. Illustrated. Map. Bibliography.**

Provides generous entries on popular customs and ceremonies of Great Britain. Covers fairs; festivals of the Church; official ceremonies; popular calendar customs; folk holidays; customs related to birth, weddings, and funerals; civic customs; sporting events; commemorations; dances; and processions. Describes customary practices and their history, notes regional variation, and discusses their significance. Arranged in alphabetical order. Gives a calendar of customs which includes fixed and movable events, a map of England, and a regional gazetteer, which lists events by region, name, and date. More than 200 photos illustrate, 12 in color.

LC: GT 4843 K53 ISBN 0-500-27537-8

♦ 625 ♦

Customs and Traditions of England. **Garry Hogg. New York: Arco Publishing Company, Inc., 1971. 112 pp. Illustrated. Map. Bibliography.**

Describes 49 yearly rituals selected by the author as among the oldest of England's still-celebrated customs. Includes festivals, fairs, contests, doles, ceremonies, dances, processions, and other unusual and interesting customs. Entries describe events, give their origins and history, and remark upon similar customs. Location, date, and nearest highways and roads also given. Arranged by county. Each entry accompanied by large black-and-white photograph. Gives map of England with counties and event locations marked. Also lists additional calendar customs for each county.

DEWEY: 914.203 ISBN 0-668-02490-9

♦ 626 ♦

Customs in Common. **E. P. Thompson. New York: The New Press, 1991. 547 pp. Illustrated. Index.**

Scholarly study of customary practices of the English working class in the eighteenth and early nineteenth centuries by the well-known British historian. Examines the historical and socioeconomic contexts for such customs as wife sale, rough music, and beating the bounds. References given in footnotes.

DEWEY: 306.0942 LC: HN398.E5T48 ISBN 1-565584-003-8

♦ 627 ♦

Echoes of Magic: A Study of Seasonal Festivals Through the Ages. **C. A. Burland. London: Peter Davies, 1972. 234 pp. Illustrated. Appendix. Index.**

Weaves together brief descriptive accounts of a wide variety of British calendar and seasonal customs. Black-and-white illustrations. Appendix gives calendar of festivals and saints' days.

LC: GT 4843 A2 B8 ISBN 432-01963-4

♦ 628 ♦

Endless Cavalcade: A Diary of British Festivals and Customs. **Alexander Howard. London: Arthur Barker, Ltd., 1964. 300 pp. Bibliography. Index.**

Describes hundreds of British annual customs and their history. Covers holiday and festival customs, royal, legal, folk, ecclesiastical, hunting, and university customs, races, doles, contests, charities, exhibits, annual dinners, sermons, and more. Illustrated with black-and-white photos. Arranged in calendar order.

♦ 629 ♦

English Custom and Usage. **Christina Hole. 1941-42. Reprint. Detroit, MI: Omnigraphics, Inc., 1990. 152 pp. Illustrated. Bibliography. Index.**

Descriptive account of English calendar customs. Covers the Christmas season, New Year, Lent, Easter, Ascension, Whitsuntide (Pentecost), May Day, and various customs associated with the seasons or other celebrated days. Also treats a number of fairs, wakes, memorials, and civic customs, as well as customs concerning land and tenancy, gifts and bequests. Notes regional variation and pre-Christian origins of some customs associated with Christian holy days.

DEWEY: 914.2 H72 LC: GR141.H593 ISBN 1-55888-851-9

♦ 630 ♦

The English Festivals. **Laurence Whistler. London: William Heinemann Ltd., 1947. 241 pp. Appendices. Bibliography. Index.**

Relates the historical development of, and customs associated with, English festivals. Some attention to religious observance when applicable. Treats Christmas, Boxing Day, New Year, Twelfth Day (or Epiphany), Plough Sunday and Monday, Candlemas, St. Valentine's Day, Shrove Tuesday, Mothering Sunday, All Fool's Day, Palm Sunday, Good Friday, Easter, May Day, Rogationtide, Whitsun (Pentecost), Midsummer's Day, Lammas, Harvest, Michaelmas, All Hallow's Day, Guy Fawkes Day, and St. Cecilia's Day. Also covers customs associated with christenings, weddings, and birthdays. Appendix A gives dates of movable festivals until 1975. Appendix B lists books of Christmas carols, titles of carols, and ranks the songs according to familiarity and difficulty.

DEWEY: 394.2 W579e LC: GT 4844.A2W5

♦ 631 ♦

The Englishman's Christmas: A Social History. **J.A.R. Pimlott. Introduction by Ben Pimlott. Atlantic Highlands, NJ: Humanities Press, 1978. 230 pp. Illustrated. Appendices. Bibliography. Index.**

A social history of English Christmas celebrations, from their antecedents in late antiquity to the twentieth century. Discusses the development of the nativity story, the lengthy medieval Christmas season, Christmas after the Reformation, the Puritan Christmas, Christmas in the eighteenth and early nineteenth centuries, the Victorian Christmas, and the twentieth-century Christmas. Traces changes in Christmas customs, beliefs, sentiments, and manner of celebration; special attention given to Christmas foods, trees, cards, carols, the figure of Father Christmas, and the commercial aspects of Christmas. Appendix C gives bibliography of sources.

DEWEY: 394.2 68282 0942 LC: GT 4987. 44 ISBN 0-391-00900-1

♦ 632 ♦

The English Mummers and Their Plays: Traces of Ancient Mystery. **Alan Brody. Philadelphia, PA: University of Pennsylvania Press, 1970. 201 pp. Illustrated. Appendices. Bibliography. Indexes.**

A comprehensive study of English seasonal folk dramas, or mummers' plays. Characterizes their performance style and plots, as well as the folklore literature about them. Describes many local variations on three main themes: the hero-combat, the sword play, and the wooing ceremony. Shows the relationship between English mummers' plays and ancient mystery rites and religious rituals. Appendices give texts to several mummers' plays, notes on the Revesby Play and the Papa Stour text, and excerpted passages from other writings describing seasonal folk dramas. References given in endnotes. Subject, character, and play indexes.

LC: PR 635 F6 B7 ISBN 0-8122-7611-6

♦ 633 ♦

The English Mummers' Play. **Alex Helm. Foreword by N. Peacock and E. C. Cawte. Totowa, NJ: Rowman and Littlefield, 1981. 116 pp. Illustrated. Maps. Appendices. Bibliography. Index.**

Provides an overview of the performance of, and folklore literature about, English mummers' plays. Discusses the three main types of plays: the wooing ceremony, the sword dance ceremony, and the hero-combat ceremony. Gives excerpts from texts, considers atypical texts and stories, and depicts costumes. Describes similar folk plays throughout modern Europe and in the ancient world. Treats historical development and fragmentation of the plays. Appendix one categorizes the chapbook texts. Appendix two provides play texts, including words and music to songs. Furnishes maps showing distribution of play types. Illustrated with black-and-white photos and drawings.

DEWEY: 398.2 LC: PR 635. F6 ISBN 0-8476-7014-7

♦ 634 ♦

English Ritual Drama: A Geographical Index. **E. C. Cawte, Alex Helm, and N. Peacock. London: The Folk-lore Society, 1967. 132 pp. Maps. Appendices. Bibliography.**

A survey of English folk plays, or mummers' plays. Tells when and where performed, date of last known performance, year of origin or first documentation, theme, and sources from which this information was obtained. Includes plays from Wales, Scotland, and Ireland, as well as plays from Canada and the United States thought to be of British origin. Gives maps with play locations marked. Chapter on origins summarizes the performance of other, similar

East and West European folk plays, and discusses play themes. Appendix I lists miscellaneous plays. Appendix II provides examples of play texts.

LC: PR 635 F6C3

♦ 635 ♦

English Traditional Customs. **Christina Hole. Illustrated by Gay John Galsworthy. Totowa, NJ: Rowman and Littlefield, 1975. 178 pp. Bibliography. Index.**

Presents a wealth of English customs associated with festivals, holidays, calendar dates, or certain times of year. Describes practices and their history. Separate chapters cover doles and charities, wakes and fairs, and customs surrounding land usage. Designed to update *English Custom and Usage,* written 40 years earlier.

DEWEY: 394.0942 LC: DA 110.H 597 ISBN 0-87471-736-1

♦ 636 ♦

Fairs and Revels. **Brian Jewell. Tunbridge Wells, Kent, England: Midas Books, 1976. 127 pp. Illustrated. Bibliography. Index.**

Reviews festivities, folk customs, ceremonies, costumes, and business practices of English fairs from the Middle Ages to the nineteenth century. Chapters focus on different kinds of fairs—such as seasonal festivals, wakes, and saints' feast days—and different aspects of traditional fairs, such as the hiring of servants, forms of entertainments, and methods of keeping order. Epilogue, by Brenda Kidman, discusses how fairs have changed in nineteenth- and twentieth-century Britain. Illustrated with reproductions of black-and-white drawings, paintings, photos, and etchings of fair activities.

LC: GT 4843 J48 ISBN 0-85936-068-7

♦ 637 ♦

Faiths and Folklore of the British Isles: A Descriptive and Historical Dictionary of the Superstitions, Beliefs, and Popular Customs of England, Scotland, Wales, and Ireland, from Norman Times to the End of the Nineteenth Century, with Classical and Foreign Analogues. **W. Carew Hazlitt. Two volumes. 1905. Reprint. New York: Benjamin Blom, 1965. Volume one, pp. 1-334. Volume two, pp. 335-672.**

Based on Brand and Ellis's 1813 *The Popular Antiquities of Great Britain,* with much editing, revision, and enlargement by Hazlitt. Brief, descriptive entries cover many aspects of British popular culture and customs, including beliefs and practices associated with common objects, nature, parts of the body, holidays and calendar customs, games, everyday practices and amusements, and more. Many entries note sources.

LC: DA 110 H38

♦ 638 ♦

The Folklore Calendar. **George Long. 1930. Reprint. Detroit, MI: Omnigraphics, Inc., 1990. 240 pp. Illustrated. Index.**

Describes 40 British calendar customs, noting associated beliefs, legends, or historical facts. Includes holidays, festivals, contests, doles, dances, yearly practices concerning wells, fire, and the agricultural cycle, and more. Arranged by month. Illustrated with black-and-white photos.

DEWEY: 398.842 L848 ISBN 1-55888-875-6

♦ 639 ♦

The Fool: His Social and Literary History. **Enid Welsford. London: Faber and Faber, 1935. 374 pp. Illustrated. Bibliography. Index.**

A historical study of the figure of the fool in literature and in society, with a special emphasis on English customs and literature. Discusses professional and mythical fools, the court fool in actuality and in literature, and stage clowns. Gives chapter on the Lord of Misrule and other fools associated with seasonal celebrations. Endnotes. Black-and-white illustrations.

DEWEY: 394.2 W 45 LC: GT 3570 W4

♦ 640 ♦

Hogmanay and Tiffany: The Names of Feasts and Fasts. **Gillian Edwards. London: Geoffrey Bles, 1970. 184 pp. Index.**

Unravels the etymology of the names of British feasts, fasts and other observed days, and in so doing conveys information about their history and their changing customs and significance. Covers Dismal Days (or Egyptian Days), Christmas, Boxing Day (or St. Stephen's Day), Tiffany (or Epiphany), Carnival, Shrovetide, Lent, Easter, Whitsunday and Pentecost, and Hogmanay (or New Year's Eve). Also address "wassail," and other words associated with the holidays covered.

LC: PE 1574 E27 ISBN 7138-0260-X

♦ 641 ♦

Holy Time: Moderate Puritanism and the Sabbath. **John H. Primus. Macon, GA: Mercer University Press, 1989. 184 pp. Index.**

Scholarly study of the historical development of, and relationship between, Puritanism, Sabbath observance, and Sabbath doctrines in sixteenth-century England.

DEWEY: 263. 4 094109031 LC: BV 111.P75 ISBN 0-86554-340-2

♦ 642 ♦

The Jack-in-the-Green: A May Day Custom. **Roy Judge. Cambridge, England: D. S. Brewer, Ltd., 1979. 145 pp. Illustrated. Bibliography. Index.**

Explores the origins and historical development of the Jack-in-the-Green figure associated with May Day celebrations in and around London. Emphasis on the late eighteenth and nineteenth centuries. Reviews the work of early folklorists and traces the changing characterization of Jack-in-the-Green. Gives many excerpts from firsthand descriptions.

DEWEY: 398.45 LC: GR 141 ISBN 0-85991-029-6

♦ 643 ♦

Masquerade Politics: Explorations in the Structure of Urban Cultural Movements. **Abner Cohen. Berkeley, CA: University of California Press, 1993. 166 pp. Bibliography. Index.**

Examines the origin and growth of the Notting Hill (London) West Indian Carnival celebrations. Analyzes the class and ethnic politics implicit in the organization and celebration of the festival, as well as those implicit in opposition to it.

DEWEY: 394.2 5 LC: GT 4244.L66 C64 ISBN 0-520-07838-1

♦ 644 ♦

Maypoles, Martyrs and Mayhem: 366 Days of British Customs, Myths and Eccentricities. **Quentin Cooper and Paul Sullivan. London: Bloomsbury Publishing, 1994. 378 pp. Appendix. Index.**

A witty catalog of British customs, holidays, fairs, myths, and paranormal or historical events, organized by calendar date. More than one entry for most dates. Most entries coded as follows: ongoing public celebration; ongoing private or irregular public celebration; weather lore; ongoing paranormal phenomena; place, custom, or event still relevant or still visible; method of divination.

LC: GR 141 C66 ISBN 0-7475-1807-6

♦ 645 ♦

Merrymaking in Great Britain. **Margaret Chittenden. Illustrated by Cary. Champaign, IL: Garrard Publishing Company, 1974. 95 pp. Index.**

Describes the folklore and festivities of 11 British holidays. Covers New Year's Eve in Scotland, Shrove Tuesday, Easter, May Day, Trooping the Colour, Eisteddfod in Wales, the Scottish Braemar Highland Gathering, Halloween, Guy Fawkes Day, Christmas, and Boxing Day. For children.

DEWEY: 394.2 6942 LC: GT4843.A2C45 ISBN 0-8116-4952-0

♦ 646 ♦

The National Trust Guide to Traditional Customs of Britain. **Brian Shuel. Exeter, Devon, England: Webb and Bower, 1985. 209 pp. Illustrated. Index.**

Presents first-hand descriptions and black-and-white photographs of more than 150 local, British calendar customs. Organized first by theme and then by time of year. Covers May customs, ritual dances, processions, musical customs, religious rituals, customs concerning wells, legal customs, bequeathed customs, sporting events, games, folk plays, and fire rituals. Includes a calendar of the events covered in the book (plus many others), giving location and date. Further reading list.

DEWEY: 394.2 6942 LC: GR 141 ISBN 0-86350-051-X

♦ 647 ♦

Old English Customs and Ceremonies. **F. J. Drake-Carnell. New York: Charles Scribner's Sons, 1938. 120 pp. Illustrated. Index.**

Describes a wide variety of traditional English customs, many of which concern annual events and celebrations. Covers parliamentary customs, royal ceremonies, London customs, city livery company customs, ceremony and the law, ecclesiastical ceremonies, doles, charities, rural customs, customs related to land tenures, and army, maritime, school, and other miscellaneous customs. Illustrated with color drawings and black-and-white photos.

DEWEY: 914.2

♦ 648 ♦

Old English Customs Extant at the Present Time: An Account of Local Observances, Festival Customs, and Ancient Ceremonies yet Surviving in Great Britain. **P. H. Ditchfield. 1896. Reprint. Detroit, MI: Omnigraphics, Inc., 1968. 344 pp. Appendices. Index.**

Discusses British calendar customs still practiced at the turn of the twentieth century. Gives ample description of a wide range of customary practices and beliefs, noting local variants, and considering their origins. Arranged in calendar order. Appendices provide texts of several mummers' plays, the melodies used by the Bampton Morris dancers, and words and music to the Boar's Head Carol.

DEWEY: 390.0942 LC: DA 110 D644 ISBN 1-55888-917-5

♦ 649 ♦

Once a Year: Some Traditional British Customs. **Homer Sykes. Introduction by Paul Smith and Georgina Smith. London: Gordon Fraser, 1977. 168 pp. Illustrated. Map. Bibliography.**

Furnishes a description and black-and-white photo for 81 British calendar customs. Covers games, contests, dances, processions, doles, fairs, and many other regularly occurring festivities. Entries give date and location; many give history of the custom and note changes in its celebration. Arranged in calendar order. Map shows locations of the 81 customs.

DEWEY: 394.2 0942 LC: GR 930 ISBN 0-900406-68-2

♦ 650 ♦

Origins of Festivals and Feasts. **Jean Harrowven. London: Kaye and Ward, 1980. 188 pp. Bibliography.**

Recounts the history and lore of 12 British festivals and seasonal celebrations: St. Valentine's Day, Shrovetide (Shrove Tuesday), Mothering Sunday, Easter, April Fool's Day, May Day, Whitsuntide (Pentecost), Harvest, Hallowe'en, Guy Fawkes Day, Christmas, and New Year's Eve (or Hogmanay). Describes customs, past and present. Offers recipes and crafts for children.

LC: GT 3930 H36 ISBN 0-7182-1251-7

♦ 651 ♦

Representative Medieval and Tudor Plays, Translated and Modernized. **Introduction by Roger Sherman Loomis and Henry Willis Wells. 1942. Reprint. Freeport, NY: Books for Libraries Press, 1970. 301 pp. Bibliography.**

Reprints translated and modernized versions of medieval plays, many of which celebrate Church festivals or saints' miracles. Includes "The Miracle of Saint Nicholas and the Schoolboys"; "The Miracle of Saint Nicholas and the Virgins"; "The Miracle of Saint Nicholas and the Image" by Hilarius; "The Miracle of the Blind Man and the Cripple" by Andrieu de la Vigne; "The

Annunciation" and "The Second Shepherds' Play" from the Wakefield Mystery Cycle; "The Mystery of the Redemption" from the Hegge Manuscript; "The Summoning of Everyman"; and "John, Tyb and Sir John" and "The Pardoner and the Friar" by John Heywood. Introduction discusses the development of medieval drama.

DEWEY: 808.8251 LC: PN6112.L57 ISBN 0-8369-8202-9

♦ 652 ♦

Rituals of Royalty: The Ceremony and Pageantry of Britain's Monarchy. **Michele Brown. Englewood Cliffs, NJ: Prentice-Hall, 1983. 178 pp. Illustrated. Maps. Index.**

Describes and documents the historical development of about 50 ceremonies of the British monarchy, including many annual events. Some coverage of Scottish traditions. Black-and-white and color photos illustrate. Arranged in alphabetical order by ceremony name. Gives calendar of annual events, maps showing locations of these events, and addresses of organizations which can provide tickets or more information.

DEWEY: 390.2209 ISBN 0-13-781047-4

♦ 653 ♦

Saint George: A Christmas Mummers' Play. **Katherine Miller. Illustrated by Wallace Tripp. Boston, MA: Houghton Mifflin Company, 1967. 62 pp. Bibliography.**

Gives an adaptation of a Christmas mummers' play, along with production notes which suggest appropriate costumes and props. Illustrated with color and black-and-white drawings. Suitable for children.

DEWEY: 792.9

♦ 654 ♦

Saint George and the Dragon: A Mummer's Play. **John Langstaff. Illustrated by David Gentleman. New York: Atheneum Press, 1973. 48 pp.**

Presents an adaptation of a Christmas mummers' play. Gives words and music to mummers' songs. Illustrated with color woodcuts. Suitable for children.

DEWEY: 822.1 ISBN 0-689-30421-8

♦ 655 ♦

A Social History of the Fool. **Sandra Billington. Sussex, England: The Harvester Press, 1984. Published in the U.S. by St. Martin's Press, New York, 1984. 150 pp. Appendix. Bibliography. Index.**

Provides a social history of the fool in English society from the Middle Ages to modern times. Offers chapter on seasonal fools and fooling. Endnotes. Appendix gives chronological list of illustrations depicting fools in English manuscripts.

DEWEY: 306.48 LC: GT 3670. B45 ISBN 0-312-73293-7

♦ 656 ♦

The Stations of the Sun: A History of the Ritual Year in Britain. **Ronald Hutton. Oxford, England: Oxford University Press, 1996. 542 pp. Illustrated. Index.**

Learned account of the origins and historical development of seasonal celebrations, customs, and festivals of the British Isles. Arranged in calendar order. Black-and-white plates. Endnotes.

DEWEY: 394.2 6 0941 LC: GT 4843 A2 H87 ISBN 0-19-820570-8

♦ 657 ♦

Yearbook of English Festivals. **Dorothy Gladys Spicer. 1954. Reprint. Detroit, MI: Omnigraphics, Inc., 1993. 298 pp. Map. Glossary. Indexes.**

Introduces the reader to the local, regional, and national festivals and celebrations of England. Entries describe customary practices and their history, when known. Provides a county map of England, a glossary of terms associated with English festivals, a list of movable feasts of the Easter cycle and their dates from 1954 through 1984, and gives the meaning and uses of liturgical colors. Further reading list. Indexed by custom, county, and region.

DEWEY: 394.2 6 0942 LC: GT 4843. S6 ISBN 0-7808-0002-8

♦ 658 ♦

A Year of Festivals: A Guide to British Calendar Customs. **Geoffrey Palmer and Noel Lloyd. Illustrated by Gareth Floyd. London: Frederick Warne, 1972. 192 pp. Index.**

Describes popular customs and celebrations associated with local and national British festivals. Separate chapter treats London customs. Also provides a calendar of fairs and a county-by-county calendar of holidays, fairs, and festivals covered in the book.

LC: GT4843 P34 ISBN 0-7232-1309-7

SCOTLAND

♦ 659 ♦

British Calendar Customs—Scotland. **Three volumes. M. Macleod Banks. Preface by J. A. MacCulloch. London: William Glaisher, Ltd., 1937-1941. Volume one, 202 pp. Index. Volume two, 253 pp. Volume three, 266 pp., including index to volumes two and three.**

Encyclopedic coverage of the calendar customs of Scotland. Volume one is subtitled *Moveable Festivals, Harvest, March Riding and Wapynshaws, Wells, Fairs.* Volume two is subtitled *The Seasons, the Quarters, Hogmanay, January to May.* Volume three is subtitled *June to December, Christmas, the Yules.* Gives celebratory practices, pranks, sayings, superstitions, beliefs about the supernatural, folk medicines, folk dramas, dances, processions, games and contests, religious customs, business transactions, and prohibitions associated with celebrated days. Also relates lore concerning the months and days.

DEWEY: 398.841 B218   LC: GT 4845 B3

♦ 660 ♦

The Folklore of the Scottish Highlands. **Anne Ross. Illustrated by Richard Feachem. Totowa, NJ: Rowman and Littlefield, 1976. 174 pp. Bibliography. Glossary. Indexes.**

Describes folk beliefs and practices of the Scottish Highlands. Treats clan lore, seers, second sight, witchcraft, social customs, superstitions, healing, the life cycle, festivals, and death. Retells associated legends and lore and gives known history of customs and beliefs. Festivals covered include Christmas, New Year's Eve, St. Bride's Day (St. Bridget's Day), St. Columba's Day, Easter, May Day (or Beltane), Lughnasa (Lughnasadh), Feast of St. Mary, Feast of St. Barr, and St. Michael's Day. Provides a general index and a folk motif index.

LC: GR 145 H6 R68   ISBN 0-87471-836-8

♦ 661 ♦

Hallowe'en: Its Origin, Rites and Ceremonies in the Scottish Tradition. **F. Marian McNeill. Illustrations by John Mackay. Edinburgh, Scotland: The Albyn Press, [1970]. 63 pp.**

Reviews the legends, practices, and pranks which characterize the celebration of Halloween in Scotland. Gives poems, songs, and recipes.

DEWEY: 394.2683   LC: GT 4965 M33   ISBN 0-284-98537-6

♦ 662 ♦

The Silver Bough: Volume Two, A Calendar of Scottish National Festivals, Candlemas to Harvest Home. **F. Marian McNeill. Glasgow, Scotland: William Maclellan, 1959. 163 pp. Illustrated. Bibliography. Index.**

Relates the history, customs, legends, beliefs, superstitions, foods, and celebrations of Scottish festivals. Covers the Day of Bride (St. Bridget's Day), Candlemas, St. Valentine's Day, Fastern's E'en (Shrove Tuesday), Easter, All Fool's Day, Beltane and May Day, St. Columba's Day, Midsummer's Eve, Lammas, Michaelmas, and the Harvest. Also describes medieval festival plays and processions. Notes regional variation in beliefs and practices. Illustrated with black-and-white photos and drawings. Arranged in calendar order. Endnotes.

LC: GR 144 M163

♦ 663 ♦

The Silver Bough: Volume Three, A Calendar of Scottish National Festivals, Hallowe'en to Yule. **F. Marian McNeill. Glasgow, Scotland: William Maclellan, 1961. 180 pp. Illustrated. Appendix. Bibliography. Index.**

Relates the history, customs, legends, beliefs, superstitions, foods, and celebrations of Scottish festivals. Covers Halloween, Martinmas, Anermas (or St. Andrew's Day), Yule (the Christmas season), Hogmanay, Auld Hansel Monday, Uphalieday (Epiphany), and the Yule season in the Shetland Islands. Special attention given to Halloween divination rites, Christmas customs, Hogmanay customs and superstitions, the history of Christmas, and the practice of guising (or mumming). Arranged in calendar order. Illustrated with black-and-white photos and drawings. Appendix gives history and description of Burns Night, a popular festival celebrating the Scottish poet Robert Burns. Endnotes.

LC: GR 144 M163

♦ 664 ♦

The Silver Bough: Volume Four, The Local Festivals of Scotland. **F. Marian McNeill. Glasgow, Scotland: William Maclellan, 1968. 272 pp. Illustrated. Index.**

Covers more than 100 local festivals of Scotland. Gives place, date (or time or year), festival history, elements of local history, and description of celebration or observance. Arranged by season. Illustrated with black-and-white photos. Endnotes.

LC: GR 144 M163

WALES

♦ 665 ♦

Welsh Folk Customs. **Trefor M. Owen. Cardiff, Wales: National Museum of Wales, Welsh Folk Museum, 1959. 258 pp. Illustrated. Bibliography. Catalogue.**

Discusses Welsh folk customs, with a particular emphasis on calendar customs. Chapters address the Christmas season, Candlemas and the movable feasts surrounding Easter, May and high summer, harvest and the beginning of winter, and birth, marriage, and death. Covers folk and religious holidays, the manner of their celebration in the past and the present, and beliefs, customs, and superstitions concerning special days or times of year. Includes a catalogue of the collection of the Welsh Folk Museum. Illustrated with black-and-white plates.

DEWEY: 398.09429

♦ 666 ♦

Welsh Folklore and Folk-Custom. **Gwynn T. Jones. 1930. Reprint. Suffolk, England: D. S. Brewer, 1979. 255 pp. Bibliography. Glossary. Index.**

Collection of Welsh folklore regarding gods, ghosts, fairies, monsters, caves, lakes, magic, marriage, birth, and death. Recounting of some folk tales. Chapters nine and ten deal with customs concerning such holidays as May Day, Midsummer, Christmas, New Year, Easter, and more. (NR)

DEWEY: 390.009429 LC: GR150.J6 ISBN 0-8476-6185-7

Latin America (Caribbean, Central and South America)

General Works

♦ 667 ♦

Black Saturnalia: Conflict and Its Ritual Expression on British West Indian Slave Plantations. **Robert Dirks. Gainesville, FL: University of Florida Presses, 1987. 228 pp. Bibliography. Index.**

Scholarly analysis of Christmas celebrations in the British West Indies from the mid-eighteenth century to 1834. Investigates ecology and social organization of West Indies society and describes Christmas revels, which resembled Roman Saturnalia in their excesses and in their temporary erasure of social hierarchy between masters and slaves. Argues these celebrations symbolized social conditions of blacks under slavery.

DEWEY: 394. 268282 LC: GT 4987.23 D57 ISBN 0-8130-0843-3

♦ 668 ♦

Caribbean Festival Arts. **John W. Nunley and Judith Bettleheim, eds. Seattle, WA: University of Washington Press, 1988. 217 pp. Illustrated. Glossary. Index.**

Explores Caribbean festivals as cultural and artistic productions, focusing on performances, costumes, and music. Examines the uniquely Caribbean blend of African, European, and Native cultural influences evident in festival celebrations, as well as documenting the work of specific artists. First chapter provides a social history of Caribbean festivals. Remaining chapters cover Jonkonnu in Jamaica, Nassau, and the Bahamas; various Christmas season masquerades, Carnival and the Hosay festival (of Muslim origin) in Trinidad; and Carnival and other festivals in Cuba, Haiti, and New Orleans. Beautifully illustrated with many large color photos.

DEWEY: 394.2 5 07409729 LC: GT 4823.N85 ISBN 0-295-96702-1

♦ 669 ♦

Feliz Nochebuena Feliz Navidad: Christmas Feasts of the Hispanic Caribbean. **Maricel E. Presilla. New York: Henry Holt and Company, 1994. Unpaginated. Illustrated. Bibliography. Glossary.**

Describes Christmas season celebrations in Cuba, Puerto Rico, and the Dominican Republic. Focuses on seasonal dishes and their origins. Gives recipes, introduces Spanish words. Color drawings illustrate. For children.

DEWEY: 394.2 663 09729 LC: GT 4987.23 P74 ISBN 0-8050-2512-X

♦ 670 ♦

Fiesta Time in Latin America. **Jean Milne. Los Angeles, CA: Ward Ritchie Press, 1965. 236 pp. Appendix.**

Describes the festivities and folklore of 100 holidays, festivals, and fairs throughout Latin America. Covers events in Argentina, Bolivia, Brazil, Chile, Colombia, Costa Rica, Dominican Republic, Ecuador, Guatemala, Haiti, Honduras, Mexico, Nicaragua, Panama, Paraguay, Peru, El Salvador, Uruguay, and Venezuela. Focuses on religious and community festivals; excludes patriotic holidays. Entries organized by month and date. Appendix gives festival calendar for each country, noting festival name, date, location, and major attraction.

DEWEY: 394.2098

♦ 671 ♦

Piñatas and Paper Flowers, Piñatas y Flores de Papel. **Lila Perl. Spanish version by Alma Flor Ada. Illustrated by Victoria de Larrea. New York: Clarion Books, 1983. 91 pp. Index.**

Describes the celebration of eight Latin American holidays. Gives English and Spanish text. Covers New Year, Three King's Day, Carnival and Easter, St. John the Baptist Day, Columbus Day, Halloween, the Festival of the Sun, and Christmas. Depicts customs, foods, and festivities of many Latin American countries and peoples, as well as those of Hispanics in the U.S. For children.

DEWEY: 394.2 698 LC: GT 4801.P47 ISBN 0-89919-112-6

Bolivia

♦ 672 ♦

The Masked Media: Aymara Fiestas and Social Interaction in the Bolivian Highlands. **Hans C. Buechler. The Hague, Netherlands: Mouton**

Publishers, 1980. 399 pp. Illustrated. Appendices. Bibliography. Glossary. Indexes.

Offers an anthropological study of the fiesta cycle of the Aymara people of Compi, Bolivia. Outlines festival structure and activities, as well as discusses festival organization and the various roles available to festival participants. Contrasts town and city festivals. Analyzes the social codes expressed in festival structure and participation. Also covers life-cycle celebrations. Appendices offer commentary on the instrument cycle in Irpa Chico, the Festival of the Skulls, the introduction of brass bands in Compi festivals, and more. Subject and author indexes. Scholarly.

LC: F2230.2 A9 B83 ISBN 90-279-7777-1

Brazil

♦ 673 ♦

Carnivals, Rogues, and Heroes: An Interpretation of the Brazilian Dilemma. **Roberto Da Matta. Translated by John Drury. Notre Dame, IN: University of Notre Dame Press, 1991. 279 pp.**

Scholarly analysis of the meaning and organization of Carnival in Brazil; results used to shed light on the nature of Brazilian society and the Brazilian nation. Some comparison of Carnival in Brazil with Mardi Gras in the U.S. List of references cited.

DEWEY: 394.2 5 0981 LC: GT 4233. A2 M38 ISBN 0-268-00780-2

♦ 674 ♦

Christmas in Brazil. **Rebecca A. Lauer. Chicago: World Book, Inc., 1991. 80 pp. Illustrated.** 📖

Tells how the Christmas season is celebrated in Brazil. Explains the history of Brazilian Christmas celebrations, noting African, Indian, and Portuguese elements and influences. Describes Papai Noel, the *Missa do Galo* (Mass of the Rooster), the preparation of nativity scenes (or *presépios*), secret friends, Christmas baskets, and other Christmas season customs and activities. Also describes typical Brazilian Christmas decorations and foods. Covers the festivities and customs associated with New Year's Eve, including St. Sylvester's Race, and New Year's Day, including the Feast of Iemanjá, the procession honoring Our Lady of Sailors, and the festival of Congada. Also covers the month-long Festival of the Kings, including the folk plays called "Beating of the Bull" (*Bumba-meu-boi*), and Three King's Day. Explains the coexistence and intermingling of Roman Catholicism, Candomblé, and Umbanda beliefs and practices. For older children. One book in a series entitled *Christmas Around the World.*

DEWEY: 394.2682 ISBN 0-7166-0891-X

Colombia

♦ 675 ♦

Caribbean Carnival: An Exploration of the Barranquilla Carnival, Colombia. **Diego Samper Martínez and Mirtha Buelvas Aldana. Bogotá, Colombia: Diego Samper Ediciones, 1994. 191 pp. Illustrated. Bibliography.**

Numerous color photos and accompanying text convey the spirit of Carnival season celebrations in Barranquilla, Colombia. Photos document costumes, makeup, masks, dances, and processions. Text considers history of Colombian Carnival; its European, African, and Native elements and influences; and the Colombian and Caribbean cultural values it embodies. Describes Guacherna Night, the Battle of the Flowers, and Carnival music and dance styles.

DEWEY: 96 00550 ISBN 9978-82-558-6

♦ 676 ♦

Fiestas: Celebrations and Rituals of Colombia. **Benjamin Villegas, Nina S. de Friedemann, and Jeremy Horner. Translated by Patricia Shaio de Pitchon. Bogotá, Colombia: Villegas Editores, 1995. Illustrated. Bibliography. Glossary.**

Photoessay and text describing many festivals and celebrations of Colombia. Covers Corpus Christi, Carnival, Easter, Fiesta de San Pacho, and corrales, rodeos, and circuses. Considers costumes, masks, processions, dances, and other festival activities. Identifies themes and analyzes their symbolic and social meanings. Some attention to history of Colombian fiestas and their mixture of European, African, and Native cultural influences.

DEWEY: 96 11947 ISBN 958-9393-14-4

Cuba

♦ 677 ♦

Cuban Festivals: An Illustrated Anthology. **Judith Bettleheim, ed. New York: Garland Publishing, Inc., 1993. 261 pp. Illustrated. Index.**

Contains several articles which analyze the festivities of Carnival and Day of the Kings (Día de los Reyes, or Epiphany) celebrations in Cuba. Examines history of festivals and festival practices, and derives insights into Cuban society. One article provides glossary of Afro-Cuban terms associated with Cuban festivals.

DEWEY: 394.2 697291 LC: GT 4825. A2 C83 ISBN 0-8153-0310-6

Haiti

♦ 678 ♦

Dances of Haiti. **Katherine Dunham. Foreword by Claude Lévi-Strauss. 1957. Reprint. Los Angeles, CA: University of California at Los Angeles Press, 1983. 78 pp. Illustrated. Glossary.**

Discusses the forms and functions of Haitian dance. Covers all types of dance, including those performed for seasonal celebrations, religious (Vodoo) ceremonies, and Mardi Gras and Holy Week observations.

DEWEY: 793.3 19729 4 LC: GV 1632. H2 D86 ISBN 0-934934-17-7

♦ 679 ♦

Haiti Through Its Holidays. **Eleanor Wong Telemaque. Illustrations by Earl Hill. New York: Edward W. Blyden, Inc., 1980. 59 pp.**

A Haitian-American grandfather tells his grandchildren about the preparations, foods, customs, festivities, beliefs, and history of seven Haitian holidays. Covers Columbus Day, Fête des Morts, Christmas, Jou d'lan (or Independence Day), Carnival, the Ra-Ra (Lent and Holy Week), and Agriculture and Labor Day. Also gives several Haitian proverbs and folk songs, and background information about Haitian family life. Illustrated with black-and-white photos and drawings. For children.

LC: GT 4826 A2 T45 ISBN 0-914110-08-X

Mexico

♦ 680 ♦

Christmas in Mexico. **Corinne Ross. Chicago: World Book Encyclopedia, Inc., 1976. 80 pp. Illustrated. Map. Glossary. Index.**

Explains the origins of Mexican Christmas celebrations, noting Indian and Spanish influences, and describes the various customs and activities associated with the celebrations of the Christmas season. Covers Las Posadas, Christmas Eve, Christmas, Day of the Innocents, New Year's Eve, Three Kings Day, and Candlemas. Describes the use of *piñatas* in Christmas festivities, the making of nativity scenes (or *nacimientos*), and the performance of Christmas folk plays called *Pastorelas* (Pastorals). Includes a discussion of distinctive regional celebrations. Identifies the foods and plants of Mexican origin which have become part of international Christmas celebrations. Provides a map of Mexico that marks locations discussed. Gives Mexican Christmas crafts, songs, and recipes. Pronunciation guide. For older children. One book in a series entitled *Christmas Around the World.*

DEWEY: 394.2682 ISBN 0-7166-2002-2

♦ 681 ♦

Days of the Dead. **Kathryn Laskey. New York: Hyperion Books for Children, 1994. 48 pp. Illustrated. Glossary.**

Depicts Day of the Dead celebrations in Mexico and explains sentiments behind them. Follows a Mexican family in their observance of the holiday. Beautifully illustrated with color photographs.

DEWEY: 394.2682 LC: GT4995. A4 L37 ISBN 0-7868-0022-4

♦ 682 ♦

The Days of the Dead: Mexico's Festival of Communion with the Departed, Los Días de Muertos: Un Festival de Comunión con los Muertos en México. **Photography by John Greenleigh. Text by Rosalind Rosoff Beimler. San Francisco, CA: CollinsPublishers, 1991. 112 pp.**

Presents a collection of beautiful color photographs which document the popular celebrations and religious devotions of the Days of the Dead in Mexico. Photos taken in four Mexican states (Michoacán, Morelos, Oaxaca, and México) between the years 1985 and 1990. Accompanying text compares the festival with celebrations of death in other cultures, summarizes the festival's history, and describes its customs, foods, and ambience. Gives text in Spanish and English.

DEWEY: 394.2 6828 LC: GT 4995. A4G74 ISBN 0-00-215962-7

♦ 683 ♦

Fiesta! Mexico's Great Celebrations. **Elizabeth Silverthorne. Illustrated by Jan Davey Ellis. Brookfield, CT: The Millbrook Press, 1992. 64 pp. Glossary. Index.**

Provides an introduction to the cultures and festivals of Mexico. Brief explanation of the geography and history of modern Mexico and its three main cultural traditions: Indian, Spanish, and Mexican. Chapters on religious, patriotic, and local fiestas describe celebrations and customs and give recipes and crafts. Covers Our Lady of Guadalupe, Christmas, Easter, the Feast of St. John, Day of the Dead, the birthday of Benito Juárez, Cinco de Mayo, Independence

Day, Día de la Raza (Columbus Day), and more. Illustrated with color drawings. Furnishes a calendar of major Mexican festivals. Further reading list. For children.

DEWEY: 394.2 6 0972 LC: GT 4814.A2S55 ISBN 1-56294-055-4

♦ 684 ♦

Fiesta in Mexico. **Erna Fergusson. Illustrated by Valentín Vidaurreta. New York: Alfred A. Knopf, 1934. 267 pp. Index, pp. i-iv.**

Offers author's firsthand description of more than 10 local Mexican fiestas. Covers the Birth of the Virgin (Tixtla), the Pilgrimage to Chalma, Moors and Christians (Tuxpan and Tinsel), the Feast of La Soledad (Oaxaca), Easter Week Passion Plays (Tzintzuntzan), the Huichol Deer Dance, the Fiesta of Santa Maria (Tehuantepec), the Yaqui Pascola, the Day of the Dead, the Lenten festivals of La Chavarrieta and Nuestro Señor de la Vera Cruz (Taxco), and El Viernes de los Dolores (Santa Anita/Mexico City). Illustrated with black-and-white drawings.

DEWEY: 917.2 F35

♦ 685 ♦

Fiestas in Mexico. **First English edition. Mexico City, Mexico: Ediciones Lara, S. A., 1978. 198 pp. Illustrated. Maps.**

Lists hundreds of local Mexican festivals and celebrations. Festivals presented first by state and then by calendar date. Entries give festival locations and briefly describe celebratory activities and other local attractions. Also furnishes map of each state with festival locations marked. Illustrated with black-and-white photos of festival activities.

LC: GT 4814 A2 F53

♦ 686 ♦

Fiesta Time in Mexico. **Rebecca B. Marcus and Judith Marcus. Illustrated by Bert Dodson. Champaign, IL: Garrard Publishing Company, 1974. 95 pp. Index.**

Introduces children to the celebrations, devotional practices, foods, spirit, and significance of 11 of Mexico's most important holidays. Covers the Day of the Dead, Our Lady of Guadalupe Day, the Christmas season, New Year's Day, Three Kings Day, St. Anthony the Abbot's Day, Holy Week and Easter, St. John's Day, Mexican Independence Day, Cinco de Mayo, and the Twentieth of November. Gives pronunciation guide.

DEWEY: 394.2 6971 LC: GT 4814. A2M37 ISBN 0-8116-4953-9

♦ 687 ♦

The Lady of Guadalupe. **Tomie de Paola. New York: Holiday House, 1980. 44 pp. Illustrated.**

Retells the story of the appearance of the Virgin of Guadalupe, Mexico's patron saint, to a poor Indian named Juan Diego. Illustrated with color drawings. For children.

DEWEY: 235.2 LC: BT 660 G8 D43 ISBN 0-8234-0373-4

♦ 688 ♦

Mexican Celebrations. **Eliot Porter and Ellen Auerbach. Essays by Donna Pierce and Marsha C. Bol. Albuquerque, NM: University of New Mexico Press, 1990. 115 pp. Illustrated.**

Presents a collection of color photos documenting religious sentiments and celebrations in Mexico. Includes two essays of commentary: one on Mexican religious ritual and one on festival organization and activities.

DEWEY: 263.9 0972 LC: BX1428.2 P67 ISBN 0-8263-1209-8

♦ 689 ♦

The Mexican Day of the Dead. **Chloë Sayer, ed. Boston, MA: Shambala Redstone Editions, 1994. 95 pp. Illustrated.**

An anthology of texts and photographs concerning the Day of the Dead celebrations in Mexico. Gives poems and excerpts from letters, journal entries, and published works that describe the celebrations and related beliefs or convey their spirit. Includes selections from Sor Juana Inéz de la Cruz, Sergei Eisenstein, Octavio Paz, and more. Many entries list suggestions for further reading. Black-and-white and color photos illustrate.

DEWEY: 394.2 64 LC: GT4995.A4 M49 ISBN 1-57062-026-1

♦ 690 ♦

Mexican Folk Toys: Festival Decorations and Ritual Objects. **Florence H. Pettit and Robert M. Pettit. New York: Hastings House, 1978. 192 pp. Illustrated. Bibliography. Glossary. Index.**

Gives an overview of the design, production, and uses of Mexican folk toys and ceremonial objects. Catalogs materials and techniques used in craft production. Provides a calendar of Mexican festivals, which offers brief descriptions of ceremonies and celebratory activities. Lists regions where specific craft items are made, shops and markets where they can be bought, and folk museums where they can be viewed. Amply illustrated with color and black-and-white photos.

DEWEY: 394.3 0972 LC: GN 560. M6 P47 ISBN 8038-4709-2

♦ 691 ♦

Power and Persuasion: Fiestas and Social Control in Rural Mexico. **Stanley Brandes. Philadelphia, PA: University of Pennsylvania Press, 1988. 212 pp. Illustrated. Bibliography. Glossary. Index.**

Anthropological study of the social functions served by rural Mexican fiestas, or festivals. Attention given to festival organization, various forms of contracts and exchanges associated with festivals, and the role of dance and fireworks displays. Special focus on Las Posadas. Concludes that, in spite of the temporary loosening of behavioral mores, festivals promote conformity with established cultural norms. Based on firsthand research in Tzintzuntzan, located in the state of Michoacán.

DEWEY: 394.2 6972 37 LC: GT 4814. T95 B7 ISBN 0-8122-8077-6

♦ 692 ♦

Rituals of Rule, Rituals of Resistance: Popular Celebrations and Popular Culture in Mexico. **William H. Beezley, Cheryl English Martin, and William E. French, eds. Wilmington, DE: Scholarly Resources, Inc., 1994. 374 pp.**

A collection of 15 scholarly essays which examine Mexican public rituals and ceremonies of many kinds, including festivals. Common goal of essays is to identify ways in which the power and authority of the state is consolidated or resisted during these public displays. Essays span 500 years of Mexican history.

DEWEY: 394.2 6972 LC: GT 4814. A2 R57 ISBN 0-8420-2416-6

♦ 693 ♦

The Skeleton at the Feast: The Day of the Dead in Mexico. **Elizabeth Carmichael and Chloë Sayer. Austin, TX: University of Texas Press, 1995. 160 pp. Illustrated. Appendix. Bibliography. Glossary. Index.**

Offers a multi-faceted perspective on the Day of the Dead festival in Mexico. Describes Day of the Dead beliefs, practices, folk and ceremonial art, and notes other thematically related Mexican festivals, customs, and observances. Discusses historical development and regional variation of the festival, noting both pre-Hispanic and Christian elements and influences. Gives 10 translated interviews with contemporary Mexicans from various regions and backgrounds on the ideas, beliefs, images, art, and sentiments encompassed by the festival. Richly illustrated with color and black-and-white photos of festival celebrations and folk art.

DEWEY: 394.2682 ISBN 0-292-77658-6

♦ 694 ♦

A Treasury of Mexican Folkways. **Frances Toor. Illustrated by Carlos Merida. New York: Crown Publishers, 1947. 566 pp. Bibliography. Glossary. Index.**

Presents a wide range of folk practices, beliefs, and customs. Treats agriculture, folk arts, the life cycle, society, fiestas, music, dance, verse, myths, and tales. Describes ceremonies and popular celebrations of more than 20 religious festivals. Illustrated with black-and-white photographs and a number of color drawings.

DEWEY: 398 T672

♦ 695 ♦

Vive tu Recuerdo: Living Traditions in the Mexican Days of the Dead. **Robert V. Childs and Patricia B. Altman. Spanish translation by Hernán Quiñones. Los Angeles, CA: Museum of Cultural History, University of California at Los Angeles, 1982. 64 pp. Illustrated.**

Presents the folk arts, festivities, customs, beliefs, and observances of the Mexican Days of the Dead in Spanish and in English. Discusses indigenous and Spanish influences and elements in the festival, and conveys its spirit and meaning. Describes celebrations in Oaxaca, Michoacán, Morelos, Tlaxcala, Chiapas, the Yucatán, and East Los Angeles, noting regional variation in folk arts, practices, and beliefs, as well as identifies the ways in which they have been influenced by local Native cultures. Many black-and-white and some color photos of folk arts and ceremonial objects.

DEWEY: 394.2682

Peru

♦ 696 ♦

Three Worlds of Peru. **Frances Toor. New York: Crown Publishers, 1949. 239 pp. Appendix. Bibliography. Index.**

A descriptive account of the peoples, lifestyles, and customs of Peru. Divided into three parts which cover the country's three distinct geographical and cultural regions: the Coast, the Sierra and the Montaña. Characterizes way of life, social groups, landscape, architecture, and folk costumes; describes popular customs and festivals. Includes chapter on the history of Peru. Appendix gives a calendar of festivals, which outlines the celebration of the major festivals of each month.

LC: F 3423 T67

Trinidad

♦ 697 ♦

The Trinidad Carnival: Mandate for a National Theatre. **Errol Hill. Austin, TX: University of Texas Press, 1972. 139 pp. Illustrated. Appendices. Bibliography. Index.**

Traces the history of Carnival celebrations in Trinidad, examining the development of its aesthetic elements and identifying the ethnic origins of various concepts and practices. Provides a brief history of the colonization of Trinidad and the beginnings of its Carnival traditions. Chapters devoted to the practice of stick games, steel drum bands, Calypso music, masquerade, Carnival tents, stage spectacles, and other elements of folk celebration which the author argues could provide the basis for a national theater. Illustrated with color photos of Carnival participants.

LC: GT 4229 T7 H5 ISBN 0-292-78000-1

Middle East and North Africa

General Works

♦ 698 ♦

Arab World Mosaic: A Curriculum Supplement for Elementary Teachers. **Lars Rodseth, Sally Howell, and Andrew Shryock. Illustrated by Michelle P. Gallagher. Sally Howell and Andrew Shryock, eds. Dearborn, MI: Arab Community Center for Economic and Social Services, 1994. 209 pp. Appendices. Bibliography.**

Offers detailed elementary school lessons on six aspects of Arab culture: names and language; family; home, neighborhood and community; plants and animals; holidays and celebrations; folktales and stories. Each unit identifies educational objectives, lists needed materials, offers lesson plans, includes student reading materials and illustrations, and provides cultural notes for teachers. Holidays covered include Ramadan, Id al-Fitr, Id al-Adha, the Hajj, Easter, and Christmas. Tells where to obtain additional teaching material. Appendix A furnishes list of Middle East Outreach programs.

ISBN 0-8187-0222-2

♦ 699 ♦

The Travelers' Guide to Middle Eastern and North African Customs and Manners. **Elizabeth Devine and Nancy L. Braganti. New York: St. Martin's Press, 1991. 244 pp.**

Alerts travelers to everyday social customs in Middle Eastern and North African countries. Covers Egypt, the Gulf States (Bahrain, Kuwait, Oman, Qatar, and the United Arab Emirates), Iraq, Israel, Jordan, the Maghreb (Algeria, Morocco, and Tunisia), Saudi Arabia, and Yemen. Lists national holidays for all countries. Other topics covered include greetings, conversation, telephones, public behavior, dress, meals, hotels, tipping, visits to private homes, business practices, transportation, legal issues, safety, and health. Gives useful phrases in Arabic and Hebrew.

DEWEY: 915.604 53 LC: DS 43.D45 ISBN 0-312-05523-4

Egypt

♦ 700 ♦

Festivals of Egypt. **Jailan Abbas. Illustrated by Abd el Wahab Bilal. Cairo, Egypt: Hoopoe Books, 1995. 49 pp. Index.**

Describes Muslim, Christian, and folk holidays of Egypt. Covers Moulid el-Nabi (Mulud al-Nabi), Ramadan, Id el-Fitr, Id el-Adha, Moulids, Christmas, Epiphany, Palm Sunday, Easter, Sham el-Nessim, and Nile Festivals. Entries depict religious observance, activities of celebration, foods, and customs; some give brief historical background. Also introduces the Islamic and Coptic calendars, offers several recipes, includes chronology of periods in Egyptian history. Illustrated with color photos and drawings. For young readers.

DEWEY: 394.2696 ISBN 977-5325-47-1

♦ 701 ♦

Ritual, Politics, and the City in Fatimid Cairo. **Paula Sanders. Albany, NY: State University of New York Press, 1994. 231 pp. Bibliography. Index.**

Uses analysis of court ceremonies and rituals, including festival celebrations, to shed light on the politics and culture of Cairo during the Fatimid period (909-1171 A.D.). Gives chapter on the New Year ceremony. Discusses Id al-Fitr, various ceremonies surrounding the rising of the Nile river, and the Festival of Ghadir.

DEWEY: 962.16 LC: DT 146. S26 ISBN 0-7914-1781-6

Israel

♦ 702 ♦

Through the Year in Israel. **Denise Bergman and Lorna Williams. London: Batsford Academic and Educational Ltd., 1983. 71 pp. Illustrated. Maps. Index.**

Provides an overview of Israeli culture and society. Covers history, politics, home life, ethnic and religious diversity, holidays, economy, and more. Illustrated with black-and-white photos and maps. Gives a suggested reading list and resources list. For young readers.

DEWEY: 956.94 ISBN 0-7134-0846-4

Morocco

♦ 703 ♦

Fasting and Feasting in Morocco: Women's Participation in Ramadan. **Marjo Buitelaar. Oxford, England: Berg Press, 1993. 203 pp. Illustrated. Appendix. Bibliography. Glossary. Index.**

In-depth anthropological study of Ramadan in Morocco, with a particular emphasis on women's observances. Describes women's devotional and preparatory practices, examines meaning participants attach to them, and relates these to formal Islamic doctrines. Considers the relationship between the values and ideas enshrined in Ramadan and those of Moroccan society as a whole. Creates wider context for the analysis of Ramadan by outlining the celebration of other Islamic holidays in Morocco, including the Feast of Immolation (in the month of Dhu al-Hijjah), Ashura (the tenth of Muharram), and the Mulud (the birthday of the Prophet, or Mulud al-Nabi).

DEWEY: 297. 36 LC: BP 186.4 B85 ISBN 0-85496-321-9

♦ 704 ♦

Ritual and Belief in Morocco. **Two volumes. Edward Westermarck. London: Macmillan and Company, 1926. Volume one, 608 pp. Illustrated. Volume two, 629 pp. Illustrated. Index.**

A comprehensive compilation of Moroccan folk practices and folk beliefs. Volume one introduces the various ethnic groups of Morocco, and presents the folklore surrounding the concept of baraka (or holiness), the Jinn (spirits), the evil eye, curses and oaths, and witchcraft. Volume two covers folklore and folk practices associated with magic, omens, dreams, childbirth, childhood, and death, as well as beliefs and rituals associated with the Islamic calendar, dates of the solar year, time of year, agriculture, and weather-influencing rites. Gives detailed description which notes regional and ethnic variations.

DEWEY: 398.864 W527

North America

General Works

♦ 705 ♦

The American Festival Guide: A Handbook of More Than 200 Colonial, Homesteading, Western, Spanish, Folk, Rodeo, Sports, Cultural and Other Annual Festivals and Celebrations in the United States and Canada, with a Calendar and a Gazetteer of Festivals for Ready Reference. **Helen B. Coates. 1956. Reprint. Detroit, MI: Omnigraphics, Inc., 1997. 299 pp.**

Covers more than 200 North American festivals. Brief chapters offer first hand accounts of the foods, festivities, people, costumes, history, and attractions of 10 American festivals: Old Spanish Days (Santa Barbara, Calif.), Patriots' Day (Lexington, Mass.), Desert Cavalcade (Calexico, Calif. and Mexicali, Mexico), Tulip-Time (Holland, Mich.), All-Indian Pow-Wow (Flagstaff, Ariz.), Seafoods Festival (Rockland, Maine), Pennsylvania Dutch Folk Festival (Kutztown, Penn.), Hyllnings Fest (Lindsborg, Kan.), Festival of the Arts (Laguna Beach, Calif.). Remaining festivals are grouped together by theme and covered in lesser detail. Further reading suggested for many festivals. Includes calendar and gazetteer of festivals.

DEWEY: 394.26973 LC: GT4803 A2C63 ISBN 0-7808-0269-1

♦ 706 ♦

Best Festivals of North America: A Performing Arts Guide. **Third edition. Carol Spivack and Richard A. Weinstock. Ventura, CA: Printwheel Press, 1989. 208 pp. Indexes.**

Lists more than 200 festivals in the United States and Canada. Includes arts festivals, dance festivals, classical music festivals, folk music festivals, jazz festivals, theater festivals, folk festivals, ethnic festivals, childrens' festivals and more. Entries give brief description of festival activities and ambience, note recent performers and performances, give performance times and ticket information, mention local sightseeing opportunities, rate local accommodations, and give organization to contact for more information. Provides an index of festival names, a geographic index, an index of nearby attractions, and an index of festivals by date. Cross-referenced.

DEWEY: 790.2097 ISBN 0-916401-08-1

♦ 707 ♦

Celebrations: America's Best Festivals, Jamborees, Carnivals and Parades. **Judith Young. Foreword by Ray Bradbury. Santa Barbara, CA: Capra Press, 1986. 183 pp. Illustrated.**

A guide to more than 200 festivals in all 50 states and Canada. Entries list date, festival name, city, contact address, and describe festival events and ambience. Provides separate listing of ethnic and Native American festivals not covered in the text. Numerous black-and-white photos illustrate.

DEWEY: 394.5 0973 LC: GT 4803Y68 ISBN 0-88496-242-3

♦ 708 ♦

Festivals Sourcebook: A Reference Guide to Fairs, Festivals and Celebrations in Agriculture, Antiques, the Arts, Theater and Drama, Arts and Crafts, Community, Dance, Ethnic Events, Film, Folk, Food and Drink, History, Indians, Marine, Music, Seasons, and Wildlife. **Paul Wasserman, ed. Detroit, MI: Gale Research, 1977. 656 pp. Indexes.**

Lists more than 3,800 local festivals in the United States and Canada. Entries give festival theme, state (or province), city, festival name, month, frequency, duration, specific location, contact organization, one-sentence description, and year begun. Arranged by the 18 festival themes included in the book title. Excludes local celebrations of national holidays, most sporting events, religious holidays, rodeos, horse shows, county fairs, and beauty pageants. Also provides a chronological listing of events and indexes of event names, locations, and specific subjects.

DEWEY: 394.2 0973 LC: GT 4802. F47 ISBN 0-8103-0311-6

♦ 709 ♦

Holy Days and Holidays: A Treasury of Historical Material, Sermons in Full and in Brief, Suggestive Thoughts, and Poetry, Relating to Holy Days and Holidays. **Rev. Edward M. Deems. 1902. Reprint. Detroit, MI: Omnigraphics, Inc., 1993. 767 pp. Bibliography. Indexes.**

A collection of descriptive materials, including sermons, quotations, poetry, historical essays, anecdotes, and personal observations relating to 19 Christian and 17 secular North American and British holidays. Reflects nineteenth sensibilities of the author.

DEWEY: 394.2 6973 LC: BV 30 D4 ISBN 1-55888-910-8

Canada

♦ 710 ♦

Christmas in Canada. **Staff of World Book, Inc. Chicago: World Book Inc., 1994. 80 pp. Illustrated.**

Describes Christmas celebrations of Canada's major ethnic groups. Relates Christmas customs and history of French Canadians, British Canadians, German Canadians, Ukrainian Canadians, and Native Canadians. Portrays pioneer and Victorian Christmas celebrations, as well as contemporary festivities and religious observance in Canada's largest cities. Gives Christmas crafts, recipes, and songs. Illustrated with color photos. For older children. One book in a series entitled *Christmas Around the World.*

DEWEY: 394.2663 ISBN 0-7166-0894-4

♦ 711 ♦

Christmas Mumming in Newfoundland. **Herbert Halpert and G. M. Story, eds. Toronto, Canada: University of Toronto Press, 1969. 246 pp. Appendices. Bibliography. Index.**

Gathers together a collection of scholarly articles on the Newfoundland folk tradition of Christmas mumming. Includes "Newfoundland: Fishermen, Hunters, Planters, and Merchants" by G. M. Story; "A Typology of Mumming" by Herbert Halpert; "Mummers and Strangers in Northern Newfoundland" by Melvin M. Firestone; "Mumming in 'Deep Harbor': Aspects of Social Organization in Mumming and Drinking" by Louis J. Charamonte; "The Mask of Friendship: Mumming as a Ritual of Social Relations" by John F. Szwed; "The 'Naluyuks' of Northern Labrador: A Mechanism of Social Control" by Shmuel Ben-Dor; "Mumming in an Outport Fishing Settlement: A Description and Suggestions on the Cognitive Complex" by James C. Faris; "The Disguises of Newfoundland Mummers" by J.D.A. Widdowson and Herbert Halpert; "Mummers in Newfoundland History: A Survey of the Printed Record" by G. M. Story; and "Newfoundland Mummers' Plays: Three Printed Texts" edited by Herbert Halpert and G. M. Story.

LC: GT 4985 H27 ISBN 8020-3200-1

♦ 712 ♦

Let's Celebrate! **Caroline Parry. Toronto, Canada: Kids Can Press, Ltd. 1987. 256 pp. Illustrated. Index.**

A multicultural, children's guide to the many holidays and festivals of Canada's religious and ethnic groups. Entries give holiday name, note date and religious or ethnic affiliation, explain holiday's significance, and tell how celebrated. Includes holidays and festivals of European, Inuit, Asian, and Caribbean Canadians, as well as those of Christians, Jews, Muslims, Hindus, Buddhists, and followers of Baha'i. Sidebars provide additional interesting facts, stories, recipes and activities. Arranged in calendar order. Brief introduction to various calendar systems and the seasons. Illustrated with black-and-white drawings.

DEWEY: 394.2 691 LC: GT 4813. A2 P37 ISBN 0-921103-38-7

Native North America

GENERAL WORKS

♦ 713 ♦

American Indian Ceremonial Dances. **John Collier. Illustrated by Ira Moskowitz. New York: Bounty Books, 1972. 192 pp.**

Noted artist's collection of more than 100 black-and-white drawings, lithographs, and etchings of scenes from Southwest Indian life, with special emphasis on ceremonies. Accompanying text recounts history of Southwest tribes, and describes Native ways of life, noting the role and meaning of ceremonies within it. Revised edition of a book originally titled *Patterns and Ceremonials of the Indians of the Southwest.*

DEWEY: 970.4 C699 a

♦ 714 ♦

American Indian Design and Decoration. **Le Roy H. Appleton. 1950. Reprint. New York: Dover Publications, 1971. 277 pp. Illustrated. Bibliography. Indexes.**

Offers more than 700 illustrations of Native North and South American designs, identifying the most common motifs of each culture area. Introductory chapter reviews art and craft skills of various Native American tribes. Also furnishes folk tales for each culture area. Four color and 79 black-and-white plates. Story index and plate index. Originally published as *Indian Art of the Americas.*

DEWEY: 970.1 ISBN 0-486-22704-9

♦ 715 ♦

Dancing Gods: Indian Ceremonials of New Mexico and Arizona. **Erna Fergusson. Foreword by Tony Hillerman. Albuquerque, NM: University of New Mexico Press, 1991. 286 pp. Illustrated. Index.**

Explains history, meaning, and describes performance of religious and social dances and ceremonies observed among the Pueblo, Hopi, Navaho, and Apache peoples, including prayers, customs, and some historical background. First printing 1931. (NR)

DEWEY: 970.67933 LC: E98.D2 F43

♦ 716 ♦

Discover Indian Reservations U.S.A.: A Visitors' Welcome Guide. **Foreword by Ben Nighthorse Campbell. Denver, CO: Council Publications, 1992. 402 pp. Illustrated. Maps. Appendices. Index.**

Travel-oriented information provided on more than 350 federal and state Indian reservations in 33 states, listed in alphabetical order by state. Entries include a brief profile on the reservation's land, population, and structure, its location and address, cultural institutes, special events (including festivals, powwows, rodeos, etc.), businesses and organizations, accommodations, and special restrictions. Appendix I lists tribes alphabetically and gives their location. Appendix II is a powwow directory by state, then month. (NR)

ISBN 0-9632580-0-1

♦ 717 ♦

Eagle Drum: On the Powwow Trail With a Young Grass Dancer. **Robert Crum. New York: Four Winds Press, 1994. 48 pp. Illustrated.**

Describes a young Indian boy's preparations for and participation in the dance competitions held during the summer powwows of the Northern Great Plains tribes. Describes powwows, dance styles, and costumes, presents beliefs and values of Native Americans. Provides a partial calendar of powwows. Written for children.

DEWEY: 394.3 LC: E99. K17 C77 ISBN 0-02-725515-8

♦ 718 ♦

Enduring Harvests: Native American Foods and Festivals for Every Season. **E. Barrie Kavasch. Illustrated by Mitzi Rawls. Old Saybrook, CT: Globe Pequot Press, 1995. 333 pp. Bibliography. Index.**

Presents brief descriptions of 68 Native American festivals, ceremonies, commemorative events, and powwows from every region of the United States, along with recipes for festival foods and other typical dishes. Also gives background information on tribal history, culture, contemporary issues, and location. Provides a directory of Native foods suppliers.

DEWEY: 641.59 297 LC: TX 715. K205 ISBN 1-56440-737-3

♦ 719 ♦

Games of the North American Indians. **Stewart Culin. 1907. Reprint. New York: Dover Publications, 1975. 846 pp. Illustrated. Appendix. Index.**

Describes games and gaming equipment of North American Indians. Games are grouped into three main categories: games of chance, games of dexterity, and amusements. Describes 36 types of games as they are played in more than 200 tribal groups, noting variations and describing gaming implements. Descriptions often taken from accounts of early white observers. Illustrated with more than 1,000 black-and-white drawings and photographs.

DEWEY: 970.679 C 967g ISBN 0-486-23125-9

♦ 720 ♦

Indian America: A Traveler's Companion. **Eagle/Walking Turtle. Santa Fe, NM: John Muir Publications, 1989. 413 pp. Illustrated. Appendix. Bibliography. Glossary. Index.**

Provides addresses, directions, visitor information, history, cultural background, and dates of public ceremonies for those wishing to visit Native American reservations and communities. Covers more than 300 tribes in the continental United States (not including Alaska). Entries organized into nine cultural and geographic groupings.

DEWEY: 917. 3049 LC: E 77. E117 ISBN 0-945465-29-7

♦ 721 ♦

Indian Festivals. **Paul Showers. Illustrated by Lorence Bjorklund. New York: Thomas Y. Crowell Company, 1969. 34 pp.**

Describes five American Indian festivals for children: the Green Corn celebration of the Seminole, the Shalako festival of the Zuni, the Sun Dance of the Great Plains tribes, an Eskimo celebration after a successful hunt, and contemporary Plains and Southwestern powwows.

DEWEY: J970.1 S559i

♦ 722 ♦

Native American Dance: Ceremonies and Social Traditions. **Charlotte Heth, ed. Washington, DC: The Smithsonian Institution, National Museum of the American Indian, 1992. 196 pp. Illustrated. Bibliography. Discography. Videography. Index.**

Describes and explains the ceremonial dance traditions of nine Native American cultural groups, traditions which include dances associated with many seasonal ceremonies and celebrations. Covers the Haudenosaunee (or Iroquois), Indians of the Mexican Sierra (featuring the Zapotec, as well as the Maya Tzotziles and Tzeltales), Indians of the Bolivian Altiplano (featuring the Aymara), the White Mountain Apache, the Tewa, the Cherokee, and Indians of the Southern Plains (featuring the Kiowa), the Northern Plains (featuring the Lakota Sioux), and Alaska. Articles reflect the combined input of scholars and practitioners. Beautifully illustrated with many color photos. Oversize.

DEWEY: 394.3 0897 LC: E 59. D35 N38 ISBN 1-56373-020-0

♦ 723 ♦

Native American Myths and Legends. **Colin F. Taylor, ed. New York: Smithmark, 1994. 144 pp. Illustrated. Bibliography. Index.**

Noted authorities contribute chapters on the myths, ceremonial life, sacred places, sacred animals, and spiritual beliefs of the tribes of nine Native American culture areas: the Southeast, the Southwest, the Plains, the Plateau and Basin, California, the Northwest Coast, the Subarctic, the Arctic, and the Northeast. Some coverage of seasonal ceremonies and festivals. Amply illustrated with color photos, black-and-white photos, and drawings.

DEWEY: 299.793 ISBN 0-8317-6290-X

♦ 724 ♦

Native American Religions: A Geographical Survey. **John James Collins. Lewiston, NY: Edwin Mellen Press, 1991. 393 pp. Maps. Bibliography. Index.**

A survey of Native North American religious beliefs and rituals at the time of European contact. Organized by culture area (groupings of culturally similar tribes). Provides overview of religious and ceremonial complex of 10 culture areas: Eastern, Eastern Sub-Arctic, Plains, Southwestern, Basin, California, Plateau, Northwest Coast, Western Sub-Arctic, and Arctic. Refers to over 150 tribes. Bibliographies provided for each culture area, featuring older, more difficult-to-locate sources.

DEWEY: 299.7 LC: E98. R3C69 ISBN 0-88946-483-9

♦ 725 ♦

1993 Powwow Calendar: Guide to North American Powwows and Gatherings U.S.A. and Canada. **Liz Campbell, comp. Summertown, TN: The Book Publishing Company, 1992. 96 pp. Illustrated.**

Lists, in chronological order, more than 400 powwows and other events observed by Native Americans in the United States and Canada. Entries include contact addresses and phone numbers.

ISBN 1-913990-99-X

♦ 726 ♦

Powwow. **George Ancona. San Diego, CA: Harcourt Brace Jovanovich, 1993. 45 pp. Illustrated.**

Depicts the celebrations at Crow Fair, the largest annual powwow in the United States. Describes processions, dances, contests, and costumes. Written for children. Illustrated with color photos.

DEWEY: 394.2 68 089975 LC: E99. C92 A53 ISBN 0-15-263268-9

♦ 727 ♦

The Rattle and the Drum: Native American Rituals and Celebrations. **Lisa Sita. Illustrated by James Watling. Brookfield, CT: The Millbrook Press, 1994. 71 pp. Glossary. Index.**

Describes a variety of rituals from different Native American tribes. Covers initiation ceremonies, daily rituals, seasonal ceremonies, healing rituals, and powwows. Seasonal celebrations covered include the Creek Green Corn Dance and the Hopi Snake Ceremony. Gives suggested activities, recipes, further reading list. Illustrated with color drawings. For children.

DEWEY: 299.7 LC: E98. R3 S46 ISBN 1-56294-420-7

♦ 728 ♦

Ritual of the Wind: North American Indian Ceremonies, Music, and Dances. **Jamake Highwater. Drawings by Asa Battles. New York: Viking Press, 1977. 192 pp. Appendices. Bibliography. Discography. Index.**

Describes seven Native American ceremonies: the Sun Dance of the Plains tribes, the Booger Dance of the Cherokee, the Mountain Spirit Dance of the Apache, the Rain Power Ceremony of the Tewa, the Hako Ceremony of the Pawnee, the Night Chant of the Navaho, and the Easter Festival of the Yaqui. Also provides some background information on Native American spiritual concepts, dance, music, and ritual. Appendices include a calendar of Indian ceremonies, with special emphasis on events in the southwest United States and notes concerning appropriate behavior for outside visitors to Indian ceremonials, a discography of Indian music, and a selected bibliography.

DEWEY: 394 LC: E98. R3H7 ISBN 0-670-59952-2

♦ 729 ♦

Southwestern Indian Ceremonials. **Tom Bashti. Flagstaff, AZ: K.C. Publications, 1970. 66 pp. Illustrated. Map.**

Introduces the most popular and publically accessible Indian ceremonials of the American Southwest. Covers ceremonies of the Navaho, Rio Grande Pueblo, Zuni, Hopi, Apache, Papago, and Yaqui tribes, as well as the Peyote cult of the Native American church. Also briefy describes deities and religious beliefs. Beautifully illustrated with color photos and drawings of ceremonies, costumes, ritual objects, and artwork. Provides suggested reading list, discography, calendar of Southwestern Indian ceremonies, and map of the Southwest showing location of tribes.

LC: E78 S7 B183 f ISBN 0-916122-02-6

♦ 730 ♦

The Spiritual Legacy of the American Indian. **Joseph Epes Brown. New York: Crossroads Books, 1982. 135 pp. Map.**

Professor of religion identifies and explains the beliefs and concepts which provide the framework for Native American spirituality. Mentions a number of festivals throughout; an entire chapter is devoted to the Plains Sun Dance. Map of North American culture areas. Endnotes. For the general reader.

DEWEY: 299.7 LC: E98.R3 B75 ISBN 0-8245-0489-5

♦ 731 ♦

Teachings from the American Earth: Indian Religion and Philosophy. **Dennis Tedlock and Barbara Tedlock, eds. New York: Liveright, 1975. 279 pp. Index.**

A collection of essays by scholars and Native Americans exploring the spirit and metaphysics of Native American religious thinking. Articles address wide-ranging practices, such as shamanism, as well as specific cultural groups, including the Eskimos, Sioux, Papago, Wintu, Ojibwa, and Tewa. Citations given in endnotes of each article.

DEWEY: 299.7 LC: E98. R3T42 ISBN 0-87140-559-7

♦ 732 ♦

They Put on Masks. **Byrd Baylor. Illustrated by Jerry Ingram. New York: Charles Scribner's Sons, 1974. 46 pp. Map.**

Conveys the spirit behind Indian mask-making and ceremonial use. Describes how mask designs are inspired, what they are made of, their meaning, and their role in various ceremonies. Makes specific reference to masks and ceremonies of the Eskimo, the Kwakiutl, the Iroquois, the Navaho, the Apache, the Hopi, the Zuni, and the Yaqui Indians. Gives map of North America marking approximate locations of these tribes. Illustrated with color drawings of actual Indian masks. Written for children.

DEWEY: 970.62 B358 ISBN 684-13767-4

APACHE

♦ 733 ♦

The Gift of Changing Woman. **Tryntje Van Ness Seymour. New York: Henry Holt and Company, 1993. 38 pp. Illustrated. Glossary.**

Describes the four-day summer *Na'íí'es,* or sunrise, ceremony of the Apache, held to celebrate a girl's coming of age. Also referred to as "the gift of changing woman." Retells the mythology behind the ceremony and provides further reading list. Illustrated with color photos of paintings by Apache artists. Written for children. Author's endnotes also describe her research and discusses the artists whose work appears in the book.

DEWEY: 299.74 LC: E99. A6 S48 ISBN 0-8050-2577-4

CHEROKEE

♦ 734 ♦

Cherokee Dance and Drama. **Frank G. Speck and Leonard Broom, in collaboration with Will West Long. Norman, OK: University of Oklahoma Press, 1983. 112 pp. Illustrated. Bibliography. Index.**

Describes the songs, movements, and meaning of Cherokee dances. Covers winter dances, such as the Booger or Mask Dance, the Eagle Dance, and the Bear Dance; also covers summer dances, such as the Green Corn Ceremony and Dance, and the Ballplayers' Dance. Also treats dances which celebrate activities or relationships, such as war, hunting, and courting, as well as various animal dances. Some discussion of dance song origins. Illustrated with black-and-white photos and diagrams.

DEWEY: 793.3 1 08997 LC: E99. C5 S66 ISBN 0-8061-1721-4

DELAWARE

♦ 735 ♦

The Delaware Indians: A History. **C. A. Weslager. New Brunswick, NJ: Rutgers University Press, 1972. 546 pp. Illustrated. Maps. Appendices. Index.**

Provides an in-depth history of the Delaware Indians since the time of European contact. Also describes traditional way of life, including some description of customs and rituals, such as the Big House Ceremony. Illustrated with black-and-white photos. Appendices furnish additional details and documents pertaining to Delaware history and customs. Endnotes for each chapter.

DEWEY: 970.3 LC: E99. D2 W39 ISBN 0-8135-0702-2

♦ 736 ♦

A Study of the Delaware Indian Big House Ceremony. **Frank G. Speck. Native text dictated by WitapanóXwe. Volume 2. Harrisburg, PA: Publications of the Pennsylvania Historical Commission, 1931. 192 pp. Illustrated. Appendices. Index.**

Explains elements of the Delaware Big House Ceremony and Delaware religion. Translates detailed description of the Ceremony given by a Delaware herbalist. Covers Delaware view of the cosmos, concept of the soul, deities, role of carved images and masks, concept of purity and defilement, religious and ceremonial symbols and objects, and more. Detailed description of the events of the 12 nights of the Big House Ceremony in English and in the Delaware language. Appendices give songs from the Ceremony, the Delaware myth of the Red Cedar and the Seven Stars, and Chief Elkhair's Vision of the Journey of the Soul. Lists references cited.

DEWEY: 974.806 P415p

ESKIMO

♦ 737 ♦

The Eskimos. **Ernest S. Burch, Jr. Photographs by Werner Forman. Norman, OK: University of Oklahoma Press, 1988. 128 pp. Index.**

Portrays the traditional way of life of the Eskimos (Yupik, Aleut, and Inuit peoples). Some coverage of the seasonal festivals of the Western Eskimo groups, including the Asking Festival, the Festival of the Dead, and the Bladder Festival. Color photos illustrate.

DEWEY: 998 B947 ISBN 0-8061-2126-2

HOPI

♦ 738 ♦

Book of the Hopi. **Frank Waters. Illustrated by Oswald White Bear Fredericks. New York: Penguin Books, 1977. 345 pp. Glossary.**

The mythology, legends, and ceremonies of the Hopi, long kept from outsiders, as dictated to the author by 30 elders of the tribe. Covers creation stories, cosmology, clan legends, the yearly cycle of ceremonies and festivals, and tribal history.

DEWEY: 970. 004 97 LC: E 99.H 7W3 ISBN 0-1400-4527-9

♦ 739 ♦

Hopi Snake Ceremonies; An Eyewitness Account, Selections from Bureau of American Ethnology Annual Reports nos. 16 and 19 for the years 1894-95 and 1897-98. **Jesse Walter Fewkes. Reprint. Albuquerque, NM: Avanyu Publishing, Inc., 1986. 159 pp. Illustrated.**

Reprint of two papers published in annual reports. Authors describes ceremonies performed by the Hopi Snake Society during the 1890s. (NR)

DEWEY: 299.74 LC: E99.H7 F329 ISBN 0-936755-00-8

♦ 740 ♦

Little Joe: A Hopi Indian Boy Learns a Hopi Indian Secret. **Terry Latterman. Gilbert, AZ: Pussywillow Publishing House, 1985. 32 pp. Illustrated.**

A story describing a young Hopi boy's participation in the Powamu ceremony, which is the first of three steps he will take in becoming an adult.

DEWEY: J 970.3 L 3642L ISBN 0-934739-01-3

♦ 741 ♦

The Snake Dance of the Hopi Indians. **Earle R. Forrest. Illustrated by Don Louis Perceval. Los Angeles, CA: Westernlore Press, 1961. 172 pp. Bibliography. Index.**

A detailed account of the various rituals involved in the yearly Snake Dance and Flute Ceremonies of the Hopi Indians. Based on ceremonies witnessed in the first decade of the twentieth century; summarizes accounts of earlier eyewitnesses. Includes rare photographs of these rituals (cameras were banned at the ceremonies several years after these were taken). Styled as an Old West adventure story.

DEWEY: 299.7

♦ 742 ♦

Tusayan Katcinas and Hopi Altars. **Jesse Walter Fewkes. Introduction by Barton Wright. Albuquerque, NM: Avanyu Publishing, Inc., 1990. 486 pp. Illustrated.**

Reprint of two texts by Fewkes, one an article, "The Katchina Altars in Hopi Worship," that appeared in the Annual Report of the Board of Regents of the Smithsonian Institution for 1926. Both represent author's endeavor to describe and analyze katchina ceremonials among the Hopis, including the Powamû Ceremony. (NR)

DEWEY: 299.784 LC: E99.H7 F423 ISBN 0-936755-15-6

IROQUOIS

♦ 743 ♦

The Iroquois Ceremonial of Midwinter. **Elisabeth Tooker. Syracuse, NY: Syracuse University Press, 1970. 189 pp. Illustrated. Appendix. Bibliography. Index.**

Description and analysis of the Iroquois Midwinter ceremonial. Documents regional variation in the ritual, change and stasis over time. Includes historical accounts of the ceremonial from previous generations and previous centuries.

LC: E99 I7T6 ISBN 8156-2149-3

LAKOTA

♦ 744 ♦

Black Elk's Religion: The Sun Dance and Lakota Catholicism. **Clyde Holler. Syracuse, NY: Syracuse University Press, 1995. 246 pp. Bibliography. Glossary. Index.**

Scholarly examination of the relationship between the Sun Dance (the central ceremony of the Lakota Sioux religion), and the teachings of Black Elk, the well-known Lakota religious thinker. Covers the history of the Sun Dance ceremony from the late 1800s to the present, including eyewitness accounts of early ceremonies. Provides biographical information on Black Elk, as well as consideration of the meaning of his acceptance of both Christianity and traditional Lakota religion.

DEWEY: 299.785 LC: E99. O3H65 ISBN 0-8156-2676-2

NAVAHO

♦ 745 ♦

Masked Gods: Navaho and Pueblo Ceremonialism. **Frank Waters. Albuquerque, NM: University of New Mexico Press, 1950. 438 pp.**

Contains a descriptive account and a philosophical and theological analysis of Navaho and Pueblo mythology and ceremony. Part one recounts the history of the Pueblo and Navaho. Part two presents and analyzes the meaning of their numerous and varied ceremonies and rituals, many of which celebrate seasonal events, comparing their underlying philosophies to Eastern philosophies. Part three describes the expression of these philosophies in everyday life.

DEWEY: 970.4 W329m   LC: E 98. R3 W4

♦ 746 ♦

The Nightway: A History and a History of Documentation of a Navajo Ceremonial. **James C. Faris. Albuquerque, NM: University of New Mexico Press, 1990. 288 pp. Bibliography. Index.**

Anthropologist presents a study of recordings of the Navaho Nightway Ceremony and its stories, songs, beliefs, prayers, and practices, including sandpainting. Charts and figures detail genealogies of medicine men who have led the Nightway, as well as specific elements of Nightways observed over the last 100 years. (NR)

DEWEY: 299.74   LC: E99.N3 F38   ISBN 0-8263-1198-9

PAWNEE

♦ 747 ♦

Ceremonies of the Pawnee. **James R. Murie. Douglas R. Parks, ed. 1981. Reprint. Lincoln, NE: University of Nebraska Press, 1989. 497 pp. Illustrated. Appendixes. Bibliography. Indexes.**

Detailed descriptions of the highly developed ceremonial system of the Pawnee Indians, gathered around the turn of the twentieth century by Muire, a Pawnee who worked closely with anthropologists. Depicts rituals, translates songs and stories, describes ceremonial objects and their uses. Many of the ceremonies covered are now extinct. One volume in a series entitled *Studies in the Anthropology of North American Indians.*

DEWEY: 299.74   LC: E99. P3M95   ISBN 0-8032-3138-5

PUEBLO

♦ 748 ♦

Pueblo Boy: Growing Up in Two Worlds. **Marcia Keegan. New York: Cobblehill Books, 1991. 44 pp. Illustrated.**

Describes everyday life of an actual Pueblo Indian boy, who participates both in Indian culture and mainstream American culture. At school he learns to use computers, and at home he learns Pueblo songs, stories, arts, and dances.

Depicts his participation in two ceremonial dances. Beautifully illustrated with color photographs. Written for children.

DEWEY: 978.9 00497 LC: E99.S213 R695 ISBN 0-525-65060-1

YAQUI

♦ 749 ♦

With Good Heart: Yaqui Beliefs and Ceremonies in Pascua Village. **Muriel Thayer Painter. Tucson, AZ: University of Arizona Press, 1986. 533 pp. Illustrated. Bibliography. Index.**

A detailed description of the religious beliefs and ceremonies of the Yaqui Indians of Arizona, with a special emphasis on Lenten and Easter rituals. Covers all aspects of the ceremonies, from their spiritual principles and symbols to their organization. Describes dances, ceremonial objects, and costumes; explores their meaning; and notes change and stasis over time. Represents decades of observation and notetaking on the part of the author.

DEWEY: 299.78 LC: E99.Y3 P29 ISBN 0-8165-0875-5

United States

GENERAL WORKS

♦ 750 ♦

All About American Holidays. **Maymie R. Krythe. New York: Harper and Brothers, Publishers, 1962. 275 pp. Bibliography. Index.**

Relates the history of more than 50 American holidays and tells how they are celebrated. Also gives holiday folklore and customs. Covers Christian and Jewish holidays, patriotic holidays, and theme holidays. Includes some lesser known days, such as Poetry Day, Citizenship Day, and Armed Forces Day.

DEWEY: 394.26

♦ 751 ♦

All Around the Year: Holidays and Celebrations in American Life. **Jack Santino. Urbana, IL: University of Illinois Press, 1994. 227 pp. Bibliography. Index.**

Discusses, in calendar order, a wide range of American holidays and celebrations, reflecting on their history, their customs, and their symbolic representation of American values. Covers well-known holidays, such as Halloween, lesser-known ethnic holidays, such as the Laotian-American Rocket Festival, and unofficial holidays and festivals, such as the Super Bowl.

DEWEY: 394. 26973 LC: GT 4803. A2S26 ISBN 0-252-02049-9

♦ 752 ♦

Almanac for Americans. **Willis Thornton. 1941. Reprint. Detroit, MI: Omnigraphics, Inc., 1973. 418 pp. Illustrated. Index.**

A "Book of Days of the Republic," arranged chronologically, focuses on patriotic holidays and historical events in the United States. (NR)

DEWEY: 973.02 LC: E174.5.T5 ISBN 1-55888-889-6

♦ 753 ♦

America Celebrates! A Patchwork of Weird and Wonderful Holiday Lore. **Hennig Cohen and Tristram Potter Coffin. Detroit, MI: Gale Research, Inc., 1991. 355 pp.**

Reviews the folklore of 61 American holidays, including lesser-known observances such as the anniversary of Elvis Presley's death, Persian New Year, the Annual Rattlesnake Roundup, and the Seneca Green Corn Dance. Lists more than 200 folkloric practices, beliefs, legends, sayings, recipes, and customs. Reprints accounts culled from such sources as newspapers, oral histories, the writings of folklorists and anthropologists, publications issued by local chambers of commerce, and journals. Holiday entries list sources and summarize the history and significance of the holiday in this country. Includes past and present celebrations, as well as a wide variety of ethnic observances. Arranged chronologically.

DEWEY: 394.2 697 C66 a ISBN 0-8103-9407-3

♦ 754 ♦

American Anniversaries: Every Day in the Year: Presenting Seven Hundred and Fifty Events in United States History, from the Discovery of America to the Present Day. **Philip Robert Dillon. 1918. Reprint. Detroit, MI: Omnigraphics, Inc., 1991. 349 pp. Index, pp. i-xv.**

Presents at least one important event from American history for every day of the year. Includes births and deaths of noted individuals, military and political events and decisions, inventions, discoveries, and holidays. Entries range from one sentence to several pages of description and explanation.

DEWEY: 973. 02 LC: E174.5 D57 ISBN 1-55888-890-X

♦ 755 ♦

The American Book of Days. **Jane M. Hatch. Third edition. New York: H. W. Wilson, 1978. 1214 pp. Appendix. Index.**

More than 700 entries describing American holidays, customs, festivities, folklore, religious celebrations, anniversaries, achievements, historic events, and observances associated with the days of the year. Also offers profiles of distinguished citizens, articles concerning U.S. history, individual states' histories, and important social movements. Provides biographies of prominent citizens, including all U.S. presidents and chief justices of the Supreme Court. Third edition adds 240 new articles, including 56 new biographies.

DEWEY: 394.2 LC: GT 4803. D6 ISBN 0-8242-0593-6

♦ 756 ♦

American Holidays and Special Days. **George Schaun and Virginia Schaun. Illustrated by David Wisniewski. Lanham, MD: Maryland Historical Press, 1986. 194 pp. Bibliography. Index.**

Offers historical and background information on the people, events, and ideas behind 67 American holidays and anniversaries. Provides alphabetical listings of holidays, chronological listing of holidays, and dates of admission of American states to the Union. Also briefly explains the history of the Gregorian, Jewish, Muslim, and Chinese calendars, and the meanings of the names of days and months.

DEWEY: 394.2 6973 LC: GT4803.S33 ISBN 0-917882-19-9

♦ 757 ♦

An Audio-Visual Guide to American Holidays. **Carol Emmens, ed. Metuchen, NJ: Scarecrow Press, 1978. 274 pp. Index.**

Annotated bibliography of audio-visual materials related to 41 American holidays. Organized by month and by holiday. Covers civic, patriotic, and folk holidays; major Christian and Jewish holidays; and the four seasons. Materials include 16 and 8 mm film, video, filmstrips, slides, multimedia kits, records, cassettes, transparencies, prints, and other visual aids. Notes recommended grade level, from kindergarten through college. Provides list of distributors. Titles index.

DEWEY: 016.3942 68 LC: GT 4803. E47 ISBN 0-8108-1140-5

♦ 758 ♦

Beyond the Interstate: Discovering the Hidden America. **Eric Model. New York: John Wiley and Sons, Inc., 1989. 242 pp. Appendices.**

A guide to 90 festivals, holiday observances, and community events celebrating America's history, foods, and folk arts. Lists lesser-known events which capture local character, such as the National Storytelling Festival in

Jonesborough, Tennessee, and the Bison Roundup in Moiese, Montana. Gives brief description of the event, contact address, and phone number; lists local eateries and lodgings; and suggests background readings and nearby sightseeing opportunities. Hotel listings include phone number, address, type of accommodations available, and prices. Appendices include directories of events by month, by state, and by type; a directory of accommodations by state; a bed-and-breakfast resources list; a bibliography of bed-and-breakfast guides; and background readings on travel in America.

DEWEY: 917.3 04927 LC: E158. M83 ISBN 0-471-61389-4

♦ 759 ♦

The Book of Festival Holidays. **Marguerite Ickis. Illustrated by Miriam F. Fabbri. New York: Dodd, Mead and Company, 1964. 178 pp.**

Reviews ways of celebrating America's festival holidays. Covers New Year's Day, St. Valentine's Day, various midwinter festivals, St. Patrick's Day, Easter, various Jewish holidays, April Fools' Day, May Day, Halloween, Thanksgiving, and Christmas. Gives traditional games, crafts, songs, and lore.

DEWEY: 394. I17 bf

♦ 760 ♦

The Book of Festivals in the Midwest, 1983 and 1984. **Carol Baker and Astri Fingerhut, ed. South Bend, IN: Icarus Press, 1983. 227 pp. Illustrated. Maps. Index.**

Lists more than 600 festivals in nine midwestern states: Ohio, Michigan, Indiana, Illinois, Wisconsin, Minnesota, Iowa, Kentucky, and Missouri. Gives map of each state with festival locations marked. Entries give festival dates for 1983 and 1984, location, contact address and phone, attendance figures, date inaugurated, admission fees, activities and attractions, concessions, nearby sightseeing opportunities, and availability of local room and board. Organized by state. Includes two-year festival calendar and list of campgrounds.

DEWEY: 394.2 6 02577 LC: GT 4807.B34 ISBN 0-89651-056-5

♦ 761 ♦

The Book of Holidays. **Revised edition. J. Walker McSpadden. Illustrated by Robert Galster. New York: Thomas Y. Crowell Company, 1958. 246 pp. Bibliography. Index.**

Presents the history and customs of 22 American holidays and days of commemoration. Covers New Year's Day, Lincoln's Birthday, St. Valentine's Day, Washington's Birthday, St. Patrick's Day, Pan-American Day, Good Friday and

Easter, May Day, Arbor Day and Bird Day, Mother's Day, Father's Day and Children's Day, Memorial Day, Flag Day, Independence Day, Labor Day, Rosh Hashanah and other Jewish holidays, Columbus Day, Halloween, Election Day, Veterans Day, Thanksgiving, and Christmas. Briefly reviews the major festivals of the British Isles, France, Germany, Italy, Japan, India, and the Islamic countries. Provides a list of holidays in the U.S., including state holidays.

DEWEY: 394

♦ 762 ♦

The Book of Patriotic Holidays. **Marguerite Ickis. New York: Dodd, Mead and Company, 1962. 178 pp. Illustrated.**

A collection of materials to aid in the celebration of American patriotic holidays, including Lincoln's and Washington's birthdays, Pan-American Day, Memorial Day, Flag Day, Independence Day, Columbus Day, and Veterans Day. Suggests songs, stories, crafts, foods, and activities. Also lists symbols of the United States and state seals, flowers, birds, trees, mottos, songs, holidays, and dates of statehood.

DEWEY: 394

♦ 763 ♦

The Book of Religious Holidays and Celebrations. **Marguerite Ickis. Illustrated by Richard E. Howard. New York: Dodd, Mead and Company, 1966. 161 pp.**

Presents customs, ceremonies, songs, legends, symbols, and prayers of the major Christian and Jewish holidays. Covers the Christmas season (including Advent, Christmas, New Year, and Epiphany), the Easter cycle (including Lent, Holy Week, and Easter), and the Pentecost cycle (including Pentecost, Holy Trinity, Corpus Christi, Mother's Day, Children's Day, and Rally Day). Also covers the Sabbath, Purim, Yom Kippur, the New Year of the Trees, Hanukkah, Passover, Shavuot, and Sukkot. Christian emphasis. Gives further reading list.

DEWEY: 394

♦ 764 ♦

California Festivals. **Carl and Katie Landau, with Kathy Kincade. San Francisco, CA: Landau Communications, 1989. 261 pp. Illustrated.**

A guide to more than 300 California festivals. Provides dates, brief description of activities and attractions, fees, attendance, years in existence, and phone number. Full descriptions given in alphabetical order by month, but also lists festivals by theme and by general location.

DEWEY: 394.2 09794 LC: GT 4810. C2 L36 ISBN 0-929881-25-7

♦ 765 ♦

Celebrate America's Diversity. **Paula Ross. Chicago, IL: American Library Association, 1993. 54 pp. Illustrated.**

A guide to producing community events which commemorate national or local holidays and festivals recognized by four minority groups. Offers programs for nine African American, eight Native American, 25 Asian and Pacific Island American, and eight Latin American festivals and holidays. Entries note festival's significance, describe how celebrated, suggest program ideas, and list additional resources, such as books and recordings. Furnishes nine unnumbered pages of graphic images and borders to aid in designing flyers and other promotional materials.

DEWEY: 394 C 392

♦ 766 ♦

Celebrating With Books. **Nancy Polette and Marjorie Hamlin. Illustrated by Patricia Gilman. Metuchen, NJ: Scarecrow Press, 1977. 175 pp. Index.**

An elementary school teacher's guide to using holiday books in the classroom. Explains how to build lessons around holiday books which will convey information, teach basic skills, and encourage children to read on their own. Gives teaching tips, including suggested activities, as well as annotated bibliographies of children's holiday books, noting appropriate grade level. Covers Columbus Day, United Nations Day, Halloween, Thanksgiving and the Fall season, Christmas, Hanukkah, the February birthday holidays, Valentine's Day, St. Patrick's Day, and Easter and the Spring season. Provides an index to book titles, authors, and illustrators.

DEWEY: 028.52 LC: Z1037.9 P64 ISBN 0-8108-1032-8

♦ 767 ♦

Celebrations: Read-Aloud Holiday and Theme Book Programs. **Caroline Feller Bauer. Illustrated by Lynn Gates Bredeson. New York: H. W. Wilson Company, 1985. 301 pp. Index.**

Presents 26 children's programs around holidays or special themes designed to inspire young people to read. Holidays covered include Calendar Day, Grandparents Day, Halloween, St. Patrick's Day, Thanksgiving, Christmas, Valentine's Day, and National Nothing Day. Themes covered include art, baseball, fishing, Jewish humor, spring, pigs, turtles, and television. Programs highlight concept behind the holiday. Each program reprints holiday stories and poems, suggests a variety of activities, offers recipes, and gives an annotated bibliography of children's books on the topic, noting appropriate age group.

DEWEY: 808.06 8 LC: Z 1037 A1B3 ISBN 0-8242-0708-4

♦ 768 ♦

Celebrations: The Complete Book of American Holidays. **Robert J. Myers, with the editors of Hallmark Cards. Illustrated by Bill Greer. Garden City, NY: Doubleday and Company, 1972. 386 pp. Bibliography. Index.**

Presents the history, manner of celebration, folklore, and symbols of 60 American holidays. Also gives stories, songs, and other background materials. Covers Christian and Jewish holidays, as well as civic holidays, such as Memorial Day, and some ethnic holidays, such as Columbus Day and Chinese New Year.

LC: GT 4803 A2 M84 ISBN 0-385-07677-0

♦ 769 ♦

Clambake: A History and Celebration of an American Tradition. **Kathy Neustadt. Amherst, MA: University of Massachusetts Press, 1992. 227 pp. Illustrated. Bibliography. Index.**

Investigates the history of the clambake as an American tradition and documents the origins, activities, organization, and significance of the yearly clambake at Allen's Neck, Massachusetts. Considers the social effects of the clambake, and its shaping by and reflection of American values. Also reviews folkloric and anthropological theories of festivity, food, and ritual which shed light on this American tradition.

DEWEY: 394.3 LC: GT2956.U6 N48 ISBN 0-87023-782-9

♦ 770 ♦

Colonial American Holidays and Entertainment. **Karen Helene Lizon. New York: Franklin Watts, 1993. 111 pp. Illustrated. Appendix. Bibliography. Glossary. Index.**

Provides an overview of colonial holidays, amusements, and social gatherings. Introduces the religious and folk holidays of many emigrant groups, as well as including Native and African Americans. Tells significance of holiday and relates main customs. Also describes other aspects of everyday life in colonial America, including sports and recreation, games and toys, socializing, pastimes, family and community observances, and communal work projects. Further reading list. Appendix gives recipes, games, and a colonial craft. For older children.

DEWEY: 394.2 6973 09032 LC: GT 4803. A2L59 ISBN 0-531-12546-7

♦ 771 ♦

***Consumer Rites: The Buying and Selling of American Holidays.* Leigh Eric Schmidt. Princeton, NJ: Princeton University Press, 1995. 363 pp. Illustrated. Index.**

Examines the increasing influence of consumerism on the celebration of American holidays, from colonial times to the twentieth century. Identifies the power of commercial culture, and the way in which the consumption patterns it encourages have shaped both the religious and secular celebration of American holidays, as well as helped to create new holidays. Special emphasis on Valentine's Day, Christmas, Easter, and Mother's Day. Also discusses New Year, the Fourth of July, and Father's Day. Illustrated with black-and-white holiday-related photos, advertisements, cards, and more.

DEWEY: 394.2 6973 LC: GT 4986. A1 S35 ISBN 0-691-02980-6

♦ 772 ♦

***Curious Customs: The Stories Behind 296 Popular American Rituals.* Tad Tuleja. New York: Harmony Books, 1987. 210 pp. Bibliography.**

Relates the origins of 296 popular American customs, symbols, and beliefs. Gives chapters on manners, gestures, rites of passage, courtship, clothes and appearance, foods, family, entertainment, holidays, superstitions, and miscellany.

DEWEY: 390.0973 LC: E161.T84 ISBN 0-517-56653-2

♦ 773 ♦

***The Days We Celebrate.* Robert Haven Schauffler, ed. New York: Dodd, Mead and Company, 1948. 397 pp.**

Offers an anthology of plays, stories, essays, poems, exercises, activities, games, and lessons for seven patriotic holidays: Lincoln's Birthday, Washington's Birthday, Memorial Day, Flag Day, Independence Day, Armistice Day, and Columbus Day. Much material appropriate for school use.

DEWEY: 394.268

♦ 774 ♦

Fairs and Festivals: A Smithsonian Guide to Celebrations in Maryland, Virginia and Washington D.C. **Elizabeth Rees Gilbert. Peter Seitel, ed. Illustrated by Daphne Shuttleworth. Washington, DC: Smithsonian Institution Press, 1982. 160 pp.**

A guide to approximately 200 fairs, festivals, and public holiday celebrations in Washington D.C., Maryland, and Virginia. Developed to accompany the Smithsonian exhibit,"Celebration: A World of Art and Ritual."Explains significance of the event, notes when and where it is celebrated, describes main events and festivities, tells how to get there, and lists address and phone of contact organization. Organized by month. Covers ethnic, religious, civic, commercial, agricultural, and nature festivals and holidays, such as Ukrainian New Year, Girl Scouts of America's Anniversary, Gandhi's Birthday, Corpus Christi, Reformation Day, Constitution Day, Fall Foliage Festival, and Bastille Day. Illustrated with black-and-white drawings.

DEWEY: 394.2 69753 LC: GT 4811. W37 G54 ISBN 0-87474-473-3

♦ 775 ♦

Feasts and Celebrations in North American Ethnic Communities. **Ramón A. Gutiérrez and Geneviève Fabre. Albuquerque, NM: University of New Mexico Press, 1995. 195 pp. Index.**

A collection of scholarly essays on regional ethnic celebrations of many kinds. Festivals covered include the Pinkster Festival (African American), the Pastorela (Mexican American), the Matachines (Mexican American), Rizal Day (Filipino American), harvest celebrations of the rural South, Carnival (Caribbean American), and Halloween in New York City's gay community. Articles offer social and political analysis of festival practices and their history.

DEWEY: 394.2 6 08693 LC: GT 4803. A2F43 ISBN 0-8263-1593-3

♦ 776 ♦

The Festival Hopper's Guide to the Rocky West. **Craig Darrin and Julie Craig. San Jose, CA: Creative Chaos, 1991. 209 pp. Maps. Indexes.**

Covers more than 150 festivals, fairs, rodeos, and arts and music events held in Arizona, Colorado, New Mexico, Utah, and Wyoming. Entries are organized alphabetically by state, then chronologically within each state. Information provided within each entry includes a map, population of the town and festival attendance, average outdoor temperature for the event, festival location, where to call for more information, and checklist of the event's features, regulations, accommodations, and fees. Town index and festival index. List of festival coordinators and vendors with addresses and phone numbers.

ISBN 0-9624538-4-6

♦ 777 ♦

Festivals of New England. **Kathy Kincade and Carl Landau. San Francisco, CA: Landau Communications, 1989. 218 pp. Illustrated.**

A guide to more than 200 festivals in Connecticut, Maine, Massachusetts, New Hampshire, Rhode Island, and Vermont. Provides dates, brief description of activities and attractions, fees, attendance, years in existence, and phone number for each festival. Full descriptions given in alphabetical order by month, followed by listings of festivals by theme and by state. Illustrated with black-and-white photos.

DEWEY: 394.2609 LC: GT 4805. K56 ISBN 0-929881-28-1

♦ 778 ♦

Festivals of the Pacific Northwest. **Kathy Kincade and Steve Rank. San Francisco, CA: Landau Communications, 1990. 218 pp.**

A guide to more than 250 Washington and Oregon festivals. Provides dates, brief description of activities and attractions, fees, attendance, years in existence, and phone number. Full descriptions given in alphabetical order by month, followed by listings of festivals by theme and by general location.

DEWEY: 394.2 09795 LC: GT 4810.W2 R36 ISBN 0-929881-26-5

♦ 779 ♦

Festivals of the Southwest. **Kathy Kincade and Carl Landau. San Francisco, CA: Landau Communications, 1990. 174 pp.**

A guide to more than 200 Arizona and New Mexico festivals. Provides dates, brief description of activities and attractions, fees, attendance, years in existence, and phone number. Full descriptions given in alphabetical order by month, followed by listings of festivals by theme and by general location.

DEWEY: 394.2 09789 LC: GT 4810.A6L36 ISBN 0-929881-27-3

♦ 780 ♦

Festivals of the West. **Nancy Meyer. Pasadena, CA: Ward Ritchie Press, 1975. 152 pp. Illustrated. Index.**

A guide to more than 170 festivals in the western states. Gives festival name, date, and location, describes festival events and ambience, and gives contact organization. Some entries also give travel directions, event history, ticket prices, and tips on local accommodations. Arranged by month. Provides addresses for the western states' tourist information offices. Index of festival themes.

DEWEY: 394.2697 ISBN 0-378-05582-8

♦ 781 ♦

Festivals U.S.A. **Kathleen Thompson Hill. Foreword by Willard Scott. New York: John Wiley and Sons, 1988. 242 pp. Glossary. Index.**

A guide to 1000 American festivals celebrating the arts, crafts, foods, plants, the harvest, folk arts, ethnic groups, local or regional identity and history, music, and the seasons. Entries give festival name, dates, focus of celebration, main activities or displays, foods served, admission fees, and address and phone number of contact organization; also note existence and type of local accommodations and restaurants.

DEWEY: 394.2 6973 LC: GT 4803. H54 ISBN 0-471-62636-8

♦ 782 ♦

Festivals U.S.A. **Robert Meyer, Jr. Illustrated by Lee Owens. New York: Ives Washburn, Inc., 1950. 438 pp. Index.**

Covers more than 1200 festivals and annual events in 49 states. Entries describe festival activities and give approximate date; many list attendance figures. Covers events celebrating food, sports, nature, the arts, community and ethnic traditions, animals, hobbies, trades, holidays, military exercises, and more. Organized by state and by festival theme.

DEWEY: 394.M57f

♦ 783 ♦

Fifty Plays for Holidays: A Collection of Royalty-Free One-Act Children's Plays for Holidays and Special Occasions. **Sylvia Kamerman, ed. Boston, MA: Plays, Inc., 1969. 652 pp.**

Offers 50 royalty-free children's plays with holiday themes. Includes plays for Columbus Day, Halloween, Book Week, Election Day, American Education Week, Thanksgiving, Christmas, Lincoln's Birthday, Valentine's Day, Washington's Birthday, Brotherhood Week, St. Patrick's Day, Easter, Pan-American Day, Arbor Day, May Day, Mother's Day, and the patriotic holidays.

Includes production notes summarizing cast, costume, properties, set, lighting, and sound requirements, as well as playing time.

DEWEY: 822.008 LC: PN 6120 H7K3

♦ 784 ♦

Folklore in America: Tales, Songs, Superstitions, Proverbs, Riddles, Games, Folk Drama and Folk Festivals. **Tristram Potter Coffin and Hennig Cohen, eds. Garden City, NY: Doubleday and Company, 1966. 256 pp. Indexes.**

Presents a compilation of American folklore from many ethnic groups. Offers tales, songs, superstitions, proverbs, riddles, games, and description of 10 folk dramas or festivals. Includes the Mexican-American Los Pastores procession, Christmas Masking in Boston, a mummers' play from Kentucky, a Slovak Harvest festival, a German-American Corpus Christi festival in New Jersey, a Los Penitentes procession from the Southwest, a Yaqui Indian Lent procession, and more. Gives notes on sources. Indexes of ethnic groups and places; collectors and translations; titles and first lines of songs; and tale types.

DEWEY: 398.0973

♦ 785 ♦

The Folklore of American Holidays: A Compilation of More Than 400 Beliefs, Legends, Superstitions, Proverbs, Riddles, Poems, Songs, Dances, Games, Plays, Pageants, Fairs, Foods, and Processions Associated with Over 100 American Calendar Customs and Festivals. **Hennig Cohen and Tristram Potter Coffin, eds. Second edition. Detroit, MI: Gale Research Company, 1991. 431 pp. Indexes.**

Covers a wide range of American holidays, from the well-known to the obscure and from the historic to the currently celebrated. Discusses hundreds of items of folklore associated with more than 120 holidays. Entries describe the origin and significance of each holiday, its important festivities, its lore and customs. Wide range of ethnic celebrations covered. Various indexes facilitate search by subject, ethnicity, geographical location, collectors, informants, translators, song titles, significant first lines, motifs, and tale types.

DEWEY: 394. 26973 LC: GT 4803 F65 ISBN 0-8103-7602-4

♦ 786 ♦

Food Festival: The Ultimate Guidebook to America's Best Regional Food Celebrations. **Alice M. Geffen and Carole Berglie. New York: Pantheon Books, 1986. 271 pp. Map. Index.**

Introduces 58 regional festivals celebrating food. Describes foods, festival ambience and history and provides travel information. Gives more than 130 recipes for featured dishes. Entries are organized by season. Geographical listing of festivals. A U.S. map shows festival locations. Recipe Index.

DEWEY: 394.6973 LC: GT 4403. G44 ISBN 0-394-72966-8

♦ 787 ♦

Foods from Harvest Festivals and Folk Fairs: The Best Recipes from and a Guide to Food Happenings Across the Nation. **Anita Borghese. New York: Thomas Y. Crowell Company, 1977. 270 pp. Index.**

Gives recipes from, description of, and travel information for 37 American and one Canadian festival. Covers food festivals, ethnic fairs, and other unusual celebrations. Describes attractions, events, foods, crafts, and festival history. Gives festival dates, location, year first held, nearest highways, and contact organization.

DEWEY: 641.5 973 LC: TX 715. B7255 ISBN 0-690-01655-7

♦ 788 ♦

Good Stories for Anniversaries. **Frances Jenkins Olcott. Illustrated by Hattie Longstreet Price. 1937. Reprint. Detroit, MI: Omnigraphics, Inc., 1990. 237 pp. Index.**

Furnishes more than 120 stories which dramatize the events, people, and spirit of American patriotic holidays and anniversaries. Gives stories for Constitution Day, Armistice Day, American Red Cross Roll Call, Aviation Days, Evacuation Day, Inauguration Day, Flag Day, Bunker Hill Day, Independence Day, Pioneer Days, and Patriot Days. Appropriate for school use. Subject index.

DEWEY: 973 LC: E178.9 053 ISBN 1-55888-876-4

♦ 789 ♦

The Great American Spectaculars: The Kentucky Derby, Mardi Gras, and Other Days of Celebration. **Jack Ludwig. Garden City, NY: Doubleday and Company, 1976. 247 pp.**

Conveys behind-the-scenes experiences and personal reflections of a writer attending five spectacular American celebrations: the Kentucky Derby, the Indianapolis 500, the Rose Bowl, the 1972 Democratic and Republican National Conventions, and Mardi Gras.

DEWEY: 394.2 LC: GT 4803. L82 ISBN 0-385-06670-8

♦ 790 ♦

A Guide to Fairs and Festivals in the United States. **Frances Shemanski. Westport, CT: Greenwood Press, 1984. 339 pp. Appendix. Index.**

Covers all 50 states as well as the U.S. Virgin Islands, American Samoa, and Puerto Rico. Festival entries provide information on origins, history, purpose, special events, and activities. Entries are organized by state. Appendix lists festivals by type.

DEWEY: 394.6 025 LC: GT 3930. S4 ISBN 0-313-21437-9

♦ 791 ♦

Guide to Fairs, Festivals, and Fun Events. **Janice Gale and Stephen Gale. Miami, FL: Sightseer Publications, 1980. 190 pp. Illustrated. Maps. Index.**

Covers more than 400 yearly celebrations in 18 states, including folk, music, food, and ethnic festivals, rodeos, expositions, races, contests, and more. Entries give approximate date, town, festival name, address and phone number of contact organization, and brief description of festival attractions. Many entries mention nearby sightseeing opportunities. Organized by state and by date. Illustrated with black-and-white photos. Index of towns.

DEWEY: 394.2 0974 LC: GT4805.G34 ISBN 0-937928-00-3

♦ 792 ♦

Highdays and Holidays. **Florence Adams and Elizabeth McCarrick. New York: E. P. Dutton, 1927. 337 pp. Indexes.**

A collection of verse on the nation's holidays. Covers New Year's Day, Lincoln's Birthday, Valentine's Day, Washington's Birthday, St. Patrick's Day, Arbor Day, Bird Day, Easter, May Day, Mother's Day, Music Week, Memorial Day, Flag Day, Independence Day, Labor Day, Columbus Day, Roosevelt's Birthday, Armistice Day, Book Week, Thanksgiving, and Christmas. Index of authors, titles, and first lines.

DEWEY: 394

♦ 793 ♦

Historic Festivals: A Traveler's Guide. **George Cantor. Detroit, MI: Gale Research, 1996. 392 pp. Illustrated. Indexes.**

A guide to almost 300 American festivals which reflect local history, culture, or character. Covers every region of the United States, including Alaska and Hawaii. Entries give festival's historical background and significance, list major events, provide contact organization and address, and note nearest roads or highways. Furnishes chronology of the historical events celebrated in the festivals, an indexed calendar of festivals, a festival index, and a subject index.

DEWEY: 394.2 69 73 LC: E 158. C 247 ISBN 0-8103-9150-3

♦ 794 ♦

The Holiday Book. **Marguerite Kohl and Frederica Young. Illustrated by Phillip Miller. 1952. Reprint. Detroit, MI: Omnigraphics, Inc., 1996. 214 pp.**

Offers craft projects, recipes, decorations, and party ideas for the celebration of 14 American holidays: Christmas, New Year, Lincoln's Birthday, Washington's Birthday, Valentine's Day, St. Patrick's Day, Easter, Passover, Purim, Mother's Day, Father's Day, Independence Day, Halloween, and Thanksgiving. Also addresses birthdays, graduations, and anniversaries.

DEWEY: 394.2 6973 LC: GT4803 K6 ISBN 0-7808-0163-6

♦ 795 ♦

The Holiday Book: America's Festivals and Celebrations. **Martin Greif. New York: The Main Street Press, 1978. 255 pp. Illustrated. Bibliography.**

Conveys the lore, history, and spirit of 20 American holidays. Covers New Year's Day, Lincoln's Birthday, St. Valentine's Day, Washington's Birthday, St. Patrick's Day, April Fools' Day, Arbor Day, Easter, May Day, Mother's Day, Memorial Day, Flag Day, Father's Day, the Fourth of July, Labor Day, Columbus Day, Halloween, Veterans Day, Thanksgiving, and Christmas. Discusses the origins of the holiday, its history, and celebration in America. Gives poems, notable quotations, anecdotes, and excerpts from essays and addresses which convey the spirit of the holiday. Reprints antique drawings and engravings addressing holiday themes. Also covers 20 minor American holidays in lesser detail.

DEWEY: 810.8 LC: PS 509. H55 H6 ISBN 0-87663-309-2

♦ 796 ♦

The Holiday Handbook. **Carol Barkin and Elizabeth James. Illustrated by Melanie Marder Parks. New York: Clarion Books, 1994. 240 pp. Appendix. Bibliography. Index.**

Presents 35 secular holidays to young readers. Gives brief history and facts about the holiday. Suggests ways to celebrate, including craft and food ideas. Includes many less observed days, such as Women's Equality Day,

Grandparents' Day, United Nation Day, Leif Eriksson Day, and Groundhog Day. Organized by season. Each season is characterized, followed by brief descriptions of the major religious holidays of various faith traditions occurring during that season given. Appendix provides list of contact organizations.

DEWEY: 394.2 6 LC: GT 4803. B37 ISBN 0-395-65011-9

♦ 797 ♦

Holiday Hullabaloo! Facts, Jokes, and Riddles. **E. Richard Churchill, with Eric Churchill and Sean Churchill. New York: Franklin Watts, 1977. 183 pp. Illustrated. Index.**

Gives holiday lore, historical facts, trivia, jokes, and riddles for 23 American holidays. Treats New Year, Benjamin Franklin's Birthday, Groundhog Day, Boy Scout Day, Lincoln's Birthday, St. Valentine's Day, Washington's Birthday, Girl Scout Day, St. Patrick's Day, April Fool's Day, Easter, Arbor Day, May Day, Mother's Day, Children's Day, Flag Day, Father's Day, Independence Day, Labor Day, Columbus Day, Halloween, Thanksgiving, and Christmas. Illustrated with black-and-white drawings.

DEWEY: 394.2 6973 LC: GT 3933. C48 ISBN 0-531-00384-1

♦ 798 ♦

Holiday Ring. **Adeline Corrigan, ed. Illustrated by Rainey Bennett. Chicago, IL: Albert Whitman and Company, 1975. 256 pp. Index.**

Presents a collection of stories, poems, and short essays which celebrate the spirit of American holidays. Covers New Year's Day, Martin Luther King's Day, Abraham Lincoln's Birthday, Valentine's Day, George Washington's Birthday, St. Patrick's Day, Earth Day and Arbor Day, Easter, Mother's Day, Memorial Day, Flag Day, Father's Day, Dominion Day, Independence Day, Labor Day, American Indian Day, Columbus Day, Veterans Day, Halloween, Thanksgiving, Hanukkah, and Christmas. Briefly introduces each holiday with notes on its origin, meaning, and customs. For children.

DEWEY: 394.26 LC: PZ 5. H723 ISBN 0-8075-3356-4

♦ 799 ♦

Holidays: Days of Significance to All Americans. **Trevor Nevitt Dupuy, ed. New York: Franklin Watts, Inc., 1965. 162 pp. Index.**

A collection of brief essays providing factual information about the people, events, and causes behind America's secular holidays. Covers 27 regional, ethnic, and national holidays, including V-J Day, Alamo Day, Patriot's Day,

Robert E. Lee's Birthday, Pan-American Day, Discovery Day, American Indian Day, and more. Directed towards teachers. Provides further reading list.

DEWEY: 394. D945 h

♦ 800 ♦

Music Festivals in America: Classical, Opera, Jazz, Pops, Country, Old-time Fiddlers, Folk, Bluegrass, Cajun. **Carol Price Rabin. Fourth edition. Illustrated by Celia Elke. Great Barrington, MA: Berkshire Traveller Press, 1990. 271 pp. Maps. Bibliography. Index.**

Lists more than 160 festivals in 39 states, Puerto Rico, Bermuda, and Canada. Entries provide history and background of festival, sample of programs and performing artists, listing of workshops and classes offered through the festival, contact addresses and telephone numbers, festival dates, and information pertaining to the reservation and purchase of tickets and lodging. Organized by musical genre. Includes seven regional maps identifying festival locations.

DEWEY: 780. 7973 LC: ML 19. R3 ISBN 0-930145-0101

♦ 801 ♦

The 1990 Festival Hopper's Guide to California. **Julie Hicks-Herman and Darrin Craig. San Jose, CA: Creative Chaos, 1990. 392 pp. Maps. Indexes.**

A guide to more than 350 California festivals. Organized by region (north, central, and south) and calendar date. Each listing provides a brief characterization of the festival, a checklist indicating festival attractions, services available, permitted activities, town population, festival location, previous year's attendance, other local attractions, and average outdoor temperature. Also lists local motels and restaurants, gives phone number to call for information, and provides a road map showing town's location and nearest highways. Includes festival index and town index.

DEWEY: 394 H631 fc ISBN 0-9624538-0-3

♦ 802 ♦

The 1990 Festival Hopper's Guide to the Great Northwest. **Julie Hicks-Herman and Darrin Craig. San Jose, CA: Creative Chaos, 1990. 167 pp. Maps. Indexes.**

A guide to more than 130 festivals in Idaho, Oregon, and Washington. Organized by state and calendar date. Each listing provides a brief characterization of the festival, a checklist indicating festival attractions, services available, permitted activities, town population, festival location, previous year's attendance, other local attractions, and average outdoor temperature. Also lists local motels and restaurants, gives phone number to call for information, and provides a road map showing town's location and nearest highways. Includes festival index and town index.

DEWEY: 394 H631 f ISBN 0-9624538-1-1

♦ 803 ♦

Norman Rockwell's American Holidays. **Milton Garrison. New York: Crescent Books, 1990. 123 pp. Illustrated.**

A collection of full-page color reproductions of Rockwell's paintings of American holiday themes. Reproduces more than 50 images. Covers a selection of national holidays, special holidays (such as Arbor Day and Bird Day), children's holidays (such as May Day and Prom Night), and family holidays. Gives brief commentaries on the holidays and the artist's view of American life as represented in his paintings.

DEWEY: 759.13 LC: ND 237 R68 G37 ISBN 0-517-03173-6

♦ 804 ♦

Our National Holidays. **Karen Spies. Brookfield, CT: The Millbrook Press, 1992. 48 pp. Illustrated. Index.**

Explains why and how we celebrate 19 national holidays honoring our nation and government, famous individuals, the armed forces, ethnic traditions, and the environment. Covers Independence Day, Flag Day, Labor Day, Citizenship Day, Martin Luther King, Jr. Day, Washington's Birthday, Lincoln's Birthday, Columbus Day, Thanksgiving Day, Chinese New Year, Cinco de Mayo, Kwanzaa, Native American Day, Arbor Day, Bird Day, and Earth Day. Also furnishes chronology of holiday observance, as well as further reading and resource list. For children.

DEWEY: 394.2 6 0973 LC: GT 2703 S66 ISBN 1-56294-109-7

♦ 805 ♦

Patriotic Holidays. **Cass R. Sandak. New York: Crestwood House, 1990. 48 pp. Illustrated. Index.**

Summarizes the history and explains the significance of 16 patriotic holidays of the United States: the Fourth of July, Martin Luther King, Jr. Day, President's Day, Memorial Day, Labor Day, Veterans Day, Inauguration Day, Arbor Day, Pan-American Day, Patriot's Day, Armed Forces Day, Flag Day, Citizenship Day, United Nations Day, and Election Day. Gives holiday trivia, and lists several patriotic holidays of other countries. Further reading list. For children.

DEWEY: 394.2 68473 LC: GT 4803. S26 ISBN 0-89686-501-0

♦ 806 ♦

Patriotic Holidays and Celebrations. **Valorie Grigoli. New York: Franklin Watts, 1985. 66 pp. Illustrated. Index.**

Explains the history and ideas behind 24 patriotic and civic holidays. Covers Independence Day, Labor Day, Inauguration Day, Pan American Day, Flag Day, Citizenship Day, United Nations Day, Bill of Rights Day, Presidents' Day, George Washington's Birthday, Abraham Lincoln's Birthday, Martin Luther King, Jr. Day, Columbus Day, Memorial Day, Veterans Day, Armed Forces Day, Arbor Day, Saint Paul Winter Carnival, Patriots' Day, Confederate Memorial Day, Cinco de Mayo, and American Indian Day. For children.

DEWEY: 394.2 684 73 LC: JK 1761. G75 ISBN 0-531-10044-8

♦ 807 ♦

Pieces for Every Day the Schools Celebrate. **Enlarged edition. Norma H. Deming and Katharine I. Bemis. New York: Noble and Noble, Publishers, 1921. 455 pp.**

Provides prose, verse, quotations, sayings, and addresses about the people, events, or ideas behind American celebrated days. Covers New Year's Day, Lincoln's Birthday, Washington's Birthday, Arbor Day and Bird Day, Mother's Day, Memorial Day, Flag Day, Father's Day, Commencement Day, Independence Day, Labor Day, Constitution Day, Columbus Day, Roosevelt's Birthday, Armistice Day, Red Cross Day, Thanksgiving Day, and Christmas Day.

DEWEY: 808.8 D38p

♦ 808 ♦

Red Letter Days: A Book of Holiday Customs. **Revised edition. Elizabeth Hough Sechrist. Illustrations by Elsie Jane McCorkell. Philadelphia, PA: Macrae Smith Company, 1965. 253 pp. Index.**

Presents a collection of lore, customs, and historical information about American holidays and their counterparts in European and other countries. Covers New Year's Day, Lincoln's Birthday, St. Valentine's Day, Washington's Birthday, St. Patrick's Day, Easter, April Fools' Day, Arbor Day, Pan-American Day, May Day, Mother's Day, Memorial Day, Children's Day, Flag Day, Independence Day, Columbus Day, Halloween, All Saints' and All Souls' Days, Veterans Day, Thanksgiving, and Christmas. Covers 26 other American holidays and days of observance or commemoration in lesser detail. Lists Jewish, Orthodox, and Catholic holidays. Includes a brief history of the Gregorian calendar. For children.

DEWEY: 394

♦ 809 ♦

Singing Holidays: The Calendar in Folk Song. **Oscar Brand. Illustrated by Roberta Moynihan. New York: Alfred A. Knopf, 1957. 258 pp. Indexes.**

Gives words and music to 90 folk songs which convey the meaning or spirit of 26 American holidays. Also gives songs for the four seasons. Index of songs and index of first lines.

DEWEY: 784

♦ 810 ♦

Stories for Every Holiday. **Carolyn Sherwin Bailey. 1919. Reprint. Detroit, MI: Omnigraphics, Inc., 1990. 277 pp.**

Twenty-seven stories for young readers about 19 American holidays: Labor Day, Columbus Day, Halloween, Election Day, Thanksgiving Day, Christmas Day, New Year's Day, Lincoln's Birthday, St. Valentine's Day, Washington's Birthday, St. Patrick's Day, April Fool's Day, Easter Day, Arbor Day, May Day, Mother's Day, Memorial Day, Flag Day, and Independence Day.

DEWEY: Fic LC: PZ7 Bi51 Ste ISBN 1-55888-880-2

♦ 811 ♦

"We Gather Together": Food and Festival in American Life. **Theodore C. Humphrey and Lin T. Humphrey, eds. Ann Arbor, MI: U. M. I. Research Press, 1988. 289 pp. Appendix. Bibliography. Index.**

A collection of articles by folklore scholars exploring the role of food in a diverse range of contemporary American family and community celebrations. Appendix give soup recipes and suggestions for starting your own Soup Night gathering.

DEWEY: 394.2 6973 LC: GT 4803. W4 ISBN 0-8357-1890-5

♦ 812 ♦

What So Proudly We Hail: All About Our American Flag, Monuments, and Symbols. **Maymie R. Krythe. New York: Harper and Row, Publishers, 1968. 278 pp. Bibliography. Index.**

Relates history, lore, and customs concerning the American flag, American monuments, and symbols. Covers the Great Seal of the United States, the Presidential Seal and Flag, "In God We Trust," the American Eagle, Uncle Sam, the Liberty Bell and Independence Hall, the White House, the Capitol building, the Statue of Liberty, the Washington Monument, the Lincoln Memorial, the Jefferson Memorial, and the Tomb of the Unknown Soldier.

DEWEY: 917.3

♦ 813 ♦

Why We Celebrate Our Holidays. **Mary I. Curtis. Illustrated by Jewel Morrison. New York: Lyons and Carnahan, 1924. 148 pp.**

Explains the meaning and describes the customs of 22 American holidays, including New Year, Lincoln's Birthday, St. Valentine's Day, Washington's Birthday, St. Patrick's Day, April Fool's Day, Good Friday and Easter, Arbor Day, Bird Day, May Day, American Indian Day, Mother's Day, Memorial Day, Flag Day, Independence Day, Labor Day, Columbus Day, Halloween, Armistice Day, Thanksgiving Day, Forefathers' Day, and Christmas. For children.

DEWEY: 394.26973

AFRICAN AMERICAN

♦ 814 ♦

African American Holidays. **Faith Winchester. Mankato, MN: Bridgestone Books, 1996. 24 pp. Illustrated. Index.**

Outlines the celebration of eight African-American holidays: Martin Luther King, Jr.'s Birthday, Black History Month, Malcolm X's Birthday, Juneteenth, Marcus Garvey's Birthday, Harambee, Junkanoo, and Kwanzaa. Gives a craft project, pronunciation guide, further reading list, and several further resources. Color photos illustrate. For children. One book in a series entitled *Ethnic Holidays.*

DEWEY: 394.2 6 08996073   LC: GT4803.A2W55   ISBN 1-56065-456-2

♦ 815 ♦

African American Holidays: A Historical Research and Resource Guide to Cultural Celebrations. **James C. Anyike. Chicago: Popular Truth, Inc., 1991. 102 pp. Appendices. Bibliography.**

Covers holidays celebrated by slaves between the seventeenth and nineteenth centuries, as well as Martin Luther King, Jr. Day, Black History Month, African Liberation Day, Juneteenth, Umoja Karamu (Unity Feast), and Kwanzaa. Appendices include timeline of important dates in history and brief historical background on major holidays observed in the U.S. List of related sources and organizations. (NR)

DEWEY: 394.2 68   LC: GT4803.A8   ISBN 0-963154-7-0-2

♦ 816 ♦

O Freedom! Afro-American Emancipation Celebrations. **William H. Wiggins. Knoxville, TN: University of Tennessee Press, 1987. 207 pp. Illustrated. Bibliography. Index.**

Describes past and present African-American celebrations of Emancipation, including Juneteenth. Traces influence of earlier Emancipation celebrations on more recent observances, such as Black History Month, Black Expo, Black Music Month, African Liberation Day, and Martin Luther King, Jr. Day. Explains how the customs and festivities of these celebrations work to enhance a sense of identity and worth in the participants, and discusses the ideological themes of African-American spiritual celebrations. Relates the history of the establishment of Martin Luther King, Jr. Day as a national holiday. References given in endnotes.

DEWEY: 973.7 14 LC: E453 W65 ISBN 0-87049-520-8

♦ 817 ♦

Santería: African Spirits in America. **Joseph M. Murphy. Boston, MA: Beacon Press, 1993. 189 pp. Glossary. Bibliography. Index.**

Traces origins and presents beliefs, rituals, ceremonies, songs, gestures, foods, and herbs associated with the practice of the Santería ("the way of the saints") religion, an Afro-Cuban outgrowth of the Yoruba religion in Nigeria, as observed by African Americans in New York. (NR)

DEWEY: 299.67 LC: BL2532.S3 M87 ISBN 0-8070-1021-9

AMERICAN INDIAN DAY

♦ 818 ♦

American Indian Myths and Legends. **Richard Erdoes and Alfonso Ortiz, eds. New York: Pantheon Books, 1984. 527 pp. Illustrated. Appendix. Bibliography. Index.**

Offers 160 myths and legends from more than 80 American Indian tribes. Organized around 10 themes: human creation, world creation, celestial objects, heros, war and warriors, love and desire, trickster tales, animals and other people, ghosts and the spirit world, and death and the end of the world. Appendix furnishes one-paragraph background for the tribes represented in the book. Title index.

DEWEY: 389.2 08997 LC: E98. F6 A47 ISBN 0-394-50796-7

♦ 819 ♦

American Indians Today: Issues and Conflicts. **Judith Harlan. New York: Franklin Watts, 1987. 128 pp. Illustrated. Index.**

Provides an introduction to the social conditions and challenges facing Native Americans today. Reviews Native history, tribal organizations, and legal status;

discusses contemporary tribal economic ventures and legal battles, difficulties arising from cultural difference and conflict, health care issues, education, and employment off the reservation. Black-and-white photos. Further reading list. For young readers.

DEWEY: 973-0497 ISBN 531-10325-0

♦ 820 ♦

The Book of Indian Crafts and Indian Lore. **Julian Harris Salomon. New York: Harper and Row, 1928. 418 pp. Illustrated. Bibliography. Index.**

Explains Indian customs and lore, and gives instructions for Indian crafts and activities. Covers clothing, headgear, ornaments, tipis, weapons, war paint, musical instruments, cooking, pipes, bags, games, dances, ceremonies, and more. Words and music to Indian songs. Tips for producing an Indian pageant. List of Indian names. Black-and-white illustrations.

DEWEY: 970.1

♦ 821 ♦

Everyday Life of the North American Indian. **Jon Manchip White. New York: Holmes and Meier Publishers, 1979. 256 pp. Illustrated. Bibliography. Index.**

Describes the everyday life of North American Indians before the arrival of Europeans. Covers hunting, home life, war, spirituality, and the arts. Also summarizes Indian history, from their arrival on the North American continent to their military defeat by Euro-Americans and assignment to reservations. Illustrated with black-and-white photos.

DEWEY: 970.004 97 LC: E98. S7 W48 ISBN 0-8419-0488-X

♦ 822 ♦

Growing Up Indian. **Evelyn Wolfson. Illustrated by William Sauts Bock. New York: Walker and Company, 1986. 81 pp. Bibliography. Index.**

Uses question-and-answer format to describe the life of children in traditional Indian society. Covers such topics as clothing, food, dress, discipline, learning, religion, family, play, and more. Black-and-white drawings illustrate. Suggested reading list. For children.

DEWEY: 306 08997073 LC: E98. C5 W68 ISBN 0-8027-6643-9

♦ 823 ♦

The Indian How Book. **Arthur C. Parker. 1927. Reprint. New York: Dover Publications, 1975. 335 pp. Illustrated.**

Describes more than 70 aspects of traditional life among the North American Indians. Tells how Indians acquired and cooked food, and how they made implements, furnishings, clothing, ornaments, and more. Discusses many activities of daily life, such as courtship, marriage, education, bathing, and recreation, as well as special activities, such as those related to warfare and ceremonial life. Black-and-white drawings illustrate.

DEWEY: 970.1 ISBN 0-486-21767-1

♦ 824 ♦

A Native American Feast. **Lucille Recht Penner. New York: Macmillan Publishing Company, 1994. 99 pp. Illustrated. Bibliography. Index.**

Explores the cuisine and food-related beliefs and customs of traditional Native American societies. Contrasts the foods eaten by various tribes, tells how animals were hunted and how plants were gathered or cultivated. Discusses food preparation and gives recipes. Discusses food lore, customs, and table manners. Black-and-white illustrations. For young readers.

DEWEY: 394.1 08997 LC: E98. F7 P46 ISBN 0-02-770902-7

♦ 825 ♦

Native Americans. **David Hurst Thomas and Lorann Pendleton, eds. Alexandria, VA: Time Life Books, 1995. 64 pp. Illustrated. Glossary. Index.**

Color photos, drawings, and text portray many aspects of daily life in traditional Native American societies. Covers origins, clothing, childhood, courtship, transportation, food, artwork, housing, games, ceremonies, and more. Touches on Native American history and reservation life. Lavishly illustrated with color drawings and photos.

DEWEY: 970.1 LC: E77.4 N38 ISBN 0-7835-4759-5

♦ 826 ♦

Native Americans and the U.S. Government. **Martha Blakely. New York: Chelsea Juniors, a Division of Chelsea House Publishers, 1995. 79 pp. Illustrated. Glossary. Index.**

Documents the treatment given Native Americans by the U.S. government for the past 200 years. Covers Euro-American attitudes towards Native Americans, government treaties, forced relocations and acculturations, the sale of Native American lands, and contemporary Native American activism. Chronology of important events in Native American history. Illustrated with color and black-and-white photos. For young readers.

DEWEY: 323.1 197073 LC: E91 B65 ISBN 0-7910-2475-X

♦ 827 ♦

Native American Stories. **Joseph Bruchac. Golden, CO: Fulcrum Publishing, 1991. 145 pp. Illustrated. Maps. Glossary.**

Presents a collection of traditional Native American stories pertaining to the relationship between human beings and the natural world. Organized by the following themes: creation, fire, earth, wind and weather, water, sky, seasons, plants and animals, life, death, spirit, and unity of earth. Stories from 16 different tribes from all regions of the United States. Gives map and paragraph of background information on each tribe. Illustrated with black-and-white drawings. Suggestions for parents, teachers, and storytellers.

DEWEY: 398.2 08997 LC: E98. F6 B9 ISBN 1-55591-094-7

♦ 828 ♦

The World of the American Indian. **Jules B. Billard, ed. Washington, DC: National Geographic Society, 1974. 399 pp. Illustrated. Map. Index.**

Explains the historical origins and describes the traditional way of life of the Northern, Woodland, Plains, Southwest, and Western Indian tribes. Also gives chapter on history and ceremonialism of Southwest tribes, as well as chapter on Euro-American colonization and conquest of Native American lands and peoples. Chapter by Vine Deloria on twentieth-century Indian history and political movements. Introductory essay on Indian identity by N. Scott Momaday. Provides list of all Indian groups in North America with accompanying map. More than 440 illustrations, 360 in color.

DEWEY: 970.1

ARBOR DAY

♦ 829 ♦

Arbor Day. **Aileen Fisher. Illustrations by Nonny Hogrogian. New York: Thomas Y. Crowell Company, 1965. 34 pp.**

Relates the history of Arbor Day in America and explains the importance of tree conservation. Written for young children.

DEWEY: 394 ISBN 0-690-09615-1

♦ 830 ♦

Arbor Day: Its History, Observance, Spirit and Significance; with Practical Selections on Tree-Planting and Conservation, and a Nature Anthology. **Robert Haven Schauffler. 1909. Reprint. Detroit, MI: Omnigraphics, Inc., 1990, 376 pp.**

An anthology of texts concerning Arbor Day. Articles and essays discuss the establishment of Arbor Day as a national holiday, offer practical advice on tree planting and conservation, and furnish material for Arbor Day programs. Also gives poems, essays, and various excerpted passages which describe, reflect, or elaborate on the meaning and spirit of Arbor Day. Includes Theodore Roosevelt's Arbor Day letter to American schoolchildren, and other texts by Washington Irving, Walt Whitman, Henry Wadsworth Longfellow, William Shakespeare, and many others. One volume in a series entitled *Our American Holidays.*

DEWEY: 394.2 68 LC: SD 363 S3 ISBN 1-55888-865-9

♦ 831 ♦

The Simple Act of Planting a Tree: Healing Your Neighborhood, Your City, and Your World. **Treepeople, with Andy Lipkis and Katie Lipkis. Foreword by Lester R. Brown. Los Angeles, CA: Jeremy P. Tarcher, Inc., 1990. 236 pp. Illustrated.**

A detailed practical guide to organizing a community tree-planting event. Explains the problem of global deforestation and the positive impact of trees on the environment. Gives instructions for tree planting and tree care. Tells how to select tree-planting sites, organize a community group, hold meetings, get publicity, acquire permits, raise money, and execute a tree-planting event. Many checklists and workbook pages.

DEWEY: 635.9 77 091732 LC: SB 436. L56 ISBN 0-87477-602-3

ASIAN AMERICAN

♦ 832 ♦

Asian Holidays. **Faith Winchester. Mankato, MN: Bridgestone Books, 1996. 24 pp. Illustrated. Index.**

Outlines celebration of eight Asian holidays: Chinese New Year, Clear and Bright Festival (Ching Ming), Japanese New Year, Buddha's Birthday, Tet, the Girls' Festival (Doll Festival), the Boys' Festival, and the Mid-Autumn Festival (Harvest Moon Festival). Gives a craft project, pronunciation guide, further reading list, and several further resources. Color photos illustrate. For children. One book in a series entitled *Ethnic Holidays.*

DEWEY: 394.2 695 LC: GT4872. A2W55 ISBN 1-56065-458-9

CAMBODIAN NEW YEAR

♦ 833 ♦

Dara's Cambodian New Year. **Sothea Chiemruom. Illustrated by Dam Nang Pin. New York: Half Moon Books, 1992. 23 pp. Glossary.**

Presents a Cambodian-American family's reminiscences about New Year celebrations in Cambodia. Briefly describes decorations and customs. Illustrated with color photos and drawings. For children.

DEWEY: 394 ISBN 0-671-88607-X

CHINESE NEW YEAR

♦ 834 ♦

Chinese New Year. **Tricia Brown. New York: Henry Holt and Company, 1987. 39 pp. Illustrated.**

Describes the symbols, customs, foods, devotions, and festivities by which American Chinese families celebrate Chinese New Year. Illustrated with black-and-white photos. For young children.

DEWEY: 394.2 683 LC: GT 4905.B76 ISBN 0-8050-0497-1

♦ 835 ♦

Chinese New Year. **Dianne M. MacMillan. Hillside, NJ: Enslow Publishers, Inc., 1994. 48 pp. Illustrated. Glossary. Index.**

Describes the preparations, beliefs, customs, symbols, foods, and festivities of the Chinese New Year season in America. Illustrated with color and black-and-white photos. For children. One book in a series entitled *Best Holiday Books.*

DEWEY: 394.2 61 LC: GT 4905.M33 ISBN 0-89490-500-7

♦ 836 ♦

Gung Hay Fat Choy. **June Behrens. Chicago: Childrens Press, 1982. 31 pp. Illustrated.**

Tells how Chinese New Year is celebrated. Treats home and street festivities and customs. Illustrated with color photos. For children. One volume in a series entitled *Festivals and Holidays.*

DEWEY: 394.2 683 LC: GT 4905. B43 ISBN 0-516-008842-4

CHRISTMAS

♦ 837 ♦

The American Christmas: A Study in National Culture. **James H. Barnett. New York: Macmillan Company, 1954. 173 pp. Bibliography. Index.**

A study of American Christmas celebrations, their format, their social effects, and their historical development. Discusses Puritan influence on Christmas in early America; the role and meaning of Santa Claus in Christmas celebrations; Christmas celebrations in homes, schools, and churches; the influence of commerical concerns on Christmas; representations of Christmas in the popular arts; and the long-standing tensions between religious and secular elements of the celebration.

LC: GT 4985 B3

♦ 838 ♦

America's Christmas Heritage. **Ruth Cole Kainen. New York: Funk and Wagnalls, 1969. 260 pp. Illustrated. Index.**

Introduces the reader to regional and ethnic diversity in American Christmas celebrations. Offers descriptions of Christmas beliefs, customs, and foods; gives recipes; and summarizes history of various American ethnic groups. Reviews the historical development of Christmas celebrations in New Amsterdam, New York, New England, Pennsylvania, Hawaii, and the South. Covers numerous ethnic groups, with special emphasis on the Germans, Moravians, French, Spanish, Mexicans, and Scandinavians. Illustrated with black-and-white photos of Christmas dishes.

DEWEY: 394 C555k

♦ 839 ♦

The Battle for Christmas. **Stephen Nissenbaum. New York: Alfred A. Knopf, 1996. 381 pp. Illustrated. Index.**

Offers a history of American Christmas celebrations from the seventeenth through the nineteenth centuries. Ties evolving sentiments and customs to social and cultural changes. Addresses the Puritan resistance to Christmas, the role of Santa Claus, the decline of public and the rise of domestic celebrations, gift giving, charity, and the celebrations of African Americans in the Antebellum and postwar South. References given in endnotes. Black-and-white illustrations.

DEWEY: 394.2 663 0973 LC: GT 4986. A1 N57 ISBN 0-679-41223-9

♦ 840 ♦

Christmas in America. **Penne L. Restad. New York: Oxford University Press, 1995. 219 pp. Index.**

A scholarly history of Christmas in the United States, from its prohibition in colonial times to its immense popularity in the late twentieth century, with emphasis on the nineteenth century. Covers diverse and changing attitudes towards Christmas, the manner in which it was celebrated, the meanings attributed to it, and the secularization of Christmas in the twentieth century. Views the development of popular Christmas celebrations as reflective of the development of a national identity, and as instrumental in unifying the disparate ethnic groups that made up the population.

DEWEY: 394.2 66309 LC: GT 4986. A1 R47 ISBN 0-19-509300-3

♦ 841 ♦

Christmas in Colonial and Early America. **Staff of World Book Encyclopedia, Inc. Chicago: World Book Encyclopedia, Inc., 1975. 80 pp. Illustrated. Index.**

Tells how Christmas was celebrated in Colonial and eighteenth- and nineteenth-century America. Describes customs, foods, decorations, toys, and attitudes towards Christmas, often drawing on historical accounts of actual Christmas celebrations, including those of George Washington and other presidents. Treats regional and ethnic variation in Christmas celebrations and customs, the integration of Santa Claus into American Christmas lore, and Victorian Christmas celebrations. Also gives recipes, crafts, and words and music to Christmas songs. Beautifully illustrated with color photos and drawings. For older children.

DEWEY: 394.2682 ISBN 0-7166-2001-4

♦ 842 ♦

Christmas in the American Southwest. **Chicago: World Book, Inc., 1996. 80 pp. Illustrated.**

Describes Christmas season celebrations, customs, and their history in the Southwest United States. Covers the traditions of many ethnic groups of the region: Hispanic, Native, Anglo, German, Czech, Polish, and Scandinavian. Also describes community events and observances in small towns and cities, such as the Chickasha (Oklahoma) Festival of Lights and Christmas Eve services at the Shrine of the Ages in Grand Canyon National Park. Gives crafts, carols, and recipes. Color photos illustrate. One book in a series entitled *Christmas Around the World.*

DEWEY: 394.2 663 0979 LC: GT 4986. S64C57 ISBN 0-7166-0896-0

♦ 843 ♦

Christmas on the American Frontier, 1800-1900. John E. Baur. 1961. Reprint. Detroit, MI: Omnigraphics, Inc., 1993. 320 pp. Illustrated.

Seventeen chapters cover such topics as "A California Festival of Good Will," "Down a Prairie Chimney," "Giving Christmas to the Indians," and more. Contains eyewitness accounts of frontier holidays. (NR)

DEWEY: 394.268 B351 LC: GT4986.W47B38 ISBN 1-55888-171-9

♦ 844 ♦

The Civil War Christmas Album. Philip Van Doren Stern, ed. New York: Hawthorn Books, 1961. 127 pp. Illustrated.

Presents a collection of writings and illustrations on the subject of Christmas during the Civil War. Addresses Christmas before the War and Christmas during the War both in the army and at home; also treats Santa Claus during the war and the first Christmas after the peace. Gives excerpts from soldiers' letters and diaries, newspaper articles and editorials, magazine articles, essays, stories, and recipes. Includes Robert E. Lee's Christmas letters. Period drawings and engravings illustrate.

DEWEY: 394.2 ST 45c

♦ 845 ♦

December 25th: The Joys of Christmas Past. Phillip Snyder. New York: Dodd, Mead, and Company, 1985. 324 pp. Illustrated. Bibliography. Index.

Depicts American Christmas festivities of the nineteenth and early twentieth centuries, the epoch in which contemporary Christmas celebrations were shaped. Presents colorful anecdotes and historical data culled from newspaper accounts and other writings of the times. Detailed descriptions of foods bought, caught, and prepared; noise-making customs; the advent of Christmas displays, shopping and gift giving, Christmas tipping, Christmas cards, displays of greenery; the revival of Christmas carols; the changing image of Santa Claus; the introduction of store-bought toys; and Church celebrations. Covers diverse elements of American society, from fashionable Easterners to rural Westerners, European immigrants, black and white Southerners. Illustrated with black-and-white nineteenth-century drawings and engravings. Good bibliography.

DEWEY: 394.268282 0973 LC: GT 4986 A1S68 ISBN 0-396-08588-1

♦ 846 ♦

The Modern Christmas in America: A Cultural History of Gift Giving. **William B. Waits. New York: New York University Press, 1993. 267 pp. Index.**

Reviews the history of gift giving as a central component of American Christmas celebrations from the nineteenth century to the mid-twentieth century. Covers the switch from homemade to store-bought gifts, shifting patterns of gift exchange between friends and family members, the rise of the Christmas card, the changing nature of gifts from parents to children, the role of community celebrations, and historical patterns of Christmas charity.

DEWEY: 394.2 68282 0973 LC: GT 4986 A1W35 ISBN 0-8147-9251-0

♦ 847 ♦

Politically Correct Holiday Stories for an Enlightened Yuletide Season. **James Finn Garner. New York: Macmillan, 1995. 99 pp.**

Humorous retelling of classic Christmas tales using contemporary American politically correct phrases and concepts. Includes, "'Twas the Night Before Solstice," "Frosty the Persun of Snow," "Rudolph the Nasally Empowered Reindeer," as well as retellings of "The Nutcracker" and "A Christmas Carol."

DEWEY: 394.2682 ISBN 0-02-860420-2

♦ 848 ♦

The Southern Christmas Book: The Full Story from Earliest Times to the Present: People, Customs, Conviviality, Carols, Cooking. **Harnett T. Kane. 1958. Reprint. Detroit, MI: Omnigraphics, Inc., 1997. 337 pp. Illustrated. Index.**

Recounts 300 years of southern Christmas season celebrations. Describes customs, lore, and foods, as well as memorable Christmas parties and anecdotes of times past. Notes differences in celebration styles between states and regions, whites and blacks. Reflects pre-Civil Rights attitudes prevalent in the South.

DEWEY: 394.2663 0975 LC: GT4986 A1K36 ISBN 0-7808-0271-3

CINCO DE MAYO

♦ 849 ♦

Fiesta! Cinco de Mayo. **June Behrens. Chicago, IL: Childrens Press, 1978. 31 pp. Illustrated.**

Depicts Mexican-American celebrations of Cinco de Mayo. Explains reason for holiday and describes dancing, music, foods, and other holiday activities. Illustrated with color photos. For children. One volume in a series entitled *Festivals and Holidays*.

DEWEY: 394.2 684 72 LC: F1233. B39 ISBN 0-516-08815-7

COLUMBUS DAY

♦ 850 ♦

Admiral of the Ocean Sea: A Life of Christopher Columbus. **Samuel Eliot Morison. Boston, MA: Little, Brown and Company, 1942. 680 pp. Illustrated. Maps. Index.**

A classic biography of Christopher Columbus, with an emphasis on the events of the voyages of discovery. Detailed descriptions. Numerous maps.

DEWEY: 970.015

♦ 851 ♦

America Discovers Columbus: How an Italian Explorer Became an American Hero. **Claudia L. Bushman. Hanover, NH: University Press of New England. 1992. 217 pp. Illustrated. Index.**

Examines the history of Columbus commemoration and celebration in the United States, focusing on the period from late eighteenth to the twentieth century. Documents the changing image of Columbus in art, poetry, ceremony, celebration, and biography. Illustrated with black-and-white photos of artwork depicting Columbus and the discovery of the New World.

DEWEY: 970.01 5 LC: E112. B95 ISBN 0-87451-576-9

♦ 852 ♦

Christopher Columbus and His Legacy: Opposing Viewpoints. **Mary Ellen Jones, ed. San Diego, CA: Greenhaven Press, 1992. 309 pp. Illustrated. Bibliography. Index.**

Presents excerpted passages from a wide range of thinkers expressing opposing viewpoints on Christopher Columbus and the historical legacy of the European conquest of the Americas. Subjects covered include the morality and actions of Columbus and the Conquistadors, the takeover of Indian lands, the value of Indian culture, the value of Euro-American culture, Indian and Euro-American cultural exchange, and twentieth-century perspectives on Columbus. Furnishes discussion questions. For young readers. One volume in a series entitled *Opposing Viewpoints*.

DEWEY: 970.01 5 LC: E111. C554 ISBN 0-89908-196-7

♦ 853 ♦

Columbus Day: The Best Prose and Verse About Columbus and the Discovery of America. With Tributes, Anecdotes, Plays, Poems, Tableaux, Exercises, and Programs for the Day's Observance. **Hilah Paulmier and Robert Haven Schauffler. New York: Dodd, Mead and Company, 1938. 319 pp. Appendix. Bibliography.**

An anthology of stories, poems, quotations, and excerpts from essays and addresses concerning the life of Christopher Columbus and the celebration of Columbus Day. Chapters devoted to Columbus as a boy, Columbus as a man, the voyages to the New World, tributes to Columbus, anecdotes, plays and tableaux, the observance of Columbus Day, the Americas, and children's poems. Includes various presidential proclamations. Appendix gives an outline of Columbus's life. One volume in a series entitled *Our American Holidays*.

DEWEY: 394.2

♦ 854 ♦

Columbus Dictionary. **Foster Provost. Detroit, MI: Omnigraphics, Inc. 1991. 142 pp. Bibliography.**

Covers a wide range of people, places, things, and events helpful to an understanding of Columbus's life and achievements. Entries highlight other entry titles occuring in text and cite sources; many list additional references. Suitable for a wide range of users, from middle school students to graduate students, as well as general readers.

DEWEY: 970.01 5 03 LC: E111 P96 ISBN 1-55888-158-1

♦ 855 ♦

Readings for the Christopher Columbus Quincentenary, Kindergarten Through Grade Twelve, An Annotated List. **Janet Lundin, ed. Sacramento, CA: Office of History—Social Science and Visual and Performing Arts and Office of Language Arts and Foreign Languages, California Department of Education, 1992. 24 pp. Appendix.**

An annotated bibliography of more than 80 books about Christopher Columbus for young readers. Selections include biography, history, fiction, essays, poetry, drama, and geography. Lists texts by appropriate grade level: kindergarten through grade three, grades four through six, grades seven through nine, and grades ten through twelve. Includes some Spanish-language texts. Appendix lists publishers and distributors of Spanish-language titles.

DEWEY: 970.015 ISBN 0-8011-0979-5

CZECH AMERICAN

♦ 856 ♦

Czechoslovak Culture: Recipes, History and Folk Arts. **Pat Martin, comp. Iowa City, IA: Penfield Press, 1989. 176 pp. Illustrated.**

Focus is on Czech-American culture, including traditions and stories carried over from Czechoslovakia. Essays on pioneer experiences, observance of holidays, including lengthy treatment of decorating Easter eggs, folk art, foods and recipes. Profiles of famous Czechs and Czech Americans. A partial list of Czech festivals throughout the United States and tips on planning Czech festivals. (NR)

DEWEY: 973.049186 LC: E184.B67 C927 ISBN 0-941016-61-7

D-DAY

♦ 857 ♦

America at D-Day: A Book of Remembrance. **Richard Goldstein. Preface by General Matthew B. Ridgway. New York: Delta Trade Paperbacks, 1994. 303 pp. Illustrated. Bibliography. Index.**

Retells the story of the Allied invasion of Normandy on D-Day, 1944, with an emphasis on American military efforts and the reactions of Americans at home to the invasion. Many firsthand accounts of battle by surviving American soldiers, sailors, journalists, and medics. Black-and-white photos illustrate.

DEWEY: 940. 54 2142 LC: D756.5N N6 G66 ISBN 0-385-31283-0

♦ 858 ♦

D-Day Normandy: The Story and the Photographs. **Donald M. Goldstein, Katherine V. Dillon, and J. Michael Wenger. Washington, DC: Brassey's, Inc., 1994. 180 pp. Illustrated. Index.**

Detailed description of the American participation in D-Day and the liberation of Normandy. Covers military leaders, weapons, preparations, the crossing of the channel, the invasion, and the advance to Cherbourg. More than 400 black-and-white photos illustrate. Explains purpose and activities of the Battle of Normandy Foundation. Prepared in commemoration of the 50th anniversary of the Battle of Normandy.

DEWEY: 940.54 214 LC: D756.5 N6 G65 ISBN 0-02-881057-0

DAY OF THE DEAD

♦ 859 ♦

Day of the Dead: A Mexican-American Celebration. **Diane Hoyt-Goldsmith. New York: Holiday House, 1994. 32 pp. Illustrated. Glossary. Index.**

Describes the Day of the Dead celebrations of a Mexican-American family. Introduces Aztec and Mexican history and beliefs, describes holiday preparations, including the preparation of altars, foods, offerings, and masks. Portrays processions, religious services, and celebrations. For children.

DEWEY: 394.2 64 LC: GT 4995. A4H69 ISBN 0-8234-1094-3

EARTH DAY

♦ 860 ♦

Celebrating Earth Day: A Sourcebook of Activities and Experiments. **Robert Gardner. Illustrations by Sharon Lane Holm. Brookfield, CT: Millbrook Press, 96 pp. Index.**

Teaches young people about environmental pollution and offers them a collection of conservation activities and experiments with which to celebrate Earth Day. Photos, drawings, and diagrams illustrate. Further reading list.

DEWEY: 333.7 LC: TD 170.2 G.37 ISBN 1-56294-070-8

♦ 861 ♦

Every Day is Earth Day. **Kathy Ross. Illustrated by Sharon Lane Holm. Brookfield, CT: Millbrook Press, 1995. 47 pp.**

Gives 20 craft ideas to help children celebrate Earth Day. Color illustrations.

DEWEY: 745.58 4 LC: TT160.R714 ISBN 1-56294-490-8

♦ 862 ♦

50 More Things You Can Do to Save the Earth. **The EarthWorks Group. Kansas City, ME: Andrews and McMeel, 1991. 120 pp.**

Provides summaries of successful conservation projects and suggests 50 additional projects benefitting individuals, neighborhoods, or communities. Projects are generally more involved than those listed in the group's previous book, *50 Simple Things You Can Do To Save The Earth.* Most entries list one or more of the following: resource organizations, activist groups, suppliers, further reading.

DEWEY: 301.3 F469 ISBN 0-8362-2302-0

♦ 863 ♦

50 Simple Things You Can Do To Save the Earth. **The EarthWorks Group. Berkeley, CA: Earthworks Press, 1989. 96 pp.**

Gives several brief summaries of major environmental problems and offers 50 simple conservation or restoration projects. Many entries list one or more of the following: resource organizations, suppliers, activist groups, further reading. (Note: This title was one of the best-selling environmental books ever.)

DEWEY: 301.3 F469 ISBN 0-929-634-06-3

♦ 864 ♦

Not in Our Backyard: The People and Events that Shaped America's Modern Environmental Movement. **Marc Mowrey and Tim Redmond. New York: William Morrow and Company, Inc., 1993. 496 pp. Index.**

Tells the story of the last 25 years of the environmental movement by recounting the events, campaigns, and individual struggles which spurred it on. Some coverage of the first Earth Day and subsequent Earth Day celebrations. References given in endnotes.

DEWEY: 363.7 0525 0973 LC: GE 180. M68 ISBN 0-688-10644-7

EMANCIPATION DAY

♦ 865 ♦

The Emancipation Proclamation. **John Hope Franklin. Garden City, NY: Doubleday and Company, 1963. 181 pp. Illustrated. Index.**

Offers a history of the Emancipation Proclamation. Discusses the issues and events which fostered it and its effect on the course of the Civil War. Considers its legacy. Gives chapter describing celebrations of the first Emancipation Day. Endnotes.

LC: E453. F8

FATHER'S DAY

♦ 866 ♦

Every Day is Father's Day: The Best Things Ever Said About Dear Old Dad. **Robert Byrne and Teressa Skelton, eds. New York: Atheneum, 1989. 177 pp. Illustrated. Index.**

An anthology of quotations and prose excerpts on the subject of fathers and fatherhood. Sentiments expressed include admiration, joy, sadness, and humor. Selections by well-known writers, such as Alice Walker, Ernest

Hemingway, and P. G. Wodehouse, as well as lesser-known individuals. Black-and-white photos illustrate.

DEWEY: 307.8 742 LC: HQ 756. E94 ISBN 0-689-12069-9

♦ 867 ♦

Faith of Our Fathers: African-American Men Reflect on Fatherhood. **Andre C. Willis, ed. Foreword by Alvin Poussaint. New York: Dutton, 1996. 227 pp.**

Presents a collection of essays by noted African-American writers and scholars which consider the meaning and experience of fatherhood for African-American men. Selections by Cornell West, Henry Louis Gates, Jr., John Edgar Wideman, and more.

DEWEY: 306.8742 LC: HQ 756 F33 ISBN 0-525-94158-4

♦ 868 ♦

Fathers. **Jon Winokur, ed. New York: Dutton, 1993. 226 pp. Index.**

Offers a collection of quotes and excerpts from prose works on the subject of fathers and fatherhood. Organized by theme: lessons, heroes, characters, lost fathers, bad fathers, work, advice, legacies, quality time, and memorable moments. Includes selections by such well-known figures as Arthur Ashe, C. S. Lewis, Kurt Vonnegut, Mark Twain, Richard Wright, and more.

DEWEY: 306.874 2 LC: HQ 755.85 F39 ISBN 0-525-93600-9

♦ 869 ♦

Fathers: A Celebration in Prose, Poetry, and Photography of Fathers and Fatherhood—Fathers Loved and Fathers Feared, Famous Fathers and Fathers Obscure, Real-life Fathers and Fathers From Fiction. A Varied and Wonderfully Human Portrait of the Men Who Are at the Heart of That Special Relationship That So Shapes Our Lives Forever: Father and Child. **Alexandra Towle, ed. New York: Simon and Schuster, 1986. 288 pp. Illustrated. Index.**

An anthology of quotations, poems, and excerpts from various prose works about fathers and fatherhood. Organized around seven themes: fatherhood, children's perspectives on fathers, paternal guidance, separating from fathers, disagreements with fathers, reflections on becoming a father, and the death of fathers. Includes selections by such writers as Thomas Hardy, Ogden Nash, Alex Haley, Mark Twain, and others. Illustrated with black-and-white photos.

DEWEY: 306.8 742 LC: HQ 756. F383 ISBN 0-671-63859-9

♦ 870 ♦

***Poems For Fathers.* Selected by Myra Cohn Livingston. Illustrated by Robert Casilla. New York: Holiday House, 1989. 32 pp.**

Presents 18 poems about fathers written from the perspective of children. Sentiments expressed include love, admiration, sadness, and humor. Drawings illustrate. For children.

DEWEY: 811.008 0352043 LC: PS 595. F39 P64 ISBN 0-8234-0729-2

FLAG DAY

♦ 871 ♦

***The Flag Book of the United States: The Story of the Stars and Stripes and the Flags of the Fifty States.* Revised edition. Whitney Smith. Illustrated by Louis Loynes and Lucien Phillipe. New York: William Morrow and Company, 1975. 306 pp. Appendices. Bibliography. Glossary. Index.**

A detailed compilation of information about the American flag, the flags of the 50 states, and other flags flown in the United States in past or present times. Provides an introduction to flags and a history of other flags flown in American territory, including the Viking, Spanish, French, British, Dutch, Swedish, Russian and Mexican flags. Describes the origins and historical evolution of the American flag. Also gives a brief history of the flags of the 50 states and the territories. Briefly treats other American flags, including government, military, city, and county flags, as well as the flags of Indian nations, the Confederacy, and private flags. Appendix provides other historical facts about the national and state flags and reviews the etiquette of flag usage.

DEWEY: 929.9097 ISBN 0-688-07977-6

♦ 872 ♦

***Our Flag.* Ann B. Chambers, ed. Washington, DC: United States Congress, U.S. Government Printing Office, 1989. 52 pp. Illustrated.**

Booklet covering the history of the American flag, as well as flag customs, regulations, and laws. Tells how to obtain flags which have flown over the Capitol and flags for veterans. Brief history of Flag Day. Relates information about the Great Seal of the United States, Fort McHenry, and the Flag House. Reprints the Pledge of Allegiance, the words to the Star Spangled Banner, and the American's Creed. Further reading list. (H. document 100-247, 100th Congress, second session.)

DEWEY: 929.9209

♦ 873 ♦

Saga of the American Flag: An Illustrated History. **Candice M. DeBarr and Jack A. Bonkowske. Illustrated by Barbara Schiefer and Antonio Castro. Tucson, AZ: Harbinger House, 1990. 84 pp. Glossary. Index.**

Gives a history of the American flag from colonial days to the present. Describes customs honoring the flag and recounts twentieth-century social and religious controversies over some of these customs. Gives chronology of important dates in the history of the American flag and summarizes flag rules and codes of etiquette.

DEWEY: 929.9 2 0973 LC: CR 113 D38 ISBN 0-943173-65-5

♦ 874 ♦

So Proudly We Hail: The History of the United States Flag. **William Rea Furlong and Byron McCandless. Washington, DC: Smithsonian Institution Press, 1981. 260 pp. Illustrated. Appendices. Bibliography. Index.**

Offers a history of the American flag from colonial times to the present, with a particular emphasis on the development of its design during the American Revolution. Includes military history as it relates to uses and development of the flag. Also discusses flags of other nations which have flown over American territory. Amply illustrated with color and black-and-white photos. Appendices give the history of the Pledge of Allegiance, the meaning of the flag's colors, the American's Creed, and codes, laws, etiquette, and customs concerning the flag.

DEWEY: 929.9 2 0973 LC: CR113. F93 ISBN 0-87474-448-2

♦ 875 ♦

Stars and Stripes Forever: The History of Our Flag. **John Winthrop Adams, ed. New York: Smithmark Publishers, Inc., 1992. 80 pp. Illustrated. Glossary. Index.**

Reviews the history, lore, customs, and literature of the American flag. Recounts the historical evolution of the flag from colonial to present times, including history and celebration of Flag Day. Relates customs concerning the use and display of the flag, and reprints poems, prose, and songs about the flag. Depicts the flags of the 50 states and lists flag anniversaries. Illustrated with black-and-white photos, color photos, and drawings.

DEWEY: 929.92 ISBN 0-8317-6658-1

FOURTH OF JULY (INDEPENDENCE DAY)

♦ 876 ♦

Celebrate America. **Jess Braillier and Sally Chabert. New York: Berkley Publishing Group, 1995. 148 pp. Illustrated.**

A collection of facts, anecdotes, poems, and trivia about the Fourth of July. Reprints the Declaration of Independence, quotations from early American patriots, and excerpts from their letters and other writings. Gives facts about the signers of the Declaration of Independence. Offers stories, anecdotes, and trivia regarding past and present celebrations of the Fourth. Furnishes holiday poems and songs.

DEWEY: 394.2 684 LC: E 286. A1253 ISBN 0-399-51943-2

♦ 877 ♦

Fireworks, Picnics, and Flags: The Story of July Symbols. **James Cross Giblin. Illustrated by Ursula Arndt. New York: Clarion Books, 1983. 90 pp. Index.**

Conveys the origins, meaning, and spirit of the Fourth of July to children. Depicts the conflicts between the American colonists and the British government, the drafting of the Declaration of Independence, the Revolutionary War, and past celebrations of the Fourth, including the centennial and bicentennial celebrations. Tells how Uncle Sam, bald eagles, the Liberty Bell, fireworks, flags, picnics, and patriotic songs have become associated with the Fourth of July.

DEWEY: 394.2684 LC: E286.A1297 ISBN 0-89919-146-0

♦ 878 ♦

The Glorious Fourth: An American Holiday, An American History. **Diana Karter Appelbaum. New York: Facts on File, 1989. 180 pp. Illustrated. Index.**

Provides a history of Fourth of July celebrations, from the events which distinguished the first Fourth of July to its celebration in the late twentieth century. Describes actual historical celebrations and conveys changing patterns of celebration and sentiment. Lists primary sources consulted. Illustrated with black-and-white reproductions of period drawings, cartoons, and photographs.

DEWEY: 394.2 684 LC: E286.A125 ISBN 0-8160-1767-0

♦ 879 ♦

Honorable Treason: The Declaration of Independence and the Men Who Signed It. **David Freeman Hawke. New York: Viking Press, 1976. 240 pp. Index.**

Tells the story of the writing and signing of the Declaration of Independence and provides brief biographical sketches of all the signers, noting their background, character, and role in the proceedings. Reprints text of the Declaration of Independence. Lists signers by state. Bibliographical notes.

DEWEY: 973.3 13 0922 LC: E221.H25 ISBN 0-670-37857-7

♦ 880 ♦

Independence Day: Its Celebration, Spirit, and Significance as Related in Prose and Verse. **Robert Haven Schauffler. New York: Moffat, Yard, and Co., 1915. 318 pp.**

An anthology of texts concerning the origins, meaning, and celebration of the Fourth of July. Reprints essays, stories, poetry, addresses, and excerpts from historical works. Includes texts by Daniel Webster, Patrick Henry, Samuel Adams, Henry Wadsworth Longfellow, Ralph Waldo Emerson, Oliver Wendell Holmes, and others. One volume in a series entitled *Our American Holidays.*

DEWEY: 394 F 781 S

♦ 881 ♦

It's the Fourth of July! **Stan Hoig. New York: Cobblehill Books, 1995. 81 pp. Illustrated. Bibliography. Index.**

Tells why and how Americans celebrate the Fourth of July. Gives chapter on the writing of the Declaration of Independence and reprints text of document. Describes eighteenth-, nineteenth-, and twentieth-century celebrations of the Fourth, including the 1876 centennial. Furnishes description of the making and assembling of the Statue of Liberty. Considers the relationship of Native Americans, women, and African Americans to past and present Independence Day celebrations. Black-and-white illustrations. For young readers.

DEWEY: 394.2 684 LC: E286.A136 ISBN 0-525-65175-6

♦ 882 ♦

A Short History of the American Revolution. **James L. Stokesbury. New York: William Morrow and Company, 1991. 304 pp. Maps. Index.**

Offers a concise history of the Revolutionary War, its causes, battles, and outcomes. Gives further reading list.

DEWEY: 973.3 LC: E208.S87 ISBN 0-688-08333-1

♦ 883 ♦

Songs and Ballads of the American Revolution. **Frank Moore. 1855. Reprint. New York: The New York Times and Arno Press, 1969. 394 pp. Index.**

Prints the words to folk songs and poems of the American Revolution, many of which address popular sentiments and events of the day, such as the repeal of the Stamp Act and the Boston Tea Party.

DEWEY: 784.7197

♦ 884 ♦

Songs of '76: A Folksinger's History of the Revolution. **Oscar Brand. New York: M. Evans and Company, 1972. 178 pp. Illustrated. Indexes.**

Provides words and music to 63 songs from the American Revolution. Songs included address well-known and lesser-known historical events, sentiments, and both revolutionary and loyalist points of view. Gives historical background for each song. Black-and-white illustrations. Historical index and index of song titles and first lines.

DEWEY: 784.7197

♦ 885 ♦

Voices of 1776. **Richard Wheeler. Foreword by Bruce Catton. New York: Thomas Y. Crowell, 1972. 430 pp. Illustrated. Appendix. Bibliography. Index.**

Excerpts from the writings of famous war leaders and ordinary colonial American and British citizens are used to narrate the story of the American Revolution as it was experienced by those who participated in it. Includes selections by Paul Revere, George Washington, Ethan Allen, Benedict Arnold, and more. Appendix gives chronology of important historical events covered in the text.

DEWEY: 973.2 ISBN 0-690-86422-1

♦ 886 ♦

The War for Independence: The Story of the American Revolution. **Albert Marrin. New York: Atheneum, 1988. 276 pp. Illustrated. Maps. Index.**

Summarizes the story of the American Revolution. Illustrated with maps, black-and-white drawings, reproductions of paintings. Gives further reading list.

DEWEY: 973.3 LC: E208. M348 ISBN 0-689-31390-X

♦ 887 ♦

The Women of '76. **Sally Smith Booth. New York: Hastings House, 1973. 329 pp. Illustrated. Bibliography. Index.**

Discusses the lives and activities of individual women during the Revolutionary War. Covers well-known figures such as Abigail Adams and Phyllis Wheatley, as well as many lesser known folk heroes of the day. Black-and-white photos illustrate.

DEWEY: 973.315 LC: E276 B66 ISBN 0-8038-8066-9

GREEK AMERICAN

♦ 888 ♦

A Guide to Greek Traditions and Customs in America. **Marilyn Rouvelas. Illustrated by Olga Angelo Deoudes. Bethesda, MD: Nea Attiki Press, 1993. 320 pp. Bibliography. Index.**

Three-part introduction to Greek cultural and Greek Orthodox religious practices in the United States. Part one reviews Church-related customs, such as the celebration of name days, fasting, use of holy day bread, and the meaning and rules of the Greek Orthodox sacraments; also summarizes the lives of the major Greek Orthodox saints. Part two reviews everyday customs, values, and beliefs. Part three explains the significance and describes the observance of 24 religious and patriotic Greek holidays. Furnishes holiday calendar.

DEWEY: 973.0489 LC: E184.G7R65 ISBN 0-9638051-0-X

HALLOWEEN

♦ 889 ♦

Halloween: An American Holiday, An American History. **Lesley Pratt Bannatyne. New York: Facts on File, 1990. 180 pp. Illustrated. Bibliography. Index.**

Offers a detailed history of American Halloween customs, legends, and traditions, from colonial times to the present. Discusses ancient European origins of the holiday, its transference to America, and the influence of many American religious and ethnic traditions on the festival's significance and celebration. Traces changing pattern of American observance, with attention to customs, legends, games and pranks, symbols, superstitions, and festivities.

DEWEY: 394.2 683 LC: GT 4965.B28 ISBN 0-8160-1846-4

♦ 890 ♦

Halloween and Other Festivals of Life and Death. **Jack Santino, ed. Knoxville, TN: University of Tennessee Press, 1994. 280 pp. Illustrated. Bibliography. Index.**

A collection of articles which investigate the contemporary celebration of Halloween. Articles treat changing Halloween practices, such as increasing adult participation, the impact of urban legends on recent celebrations, and cultural, ethnic and religious contention about the meaning of the holiday. Focus is on American Halloween, but some attention to Irish traditions and Tex-Mex Day of the Dead celebrations.

DEWEY: 394.2 646 LC: GT 4965. H32 ISBN 0-87049-812-6

♦ 891 ♦

Hallowe'en: Its Origin, Spirit, Celebration, and Significance as Related in Prose and Verse, Together with Hallowe'en Stories, Plays, Pantomimes; and Suggestions for Games, Stunts, Parties, Feasts and Decorations. **Robert Haven Schauffler. New York: Dodd, Mead and Company, 1964. 341 pp.**

Reviews Halloween customs, gives suggestions for Halloween parties, including decorations, entertainment, games, and foods. Prints Halloween stories and texts appropriate for recitation, plays, and pantomimes. One volume in a series entitled *Our American Holidays*.

DEWEY: 394 H 193 S

♦ 892 ♦

Halloween Through Twenty Centuries. **Ralph Linton and Adelin Linton. New York: Henry Schuman, 1950. 108 pp. Illustrated. Index.**

Provides a history of Halloween and its symbols. Traces origins of the holiday to ancient European festivals and connects these to the religious observance of All Saints' and All Souls' Days. Describes customs, beliefs, and mythological creatures associated with traditional Scottish and Irish Halloween celebrations. Recounts the history of belief in and persecution of witches in early modern Europe and colonial America; also summarizes beliefs of the period concerning black cats. Briefly covers origins of contemporary American Halloween customs. One volume in a series entitled *Great Religious Festivals*.

DEWEY: 394.268 L

♦ 893 ♦

Halloween: Why We Celebrate It the Way We Do. **Martin Hintz and Kate Hintz. Mankato, MN: Capstone Press, 1996. 48 pp. Illustrated. Glossary. Index.**

Relates the origins of Halloween, explains the meaning of its symbols, and tells how it is celebrated. Suggests Halloween crafts and activities. Offers further reading and resource list. Illustrated with color photos. For children.

DEWEY: 394.2 646 LC: GT 4965 H55 ISBN 1-56065-326-4

♦ 894 ♦

Heigh Ho for Halloween. **Elizabeth Hough Sechrist. Illustrated by Guy Fry. Philadelphia, PA: Macrae Smith Company, 1948. 240 pp.**

A children's anthology, containing seven stories, 21 poems, 10 plays, and seven games for Halloween. Also gives brief essay about the origins of the holiday and several suggestions for Halloween parties.

DEWEY: 394

♦ 895 ♦

Witches, Pumpkins, and Grinning Ghosts: The Story of Halloween Symbols. **Edna Barth. Illustrated by Ursula Arndt. New York: Seabury Press, 1972. 96 pp. Index.**

Uncovers the origins of Halloween and its customs and explains the history and significance of its symbols to children. Relates information about the Celtic holiday of Samhain and old European beliefs about witches and witchcraft. Tells how goblins, witches, black cats, toads, masquerading, broomsticks, ghosts, skeletons, Jack-O'-Lanterns, and the colors black and orange became associated with Halloween. Further reading list.

DEWEY: 394.2683 ISBN 0-8164-3087-X

HISPANIC AMERICAN

♦ 896 ♦

Fiesta U.S.A. **George Ancona. New York: Lodestar Books, 1995. 44 pp. Illustrated. Glossary.**

Tells how four festivals of Latin American origin are celebrated in various Hispanic communities of the United States. Covers the Day of the Dead, Las Posadas, Los Matachines, and Three Kings Day (Epiphany). Describes customary activities and explains the festival's significance. Illustrated with many color photos. For children.

DEWEY: 394.2 61 08968076 LC: GR 111.H57A63 ISBN 0-525-67498-5

♦ 897 ♦

Hispanic Holidays. **Faith Winchester. Mankato, MN: Bridgestone Books, 1996. 24 pp. Illustrated. Index.**

Outlines the celebration of eight Hispanic-American holidays: Cinco de Mayo, Easter, Corpus Christi, Saint John's Day, Day of the Dead, Posadas, Three Kings Day, and Our Lady of Guadalupe Day. Gives a craft project, pronunciation guide, further reading list, and several further resources. Color photos illustrate. For children. One book in a series entitled *Ethnic Holidays.*

DEWEY: 394.2 698 LC: GT 4813.5 A2W55 ISBN 1-56065-457-0

♦ 898 ♦

Holidays and Celebrations. **Ruth Goring. Vero Beach, FL: Rourke Publications, 1995. 48 pp. Illustrated. Glossary. Index.**

Introduces children to the celebrated days and events of Hispanic-American families and communities. Treats life-cycle celebrations, religious holidays, patriotic holidays, and folk festivals. Covers baptism, first communion, birthdays and saints' days, the quinceañera, Christmas, Holy Week, Day of the Dead, patron saints' days, September 15 and 16, Cinco de Mayo, Día de la Raza, Birthday of José Martí, Cuban Independence Day, and various ethnic festivals across the United States. Entries explain significance of the holiday or celebration and describe customs, foods and festivities. Gives calendar of Latino holidays and celebrations in the United States, lists national holidays of Latin American countries, and suggests further reading. Illustrated with color photos. One volume in a series entitled *Latino Life.*

DEWEY: 394.2 6 08968073 LC: GR 111.H57G67 ISBN 0-86625-542-7

♦ 899 ♦

Mexican-American Folklore: Legends, Songs, Proverbs, Crafts, Tales of Saints, of Revolutionaries, and More. **John O. West, ed. Little Rock, AR: August House, 1988. 314 pp. Illustrated. Indexes.**

A comprehensive compilation of the folk beliefs and practices of Mexican Americans. Gives chapters on Mexican-American social and cultural life, folk speech and names, proverbs, riddles, rhymes and poetry, stories and legends, songs, superstitions and beliefs, folk practices and festivals, plays and dances, games, architecture, foods, and crafts. Information on holidays and festivals found in various chapters. References given in endnotes. Furnishes an index of tale types and motifs, a song index, and a general index. Illustrated with black-and-white photos.

DEWEY: 398.08968073 LC: GR 111.M49 W47 ISBN 0-87483-060-5

♦ 900 ♦

St. James in the Streets: The Religious Processions of Loíza Aldea, Puerto Rico. **Edward C. Zaragoza. Lanham, MD: Scarecrow Press, 1995. 180 pp. Illustrated. Bibliography. Index.**

Describes and analyzes the patron saint festival (St. James Festival) of a Puerto Rican village. Focuses on religious processions and ritual clowns, with attention to saints' images, the roles and masks of the clowns, the organization and experience of procession, and the Indian cultural influences on the festival. Gives chapter on the economic and political history of Puerto Rico. Number two in the Drew Studies in Liturgy series.

DEWEY: 394.2 66 LC: GT 4995 J35 Z37 ISBN 0-8108-3070-1

♦ 901 ♦

The Silver Cradle: Las Posadas, Los Pastores, and Other Mexican American Traditions. **Julia Nott Waugh. Foreword by Félix D. Almaráz, Jr. Illustrated by Bob Winn. 1955. Reprint. Austin, TX: University of Texas Press, 1988. 160 pp.**

Portrays the observance of religious and secular Mexican-American holidays in San Antonio, Texas, through the stories of individuals who celebrate them. Covers Las Posadas, Los Pastores, and other Christmas traditions, Candlemas, the Blessing of the Animals (associated with St. Anthony the Abbot's Day), Holy Week, Mexican Independence Day, the Days of the Dead, and Our Lady of Guadalupe Day.

DEWEY: 398.2 6 09764351 LC: GT 4811. S25 W 38 ISBN 0-292-77625-X

ITALIAN AMERICAN

♦ 902 ♦

Italian American Material Culture: A Directory of Collections, Sites, and Festivals in the United States and Canada. **Margaret Hobbie, comp. Westport, CT: Greenwood Press, 1992. 173 pp. Bibliography. Indexes.**

Lists nearly 100 museum collections related to Italian-American culture, over forty sites around the U.S. significant in Italian-American history, and more than 100 religious, folk, agricultural, art, music, food, and commemorative festivals associated with Italian-American material culture. Festival entries provide information on event's location, sponsor address and phone number, dates observed, estimated annual attendance and year first observed, and brief description of festival activities. Sponsor name index. Subject index. (NR)

DEWEY: 973.0451 LC: E184.I8 H64 ISBN 0-313-27200-X

JAPANESE AMERICAN

♦ 903 ♦

Matsuri: Festival; Japanese American Celebrations and Activities. **Nancy K. Araki and Jane M. Horii. Union City, CA: Heian International, Inc., 1978. 140 pp. Illustrated. Index.**

Presents five festivals celebrated by Japanese Americans to children. Covers New Year celebrations, the Girls' Festival (Doll Festival or Peach Blossom Festival), Boys' Festival, Star Festival (or Weaving Loom Festival), and the Bon Festival (Bon Odori, or Obon Festival). Explains holiday history, activities, and symbols. Offers many traditional Japanese craft activities and recipes.

DEWEY: 394. 26 ISBN 0-89346-019-2

♦ 904 ♦

Things Japanese in Hawaii. **John DeFrancis. Honolulu, HI: University of Hawaii Press, 1973. 210 pp. Illustrated. Appendix. Glossary. Index.**

Describes Japanese cultural traditions maintained by Japanese Americans in Hawaii. Covers annual events, such as festivals; permanent or unscheduled attractions, such as Japanese temples, gardens, music, and theater performances; and elements of daily lifestyle. Treats New Year celebrations, Girls' Day, Boys' Day, the Cherry Blossom Festival, Buddha Day, Bodhi Day, the East-West Arts and Cultural Festival, the Bon Festival, the Floating Lantern Ceremony, and the Shinto Thanksgiving Festival. Tells how these festivals are celebrated and provides background information on associated legends and beliefs, as well as a brief history of the Japanese in Hawaii. Appendix lists further resources for those interested in things Japanese in Hawaii, including community organizations, schools and academies, stores, and books.

DEWEY: 919.6906 ISBN 0-8248-0233-0

JUNETEENTH

♦ 905 ♦

Juneteenth: A Celebration of Freedom. **Charles A. Taylor. Illustrated by Charles A. Taylor, II. Madison, WI: Praxis Publications, 1995. 28 pp. Glossary.**

Relates the history and meaning of Juneteenth and tells how it is celebrated. Reviews the conditions of African Americans under slavery, the conflict between the value Americans placed on freedom and the existence of slavery, and the events at the end of the Civil War. Tells how Juneteenth celebrations were started and gives suggestions for meaningful home and public observances. Reprints the Emancipation Proclamation and furnishes prayers for Juneteenth. Illustrated with photos and drawings. One title in a series devoted to Black American Celebrations. For children.

DEWEY: 394.2 63 LC: E 185. 93 T4 T39 ISBN 0-935483-23-3

KWANZAA

♦ 906 ♦

The African American Holiday of Kwanzaa: A Celebration of Family, Community and Culture. **Maulana Karenga. Los Angeles: University of Sankore Press, 1988. 116 pp.**

Founder of the American holiday of Kwanzaa explains the logic behind its creation. Identifies the African and African-American themes built into Kwanzaa and discusses the seven principles celebrated, Kwanzaa symbols, and Kwanzaa activities.

DEWEY: 394.2 68 LC: GT 4403.K37 ISBN 0-943412-09-9

♦ 907 ♦

The Complete Kwanzaa: Celebrating Our Cultural Harvest. **Dorothy Winbush Riley. New York: HarperCollins Publishers, 1995. 387 pp. Illustrated. Bibliography. Glossary. Index.**

Provides a guide to celebrating Kwanzaa and incorporating Kwanzaa principles into one's lifestyle. Introduces the seven principles and their meaning, Kwanzaa history, and symbols. Uses African folktales and parables, brief biographies of noted African Americans, quotations, excerpts from novels, essays, and other prose works, inspirational thoughts, and poetry to deepen understanding and appreciation of Kwanzaa principles.

DEWEY: 394.2 61 LC: GT 4403.R56 ISBN 0-06-017215-0

♦ 908 ♦

The Complete Kwanzaa Celebration Book. **Linda Robertson. Revised edition. Detroit, MI: Creative Acrylic Concepts, 1994. 80 pp. Bibliography. Index.**

A brief, practical orientation to celebrating Kwanzaa. Explains Kwanzaa symbols and the seven principles behind the holiday, giving practical suggestions on how to incorporate these into Kwanzaa celebrations and year-long consciousness.

DEWEY: 394.261 ISBN 0-9639026-8-7

♦ 909 ♦

Kwanzaa. **Dorothy Rhodes Freeman and Dianne M. MacMillan. Hillside, NJ: Enslow Publishers, 1992. 48 pp. Illustrated. Glossary. Index.**

Teaches children the meaning of Kwanzaa and its customs. Presents the seven principles of Kwanzaa, Kwanzaa symbols, and appropriate Kwanzaa activities. Introduces Swahili words. One book in a series entitled *Best Holiday Books.*

DEWEY: 394.2 68 LC: GT 4403. F74 ISBN 0-89490-381-0

♦ 910 ♦

Kwanzaa: An African American Celebration of Culture and Cooking. **Eric V. Copage. Illustrations by Cheryl Carrington. New York: William Morrow and Company, 1991. 356 pp. Glossary. Index.**

Celebrates and illustrates each of the seven Kwanzaa principles with a collection of stories from the lives of noted African Americans, folktales, and recipes from Africa and the African diaspora. More than 125 recipes in all. Glossary describes recipe ingredients.

DEWEY: 641.59 29073 LC: TX 715. C7865 ISBN 0-688-10939-X

♦ 911 ♦

Kwanzaa: An Everyday Resource and Instructional Guide. **David A. Anderson. New York: Gumbs and Thomas Publishers, Inc., 1992. 63 pp. Illustrated. Index.**

Provides a teaching guide for Kwanzaa. Suggests lesson plans and activities for each of the seven principles. Offers a select bibliography of books and audio and videotapes useful in teaching about Kwanzaa. Illustrated with black-and-white drawings and photos.

DEWEY: 394.268 LC: GT4403.A5 ISBN 9-936073-15-2

♦ 912 ♦

Kwanzaa: Everything You Always Wanted to Know But Didn't Know Where To Ask. **Revised edition. Cedric McClester. New York: Gumbs and Thomas Publishers, 1993. 36 pp.**

Answers most commonly asked questions about the origins and celebration of Kwanzaa. Lists the seven principles behind Kwanzaa, explains Kwanzaa symbols, gives menu suggestions and hairstyles for women based on the technique of cornrowing, and provides a list of stores throughout the country that sell Kwanzaa books, cards, and related items. Suggested reading list.

DEWEY: 394.268 ISBN 0-936073-08-X

♦ 913 ♦

A Kwanzaa Keepsake. **Jessica B. Harris. New York: Simon and Schuster, 1995. 176 pp. Illustrated. Index.**

Offers recipes, brief biographies of Africans and African Americans, proverbs, and projects for the celebration of Kwanzaa. Also covers the history and meaning of Kwanzaa, and provides blank pages for the reader to inscribe her own family history, recipes, photos, and notes. Gives chapter for each of the seven days of Kwanzaa, organized around that day's theme. Two-tone drawings illustrate.

DEWEY: 394.2 61 LC: GT 4403. H37 ISBN 0-684-80045-4

♦ 914 ♦

Kwanzaa: Why We Celebrate It the Way We Do. **Martin Hintz and Kate Hintz. Mankato, MN: Capstone Press, 1996. 48 pp. Illustrated. Glossary. Index.**

Explains the history, symbols, principles, and celebration of Kwanzaa. Gives suggested Kwanzaa activities, further reading and resource list. Illustrated with color photos. For children. One volume in a series entitled *Celebrate!*.

DEWEY: 394.2 61 LC: GT 4403 H55 ISBN 1-56065-329-9

LABOR DAY

♦ 915 ♦

Bread and Roses: The Struggle of American Labor, 1865-1915. **Milton Meltzer. New York: Alfred A. Knopf, 1967. 231 pp. Illustrated. Dictionary. Bibliography. Index.**

Provides a history of the early years of American industrialization and labor activism. Brief dictionary of labor-related terms. Black-and-white photos illustrate.

DEWEY: 331.0973 ISBN 0-451-62770-9

♦ 916 ♦

Carry It On! A History in Song and Picture of the Working Men and Women of America. **Pete Seeger and Bob Reiser. New York: Simon and Schuster, 1985. 256 pp. Illustrated. Index.**

Gathers together words and music to more than 80 American folk songs about the lives and struggles of working men and women from Revolutionary times to the present. Songs accompanied by black-and-white photos, illustrations, and commentary on the issues represented in the songs and the eras in which they were written. Further reading and listening list. Index of song titles.

DEWEY: 784.4973 C319 LC: M1977. L3 C33 ISBN 0-671-49963-7

♦ 917 ♦

Labor Day. **Geoffrey Scott. Illustrated by Cherie R. Wyman. Minneapolis, MN: Carolrhoda Books, 1982. 48 pp.**

Explains the origins of Labor Day, describes the first Labor Day celebration in New York City, and tells why we celebrate the holiday today. Illustrated with two-tone drawings. For children.

DEWEY: 394. 2 68 LC: HD 7791.S38 ISBN 0-87614-178-5

♦ 918 ♦

The Labor Movement in the United States. **John J. Flagler. M. Barbara Killen, series editor. Minneapolis, MN: Lerner Publications Company, 1990. 112 pp. Illustrated. Glossary. Index.**

Provides a brief history of labor conditions and the labor movement in the United States, from the early 1800s to the 1980s. Identifies the contributions of organized labor to American life. Illustrated with color photos, black-and-white photos, and drawings. For older children. One volume in a series entitled *Economics for Today*.

DEWEY: 331.88 0973 LC: HD6508.25 F57 ISBN 0-8225-1778-7

LEIF ERIKSSON DAY

♦ 919 ♦

The Age of Leif Eriksson. **Richard Humble. Illustrated by Richard Hook. New York: Franklin Watts, 1989. 32 pp. Maps. Glossary. Index.**

Tells the story of the Viking voyages of exploration to North America, focusing on the deeds of Leif Eriksson. Provides background information on Viking ships and seamanship. Illustrated with color drawings. Chronology of

Viking/Norwegian settlement in North America. For children. One volume in a series entitled *Exploration Through the Ages.*

DEWEY: 970.01 3 LC: E105. L47 H86 ISBN 0-531-10741-8

♦ 920 ♦

Strange Footprints on the Land: Vikings in America. **Constance Irwin. New York: Harper and Row, Publishers, 1980. 182 pp. Index.**

Reviews the archeological evidence for the Viking discovery of North America. Also discusses the evidence of Norse and later European settlements from the eleventh to the fifteenth century.

DEWEY: 970.01 3 LC: E105 I78 ISBN 0-06-022772-9

MARDI GRAS

♦ 921 ♦

All on a Mardi Gras Day: Episodes in the History of New Orleans Carnival. **Reid Mitchell. Cambridge, MA: Harvard University Press, 1995. 243 pp. Illustrated. Index.**

Retells the story of a number of incidents occurring on or around Mardi Gras, from the early 1800s to the 1990s. Provides a unique window on the history of Mardi Gras, its meaning to various ethnic and social groups across time, and the history and culture of New Orleans. Give suggested reading list.

DEWEY: 394.2 5 LC: GT 4211.N4 M57 ISBN 0-674-01622-X

♦ 922 ♦

Carnival, American Style: Mardi Gras at New Orleans and Mobile. **Samuel Kinser. Chicago: University of Chicago Press, 1990. 415 pp. Illustrated. Appendix. Bibliography. Index.**

Offers a detailed history of southern Carnival celebrations, as well as an analysis of the way in which they reflect American class distinctions, race relations, sexuality, and gender ideology. Some discussion of past Epiphany celebrations as well. Illustrated with black-and-white photos. References cited given in endnotes.

DEWEY: 394.2 5 LC: GT 4211. N4 K56 ISBN 0-226-43729-9

♦ 923 ♦

Lords of Misrule: Mardi Gras and the Politics of Race in New Orleans. **James Gill. Jackson, MS: University Press of Mississippi, 1997. 303 pp. Index.**

Reveals the history of racial exclusion and strife which has been a part of New Orleans Mardi Gras celebrations and documents the effects of these racial struggles on the city. Also discusses recent attempts to desegregate Mardi Gras celebrations. Bibliographic notes.

DEWEY: 394.2 5 LC: GT 4211. N4G55 ISBN 0-87805-916-4

♦ 924 ♦

Mardi Gras! **Suzanne M. Coil. New York: Macmillan Publishing Company, 1994. 48 pp. Illustrated. Index.**

Depicts New Orleans Mardi Gras preparations and celebrations. Gives history of celebrations and tells how organized. Describes parades, floats, and costumes. Illustrated with color photos. For children.

DEWEY: 394.2 5 LC: GT 4211. N4C65 ISBN 0-02-722805-3

♦ 925 ♦

New Orleans: Behind the Masks of America's Most Exotic City. **Carol Flake. New York: Grove Press, 1994. 351 pp.**

In-depth account of individuals and groups that organize and participate in New Orleans Mardi Gras celebrations. Weaves together anecdotes, interviews, description, and history. Provides a window on contemporary New Orleans society, politics, and culture.

DEWEY: 394.2 5 LC: GT 4211.N4 F53 ISBN 0-8021-1406-7

MARTIN LUTHER KING, JR. DAY

♦ 926 ♦

About Martin Luther King Day. **Mary Virginia Fox. Hillside, NJ: Enslow Publishers, 1989. 64 pp. Illustrated. Index.**

Introduces children to the significance and spirit of Martin Luther King, Jr. Day. Tells how the day became a national holiday, noting resistance. Discusses the history of slavery and racial prejudice in the United States, and identifies distinguished black Americans and their achievements. Summarizes King's life, emphasizing his role in the civil rights movement. Describes the Martin Luther King, Jr. Center for Nonviolent Social Change, its activities, and ways of celebrating Martin Luther King, Jr. Day. Furnishes a chronology of dates in the life of Dr. King, and a further reading list.

DEWEY: 394.2 68 LC: E185.97. K5 F68 ISBN 0-89490-200-8

♦ 927 ♦

I Have a Dream: The Life and Words of Martin Luther King, Jr. **Jim Haskins. Introduction by Rosa Parks. Brookfield, CT: Millbrook Press, 1992. 111 pp. Illustrated. Bibliography. Index.**

Gives a biography of Martin Luther King, Jr., emphasizing the spiritual inspiration, political vision, and oratory that propelled him to his position of leadership in the civil rights movement. Includes many excerpts from King's speeches and writings. Illustrated with black-and-white photos. Includes chronology of important events in the life of Martin Luther King, Jr.

DEWEY: 323. 092 LC: E 185.97 K5H32 ISBN 1-56294-087-2

♦ 928 ♦

Let the Trumpet Sound: The Life of Martin Luther King, Jr. **Stephen B. Oates. New York: Harper and Row, 1982. 560 pp. Illustrated. Index.**

A comprehensive biography of Martin Luther King, Jr. Integrates an account of his personal life, philosophy, and civil rights activism. References given in endnotes.

DEWEY: 323.4 092 4 LC: E 185.97 K 5018 ISBN 0-06-014993-0

♦ 929 ♦

Martin Luther King, Jr. **Robert Jakoubek. Nathan Irvin Huggins, ed. Introduction by Coretta Scott King. New York: Chelsea House Publishers, 1989. 143 pp. Illustrated. Appendix. Index.**

Offers a biography of Martin Luther King, Jr., emphasizing his role in the civil rights movement. Appendix lists books written by Dr. King. Gives a chronology of King's life and a further reading list. Illustrated with black-and-white photos. For older children or teens. One volume in a series entitled *Black Americans of Achievement.*

DEWEY: 301.451 LC: E 185.97 K5 J35 ISBN 1-55546-597-8

♦ 930 ♦

Martin Luther King, Jr. and the Freedom Movement. **Lillie Patterson. New York: Facts on File, 1989. 178 pp. Illustrated. Index.**

Tells the story of Martin Luther King, Jr.'s role in the civil rights movement of the 1950s and 1960s. Appropriate for young readers or the general reader. Includes chronology of important events in the life of Martin Luther King, Jr., and the civil rights movement, as well as suggestions for further reading.

DEWEY: 323.4 092 4 ISBN 0-8160-1605-4

♦ 931 ♦

Search for the Beloved Community: The Thinking of Martin Luther King, Jr. **Kenneth L. Smith and Ira G. Zepp, Jr. Valley Forge, PA: Judson Press, 1974. 159 pp. Bibliography.**

Traces the influence of various Christian theologians and schools of thought on Martin Luther King, Jr.'s religious philosophy and social activism. Identifies the "beloved community" as the ideal for which he strove. Endnotes.

DEWEY: 301.6 32 0924 LC: E185.97 K5 S58 ISBN 0-8170-0611-7

♦ 932 ♦

Strength To Love. **Martin Luther King, Jr. 1963. Reprint. Foreword by Coretta Scott King. Philadelphia, PA: Fortress Press, 1981. 155 pp.**

A collection of 15 of Martin Luther King, Jr.'s sermons on love and nonviolence.

DEWEY: 252.0613 LC: BX 6452 K5 ISBN 0-8006-1441-0

♦ 933 ♦

A Testament of Hope: The Essential Writings of Martin Luther King, Jr. **James Melvin Washington, ed. San Francisco, CA: Harper and Row, Publishers, 1986. 676 pp. Bibliography. Index.**

Gathers together the core of King's speeches, writings, sermons, addresses, and interviews. Also prints book excerpts. Topics explored include civil rights, nonviolence, civil disobedience, integration, black nationalism, democracy, Christianity, love, and ethics.

DEWEY: 323.4 092 4 LC: E185.97 K5 A25 ISBN 0-06-250931-4

♦ 934 ♦

Voice of Deliverance: The Language of Martin Luther King and Its Sources. **Keith D. Miller. New York: The Free Press, 1992. Appendices. Bibliography. Index.**

Traces the influence of African-American spiritual traditions and noted African-American preachers on the language of Martin Luther King, Jr. Identifies the often unacknowledged sources from which King borrowed ideas and imagery. Appendix one lists individuals who influenced King. Appendix two gives precedents for titles of King's sermons.

DEWEY: 323.092 LC: E185.97 K5 M49 ISBN 0-02-921521-8

MEMORIAL DAY

♦ 935 ♦

Memorial Day. **Geoffrey Scott. Illustrated by Peter E. Hanson. Minneapolis, MN: Carolrhoda Books, 1983. 48 pp.**

Explains the origins and historical development of Memorial Day and depicts its celebration. Includes description of a school and community celebration of Decoration Day in a small American town in 1878. For young children.

DEWEY: 394.2 684 LC: E 642. S38 ISBN 0-87614-219-6

♦ 936 ♦

Memorial Day (Decoration Day): Its Celebration, Spirit and Significance as Related in Prose and Verse, with a Non-Sectional Anthology of the Civil War. **Robert Haven Schauffler. 1930. Reprint. Detroit, MI: Omnigraphics, Inc., 1990. 339 pp.**

An anthology of texts concerning or relevant to the celebration of Memorial Day. Gives poetry, essays, articles, addresses, and observations concerning the spirit and meaning of Memorial Day and the Civil War. Includes selections by Paul Lawrence Dunbar, Theodore Roosevelt, William T. Sherman, Oliver Wendell Holmes, Walt Whitman, James Longstreet, and others. One volume in a series entitled *Our American Holidays.*

DEWEY: 394. M 553 S LC: PS509.M45M46 ISBN 1-55888-274-X

♦ 937 ♦

Memorial Day in Poetry. **Carnegie Library School Association. New York: H. W. Wilson Company, 1927. 60 pp.**

An anthology of 47 poems appropriate for Memorial Day programs. Emphasis on poems about the American Civil War. Includes selections by Julia Ward Howe, Emily Dickinson, Henry Wadsworth Longfellow, Bret Harte, and others.

DEWEY: 811.08 C289m

♦ 938 ♦

The Wall: A Day at the Vietnam Veterans Memorial. **Peter Meyer and editors of Life. New York: St. Martin's Press, 1993. 96 pp. Illustrated.**

Journalists spent 24 hours at the Vietnam Veterans Memorial, recording the events, experiences, and individuals who visit, their stories and their sentiments. Amply illustrated with color photos.

DEWEY: 959.704 36 LC: DS 559. 83 W18 W35 ISBN 0-312-09478-7

MOTHER'S DAY

♦ 939 ♦

***Mother and Child.* Mary Lawrence, comp. New York: Thomas Y. Crowell Company, 1975. 223 pp. Illustrated. Indexes.**

Presents 100 large color prints of paintings and other works of art depicting a mother and child. Accompanied by commentaries from a wide range of noted individuals. Emphasis is on European artwork, but also includes art from the Americas, Asia, Africa, the Middle East, and Oceania. Works range from ancient to contemporary. Commentaries by art historians, museum directors, curators, and also by noted actors, writers, and personalities, such as Kirk Douglas, Anaïs Nin, and Oleg Cassini.

DEWEY: 757.4 LC: N7632 M67 ISBN 0-690-00970-4

♦ 940 ♦

***Motherhood: A Celebration.* Bill Adler, ed. New York: Carroll and Graf Publishers, Inc., 1987. 116 pp.**

A collection of quotations celebrating mothers and motherhood. Includes selections from a wide variety of noted individuals of past and present times: George Bernard Shaw, Golda Meir, Danielle Steele, Shakespeare, Sigmund Freud, and more.

DEWEY: 082 LC: PN6084 M6 A34 ISBN 0-88184-307-5

♦ 941 ♦

***Mothers: A Celebration in Prose, Poetry, and Photographs of Mothers and Motherhood.* Alexandra Towle, ed. New York: Simon and Schuster, 1988. 281 pp. Illustrated. Index.**

Presents a collection of quotations and prose excerpts on the subject of mothers and motherhood. Organized around the following themes: maternal instinct, mothers and sons, mothers and daughters, mother's faults, observations on mothers, lessons, new mothers, and the death of mothers. Selections by lesser-known and well-known individuals, such as Oscar Wilde, Nora Ephron, Queen Victoria, Billie Holiday, and more. Illustrated with black-and-white photos.

DEWEY: 808.8035 ISBN 0-671-66056-X

♦ 942 ♦

***Mother's Day.* Mary Kay Phelan. Illustrated by Aliki. New York: Thomas Y. Crowell Company, 1965. 34 pp.**

Tells how Mother's Day became an American holiday and how it is celebrated. Describes other festivals from around the world, ancient and contemporary, which honor mothers. For children.

DEWEY: 394 M918p ISBN 0-690-56194-6

♦ 943 ♦

Mother's Day: Its History, Origin, Celebration, Spirit, and Significance as Related in Prose and Verse. **Susan Tracy Rice. Robert Haven Schauffler, ed. 1915. Reprint. Detroit, MI: Omnigraphics, Inc., 1990. 380 pp.**

Gathers together poems, songs, stories, and excerpts from essays, letters, and legislation concerning Mother's Day. Topics include the founding of Mother's Day in the United States, motherhood, sentiments between mothers and children, the mothers of famous individuals, lullabies, and suggestions for Mother's Day programs. Selections by Rabindranath Tagore, Elizabeth Barrett Browning, Plutarch, Tennyson, and more. One volume in a series entitled *Our American Holidays*.

DEWEY: 808.8 03520431 LC: PN 6071 M7 R52 ISBN 1-55888-864-0

PATRIOTS' DAY

♦ 944 ♦

The Battle of Lexington and Concord. **Neil Johnson. New York: Four Winds Press, 1992. 40 pp. Illustrated. Bibliography.**

Tells the story of the Battles of Lexington and Concord, the first battles of the American Revolution. Also explains the events which led to armed conflict. Illustrated with color photos from annual reenactments of these events in colonial costume. For children.

DEWEY: 973.3 31 LC: E241. C7 J64 ISBN 0-02-747841-6

♦ 945 ♦

Concord and Lexington. **Judy Nordstrom. New York: Dillon Press, 1993. 72 pp. Illustrated. Index.**

Summarizes the events leading up to the American Revolution and describes its first battles at Lexington and Concord. Tells why the British attacked at Concord and shows the historical sites and attractions of Lexington and Concord today. Provides addresses and phone numbers for historical sites, attractions, and information centers. Illustrated with color photos. For children.

DEWEY: 973.3 311 LC: E241. C7 N66 ISBN 0-87518-567-3

♦ 946 ♦

Lexington, Concord and Bunker Hill. **Francis Russell. Fourth edition. New York: American Heritage Publishing Co., 1963. 153 pp. Illustrated. Maps. Index.**

Retells the story of Paul Revere's ride and describes the battles of Lexington, Concord, and Bunker Hill which followed. Black-and-white and color illustrations. Further reading list. For young readers.

DEWEY: 974.4

♦ 947 ♦

Paul Revere's Ride. **David Hackett Fischer. New York: Oxford University Press, 1994. 445 pp. Illustrated. Maps. Appendices. Bibliography. Index.**

Offers an in-depth historical study and narrative account of Paul Revere's ride, other Revolutionary American and British activities that took place on the night of April 18, 1775, and the Battles of Lexington and Concord. Illustrated with reproductions of documents, portraits, and black-and-white photos. Endnotes.

DEWEY: 973.3 311 092 LC: F69 R43 F57 ISBN 0-19-508847-6

PEARL HARBOR DAY

♦ 948 ♦

Day of Infamy. **Walter Lord. New York: Henry Holt and Company, 1957. Reissued in 1991. 243 pp. Illustrated. Index.**

Dramatized retelling of the Japanese attack on Pearl Harbor, December 7, 1941. Based on interviews with more than 500 people who were there and other firsthand research. Includes both Japanese and American perspectives. Black-and-white photos. Book was reissued for the 50th anniversary of the attack on Pearl Harbor.

DEWEY: 940.542 ISBN 0-8050-1898-0

♦ 949 ♦

December 7, 1941: The Day the Japanese Attacked Pearl Harbor. **Gordon W. Prange, with Donald M. Goldstein and Katherine V. Dillon. New York: McGraw-Hill Book Company, 1987. 493 pp. Illustrated. Index.**

Detailed historical account of the Japanese attack on Pearl Harbor, focusing on the events of December 6 and December 7, 1941. Includes both American and Japanese perspectives. Based on interviews with participants, government documents, and published works. Endnotes. Third volume by the same authors in a series of books about Pearl Harbor which also includes *At Dawn We Slept* (1981) and *Pearl Harbor: The Verdict of History* (1986).

DEWEY: 940.54 26 LC: D767.92 P7215 ISBN 0-07-050682-5

♦ 950 ♦

Pearl Harbor. **William E. Shapiro. New York: Franklin Watts, 1984. 103 pp. Illustrated. Index.**

Furnishes historical background to and description of the Japanese attack on Pearl Harbor. Summarizes Japanese-American relations in the nineteenth and twentieth centuries, and depicts the Japanese military buildup of the early twentieth century. Explains why the Japanese attacked and why the United States was unprepared. Chronology of events and further reading list. Illustrated with black-and-white photos. One volume in a series for young readers entitled *Turning Points of World War II.*

DEWEY: 940.54 26 LC: DS767.92 S43 ISBN 0-531-04865-9

♦ 951 ♦

Pearl Harbor: America Enters the War. **Terry Dunnahoo. Foreword by Jesse E. Pond, Jr. New York: Franklin Watts, 1991. 112 pp. Illustrated. Bibliography. Index.**

Describes the attack on Pearl Harbor, and the Japanese military buildup and American complacency which preceded it. Also treats political and military consequences of the attack. Black-and-white photos illustrate. For young readers.

DEWEY: 940.54 26 LC: D767.92 D86 ISBN 0-531-11010-9

PRESIDENTS' DAYS

♦ 952 ♦

Abraham Lincoln: The Prairie Years and the War Years. **One-volume edition. Carl Sandburg. New York: Harcourt, Brace and Company, 1954. 762 pp. Illustrated. Index.**

American poet's classic two-volume biography of Lincoln issued as a single volume. Covers Lincoln's life from birth to death. Lists sources.

LC: E457 S215

♦ 953 ♦

The First of Men: A Life of George Washington. **John E. Ferling. Knoxville, TN: University of Tennessee Press, 1988. 598 pp. Illustrated. Bibliography. Index.**

Offers an in-depth biography of George Washington which assesses his character in addition to his achievements.

DEWEY: 973.4 1 0924 LC: E312. F47 ISBN 0-87049-562-3

♦ 954 ♦

Founding Father: Rediscovering George Washington. **Richard Brookhiser. New York: The Free Press, 1996. 230 pp. Index.**

Furnishes a moral biography of Washington, linking his political and military achievements to his values and ideas and examining his role as founding father. References given in endnotes.

DEWEY: 973.4 1 092 LC: E312. B85 ISBN 0-684-82291-1

♦ 955 ♦

The Genius of George Washington. **Edmund S. Morgan. New York: W. W. Norton and Company, 1981. 94 pp. Index.**

Historian briefly describes George Washington's political and military abilities and comments on his character. Reprints many of Washington's letters. For the general reader.

DEWEY: 973.4 1 0924 LC: E312. 63 M839 ISBN 0-393-01440-1

♦ 956 ♦

George Washington. **Tom McGowen. New York: Franklin Watts, 1986. 64 pp. Illustrated. Index.** 📖

Describes the life and times of George Washington. Black-and-white illustrations. Further reading list. For children.

DEWEY: 973.4 1 0924 LC: E312.66. M34 ISBN 0-531-10108-8

♦ 957 ♦

George Washington: A Biography. **John R. Alden. Baton Rouge, LA: Louisiana State University Press, 1984. 326 pp. Illustrated. Bibliography. Index.**

Provides a biography of Washington's life, from his childhood to his retirement from political office. For the general reader. Bibliographical essay.

DEWEY: 973.4 1 0924 LC: E312 A58 ISBN 0-8071-1153-8

♦ 958 ♦

George Washington and the Birth of Our Nation. **Milton Meltzer. New York: Franklin Watts, 1986. 188 pp. Illustrated. Index.**

Offers a biography of George Washington which conveys a sense of his character as well as his role in American history. Black-and-white illustrations. Suggestions for further reading. For teens.

DEWEY: 973.4 1 0924 LC: E312.66 M45 ISBN 0-531-10253

♦ 959 ♦

George Washington: Leader of a New Nation. **Mary Pope Osborne. New York: Dial Books for Young Readers, 1991. 117 pp. Illustrated. Bibliography. Index.**

Furnishes a biography of George Washington for young readers. Also gives chronology of Washington's life. Black-and-white illustrations.

DEWEY: 973.4 1 092 LC: E332.79.082 ISBN 0-8037-0947-1

♦ 960 ♦

The Humorous Mr. Lincoln. **Keith W. Jennison. New York: Thomas Y. Crowell and Company, 1965. 163 pp. Illustrated. Bibliography. Index.**

Outlines the story of Lincoln's life in a collection of the jokes and humorous tales told by him and about him. Black-and-white illustrations. Chronology of Lincoln's life. Select bibliography.

DEWEY: 923.1

♦ 961 ♦

The Last Best Hope of Earth: Abraham Lincoln and the Promise of America. **Mark E. Neely, Jr. Cambridge, MA: Harvard University Press, 1993. 214 pp. Illustrated. Index.**

Provides a succinct, authoritative biography of Lincoln for the general reader. Emphasizes Lincoln's political views, actions, and achievements. Endnotes.

DEWEY: 973.7 092 LC: E457.N49 ISBN 0-674-51125-5

♦ 962 ♦

Lincoln in His Own Words. **Milton Meltzer, ed. Illustrated by Stephen Alcorn. San Diego, CA: Harcourt Brace and Company, 1993. 226 pp. Illustrated. Index.**

Provides a collection of excerpts from the speeches and writings of Abraham Lincoln. Arranged in chronological order, following the major events in Lincoln's life. Includes profiles of other influential individuals who were Lincoln's contemporaries, a chronology of Lincoln's life, and a review of sources which includes suggestions for further reading. For young readers.

DEWEY: 973.7 092 LC: E457.92 ISBN 0-15-245437-3

♦ 963 ♦

Lincoln on Democracy. **Mario M. Cuomo and Harold Holzer, eds. New York: A Cornelia and Michael Bessie Book, an imprint of HarperCollins Publishers, 1990. 416 pp. Index.**

A collection of the words of Abraham Lincoln: addresses, notes, letters, eulogies, proclamations, remarks, and speeches. Themes covered include the American Dream, slavery, the Union, the Civil War, liberty, democracy, and the presidential campaign. Chapters introduced by various authorities. Gives detailed chronology of Lincoln's life, setting events in the context of national and world history.

DEWEY: 973.7 092 LC: E457.92 ISBN 0-06-039126-X

♦ 964 ♦

The Living Land of Lincoln: A Celebration of Our 16th President and His Abiding Presence. **Thomas Fleming. New York: Reader's Digest Press, 1980. 128 pp. Illustrated.**

Conveys the character of Abraham Lincoln in words and photos. Features 24 pages of color photos documenting important places in Lincoln's life. Also offers a Lincoln biography composed largely of quotes from Lincoln and people who knew or met him. Endnotes.

DEWEY: 973.7 092 4 LC: E457.F56 ISBN 0-07-021297-X

♦ 965 ♦

The Presidency of Abraham Lincoln. **Phillip Shaw Paludan. Lawrence, KS: University of Kansas Press, 1994. 384 pp. Bibliography. Index.**

Explains the political issues dividing America during Lincoln's presidency, explores the political views of Abraham Lincoln, describes the events and achievements of his presidency, and notes Lincoln's impact on the institution of the presidency. Bibliographic essay. One volume in a series entitled *American Presidency*.

DEWEY: 973.7 092 LC: E457. P18 ISBN 0-7006-0671-8

♦ 966 ♦

Washington's Birthday. **Dennis Brindell Fradin. Hillside, NJ: Enslow Publishers, 1990. 48 pp. Illustrated. Glossary. Index.**

Provides a summary of the life and achievements of George Washington. Also tells how his birthday is celebrated. Illustrated with black-and-white and color photos and drawings. For children. One book in a series entitled *Best Holiday Books.*

DEWEY: 973.4 1 092 LC: E312.6 F83 ISBN 0-89490-235-0

♦ 967 ♦

"We Cannot Escape History": Lincoln and the Last Best Hope of Earth. **James M. McPherson, ed. Urbana, IL: University of Illinois Press, 1995. 176 pp. Illustrated.**

New essays by leading historians explore Lincoln's views on democracy, the Union, and his legacy to the United States and the world.

DEWEY: 973.7 092 LC: E457.8 W38 ISBN 0-252-02190-8

ROBERT E. LEE DAY

♦ 968 ♦

Robert E. Lee. **Nathan Aaseng. Minneapolis, MN: Lerner Publications, 1991. 112 pp. Illustrated. Index.**

Reviews the life, achievements, and character of Robert E. Lee. Black-and-white photos illustrate. For young readers. Further reading list.

DEWEY: 973.7309 LC: E467.1 L4 A15 ISBN 0-8225-4909-3

♦ 969 ♦

Robert E. Lee. **Manfred Weidhorn. New York: Atheneum, 1988. 150 pp. Illustrated. Index.**

Furnishes a concise biography of Robert E. Lee for young readers. Illustrated with black-and-white photos. Further reading list.

DEWEY: 973.7 3 0924 LC: E467.1 L4 W33 ISBN 0-689-31340-3

♦ 970 ♦

Robert E. Lee: A Biography. **Emory M. Thomas. New York: W. W. Norton and Company, 1995. 472 pp. Illustrated. Maps. Bibliography. Index.**

Examines the life of Robert E. Lee from his birth to his death. Attention to his achievements as well as to his complex character, as it is revealed in his thoughts, words, and deeds. References given in endnotes. Extensive bibliography.

DEWEY: 973.7309 ISBN 0-393-03730-4

♦ 971 ♦

Virginia's General: Robert E. Lee and the Civil War. **Albert Marrin. New York: Atheneum, 1994. 218 pp. Illustrated. Index.**

Offers a biography of Lee which focuses on the Civil War years. Also describes the battle experiences and daily life of Civil War soldiers. Generously illustrated. Further reading list. Endnotes.

DEWEY: 973.7 3 092 LC: E467.1 L4 M36 ISBN 0-689-31838-3

SABBATH

♦ 972 ♦

Redeem the Time: The Puritan Sabbath in Early America. **Winton U. Solberg. Cambridge, MA: Harvard University Press, 1977. 406 pp. Bibliography. Index.**

Scholarly study of Puritan Sabbath observance in colonial times. Chapter on history of the Christian Sabbath and debates over its proper observance. References cited in endnotes. Bibliographical essay.

DEWEY: 263.0973 LC: BV111 S64 ISBN 0-674-75130-2

ST. PATRICK'S DAY

♦ 973 ♦

St. Patrick's Day: Its Celebration in New York and Other American Places, 1737–1845. **John D. Crimmins. New York: The Author, 1902. 502 pp. Indexes.**

Detailed documentation of early American celebrations of St. Patrick's Day drawn from the records of various Irish-American organizations, diaries, histories, and newspapers. Provides brief biographical sketches of more than 550 individuals whose names are mentioned in the book. General index, name index, and index of Irish places.

DEWEY: 394.26 C925 LC: GT4995 S3 C7

♦ 974 ♦

Shamrocks, Harps, and Shillelaghs: The Story of St. Patrick's Day Symbols. **Edna Barth. Illustrated by Ursula Arndt. New York: The Seabury Press, 1977. 96 pp. Index.**

Tells the story of St. Patrick's Day and its symbols to children. Summarizes St. Patrick's life and deeds and explores the history of St. Patrick's Day celebrations. Explains how St. Patrick, along with shamrocks, the color green, harps, shillelaghs, pipes, fiddles, poetry, Leprechauns, potatoes, and other items became symbols of Ireland and Irish culture. Introduces elements of Irish and Irish-American history and culture. Further reading list suggests stories for St. Patrick's Day. Lists sources.

DEWEY: 394.2 6 LC: GT 4995. P3 B37 ISBN 0-8164-3195-7

SPECIAL EVENTS FESTIVALS

♦ 975 ♦

As I Remember Adam: An Autobiography of a Festival. **Angus L. Bowmer. Ashland, OR: The Oregon Shakespearean Festival Association, 1975. 272 pp. Illustrated.**

Founder of the Oregon Shakespearean Festival at Ashland recounts the history of the festival and his role in its development.

DEWEY: 792.0979 LC: PR3105.B6

♦ 976 ♦

Best-Loved Stories Told at the National Storytelling Festival. **Selected by the National Association for the Preservation and Perpetuation of Storytelling. Jonesborough, TN: National Storytelling Press, 1991. 224 pp. Indexes.**

Presents 37 stories told during the first 20 years of the National Storytelling Festival. Includes traditional and original stories from many regions of the United States and the world. Title index and author index.

DEWEY: 398.2 LC: GR 73 B47 ISBN 1-879991-01-2

♦ 977 ♦

Ethnomimesis: Folklife and the Representation of Culture. **Robert Cantwell. Chapel Hill, NC: University of North Carolina Press, 1993. 323 pp. Bibliography. Index.**

Considers the process of cultural production, or ethnomimesis, through a detailed analysis of the Festival of American Folklife. Scholarly and theoretical.

DEWEY: 394.2 6 0973 LC: GT4802.C36 ISBN 0-8078-2112-8

♦ 978 ♦

Inaugural Cavalcade. **Louise Durbin. New York: Dodd, Mead and Company, 1971. 210 pp. Illustrated. Bibliography. Index.**

Describes the inaugural ceremony and accompanying festivities of 37 American presidents, from George Washington to Richard Nixon. Black-and-white illustrations.

DEWEY: 394.4 ISBN 0-396-06421-3

♦ 979 ♦

New Orleans Jazz Fest: A Pictorial History. **Michael P. Smith. Foreword by Ben Sandmel. Gretna, LA: Pelican Publishing Company, 1991. 207 pp. Illustrated. Index.**

Captures the spirit of first 20 years (1970-1990) of the New Orleans Jazz Fest in black-and-white photographs. Includes photos of many famous musicians, such as Duke Ellington, Dizzy Gillespie, Wynton Marsalis, Stevie Wonder, and B. B. King.

DEWEY: 781.65 079 76335 LC: ML 38. N28 N447 ISBN 0-88289-810-8

♦ 980 ♦

Newport Jazz Festival: The Illustrated History. **Burt Goldblatt. New York: Dial Press, 1977. 287 pp. Illustrated. Appendices.**

Furnishes a detailed history of the Newport Jazz Festival, from its founding in 1954 to 1976. Discusses each year's performers and performances and conveys behind-the-scenes insights into the musicians, the festival, and the jazz scene. Generously illustrated with black-and-white photos. Appendices provide a discography of albums recorded at Newport and a list of festival programs.

DEWEY: 785.4207 LC: ML 38.N4N44 ISBN 0-8037-6440-5

♦ 981 ♦

Scenes From Tanglewood. **Andrew L. Pincus. Foreword by Seiji Ozawa. Boston, MA: Northeastern University Press, 1989. 287 pp. Illustrated. Index.**

Discusses the experiences of the conductors, musicians, and organizers of the Berkshire Festival at Tanglewood. Festival participants give many anecdotes and recall challenges. Also gives a history of the festival. Emphasis given to the 1970s and 1980s. Illustrated with black-and-white photos.

DEWEY: 780.7 97441 LC: ML200.8 B5 P56 ISBN 1-55553-049-4

♦ 982 ♦

Tanglewood. **Herbert Kupferberg. New York: McGraw-Hill Book Company, 1976. 280 pp. Illustrated. Bibliography. Index.**

Provides a history of the first 40 years of the Berkshire Festival at Tanglewood. Documents the festival's founding and offers behind-the-scenes insights into the organizers, musicians, conductors, composers, students, and concert-goers who have participated in this American institution. Discusses the music played, the influence of the festival on the American classical music scene, and how participation at Tanglewood has shaped the careers of America's great musicians. Provides a festival chronology. Illustrated with black-and-white photos.

DEWEY: 780.79 7441 LC: ML 200.8 B5 K86 ISBN 0-07-035643-2

♦ 983 ♦

The Tournament of Roses: A Pictorial History. **Joe Hendrickson. Los Angeles, CA: Brooke House Publishers, 1971. 300 pp. Illustrated. Appendices. Index.**

Offers a history of the Tournament of Roses, from its inception in the 1890s to 1970. Reviews the long line of organizers, parade participants, and athletes who have shaped this festival, as well as the memorable floats, football matches, athletic achievements, and parade queens of years past. Amply illustrated with black-and-white photos. Appendices list Rose Bowl scores, individual records, tournament presidents, parade queens and grand marshals, and participating bands.

DEWEY: 796.3327 ISBN 0-912588-00-4

♦ 984 ♦

The Urban Fair: How Cities Celebrate Themselves. **U.S. Department of Housing and Urban Development, Office of Public Affairs, 1981. 73 pp. Illustrated. Index.**

Profiles 10 successful urban fairs throughout the United States and tells how to organize one in your town. Describes fairs in Baltimore, Petersburg (Va.), San Antonio, Ithaca, Austin, Sioux City, Knoxville, Dayton, Minneapolis, and

Gilroy (Calif.). Part two gives information on fair organization, planning, programming, logistics, publicity, promotion, evaluation, and accommodating children, the elderly, and the disabled.

DEWEY: 394.6097

TET

♦ 985 ♦

***Tet: Vietnamese New Year.* Dianne M. MacMillan. Hillside, NJ: Enslow Publishers, Inc., 1994. 48 pp. Illustrated. Glossary. Index.**

Tells how Vietnamese Americans prepare for and celebrate Tet. Describes food, customs, religious observance, and festivities, retells legends, and explains significance of the holiday. Introduces Vietnamese words. Illustrated with color photos. One book in a series entitled *Best Holiday Books*.

DEWEY: 394.2 61 LC: GT 4905.M34 ISBN 0-89490-501-5

THANKSGIVING

♦ 986 ♦

***The First Thanksgiving Feast.* Joan Anderson. New York: Clarion Books, 1984. 46 pp. Illustrated.**

Dramatizes the story of the first Thanksgiving with stylized dialogue and photos of costumed interpreters from Plimoth Plantation, a museum which recreates the environment and daily life of Plymouth colony. Based on historical accounts of the first Thanksgiving. Black-and-white photos. For children.

DEWEY: 974.4 02 LC: F68 A54 ISBN 0-89919-287-4

♦ 987 ♦

***It's Time for Thanksgiving.* Elizabeth Hough Sechrist and Janette Woolsey. Philadelphia, PA: Macrae Smith Company, 1957. 251 pp.**

A Thanksgiving anthology for children. Contains two essays on Thanksgiving history, plus six stories, six plays and 27 poems on Thanksgiving themes. Includes poems by Ralph Waldo Emerson, Charles Dickens, Robert Louis Stevenson, selections from the Bible, and more. Also gives 30 Thanksgiving games and 30 Thanksgiving recipes.

DEWEY: 394.268

♦ 988 ♦

The Plymouth Thanksgiving. **Leonard Weisgard. New York: Doubleday, 1967. 60 pp. Illustrated.** 📖

Award-winning children's author tells the story of the Pilgrims' voyage to America, their first year in the New World, and the first Thanksgiving. Amply illustrated with author's drawings. For children.

DEWEY: 973.2 ISBN 0-385-26753-3

♦ 989 ♦

Thanksgiving. **Jane Duden. New York: Crestwood House, 1990. 48 pp. Illustrated. Index.** 📖

Offers a history of Thanksgiving for children. Tells why the Pilgrims came to America, portrays the first Thanksgiving, and shows how Thanksgiving celebrations have changed over the last three centuries. Introduces Thanksgiving and harvest festivals from other times and lands and describes contemporary Thanksgiving celebrations, including symbols, activities, and sentiments. Further reading list. One volume in a series entitled *Holidays*.

DEWEY: 394.2 683 LC: GT 4975 D83 ISBN 0-89686-503-7

♦ 990 ♦

Thanksgiving: An American Holiday, An American History. **Diana Karter Appelbaum. New York: Facts on File Publications, 1984. 305 pp. Illustrated. Appendix. Bibliography. Index.**

Provides an in-depth history of Thanksgiving in the U.S., noting how its celebration reflects the beliefs, spirit, and political climate of every era from colonial to present times. Also traces the historical development of contemporary Thanksgiving customs. Appendix reviews history of Thanksgiving dishes. Annotated bibliography.

DEWEY: 394.2 683 LC: GT 4975. A66 ISBN 0-87196-974-2

♦ 991 ♦

The Thanksgiving Book. **Lucille Recht Penner. New York: Hastings House, 1986. 160 pp. Illustrated. Bibliography. Index.** 📖

Places American Thanksgiving celebrations in the wider context of harvest festivals from around the world and throughout history. Gives the history of the first American Thanksgiving and tells how the holiday developed over time. Describes the harvest festivals of ancient Egypt, Rome, Greece, China and Israel, as well as traditional celebrations of Native North and Central

America, Europe, Africa, and India. Identifies Native American foods and features them in a wide variety of Thanksgiving recipes. Written for children.

DEWEY: 394.2 683 LC: GT 4975. P46 ISBN 0-8038-7228-3

♦ 992 ♦

Thanksgiving: Its Origins, Celebration and Significance as Related in Prose and Verse. **Robert Haven Schauffler, ed. New York: Moffat, Yard and Company, 1910. 265 pp.**

An anthology of stories, poems, essays, and other texts concerning Thanksgiving. Themes covered include the fall season, and the origin, celebration, and spirit of Thanksgiving. Includes selections by Nathaniel Hawthorne, John Keats, Harriet Beecher Stowe, and others. Also gives recitations suitable for children's Thanksgiving programs. One volume in a series entitled *Our American Holidays.*

DEWEY: 394 T367 s

♦ 993 ♦

Thanksgiving: Why We Celebrate It the Way We Do. **Martin Hintz and Kate Hintz. Mankato, MN: Capstone Press, 1996. 48 pp. Illustrated. Glossary. Index.**

Relates the history of the first American Thanksgiving, tells how it became an American holiday, and explains why and how we celebrate this holiday. Introduces thanksgiving festivals from other times and lands. Gives Thanksgiving recipes, craft idea, and suggested activities. Offers further reading and resource list. For children. One book in a series entitled *Celebrate!.*

DEWEY: 394.2 649 LC: GT 4975.H57 ISBN 1-56065-328-0

♦ 994 ♦

Turkeys, Pilgrims, and Indian Corn: The Story of Thanksgiving Symbols. **Edna Barth. Illustrated by Ursula Arndt. New York: Seabury Press, 1975. 96 pp. Index.**

Teaches the history and symbols of Thanksgiving to children. Tells the story of the first Thanksgiving, presents aspects of everyday life in Pilgrim society, relates the history of Thanksgiving celebrations in America, and explains how Pilgrims, Plymouth Rock, Indian corn, turkeys, and cranberries became Thanksgiving symbols. Compares Thanksgiving to other harvest festivals. Gives suggestions for further reading and sources.

DEWEY: 394.2683 ISBN 0-8164-3149-3

♦ 995 ♦

We Gather Together: The Story of Thanksgiving. **Ralph Linton and Adelin Linton. 1949. Reprint. Detroit, MI: Omnigraphics, Inc., 1990. 100 pp. Illustrated. Index.**

Tells the story of the American holiday of Thanksgiving, and places it in context by reviewing Thanksgiving festivals of other times and cultures. Presents the history of the first Thanksgiving and its commemoration from colonial times until 1863, when President Lincoln issued a proclamation declaring it a national holiday. Reprints Lincoln's proclamation. One volume in a series entitled *Great Religious Festivals.*

DEWEY: 394 L LC: GT4975.L5 ISBN 1-55888-883-7

VALENTINE'S DAY

♦ 996 ♦

Hearts, Cupids, and Red Roses: The Story of the Valentine Symbols. **Edna Barth. Illustrated by Ursula Arndt. New York: Clarion Books, 1974. 64 pp. Illustrated. Bibliography. Index.** 📖

Explains the origins of Valentine's Day and the meaning of its symbols to children. Introduces the Roman festival of Lupercalia and its customs, the deeds of St. Valentine, and the legend of Cupid and Psyche. Describes how the holiday was celebrated in many countries of medieval and later Europe. Tells how the custom of exchanging Valentine's Day cards developed and describes antique cards. Shows how such symbols as hearts, birds, roses, lace, candy, and the colors red, pink, and white became associated with Valentine's Day. Further reading list.

DEWEY: 394.2 683 LC: GT 4925. B52 ISBN 0-8164-3111-6

♦ 997 ♦

The Valentine and Its Origins. **Frank Staff. New York: Frederick A. Praeger, Publishers, 1969. 144 pp. Illustrated. Appendices. Bibliography. Index.**

Documents the history of Valentine's Day cards. Provides brief biography of St. Valentine. Discusses early European custom of exchanging Valentine's Day tokens and gives a detailed history of Valentine's Day cards, from their advent in the eighteenth century through the early twentieth century. Color and black-and-white photos of antique Valentine cards illustrate.

DEWEY: 394.268

♦ 998 ♦

Valentine's Day. **Elizabeth Guilfoile. Illustrated by Gordon Laite. Champaign, IL: Garrard Publishing Company, 1965. 64 pp.**

Tells the story of Valentine's Day and its customs to children. Covers Roman celebration of Lupercalia, the legends associated with St. Valentine, and old European customs concerning the day. Describes the first paper Valentines, their increasing popularity, and early American Valentine customs. Illustrated with many two-tone drawings.

DEWEY: 394.26

♦ 999 ♦

Valentine's Day. **Cass R. Sandak. New York: Crestwood House, 1990. 47 pp. Illustrated. Index.**

Provides children with a thorough introduction to Valentine's Day, its historical development, customs, symbols, and meaning. Describes ancient Roman festival of Lupercalia and its customs, the deeds of St. Valentine, and Valentine customs of medieval and later Europe. Also explains how hearts, flowers, Cupid, cards, and candy are used to represent and celebrate the holiday. Illustrated with color and black-and-white reproductions of artwork, antique Valentines, etc. Further reading list.

DEWEY: 394.2 683 LC: GT 4925.S26 ISBN 0-89686-504-5

VETERANS DAY

♦ 1000 ♦

An Album of Black Americans in the Armed Forces. **Donald L. Miller. New York: Franklin Watts, Inc., 1969. 72 pp. Illustrated. Glossary.**

Presents a brief history of the participation of Black Americans in the armed forces from colonial times to the Vietnam War. Illustrated with black-and-white photos and drawings of African Americans who served their country in times of war. For children.

DEWEY: J973.0974

♦ 1001 ♦

Armistice Day: An Anthology of the Best Prose and Verse on Patriotism, the Great War, the Armistice,—its History, Observance, Spirit and Significance; Victory, the Unknown Soldier and his Brothers, and Peace. With Fiction, Drama, Pageantry and Programs for Armistice Day Observance. **Robert Haven Schauffler. New York: Dodd, Mead and Company, 1928. 457 pp.**

An anthology of texts concerning Armistice Day, peace, patriotism, and war. Gives excerpts from articles, essays, and speeches, reprints poems, stories, and plays, and suggests program ideas. Selections by Woodrow Wilson, Alfred Tennyson, Rupert Brooke and many others. One volume in a series entitled *Our American Holidays.*

DEWEY: 807.3 792 LC: D 526.2 S32

♦ 1002 ♦

Blacks in America's Wars: The Shift in Attitudes from the Revolutionary War to Vietnam. **Robert W. Mullen. New York: Monad Press, 1973. 96 pp. Illustrated. Bibliography. Index.**

Reviews the history of service by and discrimination against Black Americans in the armed services, from the Revolutionary War to the Vietnam War. Emphasis on the Vietnam War and the shift in attitudes of many Black Americans towards military service.

DEWEY: 301.4444 LC: E185.63.M77

♦ 1003 ♦

For Our Beloved Country: American War Diaries from the Revolution to the Persian Gulf. **Speer Morgan and Greg Michalson, eds. New York: Atlantic Monthly Press, 1994. Bibliography.**

Reproduces the war diary of one ordinary soldier from each of seven American wars: the War of American Independence, the Civil War, the Spanish-American War, World War I, World War II, the Vietnam War, and the Gulf War. Conveys the unique circumstances of each war and the common experiences of men in battle. Bibliography of books on American wars.

DEWEY: 973 LC: E181. F67 ISBN 0-87113-549-3

♦ 1004 ♦

The Wages of War: When America's Soldiers Came Home, From Valley Forge to Vietnam. **Richard Severo and Lewis Milford. New York: Simon and Schuster, 1989. 495 pp. Index.**

Documents the generally poor treatment given returning war veterans by their government and society. Also discusses the efforts of veterans to organize and effect change. Includes original reporting on the Agent Orange controversy. Covers the period from the Revolutionary War through the Vietnam War. Endnotes.

DEWEY: 355.1 15 0973 LC: UB 357 S48 ISBN 0-671-54325-3

WOMEN'S HISTORY MONTH

♦ 1005 ♦

Celebrating Women's History: A Woman's History Month Resource Book. **Mary Ellen Snodgrass, ed. Foreword by Mary Ruthsdotter. Detroit, MI: Gale Research, 1995. 517 pp. Appendices. Indexes.**

A guide to organizing events in celebration of Women's History Month. Events are designed to raise awareness of the contributions and achievements of women in many fields of endeavor. Offers 300 suggested programs; each entry describes program activity, notes appropriate age level or audience, gives approximate budget, tells how to organize it, offers suggestions for alternative activities, and lists additional resources. Organized by 29 professional fields, such as business, film, dance, education, and politics. Appendices list books and CD-ROMs on the subject of women's history, as well as a wide variety of resources, including archives, associations, centers, groups, electronic packagers, multimedia supplies, museums, music distributors, newsletters, on-line sites, periodicals, publishers, and video distributors. Gives program index, age and audience index, budget index, and general index.

DEWEY: 305.4 09 LC: HQ 1122. C45 ISBN 0-7876-0605-7

The Pacific Islands and Australia

♦ 1006 ♦

The Fijian Way of Life. **G. K. Roth. Introduction by G. B. Milner. Second edition. Melbourne, Australia: Oxford University Press, 1973. 176 pp. Illustrated. Maps. Appendices. Bibliography. Glossary. Index.**

Outlines Fijian social, economic, ceremonial, and political life. Also discusses houses, furniture, and other aspects of material culture. Describes ceremonies performed for special events or high-ranking visitors, including the Tambua Ceremony and the Yanggona Ceremony.

DEWEY: 301.299611 LC: GN 671 F5 R68 ISBN 0-19-550449-6

♦ 1007 ♦

The Melanesians: People of the South Pacific. **Albert B. Lewis. Chicago: Chicago Natural History Museum Press, 1951. 259 pp. Illustrated. Appendix. Bibliography. Index.**

Provides an overview of the natural environment and traditional way of life of the peoples of Melanesia. Gives chapters on food, clothing, weapons, warfare, tools, transportation, trade, history, music, toys, religion, death, and more. Offers chapter on ceremonies and ceremonial objects, which supplies general description of festival and ceremonial activities, depicts ceremonial masks and figures, and briefly describes the Semese Festival (New Guinea). Black-and-white photos illustrate. Appendix furnishes notes on the physical anthropology of Melanesia. First published in 1932; based on firsthand research in the first two decades of the twentieth century.

LC: GN 668.L67

♦ 1008 ♦

Russ Tyson's Australian Christmas Book. **Russ Tyson. Melbourne, Australia: Landsdowne Press, 1965. 112 pp.**

A collection of short stories and verse about Christmas which reflects the spirit, ambience, and customs of the holiday in Australia.

DEWEY: 394.2 T988a

♦ 1009 ♦

***Samoans!* June Behrens. Chicago: Children's Press, 1986. 31 pp. Illustrated. Maps.**

Introduces young children to aspects of Samoan life, including celebrations. Contrasts Samoan and Samoan-American lifestyles, introduces Samoan words, and describes a Samoan wedding as well as the history and festivities of Samoan Flag Day. Beautifully illustrated with color photos of Samoa and Samoan-American celebrations. One volume in a series entitled *Festivals and Holidays.*

DEWEY: 996.13 LC: DU 813. B44 ISBN 0-516-02388-8

♦ 1010 ♦

***Tahiti and French Polynesia: A Travel Survival Kit.* Robert F. Kay. South Yarra, Victoria, Australia: Lonely Planet Publications, 1985. 136 pp. Illustrated. Maps. Glossary. Index.**

A travel guide for Tahiti and French Polynesia. Lists major festivals, noting dates and central activities, and describes the month-long celebration of Bastille Day. Lists accommodations, describes attractions, and tells how to travel within Polynesia. Illustrated with color photos.

DEWEY: 996.211 K23 ISBN 0-908086-80-6

♦ 1011 ♦

***A World of Islands.* June Knox-Mawer. Photographs by Peter Carmichael. New York: The Viking Press, 1969. 78 pp.**

Describes traditional customs and ways of life in the South Pacific. Covers Fiji, the Gilbert Islands, Ellice Islands, and Tonga. Some coverage of festivals and ceremonial customs. Treats the Yanggona Ceremony and firewalking rituals (Fiji), and coronation ceremonies and the Sabbath (Tonga). Amply illustrated with color and black-and-white photos.

DEWEY: 996 C287 W ISBN 670-78680-2

CHAPTER FOUR

Calendars and Time-Reckoning Systems

General Works

♦ 1012 ♦

Anno's Sundial. **Mitsumasa Anno. New York: Philomel Books, 1987. 28 pp. Illustrated.**

A pop-up book explaining the astronomy, geography, and geometry of sundials and solar time measurement to children. Pop-up diagrams include sundials and shadow-measuring experiments. Gives instructions for making a sundial.

DEWEY: 529.7 LC: QB215. A66 ISBN 0-399-21374

♦ 1013 ♦

The Book of Calendars. **Frank Parise, ed. New York: Facts on File, 1982. 387 pp. Index.**

Summarizes the history and organization of the Babylonian, Macedonian, Hebrew, Seleucid, Olympiad, Roman, Armenian, Islamic, Fasli, Zoroastrian, Yezdezred, Jelali, Egyptian, Coptic, Ethiopian, Iranian, Afghan, Akbar, Fasli Deccan, Parasuram, Burmese and Arakanese, Chinese, Tibetan, Mayan, Julian, Gregorian, and Christian eras and calendars. Tables throughout convert the various ancient and multinational calendars to Julian or Gregorian dates or years. Dates of Easter are provided from the year 1 A.D. through 1999. Calendar of Christian saints. Explanations of the French Revolutionary calendar and the Soviet calendar. Table depicts dates of European New Year's celebrations.

DEWEY: 529.3 LC: CE 11.K4 ISBN 0-98196-467-8

♦ 1014 ♦

A Book of Time. **Lesley Coleman. Camden, NJ: Thomas Nelson, Inc., 1971. 144 pp. Illustrated. Bibliography. Index.**

Survey of the ancient Sumerian, Babylonian, Muslim, Christian, Jewish, Egyptian, Roman, Julian, Gregorian, French Revolutionary, and proposed World calendar. Includes discussion of timepieces, clockmakers, navigation, and some theories and literature dealing with time. (NR)

DEWEY: 529 LC: QB213.C66 ISBN 0-8407-6144-9

♦ 1015 ♦

Calendar Art: Thirteen Days, Weeks, Months, and Years from Around the World. **Leonard Everett Fisher. New York: Four Winds Press, 1987. 64 pp. Illustrated.** 📖

Explains 13 different calendar systems from around the world and throughout history. Covers Aztec, Babylonian, Chinese, ancient Egyptian, French Revolutionary, Gregorian, Hebrew, Islamic, Julian, Mayan, Roman, Stonehenge, and World calendars. Tables, drawings, and diagrams illustrate. For children.

DEWEY: 529.3 LC: CE 11.F57 ISBN 0-02-735350-8

♦ 1016 ♦

The Calendar for Everybody. **Elizabeth Achelis. 1943. Reprint. Detroit, MI: Omnigraphics, Inc., 1990. 141 pp. Index.**

Traces the calendar from its beginning, relating little-known facts about our present calendar and presenting advantages to be gained from one that is newer and simplified. Discusses the earth's time, the Egyptian, Julian, Gregorian, the 13-Month, and World calendars. Includes chronology of important events in the history of the calendar.

DEWEY: 529.3 LC: CE11 A34 ISBN 1-55888-849-7

♦ 1017 ♦

Calendars. **Necia Apfel. New York: Franklin Watts, 1985. 88 pp. Illustrated. Index.** 📖

Explains the history and science of Western calendar systems, from ancient attempts to reckon time by the cycles of the moon, sun, and stars to the establishment of the Gregorian calendar. Introduces the Egyptian, Roman, Julian, Gregorian, traditional Chinese, Mayan/Aztec, and World calendars. Also examines the historical development of the week and the hour as units of time, as well as the names of months and days. Written for children.

DEWEY: 529 LC: CE 13. A64 ISBN 0-531-10034-0

♦ 1018 ♦

The Clock We Live On. **Revised edition. Isaac Asimov. Illustrated by John Bradford. London: Abelard-Schuman, 1965. 172 pp. Index.**

The scientist-science fiction writer explains the solar and lunar systems by which humans have learned to tell time. Surveys devices for keeping time, from ancient to modern clocks and calendars. Discussion of solar, lunar, Egyptian, Hebrew, Christian, Julian, Gregorian, and French Revolutionary calendars, and chronological eras. (NR)

♦ 1019 ♦

Empires of Time: Calendars, Clocks, and Cultures. **Anthony Aveni. New York: Basic Books, 1989. 379 pp. Illustrated. Index.**

A far-reaching examination of concepts of time and calendar systems across cultures and throughout history. Discusses historical development and workings of various calendar and time-reckoning schemes, pointing out their contribution to cultural systems as well as illustrating the connection between political power and control over the calendar. Explores the evidence for the earliest known calendar systems, including evidence of Neolithic time-reckoning systems, calendar systems of the ancient Greeks, and the Stonehenge controversy. Detailed coverage of the Western (Gregorian), Mayan, Aztec, Inca, and Chinese calendars, as well as discussion of the calendar system of two tribal groups, the Nuer of East Africa and the Trobriand Islanders of the Pacific.

DEWEY: 529 LC: QB 209.A94 ISBN 0-465-01950-1

♦ 1020 ♦

The Mystery of Time. **Harry Edward Neal. New York: Julian Messner, 1966. 190 pp. Illustrated. Bibliography. Index.**

Relates episodes in the history of time measurement, from the invention of the first calendars and sundials to the atomic clock.

DEWEY: 529 N252 m

♦ 1021 ♦

The Romance of the Calendar. **P. W. Wilson. New York: W. W. Norton and Co., 1937. 351 pp. Index.**

Tells the story of the development of calendar systems in the West, beginning with the early innovations of the Babylonians and Egyptians, continuing through the various developments of the Greeks and Romans, and culminating with the establishment of the Gregorian calendar. Also describes Mayan, Hindu, Chinese, and Jewish calendars. Reviews different ways of reckoning days and dividing them into hours and minutes, as well as the various devices that people have invented to measure time. Explains the proposed World calendar and considers the advantages obtained by adopting it. Offers world chronology of significant events in the history of calendars.

DEWEY: 902.3 W 752

♦ 1022 ♦

The 365 Days. **Keith Gordon Irwin. Illustrated by Guy Fleming. New York: Thomas Y. Crowell Company, 1963. 182 pp. Maps. Index.**

Discusses solar, lunar, and astronomical cycles, ancient calendars of Egypt, Babylon, Chaldea, Rome, and the Mayas. Traces origin and development of the Julian and the Gregorian calendars. Notes on various calendars proposed in recent history. Section on dating the observance of Easter and Christmas. Discussion of carbon-dating and tree rings. (NR)

♦ 1023 ♦

Time and the Calendars. **W. M. O'Neil. Sydney, Australia: Sydney University Press, 1975. 138 pp. Illustrated. Appendix. Bibliography. Index.**

Learned account of the astronomy and history of various calendars and systems of time measurement. Treats the Eygptian, Roman, Babylonian, Indian, Chinese, and Meso-American calendars. Appendix gives the names of the days in 13 languages.

DEWEY: 529.3 LC: CE 6. 053 ISBN 0-424-00003-2

♦ 1024 ♦

Understanding Time: The Science of Clocks and Calendars. **Beulah Tannenbaum and Myra Stillman. Illustrated by William D. Hayes. New York: Whittlesey House, 1958. 143 pp. Index.**

Explanation for young readers of time and clocks, calendars, and other measuring systems used throughout history. Each chapter includes suggested experiments. (NR)

Days, Weeks, and Months

♦ 1025 ♦

All About the Months. **Maymie R. Krythe. New York: Harper and Row, 1966. 222 pp. Bibliography. Index.**

Presents a collection of lore, customs, holidays, famous birthdays, and historic events associated with the months of the year. Explains the origins of month names and provides information about each month's birthstone and flower.

DEWEY: 529.2

♦ 1026 ♦

The Days of the Week: Stories, Songs, Traditions, Festivals, and Surprising Facts About the Days of the Week All Over the World. **Paul Hughes. Illustrated by Jeffrey Burn. Ada, OK: Garrett Educational Corporation, 1989. 62 pp. Glossary. Index.**

Explains the history of the week as a unit of time and tells how the days of the week were named. Presents a collection of lore, rhymes, sayings, holidays, traditions, and customs associated with the days of the week. Gives names of the days in 16 foreign languages, furnishes a perpetual calendar of days and explains its use. Written for children.

DEWEY: 398.27 LC: GR 930. H84 ISBN 0-944483-32-1

♦ 1027 ♦

The Months of the Year: Stories, Songs, Traditions, Festivals, and Surprising Facts About the Months of the Year All Over the World. **Paul Hughes. Illustrated by Jeffrey Burn. Ada, OK: Garrett Educational Corporation, 1989. 63 pp. Glossary. Index.**

Presents the history and the folklore of the months of the year to children. Explains the relationship between months and the moon, the difference between a lunar year and a solar year, the Julian and Gregorian calendars. Explores the history and mythology behind the names of the months, describes important holidays and festivals occurring in each month, and lists the flower and gemstone of each month. Gives the names of the months in 13 European languages. Introduces the months of the Hindu, Muslim, Jewish, and Chinese calendars, as well as the 12 signs of the Zodiac.

DEWEY: 398.27 LC: GR 930. H85 ISBN 0-944483-33-X

♦ 1028 ♦

The Seven Day Circle: The History and Meaning of the Week. **Eviatar Zerubavel. New York: The Free Press, 1985. 206 pp. Bibliography. Indexes.**

Reviews the origins and history of the seven-day week, with special emphasis on the spiritual and social implications of its adoption by Judaism, Christianity, and Islam. Contrasts stability of the seven-day week in the West with the failed calendar reforms of the French Revolution and the Soviet Union. Also contrasts with the weekly cycles of ancient Meso-America, Indonesia, ancient China, ancient Rome, and West Africa. Discusses the way in which the seven-day week shapes social life in the contemporary West.

DEWEY: 394 LC: CE 85. Z47 ISBN 0-02-934680-0

♦ 1029 ♦

The Stories of the Months and Days. **Reginald C. Couzens. 1923. Reprint. Detroit, MI: Omnigraphics, Inc., 1990. 160 pp. Illustrated.**

Explains how the months and days were named, telling stories about the Greek, Roman, Anglo, and Saxon gods, goddesses, heroes, kings, and other legendary figures with whom they are associated.

DEWEY: 398.33 LC: GR 930 C6 ISBN 1-55888-881-0

♦ 1030 ♦

The Week: An Essay on the Origin and Development of the Seven Day Cycle. **F. H. Colson. Cambridge, England: Cambridge University Press, 1926. 126 pp. Appendix.**

Traces the history of the seven-day week, outlining the difference between the planetary week and the Jewish week, and exploring their adoption or rejection first by other ancient peoples, and later by Christian Europe. Discusses history of day names. Appendix gives names of days in 15 European languages.

DEWEY: 902.3 C723

Ancient Peoples

General Works

♦ 1031 ♦

Echoes of Ancient Skies: The Astronomy of Lost Civilizations. **E. C. Krupp. 1983. Reprint. New York: New American Library, Inc., 1984. 386 pp. Illustrated. Bibliography. Index.**

Reviews the astronomy of ancient civilizations around the world, drawing connections between their mythology, astronomy, and the design of their monuments and artifacts. Tells how ancient sites were used as observatories and examines geometrical and astronomical elements in their design. Explores ancient mythologies, their connection to astronomical systems, and their symbols. Reconstructs astronomically related rituals and observances and discusses ancient calendar systems. Covers ancient Egypt, Britain, Central American, North America, and China. Diagrams and black-and-white photos illustrate.

DEWEY: 520.93 LC: QB16. K78 ISBN 0-452-00679-1

♦ 1032 ♦

In Search of Ancient Astronomies. **E. C. Krupp, ed. Garden City, NY: Doubleday and Company, 1977. 300 pp. Illustrated. Bibliography. Index.**

A collection of articles by noted authorities introducing the general reader to the astronomical and time-measurement systems of the ancient Egyptians, Native Central Americans, Native North Americans, and inhabitants of the British Isles. First chapter introduces basic astronomical terms and concepts. Contributions include "Rings and Menhirs: Geometry and Astronomy in the Neolithic Age" by Alexander Thom and Archibald Stevens Thom; "The Stonehenge Chronicles" by E. C. Krupp; "Archaeoastronomy of North America: Cliffs, Mounds, and Medicine Wheels" by John A. Eddy; "Astronomy in Ancient Mesoamerica" by Anthony Aveni; and "Astronomers, Pyramids, and Priests" by E. C. Krupp.

DEWEY: 520.93 ISBN 0-385-11639-X

♦ 1033 ♦

Megaliths and Masterminds. **Peter Lancaster Brown. New York: Charles Scribner's Sons, 1979. 246 pp. Illustrated. Bibliography. Index.**

Summarizes for the general reader the history of learned debate over the purpose of ancient stone monuments. Covers Stonehenge and other ancient British monuments in depth; also considers the monuments and inscriptions of the ancient Egyptians, Babylonians, Mayans, Native North Americans, and peoples of Paleolithic Europe. Reviews the evidence that these monuments were built for astronomical, calendrical, and ritual purposes.

DEWEY: 930.1028 ISBN 0-684-15908-2

♦ 1034 ♦

New Year's Day: The Story of the Calendar. **S. H. Hooke. New York: William Morrow and Company, 1928. 78 pp. Bibliography.**

Considers the basic outlines, origins, and functions of seven ancient calendar systems: Babylonian, Greek, Egyptian, early Christian, Jewish, Mayan, and Native North American. Also mentions elements of several calendar systems of the ancient Far East and Africa. Identifies the cultural and social elements which give rise to calendar formation. Describes the ancient Babylonian New Year Festival.

DEWEY: 902.3 H782

Central American (Mayan, Aztec, Mextec, Zapotec)

♦ 1035 ♦

The Book of the Year: Middle American Calendrical Systems. **Munro S. Edmonson. Salt Lake City, UT: University of Utah Press, 1988. 313 pp. Bibliography. Index.**

Analyzes the calendar systems of native Central America, drawing on 60 calendars of Native Central American peoples, such as the Mayas, Aztecs, Mixtecs, and Zapotecs. Explains the basic structure, divisions, and cycles of the Central American calendar, correlates Central American with European dates, sketches the historical development of the Central American calendar, and examines the relationship between the calendar and solar astronomy. Lengthy calendrical index reports information known about each of the Native American calendars mentioned in the book.

DEWEY: 529.3 09728 LC: F 1219.3 C2 E3 ISBN 0-87480-288-1

♦ 1036 ♦

The Calendar of the Mayas: Broken Cogwheels of Eternity. **Wolfgang Alexander Schoken. Brookline, MA: The Book Department, Inc., 1986. 61 pp. Index.**

Provides a concise explanation of the Mayan calendar system for the general reader. Retraces history of progress made by scholars of Mayan calendrics and teaches how to convert Mayan and Christian dates.

DEWEY: 529.329792 LC: F 1435.3 C14 S36 ISBN 0-9615883-0-6

♦ 1037 ♦

Maya Hieroglyphic Writing. **Second edition. J. Eric S. Thompson. Norman, OK: University of Oklahoma Press, 1960. 347 pp. Illustrated. Appendices. Bibliography. Glossary. Index.**

Scholarly explanation of the Maya hieroglyphic writing system and summary of information gleaned from these writings. Begins with brief introduction to Mayan society. Covers sources of inscriptions, glyph composition, Mayan graphology, and counting systems. Special emphasis on Mayan calendrics. Treats many issues regarding the names, glyphs, ordering, and ritual recognition of days and months, the 260-day cycle, the long count, distance numbers, period endings, anniversaries and Katun counts, ritual and astronomical cycles, and more. Appendices include the divinatory almanacs from the Books of Chilam Balam and additional commentary on the problems of decipherment and date calculations. Furnishes glossary of hieroglyphs. Includes more than 100 unnumbered pages of figures representing actual hieroglyphic inscriptions. Oversize.

DEWEY: 972.015 T473 m

♦ 1038 ♦

The Sky in Mayan Literature. **Anthony Aveni, ed. Oxford, England: Oxford University Press, 1992. 297 pp. Illustrated. Index.**

A collection of scholarly articles attempting to incorporate knowledge derived from recently discovered and translated Mayan texts into our understanding of Mayan astronomy and calendrics.

DEWEY: 972.81 016 LC: F1435.3 W75S55 ISBN 0-19-506844-0

♦ 1039 ♦

Time and Reality in the Thought of the Maya. **Second edition, enlarged. Miguel León-Portilla. Translated by Charles L. Boilès, Fernando**

Horcasitas, and the author. Foreword by Eric S. Thompson. Norman, OK: University of Oklahoma Press, 1988. 229 pp. Illustrated. Appendices. Bibliography. Index.

Considers how Mayan concepts of time shaped their religious beliefs, way of life, and world view. Notes Mayan preoccupation with time, reviews aspects of the Mayan calendar and astronomical knowledge. Explores the meaning of the deities, symbols, philosophy, and spatial representations implicit in or associated with Mayan notions of time. Appendix A contains brief article on contemporary Maya by Alfonso Villa Rojas. Second edition features new appendix in which author reviews work done on this subject since the original publication of the book in 1968.

DEWEY: 529.32 LC: F1435.3 C14L413 ISBN 0-8061-2128-9

Greek

♦ 1040 ♦

The Calendars of Athens. **W. Kendrick Pritchett and O. Neugebauer. Cambridge, MA: Harvard University Press, 1947. 115 pp. Appendix.**

Scholarly reconstruction of the calendar system of ancient Athens from fragments of ancient inscriptions. Authors offer their approach to the problem of understanding how the Athenians reconciled the lunar and solar years and the religious and civil calendars. Appendix provides index of inscriptions cited and discusses months appearing on Athenian coins.

LC: CE 42 P75

♦ 1041 ♦

The Sacred and Civil Calendar of the Athenian Year. **Jon D. Mikalson. Princeton, NJ: Princeton University Press, 1975. 226 pp. Appendices. Index.**

Scholarly reconstruction of the calendar of ancient Athens. Furnishes names of months and days and lists in chronological order the festivals, religious devotions, administrative and financial affairs associated with specific dates or days of the month. Cites primary sources in text.

DEWEY: 529.32 208 LC: CE 42. M52 ISBN 0-691-03458-8

Near Eastern (Amorite, Assyrian, Egyptian, Semetic, Sippar, Sumerian)

♦ 1042 ♦

The Calendars of Ancient Egypt. **Richard A. Parker. Chicago: University of Chicago Press, 1950. 83 pp. Illustrated.**

Scholarly reconstruction of the calendar system of ancient Egypt. Introduces basic astronomical terms. Explains original lunar calendar, later lunar calendar, and civil calendar. Proposes theories for starting point of Egyptian lunar month and the method whereby the Egyptians synchronized their calendar systems. Tables give chart converting Julian into Gregorian dates, names of Egyptian days and months, and more. Black-and-white plates show papyrus fragments and hieroglyphic inscriptions constituting primary data sources.

DEWEY: 529.3 P242

♦ 1043 ♦

The Cultic Calendars of the Ancient Near East. **Mark E. Cohen. Bethesda, MD: C.D.L. Press, 1993. 504 pp. Bibliography. Index.**

Scholarly reconstruction of ritual calendar systems of ancient Mesopotamia. Presents early Semitic calendars from the third millennium B.C., the Sumerian, Assyrian, Amorite, and Sippar calendars from the second millennium B.C., the standard Mesopotamian calendar from the second and first millennium B.C., as well as calendars specific to individual settlements. Identifies festival themes and outlines what is known of the practices associated with major celebrations. Lists primary sources consulted.

DEWEY: 529.32 921 LC: CE 33. C 64 ISBN 1-883053-00-5

Northern European

♦ 1044 ♦

The Stones of Time: Calendars, Sundials, and Stone Chambers of Ancient Ireland. **Martin Brennan. Rochester, VT: Inner Traditions International, 1994. 216 pp. Illustrated. Bibliography. Index.**

Tells story of author's research and discoveries and provides a systematic exposition of the theory that Ireland's megalithic stone chambers constitute calendrical devices which are aligned with the solstices, equinoxes, and other astronomical phenomena. Argues that the artwork decorating these monuments also relates to calendrical and astronomical cycles and events. Many diagrams and black-and-white photos.

DEWEY: 936.1 5 LC: GN 806.5 B74 ISBN 0-89281-509-4

Roman

♦ 1045 ♦

The Calendar of the Roman Republic. **Agnes Kirsopp Michels. Princeton, NJ: Princeton University Press, 1967. 227 pp. Illustrated. Appendices. Index.**

Scholarly interpretation of the calendar system of the Roman Republic. Discusses original sources and their meaning, how the calendar was arranged, and the various characters which the Romans ascribed to days. Addresses historical development of the calendar system from the fifth to the first century B.C. Appendices describe the Roman system of intercalation, give the characters ascribed to specific dates, and present the controversies over the *nundinae* (market-days held every ninth day) and *trinum nundinum* and the dating of the Roman calendar system. Offers pull-out reproduction of an actual Roman calendar, as well as author's schematic reconstruction of the Roman calendar.

DEWEY: 529.32 LC: CE 46 M5

♦ 1046 ♦

On Roman Time: The Codex-Calendar of 354 and the Rhythms of Urban Life in Late Antiquity. **Michele Renee Salzman. Berkeley, CA: University of California Press, 1990. 315 pp. Illustrated. Appendices. Index.**

Study of a single, rare document, an intact Roman calendar from 354 A.D. Sheds light on Pagan and Christian ritual and belief in late antiquity. Discusses seasons, holidays, festivals, and cults as characterized in the calendar, noting change over time. Illustrated with black-and-white photos of artifacts, documents, and artwork of the time. Lists frequently cited works.

DEWEY: 529.3 0937 LC: CE 46. S25 ISBN 0-520-06566-2

♦ 1047 ♦

Ovid's Fasti: Roman Holidays. **Ovid. Translated with notes and introduction by Betty Rose Nagle. Bloomington, IN: Indiana University Press, 1995. 209 pp. Glossary.**

Furnishes a translation of the *Fasti,* an epic poem about the calendar and holidays of ancient Rome by the famous Roman poet Ovid. *Fasti* is divided into six books, each addressing one of the first six months of the year and containing verses about days of note. Legends, myths, religious practices, and history associated with these days and events retold in verse. Topics include festivals, astronomical phenomena, anniversaries, and agricultural events occurring on, near, or associated with calendar dates. Also addresses the calendar system.

Translator's introduction provides a brief biography of Ovid, characterizes the *Fasti* in relation to the rest of Ovid's work and the work of other Roman and Greek poets, and introduces aspects of the Roman religion and calendar system.

DEWEY: 871.01 LC: PA 6522.F2N34 ISBN 0-253-33967-7

♦ 1048 ♦

***The Roman Festival Calendar of Numa Pompilius.* Michael York. New York: Peter Lang, 1986. 383 pp. Appendices. Bibliography. Indexes.**

Discusses the ancient Roman calendar with its yearly round of festivals, which Romans credited to the legendary figure of Numa Pompilius. Separate chapters treat the Roman day, the Roman year, the arrangement of the calendar, festal deities, the various holidays and festivals of each month, and Carnival. Appendices address foreign influences on and changes to the calendar and suggest current uses of the calendar. Provides indexes of dates, festivals, gods and legendary figures, persons, and places, as well as a general index.

DEWEY: 529. 32 207 LC: CE 46.Y 67 ISBN 0-8204-0307-5

Modern Peoples

Asian (Cambodian, Chinese, Burmese, Thai)

♦ 1049 ♦

The Calendrical Systems of Mainland South-East Asia. **J. C. Eade. Leiden, The Netherlands: E. J. Brill, 1995. 182 pp. Illustrated. Appendices. Bibliography. Index.**

Scholarly explanation of the calendar system of mainland Southeast Asia (Cambodia, Thailand, Burma). Covers eras, years, months, days, elements of astrology, and the system of intercalation. Demonstrates how to convert Western and Southeast Asian dates. Author also advises that interested readers can access a public domain computer program (Macintosh version) which can provide calendrical and astronomical information from the Southeast Asian calendar system on any date after 690 B.C. at the following address: ftp://coombs.anu.edu.au/coombspapers/otherarchives/asian-studies-archives/seasia-archives/software

DEWEY: 529.3 0959 LC: CE61.A43 E23 ISBN 90-04-10437-2

♦ 1050 ♦

Cat and Rat: The Legend of the Chinese Zodiac. **Ed Young. New York: Henry Holt and Company, 1995. 31 pp. Illustrated.**

Retells the legend concerning the creation of the 12-year Chinese zodiac. Lists the 12 animal signs of the Chinese zodiac and gives the characteristics of people born under each sign. Illustrated with color drawings. For children.

DEWEY: 133.5 LC: BF 1714.C5 Y68 ISBN 0-8050-2977-X

♦ 1051 ♦

T'ung Shu: The Ancient Chinese Almanac. **Edited and translated by Martin Palmer, with Mak Hin Chung, Kwok Man Ho, and Angela Smith. Kuala Lumpur, Malaysia: Vinpress, 1990. 240 pp. Bibliography. Glossary. Index.**

Translates selections from the *T'ung Shu,* or *The Book of Myriad Things,* an ancient Chinese almanac still widely used by Chinese populations around the world. Almanac consists of a compilation of lore associated with the Chinese lunar calendar, the seasons, and various forms of divination. Chinese text printed alongside translation. Translator also provides commentary and explanation.

LC: AY 1148 A8 L513 ISBN 967-81-0106-8

European

♦ 1052 ♦

***Medii Æni Kalendarium, or Dates, Charters, and Customs of the Middle Ages, with Kalendars from the 10th to the 15th Century; and an Alphabetical Digest of Obsolete Names of Days: Forming a Glossary of Dates of the Middle Ages, with Tables and Other Aides for Ascertaining Dates.* Robert Thomas Hampson. Two volumes. 1841. Reprint. New York: A.M.S. Press, 1978. Volume one, 492 pp. Volume two, 430 pp. Glossary. Index.**

Covers all aspects of calendar systems and named days of medieval Britain. Volume one contain three books. Book one discusses medieval chronology as it can be derived from medieval charters and other historical documents. Book two covers beliefs, practices, and lore associated with dates, seasons, or festivals. Book three reviews and reproduces ancient calendars (in the original Latin). Second volume contains book four, a glossary, which functions as an abbreviated encyclopedia of names, terms, and dates occurring in or associated with medieval calendars.

DEWEY: 909.07 02 02 LC: CB 353. H34 ISBN 0-404-16970-8

Native North American

♦ 1053 ♦

***The Big Missouri Winter Count.* Roberta Carkeek Cheney. Traditional interpretations by Kills Two. Illustrations by Ralph Shane. Happy Camp, CA: Naturegraph Publishers, Inc., 1979. 63 pp. Bibliography.**

Explains the Dakota (Sioux) winter count, or historical calendar, system. Reproduces and interprets pictographs from the Big Missouri Winter Count.

DEWEY: 529.32 97 LC: E99.D1 C47 ISBN 0-87961-082-4

♦ 1054 ♦

***Living the Sky: The Cosmos of the American Indian.* Ray A. Williamson. Illustrations by Snowden Hodges. Norman, OK: University of Oklahoma Press, 1987. 366 pp. Bibliography. Index.**

Presents the archaeoastronomy of Native North America for the general reader. Identifies various archeological remains as observatories, describes the Native American view of the heavens, and explains how it molded their cultural and social life, mythology, conception of time, and calendar system. Separate chapters treat tribes of the Southwest, the East, the Plains, and California, with special attention to beliefs of the Pawnee and the Navaho.

DEWEY: 970.004 97 LC: E98. A88 W54 ISBN 0-8061-2034-7

Religious

Christian

♦ 1055 ♦

The Christian Calendar and the Gregorian Reform. **Peter Archer. New York: Fordham University Press, 1941. 124 pp. Appendix. Index. Supplement.**

Demonstrates the workings of the Julian and Gregorian calendars, with special attention to the Christian features and uses of these calendars. Explains the establishment of the Christian era, golden numbers, dominical letters, the calendar reform of 1582, the setting of Easter dates, solar and lunar cycles and their reconciliation, the epact and its relationship to Roman martyrology, the history of the Julian and Gregorian calendars, and more. Gives many formulas and tables. Appendix reconstructs Passover dates for the years 25 to 33 A.D. Eight-page supplement discusses proposed reforms to the yearly civil calendar.

LC: CE 73 A67

Jewish

♦ 1056 ♦

The Comprehensive Hebrew Calendar: Its Structure, History, and One Hundred Years of Corresponding Dates, 5660-5760, 1900-2000. **Arthur Spier. New York: Behrman House, 1952. 228 pp.**

Gives a brief explanation and history of the Jewish calendar system. Tells when days and months begin and how the hour is divided. Furnishes tables of corresponding Jewish and Gregorian dates from the Gregorian year 1900 to 2000, with dates of Jewish holidays marked.

DEWEY: 529.3 Sp44c

♦ 1057 ♦

The Story of the Jewish Calendar. **Azriel Eisenberg. Wood engravings by Elisabeth Friedlander. London: Abelard-Schuman, 1958. 62 pp. Glossary.**

A short story of two teenaged boys watching for the new moon prefaces a history and explanation of the Jewish calendar. Also explains Jewish holidays, the Sabbath, and names of months. Glossary of Hebrew terms and place names.

DEWEY: 529.3

Appendix

Periodicals

African Arts. UCLA James S. Coleman African Studies Center, 1967-

African Studies. Witwatersrand University Press, 1921-

American Anthropologist. American Anthropological Association, Arlington, VA, 1899-

American Folklore Society Newsletter. American Anthropological Association, Arlington, VA

Anthropology and Archeology of Eurasia; a Journal of Translations from Soviet Sources. M. E. Sharpe, Inc., 1962-

Asian Folklore Studies. Nanzan University, Nanzan Anthropological Institute, 1942-

British Federation of Festivals Yearbook. British Federation of Festivals, 1921-

Canadian Geographic. Royal Canadian Geographic Society, 1930-

Cavalcade of Arts and Attractions. BPI Communications, 1894-

Comparative Studies in Society and History. Cambridge University Press, 1959-

Dance Magazine. Dance Magazine, Inc., 1926-

Directory of North American Fairs, Festivals and Expositions (Amusement Business's Directory of North American Fairs; until 1972, known as *Cavalcade and Directory of Fairs*). BPI Communications, 1988-

The Drama Review. MIT Press, 1955-

English Dance and Song. English Dance and Song Society, London, England, 1936-

Ethnos. Folkens Museum, National Museum of Ethnography, Stockholm, Sweden, 1936-

Fairs and Expositions. International Association of Fairs and Expositions, Springfield, MO

Folklife Center News. U.S. Library of Congress, American Folklife Center, Washington, D.C., 1978-

Folklore. Folklore Society, 1878-

Folklore Forum. Folklore Institute, Bloomington, IN, 1968-

Folklore of American Holidays. Gale Research, Inc., Detroit, MI, 1986-

Folklore of World Holidays. Gale Research, Inc., Detroit, MI, 1991-

International Migration Review (International Migration Digest). Center for Migration Studies of New York, Inc., 1964-

Jewish Folklore and Ethnology Review. YIVO Institute for Jewish Research, 1978-

Journal of American Culture. Bowling Green Popular Press, 1967-

Journal of American Folklore. American Folklore Society, 1888-

Journal of Ethnic Studies. Western Washington University, 1973-

Journal of Folklore Research. Indiana University, Folklore Institute, 1964-

Journal of Latin American Lore. UCLA Latin American Center, 1974-

Journal of the English Folk Dance and Song Society, 1932-1964

The Journal of the Polynesian Society. Polynesian Society, Inc., 1892-

Journal of Popular Culture. Bowling Green State University, 1967-

Lore and Language. Centre for English Cultural Tradition and Language, 1969-

National Geographic Society. National Geographic Society, 1888-

Native American Directory. National Native American Co-op, 1969-

Nigeria Magazine. Ministry of Culture and Social Welfare, Lagos, Nigeria, 1927-1988

Southwestern Lore. Colorado Archeological Association, Cortez, CO, 1935-

Trinidad Carnival. Key Caribbean Publications, Ltd., Port-au-Spain, Trinidad.

Western Folklore. California Folklore Society, 1942-

World's Fair. World's Fair, Inc., 1981

Associations

Alternative Resource Center. **P.O. Box 429, 5263 Bouldercrest Road, Ellenwood, GA 30049. Telephone: 404-961-0102. Publications:** ***Shalom Connections; To Celebrate: Reshaping Holidays and Rites of Passage; Wedding Alternatives; Whose Birthday is it, Anyway?***

Offers resources which encourage non-commercial holiday observance and responsible living. Campaigns yearly for a decommercialized Easter and Christmas.

Celtic League, American Branch. **P.O. Box 20153 Dag Hammarskjold Center, New York, NY 10017. Stephen Paul DeVillo, secretary. Publications:** ***Guide to Learning Celtic Languages in the U.S. and Canada; Keltoi: A Pan-Celtic Review; Pan-Celtic Calendar; Six Nations, One Soul.***

Distributes information about Celtic civilization, ancient and contemporary. Promotes the revival of Celtic holiday observances, sponsors concerts, speakers, and films.

Committee for National Arbor Day. **P.O. Box 333, West Orange, NJ 07052. Harry J. Banker, chairman. Telephone: 201-731-0840. Fax: 201-731-6020. Publications: booklets, newsletter, and Arbor Day kits.**

Promotes awareness of the environmental, economic, and aesthetic importance of trees. Holds semiannual meetings, one in conjunction with the International Society of Aboriculture.

Father's Day/Mother's Day Council. **1328 Broadway, New York, NY 10001. Theodore M. Kaufman, executive director. Telephone: 212-594-6421. Fax: 212-594-9349.**

Promotes awareness and observance of Mother's Day and Father's Day through advertising. Also carries out market research and surveys on Mother's Day and Father's Day observance. Grants Outstanding Mother and Father of the Year awards.

Holiday Institute of Yonkers. **Box 73, Maplewood, NJ 07040-0073. William Bickel, president. Publications:** ***Holidagology Today*****.**

Fosters interest in and celebration of holidays. Promotes December 10 as Humanities Day, an international holiday.

International Council of Folklore Festival Organizations and Folk Art. **c/o Rolf Leander, secretary general, Badstugrand 4, S-824 00 Hudiksvall, Sweden. Telephone: 650-93227. Fax: 650-93227. Publications: newsletter, annual festival calendar,** ***Entre Nous*****, and seminar proceedings.**

Works to enhance the quality of folklore festivals worldwide, thereby promoting international friendship, understanding, and peace. Monitors festivals, sponsors educational programs and exhibitions.

National Arbor Day Foundation. **100 Arbor Ave., Nebraska City, NE 68410. John Rosenow, executive director. Telephone: 402-474-5655. Fax: 402-474-0820. Publications:** ***Arbor Day*** **and** ***Tree City U.S.A.*** **(bimonthly newsletters);** ***Celebrate Arbor Day*** **and other booklets.**

Promotes tree-planting and tree-education programs, and advocates the observance of Arbor Day. Sponsors conferences and training, and grants awards to individuals, associations, corporations and the media for spreading information about and appreciation of the nation's trees.

National Council for the Traditional Arts. **1320 Fenwick Lane, suite 200, Silver Spring, MD 20910. Joseph T. Wilson, executive director. Telephone: 301-565-0654. Fax: 301-565-0472.**

Aids national and state governmental bodies, as well as local organizations, in staging presentations of folk art and artists. Sponsors appearance of folk artists in tours and festivals. Formerly known as the "National Folk Festival Association."

National Father's Day Committee. **47 W. 34th Street. New York, NY 10001. Theodore M. Kaufman, executive director. Telephone: 212-594-5977. Fax: 212-594-9349.**

Supports the observance of Father's Day. Grants Father of the Year award.

National Mother's Day Committee. **1328 Broadway, New York, NY 10001. Theodore M. Kaufman, executive director. Telephone: 212-594-6421. Fax: 212-594-9349.**

Supports the observance of Mother's Day. Grants Mother of the Year award. Affiliated with the Father's Day/Mother's Day Council. Formerly "National Committee for the Observance of Mother's Day."

National Peace Day Celebrations. **93 Pilgrim Road, Concord, MA 01742. Telephone: 508-369-3751. Publications: Peace Day newsletter, Ideas for Celebration of Peace.**

Works for the recognition of the first Sunday in August as National Day of Peace. Promotes the celebration of Peace Day and offers information and advice to churches, schools, peace organizations, and individuals on how to organize Peace Day celebrations. Speakers bureau. Peace Day award. Formerly "National Peace Day Campaign."

National Society for Shut-Ins. **P.O. Box 1392, Reading, PA 19603. Mary Lou Pollock, president. Telephone: 215-374-2930. Publications:** ***Sunshine News*** **(quarterly).**

Organizes local chapters throughout the United States which educate the populace on the plight of shut-ins and promote visits to shut-ins. Recognizes the third Sunday in October as National Shut-in Day, and encourages visits to shut-ins on that day. Formerly "National Shut-in Day Society."

National Spiritual Assembly of the Baha'is of the United States. **536 Sheridan Road, Wilmette, IL 60091. Telephone: 708-869-9039. Fax: 708-869-0247. Robert C. Henderson, secretary general. Publications:** ***The American Baha'i*** **(a monthly newspaper) and** ***World Order*** **(a quarterly journal).**

National administrative center for the Baha'i faith in the United States. Maintains schools and sponsors educational programs.

National Thanksgiving Commission. **P.O. Box 1770, Dallas, TX 75221. Elizabeth Espersen, executive director. Telephone: 214-969-1977. Fax: 214-754-0152. Publications: brochures.**

Encourages the celebration of a traditional American Thanksgiving which emphasizes gratitude to God. Drafts presidential proclamations for National Day of Prayer and Thanksgiving. Reference library.

North American Native American Indian Information and Trade Center. **P.O. Box 1000, San Carlos, AZ 85550-1000. Telephone: 602-622-4900. Fax: 602-292-0779. Publications:** ***American Indian Information Packet; Indian***

America **(annual);** ***Native American Directory; Powwow on the Red Road*** **(a listing of Native American special events).**

Offers educational programs for those interested in the culture of Native North Americans and acts as a clearinghouse of information about Native American events and activities, including powwows and craft sales. Operates speakers bureau, maintains reference library, collects statistics. Semiannual meetings at Thanksgiving and New Year.

Society to Curtail Ridiculous, Outrageous, and Ostentatious Gift Exchanges (SCROOGE). **1447 Westwood Road, Charlottesville, VA 22903-5151. Telephone: 804-977-4645. Charles G. Langham, executive director. Publications:** ***Scrooge Report*** **(annual).**

Promotes the de-commercialization of Christmas celebrations. Advocates modest, charitable, or homemade gifts and visits.

U.S. National Committee for World Food Day. **1001 22nd St. NW, Washington, DC 20437. Patricia Young, coordinator. Telephone: 202-653-2404. Fax: 202-653-5760. Publications:** ***World Food Day Directory*** **(periodic), various materials for World Food Day.**

A resource center serving a wide variety of individuals and groups interested in local, national, foreign, and international food issues and policy options. Organizes activities for World Food Day (October 16), including satellite teleconferences, and encourages community groups to sponsor educational and political activities for World Food Day and beyond. Library on food- and hunger-related topics. Formerly known as "National Committee for World Food Day."

World Day for Peace. **3570 Williams Pond Lane, Loomis, CA 95650. Evan Jones, coordinator. Telephone: 916-652-9056. Publications:** ***A Day for Peace*** **(annual), brochures, pamphlets, posters.**

Advocates the observance of World Peace Day, the fourth Wednesday of October. Helps community groups and individuals organize events for this day, including vigils, demonstrations, marches, symposia, and phone call or letter-writing campaigns to political representatives. Library on nuclear weapons and disarmament. Annual meeting and symposium. Formerly known as "Strike for Peace."

Web Sites

Blake & Associates: First Tier Sites
URL: http://banzai.neosoft.com/citylink/blake/ftier.html
Sponsor: Blake & Associates
Phone: 504-898-2158; fax: 504-892-8535
E-mail: citylink@neosoft.com

This site will link visitors to sites about Halloween, Christmas, Valentine's Day, Mardi Gras, the Fourth of July, and St. Patrick's Day. Each of these sites is hosted by Blake & Associates, a group of Internet marketing consultants headed by Carol Blake, who is responsible for founding the massive **USA CityLink** site, which may be found at http://usacitylink.com/. These holiday sites all tie back to **USA CityLink**, but each offers some combination of commercial products and services, traditional recipes, crafts, music, history, celebration ideas, and links to related sites. According to Carol Blake, "all of our seasonal sites are into their third year and we have no plans of taking them down."

Chinese New Year
URL: http://www.chinascape.org/chinascape/ChineseNewYear/
Sponsor: Chinascape
E-mail: china@chinascape.org

This site, one page from Chinascape's home page (found at http://www.chinascape.org), is a growing list of links to information on the Chinese New Year. Besides links to essays on the history and celebration of the Chinese New Year, visitors will find links to Chinese calendars, songs, astrology, and information on specific celebrations planned around the world. This site also contains a Holidays section with links to information on official, traditional, and minority nationality holidays celebrated by the Chinese. Finally, there is a growing list of links—in the What's New section—to such far flung topics of Chinese interest as hotels in China, the folk art of the Taiwan Traditional Puppet Show (Bo-De-Hi), and Chinese newsgroups and mailing lists.

Festival Finder: Music Festivals of North America
URL: http://www.festivalfinder.com/fest.home.html
Sponsor: The Clyness Group
5616 N. Broadway
Chicago, IL 60640
Phone: 312-878-2523
E-mail: rudy@festivalfinder.com

Festival Finder is a massive, well-indexed page listing hundreds of music festivals in the United States and Canada. Visitors can locate information by linking to Alternative, Bluegrass, Blues, Cajun Zydeco, Classical, Country, Eclectic, Folk, Jazz, Reggae and World Music, Rock, and Miscellaneous subject categories. The site is organized as a database where visitors can search by festival name, performer, genre, date, state/province, or region. Each of the twelve subject categories has a search option, a list of the current month's offerings, an index of all the festivals in the particular category, and a newsgroup-style discussion area. Links to individual festivals yield dates, artists scheduled to appear, location, directions, contact information for tickets and tourists, and detailed descriptions of the history and happenings of each festival.

Good Stories for Great Holidays: Arranged for Story-Telling and Reading Aloud and for the Children's Own Reading **by Frances Jenkins Olcott**
URL: http://ftp.sunet.se/ftp/pub/etext/gutenberg/etext95/sthol10.txt
Sponsor: Project Gutenberg
P. O. Box 2782
Champaign, IL 61825
E-mail: dircompg@ux1.cso.uiuc.edu

Visitors to this site will find the entire ASCII text of *Good Stories for Great Holidays* (originally published in 1914), by Frances Jenkins Olcott. In this book, the author "endeavored to bring together myths, legends, tales, and historical stories suitable to holiday occasions." The text contains over 100 traditional stories to be read or told for New Year's Day, Abraham Lincoln's Birthday, St. Valentine's Day, George Washington's Birthday, Easter, May Day, Mother's Day, Memorial Day, Independence Day, Labor Day, Columbus Day, Halloween, Thanksgiving, Christmas, and Arbor Day. This title is one of hundreds of complete "Etexts" (electronic texts) made available by Project Gutenberg, found at http://gutenberg.etext.org/. Project Gutenberg is a nonprofit organization whose goal is to make 10,000 public domain titles available in electronic format by the end of the year 2001.

Holidays on the Net
URL: http://www.holidays.net/
Sponsor: Studio Melizo
53 Meadow Lane
Levittown
New York, NY 11756
Phone: 516-520-0366; fax: 516-520-0379
E-mail: infojp@melizo.com

Studio Melizo's *Holidays on the Net* site is rich in the current multi-media technologies available to Web authors today, including 3-D animation, sound, and video. This site offers links to Studio Melizo's own sites on Christmas, Hanukkah, Thanksgiving, Halloween, Rosh Hashanah and Yom Kippur, Independence Day, Father's Day, Shavuot, Mother's Day, Easter, Passover, Purim, and St. Valentine's Day. Each site provides a history of the particular holiday and its traditional elements, and many include information on legends and customs, ideas for celebrations, and traditional recipes and songs. Studio Melizo also announces the release of *Holidays on the Net* on CD and *Jewish Holidays on the Net* on CD.

The Jewish Holidays
URL: http://bnaibrith.org/caln.html
Sponsor: B'nai B'rith, Washington, D.C.
E-mail: internet@bnaibrith.org

This site is a calendar listing the specific days on which major Jewish holidays will fall from 1996–2006 (or the traditional Jewish years of 5757–5766). A brief description follows each of the nine holidays listed. This site is a single page, originating from **B'nai B'rith Interactive**, found at http://bnaibrith.org/index.html. B'nai B'rith is an international organization of volunteers supporting the Jewish community around the world. See **B'nai B'rith Interactive** for contact information in each of the United States and 54 other countries around the world.

Merry Christmas
URL: http://www.algonet.se/~bernadot/christmas/calendar.html
E-mail: bernadot@algonet.se
Sponsor: Beradottesdolen
E2 (Christmas Calendar)
Bernadotte School
Hellerupvej 11
2900 Hellerup
Denmark

This site is a project hosted by children and teachers at Bernadotteskolen: The International School in Denmark. Visitors will find an advent calendar of links—23 of which appear in the shape of presents under the 24th link, the Christmas tree. The hosts invite visitors to "open a new page every day to find out how Christmas and other winter holidays are celebrated in different countries and cultures." The links contain submissions from students at Bernadotteskolen, as well as those solicited from children around the world. Within these links are recipes, songs (some with audio files), and children's drawings, pictures, and descriptions of holiday traditions and legends from around the world.

The National Arbor Day Foundation
URL: http://www.arborday.org/
Sponsor: The National Arbor Day Foundation
100 Arbor Ave.
Nebraska City, NE 68410
Phone: 402-474-5655

Visitors to this site will find information on the history of Arbor Day, suggestions for celebrations, and—since Arbor Day is celebrated on different dates in different states according to the best tree-planting times in various regions—the specific dates on which Arbor Day is celebrated in each of the fifty states, the Virgin Islands, and Guam. Main sections at this site include Planting & Caring for Trees, Teaching Youth About Trees, and Conferences & Workshops. This site also contains membership information and descriptions of major Foundation programs and awards.

The Sikhism Home Page
URL: http://www.sikhs.org/topics.htm
Sponsor: Sandeep Singh Brar
E-mail: sandeep@sikhs.org

This page is a storehouse of information on the Sikh religion, including in its many sections: Philosophy, The Sikh Gurus, Translations of Selected Scriptures, Audio Prayers, Sikh Ceremonies and Festivals, and Dates in Sikh History. The Ceremonies section contains descriptions of ceremonies and festivals for the naming of children, baptism, marriage, funerals, anniversaries associated with the lives of gurus, and the traditional celebrations of Baisakhi, Diwali, Maghi, Hola Mohalla, and Sangrand. The Dates section lists the calendar dates on which major Sikh holidays and festivals will fall through the year 2000, a descriptive overview of the Sikh calendar, and actual historical dates associated with the lives of Sikh gurus. This page is well organized into major sections and includes an extensive bibliography as well as a section containing additional resources such as Sikh organizations, student groups, and other Sikh-related sites.

Web Home for UU/Pagans
URL: http://world.std.com/~notelrac/cuups.dir/index.html
Sponsor: Notelrac Starshine
E-mail: notelrac@starshine.ziplink.net

This page contains"information of interest to Unitarian Universalists, Pagans, Wiccans, and followers of various other alternative religious paths."Main sections in this site include: What is Unitarian Universalism, What is Paganism, and an expansive Essay section with links to essays on subjects such as Unitarian Universalism, Paganism, Wicca, and Rituals. The Rituals section contains a calendar of Pagan holidays and festivals, and links to over 50 essays on subjects such as the Winter Solstice, February Eve, the Vernal Equinox, May Eve, the Summer Solstice, August Eve, the Autumnal Equinox, Samhain, and various rituals.

The World Wide Holiday and Festival Page
URL: http://smiley.logos.cy.net/bdecie/
Sponsor: Brian Prescott-Decie
P. O. Box 5704
1311 Nicosia, Cyprus
E-mail: bdecie@logos.cy.net

One of the most thorough and well-indexed holiday sites on the Web, **The World Wide Holiday and Festival Page** contains over 300 links divided among movable holidays, national holidays, and links. Movable holidays contains links to the Chinese New Year calculated through the year 2000, Christian fixed and movable feasts for both the Western and Orthodox calendars, Hindu festivals for the coming year, Sikh holidays and festivals through the year 2000 (four of which have links to more detailed information), and links to other organizations' pages providing similar information for Islam, Jainism, and Judaism. The national holidays section provides separate links for more than 200 countries, each listing national holidays, and, where a particular religion dominates, movable holidays for that particular religion. Finally, the manageable links section points visitors to related pages for more information.

Year 2000 and Millennium Threshold Observances Around the World
URL: http://www.igc.org/millennium/events/index.html
Sponsor: The Millennium Institute
1117 N. 19th St., Ste. 900
Arlington, VA 22209-1708
Phone: 703-841-0048; fax: 703-841-0050
E-mail: millennium@igc.apc.org

Toward its goal of helping to "create the conditions for the peoples of the world to achieve a sustainable future for Earth and to use the energy of the year 2000 to begin building a diverse alliance committed to this task," The Millennium Institute, whose home page is found at http://www.igc.org/millennium, has published this page of events for the coming millennium. This site lists contact information for millennium events by region, country, and major city. Other sections include: International and/or Synchronized Millennium Activities, listing organizations planning events leading up to and during the year 2000; Special Events, highlighting individual events; and Mega Events, in which the Institute expects more than one million people to participate (for instance, Earth Day 2000 and the Olympics). Finally, visitors will find links to further information about the Millennium Institute, as well as more than 50 links to millennium-related sites on the Web.

Author Index

This index lists authors of the annotated books as well as authors of essays and other materials contained in those books. References are to **entry numbers**, not page numbers.

A

B

All references are to **entry numbers**, not page numbers.

C

All references are to **entry numbers**, not page numbers.

D

All references are to **entry numbers**, not page numbers.

All references are to **entry numbers**, not page numbers.

G

All references are to **entry numbers**, not page numbers.

H

All references are to **entry numbers**, not page numbers.

I

J

K

All references are to **entry numbers**, not page numbers.

L

All references are to **entry numbers**, not page numbers.

M

All references are to **entry numbers**, not page numbers.

N

O

P

All references are to **entry numbers**, not page numbers.

Q

R

S

All references are to **entry numbers**, not page numbers.

All references are to **entry numbers**, not page numbers.

T

All references are to **entry numbers**, not page numbers.

U

V

W

All references are to **entry numbers**, not page numbers.

Y

Z

All references are to **entry numbers**, not page numbers.

Title Index

This index lists titles of annotated books, titles of essays contained in the books, and series titles when two or more books in a series are listed in *World Holiday, Festival, and Calendar Books.* All references are to **entry numbers**, not page numbers.

A

B

All references are to **entry numbers**, not page numbers.

C

All references are to **entry numbers**, not page numbers.

All references are to **entry numbers**, not page numbers.

All references are to **entry numbers**, not page numbers.

All references are to **entry numbers**, not page numbers.

D

E

All references are to **entry numbers**, not page numbers.

F

G

All references are to **entry numbers**, not page numbers.

H

All references are to **entry numbers**, not page numbers.

I

All references are to **entry numbers**, not page numbers.

J

All references are to **entry numbers**, not page numbers.

K

L

All references are to **entry numbers**, not page numbers.

M

All references are to **entry numbers**, not page numbers.

All references are to **entry numbers**, not page numbers.

N

O

P

All references are to **entry numbers**, not page numbers.

Q

R

All references are to **entry numbers**, not page numbers.

S

All references are to **entry numbers**, not page numbers.

All references are to **entry numbers**, not page numbers.

All references are to **entry numbers**, not page numbers.

T

All references are to **entry numbers**, not page numbers.

U

V

W

All references are to **entry numbers**, not page numbers.

Y

Z

All references are to **entry numbers**, not page numbers.

Subject Index

This index lists holidays, festivals, calendars, geographical places, ethnic groups, religious groups, activities, people, objects, and other events. All references are to **entry numbers**, not page numbers.

A

All references are to **entry numbers**, not page numbers.

All references are to **entry numbers**, not page numbers.

All references are to **entry numbers**, not page numbers.

All references are to **entry numbers**, not page numbers.

All references are to **entry numbers**, not page numbers.

All references are to **entry numbers**, not page numbers.

B

All references are to **entry numbers**, not page numbers.

All references are to **entry numbers**, not page numbers.

C

All references are to **entry numbers**, not page numbers.

All references are to **entry numbers**, not page numbers.

All references are to **entry numbers**, not page numbers.

All references are to **entry numbers**, not page numbers.

All references are to **entry numbers**, not page numbers.

All references are to **entry numbers**, not page numbers.

All references are to **entry numbers**, not page numbers.

All references are to **entry numbers**, not page numbers.

All references are to **entry numbers**, not page numbers.

All references are to **entry numbers**, not page numbers.

All references are to **entry numbers**, not page numbers.

All references are to **entry numbers**, not page numbers.

D

All references are to **entry numbers**, not page numbers.

All references are to **entry numbers**, not page numbers.

E

All references are to **entry numbers**, not page numbers.

All references are to **entry numbers**, not page numbers.

All references are to **entry numbers**, not page numbers.

F

All references are to **entry numbers**, not page numbers.

All references are to **entry numbers**, not page numbers.

All references are to **entry numbers**, not page numbers.

All references are to **entry numbers**, not page numbers.

G

All references are to **entry numbers**, not page numbers.

All references are to **entry numbers**, not page numbers.

H

All references are to **entry numbers**, not page numbers.

All references are to **entry numbers**, not page numbers.

All references are to **entry numbers**, not page numbers.

I

All references are to **entry numbers**, not page numbers.

All references are to **entry numbers**, not page numbers.

All references are to **entry numbers**, not page numbers.

J

All references are to **entry numbers**, not page numbers.

All references are to **entry numbers**, not page numbers.

K

L

All references are to **entry numbers**, not page numbers.

All references are to **entry numbers**, not page numbers.

M

All references are to **entry numbers**, not page numbers.

All references are to **entry numbers**, not page numbers.

All references are to **entry numbers**, not page numbers.

All references are to **entry numbers**, not page numbers.

All references are to **entry numbers**, not page numbers.

N

All references are to **entry numbers**, not page numbers.

All references are to **entry numbers**, not page numbers.

All references are to **entry numbers**, not page numbers.

All references are to **entry numbers**, not page numbers.

All references are to **entry numbers**, not page numbers.

P

All references are to **entry numbers**, not page numbers.

All references are to **entry numbers**, not page numbers.

All references are to **entry numbers**, not page numbers.

Q

R

All references are to **entry numbers**, not page numbers.

S

All references are to **entry numbers**, not page numbers.

All references are to **entry numbers**, not page numbers.

All references are to **entry numbers**, not page numbers.

All references are to **entry numbers**, not page numbers.

All references are to **entry numbers**, not page numbers.

All references are to **entry numbers**, not page numbers.

T

All references are to **entry numbers**, not page numbers.

All references are to **entry numbers**, not page numbers.

All references are to **entry numbers**, not page numbers.

All references are to **entry numbers**, not page numbers.

All references are to **entry numbers**, not page numbers.

V

All references are to **entry numbers**, not page numbers.

W

All references are to **entry numbers**, not page numbers.

All references are to **entry numbers**, not page numbers.

About the Author

Growing up in the culturally diverse San Francisco Bay area and listening to the stories of her immigrant grandparents kindled Tanya Gulevich's interest in the study of other cultures. At Oberlin College she pursued interests in European history, sociology, and Asian Studies. Later she obtained an M.A. and Ph.D. in cultural anthropology from the University of Michigan.

Dr. Gulevich has always enjoyed learning about other ways of life through first-hand experience and has traveled in many countries, including France, Greece, Turkey, India, Sri Lanka, Thailand, Singapore, Hong Kong, China, and Tibet. In addition, she lived in northwestern Spain for a year and a half while researching her dissertation. She speaks Spanish and has also studied French and Chinese. Other interests include music, dance, ritual, celebration, and cuisine. Her favorite holidays are Christmas and Halloween.

This is her first book for Omnigraphics, Inc. She is currently working on a forthcoming Omnigraphics title, *The Encyclopedia of Christmas*.